D1308626

Edited by two leading analysts of postcommunist politics, this book brings together distinguished specialists on the Baltic states (Estonia, Latvia, and Lithuania), Poland, the Czech Republic, Slovakia, and Hungary. The authors analyze the patterns of postcommunist democratization in these countries, paying particular attention to the process of party formation, electoral politics, the growth of civil society, and the impact of economic reform on the emergence of interest groups. Karen Dawisha and Bruce Parrott contribute theoretical and comparative chapters on postcommunist political development. This book will provide students and scholars with detailed analysis by leading authorities, plus the latest research data on recent political trends in each country.

Democratization and Authoritarianism in Postcommunist Societies: 1

The consolidation of democracy in East–Central Europe

Editors

Karen Dawisha
University of Maryland at College Park

Bruce Parrott
The Paul H. Nitze School of Advanced International Studies
The Johns Hopkins University

These four volumes, edited by two leading analysts of postcommunist politics, bring together distinguished specialists to provide specially commissioned, up-to-date essays on the postcommunist countries of Eastern Europe and the former Soviet Union. Each contributor analyzes both progress made toward democratization, and the underlying social, economic, and cultural factors that have shaped the process of political change. All chapters contain information on the emergence of political parties, elections, institutional reform, and socioeconomic trends. Each volume also contains chapters by the editors juxtaposing the overall trends in the postcommunist countries with comparable transitions and processes of democratization elsewhere.

1. *The consolidation of democracy in East–Central Europe*

2. *Politics, power, and the struggle for democracy in South-East Europe*

3. *Democratic changes and authoritarian reactions in Russia, Ukraine, Belarus, and Moldova*

4. *Conflict, cleavage, and change in Central Asia and the Caucasus*

The consolidation of democracy in East–Central Europe

edited by

Karen Dawisha

University of Maryland at College Park

and

Bruce Parrott

The Paul H. Nitze School of Advanced International Studies
The Johns Hopkins University

CAMBRIDGE
UNIVERSITY PRESS

PUBLISHED BY THE PRESS SYNDICATE OF THE UNIVERSITY OF CAMBRIDGE
The Pitt Building, Trumpington Street, Cambridge CB2 1RP, United Kingdom

CAMBRIDGE UNIVERSITY PRESS
The Edinburgh Building, Cambridge, CB2 2RU, United Kingdom
40 West 20th Street, New York, NY 10011-4211, USA
10 Stamford Road, Oakleigh, Melbourne 3166, Australia

First published 1997

Printed in the United Kingdom at the University Press, Cambridge

Typeset in 10/12 pt CG Times

A catalogue record for this book is available from the British Library

Library of Congress Cataloguing in Publication data applied for

ISBN 0 521 59064 7 hardback
ISBN 0 521 59938 5 paperback

To Florence Rotz,
a woman of exceptional wisdom and talent
with affection and gratitude

Contents

Tables

Contributors

KAREN DAWISHA is Professor of Government and Director of the Center for the Study of Postcommunist Societies at the University of Maryland at College Park. She graduated with degrees in Russian and politics from the University of Lancaster in England and received her Ph.D. from the London School of Economics. She has served as an advisor to the British House of Commons Foreign Affairs Committee and was a member of the policy planning staff of the US State Department. Her publications include *Russia and the New States of Eurasia: The Politics of Upheaval* (co-authored with Bruce Parrott, 1994), *Eastern Europe, Gorbachev and Reform: The Great Challenge* (1989, 2d ed., 1990), *The Kremlin and the Prague Spring* (1984), *The Soviet Union in the Middle East: Politics and Perspectives* (1982), *Soviet–East European Dilemmas: Coercion, Competition, and Consent* (1981), and *Soviet Foreign Policy toward Egypt* (1979).

RICHARD J. KRICKUS is Distinguished Professor of Political Science at Mary Washington College and has held the H. L. Oppenheimer Chair for Warfighting Strategy at the US Marine Corps University. Since 1990, when he served as an international monitor of the Lithuanian elections, he has visited the Baltic countries on numerous occasions. In addition to his publications in academic journals, Dr. Krickus's work has appeared in *The Washington Post, The Wall Street Journal, The Christian Science Monitor*, and Lithuania's leading daily, *Lietuvos Rytas*. His latest book is *Showdown: The Lithuanian Rebellion and the Breakup of the Soviet Empire* (1996). He received his Ph.D. in political science from Georgetown University.

ANDREW A. MICHTA is Associate Professor of International Studies at Rhodes College in Memphis, Tennessee, where he holds the Mertie Willigar Buckman Chair of International Studies. He is the author of *Soldier Citizens: The Politics of the Polish Army after Communism* (forthcoming 1997), *The Government and Politics of Postcommunist Europe* (1994), *East Central Europe after the Warsaw*

Pact: Security Dilemmas in the 1990s (1992), and *Red Eagle: The Army in Polish Politics, 1944–1988* (1990). He is also co-editor with Ilya Prizel of *Postcommunist Eastern Europe: Crisis and Reform* (1992) and *Polish Foreign Policy Reconsidered: Challenges of Independence* (1995). He has written articles and book chapters on Russian and East European security and politics and on civil–military relations. He holds a Ph.D. degree in international relations from The Johns Hopkins University School of Advanced International Studies in Washington, DC.

DAVID M. OLSON is Professor of Political Science at the University of North Carolina in Greensboro. His research interests include comparative parliaments, political parties, and the democratization process in Central Europe. He is the author of *Democratic Legislative Institutions* (1994), and editor of *The New Parliaments of Central and Eastern Europe* (with Philip Norton, 1996) and *Representation and Policy Formation in Federal Systems: Canada and the United States* (with C. E. S. Franks, 1993). He was a Fulbright Scholar at Charles University, Prague, in 1992. He received his Ph.D. from the University of California at Berkeley.

BRUCE PARROTT is Professor and Director of Russian Area and East European Studies at the Paul H. Nitze School of Advanced International Studies of The Johns Hopkins University. He is author of *Russia and the New States of Eurasia: The Politics of Upheaval* (with Karen Dawisha, 1994), *The Soviet Union and Ballistic Missile Defense* (1987), and *Politics and Technology in the Soviet Union* (1983). He is editor of *The End of Empire? The Transformation of the USSR in Comparative Perspective* (with Karen Dawisha, 1996), *State-Building and Military Power in Russia and the New States of Eurasia* (1995), *The Dynamics of Soviet Defense Policy* (1990), and *Trade, Technology, and Soviet–American Relations* (1985). He received his Ph.D. in political science from Columbia University.

ANDREJS PLAKANS is Professor of History at Iowa State University, a foreign member of the Latvian Academy of Sciences, and former president of the Association for the Advancement of Baltic Studies in the United States. He has also been a visiting professor of history at the University of Latvia (spring 1993), and since 1991 has been a member of the editorial board of the *Journal of the Latvian Institute of History*, published in Riga. He is the author of *The Latvians: A Short History (1995)* and *Kinship in the Past: An Anthropology of European Family Life, 1500-1900* (1984); he is co-editor of *Family History at the Crossroads: Linking Familial and Historical Change* (with Tamara K. Hareven, 1987), and *Bevölkerungsverschiebungen und sozialer Wandel in den baltischen Provinzen Russlands, 1850-1914* (with Gert von Pistohlkors and Paul Kaegbein, 1995). He received his Ph.D. in history from Harvard University.

TOIVO U. RAUN is Professor and Chair of the Department of Central Eurasian Studies at Indiana University. He is author of *Estonia and the Estonians* (1991), and co-author with Edward C. Thaden, et al., of *Russification in the Baltic Provinces and Finland, 1855-1914* (1981). He received his Ph.D. in Russian, German, and US history from Princeton University.

RUDOLF L. TŐKÉS is Professor of Political Science at the University of Connecticut. His most recent publications are *Hungary's Negotiated Revolution: Economic Reforms, Social Change and Political Succession, 1957-1990* (1996), and *Murmurs and Whispers: Public Opinion and Legitimacy Crisis in Hungary, 1972-1989* (1996).

SHARON L. WOLCHIK is Professor of Political Science and International Affairs at the George Washington University. She has written extensively on political and social issues, policy-making, and ethnic relations in Central and Eastern Europe. She is the author of *Czechoslovakia in Transition: Politics, Economics, and Society* (1991) and co-editor of *The Social Legacy of Communism* (with James Millar, 1994), *Women, State and Party in Eastern Europe* (with Alfred G. Meyer, 1985), and *Foreign and Domestic Politics in Eastern Europe in the 1980s* (with Michael J. Sodaro, 1983). Her current research focuses on several aspects of the transition to postcommunist rule, including gender issues, mass and elite political values and attitudes, and the international relations of the Visegrad countries and their neighbors. She received her Ph.D. in political science from the University of Michigan.

Preface

This study of democratization in East-Central Europe is the first of four books produced by the Project on Democratization and Political Participation in Postcommunist Societies. The project has been sponsored jointly by the Paul H. Nitze School of Advanced International Studies of The Johns Hopkins University and the University of Maryland at College Park. It draws on the talents of scholars from a wide array of other universities and research institutions.

As codirectors of the project, we are grateful for material support furnished by two organizations. Principal funding for the project has been provided by the United States Department of State as part of its external research program. In addition, the intellectual planning of the project was aided at a crucial juncture by a grant from the Joint Committee on Eastern Europe of the American Council of Learned Societies. However, none of the views or conclusions contained in the book should be interpreted as representing the official opinion or policy of the Department of State or of the Joint Committee.

The three other volumes in the series deal with the countries of South-East Europe; with the countries of Central Asia and the Caucasus; and with Russia, Ukraine, Belarus, and Moldova. Any student of contemporary international affairs knows that the delineation of "Europe" and its constituent regions frequently generates intellectual controversy about which countries belong to Europe or to "the West." We adopted our quadripartite grouping of countries to facilitate the management of a large research project, and because the grouping has yielded books that match the curricular structure of many college and university courses devoted to the countries of the postcommunist world. Neither the grouping nor the names were chosen with any intention of suggesting that some countries are necessarily more "advanced" or "backward" politically than others. Most of the regional groups exhibit considerable internal political diversity among the member countries, and the comparative judgments presented in the volumes are based on the findings of individual country-studies, not on preconceptions about one or another region.

In the course of this project we have received assistance from many individuals and incurred many personal obligations. We wish to thank John Parker and Susan Nelson of the Department of State for proposing the general idea of the project to us, for making helpful suggestions about how it could be carried out, and for encouraging the project participants to draw whatever conclusions the evidence supports. We are grateful to Jason Parker of the ACLS Joint Committee on Eastern Europe for his assistance. We also wish to thank several scholars for their valuable help in sorting out the basic issues at an initial planning workshop: Nancy Bermeo, Valerie Bunce, Ted Robert Gurr, Joan Nelson, and Robert Putnam. Herbert Kitschelt was likewise very helpful in this regard.

We are deeply indebted to the country-study writers for the high level of effort that they invested in writing their chapters, for their active participation in the project workshops, and for undertaking more extensive revisions than are customary in collective enterprises of this kind. We also are grateful to the four authors who served as coordinators of the workshops: Sharon Wolchik, Vladimir Tismaneanu, Ilya Prizel, and Muriel Atkin. We benefited from their advice during the organizational stage of the project, and we profited from the written comments that they made on the draft chapters presented at the workshops.

We express our special thanks to Griffin Hathaway, the Executive Director of the project, who performed a nearly endless series of administrative and intellectual tasks with exemplary efficiency; to Florence Rotz, staff person of the SAIS Russian Area and East European Studies program, who managed the production and revision of several versions of the chapters with admirable calmness and consummate skill; to Paula Smith, who proofread the manuscript; and to Steve Guenther, who helped with the logistics of the workshops. Not least, we are grateful to Murray Feshbach for generously providing demographic data for a number of the country-studies.

Finally, we express our thanks to Michael Holdsworth of Cambridge University Press for his willingness to take on this large publishing project and see it through to the end. Bruce Parrott also thanks Gordon Livingston, without whose help he could not have completed his portion of the project.

K. D.
B. P.

1 Perspectives on postcommunist democratization

Bruce Parrott

Of all the elements of the international wave of democratization that began some two decades ago, the transformation of communist political systems, once thought impervious to liberalization, is the most dramatic.[1] Since 1989, more than two dozen countries within the former Soviet bloc have officially disavowed Marxist–Leninist ideology and have dismantled, in varying degrees, the apparatus of communist dictatorship and socialist economic planning. In many cases this transformation has led to a reinvention of politics, in the sense of genuine public debate about the purposes of society and the state, and has produced significant progress toward the establishment of a liberal–democratic order.[2]

This extraordinary turn of events has evoked a surge of scholarly research and writing from specialists on the former communist countries and other social scientists. Analysts have probed the causes of the demise of communism in Eastern Europe and the former Soviet Union.[3] They have examined the communist legacies inherited by the East European and Soviet successor states and have constructed parallel narratives of early postcommunist developments in regional groupings of these states.[4] They also have produced detailed studies of recent trends in individual countries.[5] Extensive analysis and debate have likewise been devoted to the political and institutional aspects of market reform.[6]

To date, however, scholars have devoted relatively little effort to systematic cross-country comparisons of political change in the postcommunist states. With some notable exceptions, Western thinking about attempts to democratize these polities has generally been based on the experience of the countries of North America, Western and Southern Europe, and Latin America.[7] Among scholars and laypersons alike, there has been an unconscious tendency to view postcommunist political developments through interpretive lenses derived from the experiences of countries that have not undergone the historical transformations and traumas associated with

1

communism. Yet the relevance of the paradigms of democratization (and failed democratization) derived from these countries is far from self-evident. Just as some economists have challenged the applicability of models drawn from noncommunist societies to the dilemmas of economic reform in postcommunist states, some political scientists have questioned whether paradigms of democratization drawn from noncommunist countries are relevant to the study of postcommunist political change.[8] This is an issue of central importance both for social theory and for the day-to-day policies of Western governments and nongovernmental organizations.

An adequate understanding of this exceptionally complex theoretical issue, however, requires a better understanding of the nature of the political changes occurring inside the postcommunist countries themselves. Because the communist era saddled these countries with many similar political and socioeconomic dilemmas, it is logical to examine them for similar processes of political change. A strong case can be made that communist countries passed through a distinctive set of profound political and socioeconomic alterations that makes comparisons among postcommunist patterns of political development especially fruitful. On the other hand, these societies also have been shaped by dissimilar processes – witness the contrast between the Czech Republic and Turkmenistan, which today have little in common besides the fact that they were once called communist – and analysts cannot assume that they are destined to follow identical political trajectories. Controlled comparisons among postcommunist countries can help us identify the causes of the varying national outcomes that have begun to crystallize roughly a half-decade after the demise of communism.

Some valuable comparative work on postcommunist political development has already been done.[9] But the immense forces that have been unleashed and the profound questions that they raise demand much fuller exploration. Only a sustained research effort by the broad community of scholars can provide a surer baseline for evaluating recent trends and the prospects for democracy in particular postcommunist states. This long-term effort must address many aspects of each country's political life – its constitutional arrangements, the objectives of its leaders, public attitudes toward politics, ethnonational sentiments, the interplay of politics and economics, and the effects of international influences, to name only a few – and juxtapose them with comparable phenomena in other postcommunist states.

Although the project that produced this book touches on a number of these themes, the central goal has been to trace changes and continuities in elite and mass political participation in each of the postcommunist countries of Eastern Europe and the former Soviet Union.[10] By examining the major political actors and the means through which they exercise power, the project has sought to assess the extent of democratization in each country and the strength of countervailing authoritarian tendencies. In particular, we have examined the degree to which postcommunist political arrangements have fostered or inhibited an expansion of popular political participation through the introduction of competitive elections and the formation of competitive political parties. Where feasible, we also have offered preliminary assessments of the strength and orientation of the network of groups and institutions sometimes known as "civil society" – or, more generally, as political society.[11] The writers of the country-studies have necessarily approached these topics from various angles, depending on the particulars of the country being analyzed. In each instance, however, the writer has sought to clarify whether formative influences and political choices have propelled the country's postcommunist politics in a democratic or an authoritarian direction, and how durable the new constellation of power appears to be.

This approach has both intellectual advantages and limitations. The contributors to the project have harbored no illusions that we could treat all the relevant issues in the necessary depth. Separate volumes could easily have been written on particular facets of the overall comparisons we have undertaken. The value of our enterprise is that it presents a comprehensive set of carefully researched case-studies based on a common research agenda and on close interaction among the country-study writers and editors. The project provides a useful picture of each country's political development up to the mid-1990s, along with a sense of the national trends that may prevail during the next few years. In addition, it lays the groundwork for delineating and explaining alternative paths of democratic and nondemocratic change in postcommunist societies. Today, less than a decade since communist regimes began to fall, the challenge of charting these paths remains daunting. In the words of one scholar, "it is a peculiarity of political scientists that we spend much of our time explaining events that have not finished happening."[12] Identifying and explaining patterns of postcommunist political development will become easier as additional events and a longer historical perspective make those patterns more distinct; but it is not too early to begin the task.

The remainder of this chapter situates the country-studies in a general intellectual framework and highlights some of the principal themes they address. First it examines the meaning of key concepts, such as democracy and democratic transition, and sketches the types of regimes that may emerge from the wreckage of communism. Next the chapter explores the impact of the international environment and of national historical legacies on the evolution of postcommunist regimes. It then turns to a discussion of elections, party systems, and their role in the success or failure of democratization. Finally, the chapter surveys the potential effects of political culture and the intermediate groups that constitute a country's political society. In treating each theme, I draw on the chapters included in this book and the companion volumes.[13]

Democracy and the alternatives

Because the general notion of democracy has been interpreted in many different ways, it is essential to begin by discussing some of these variations and their implications for the study of postcommunist countries. After all, during their heyday Marxist–Leninist regimes claimed to be quintessentially democratic and ridiculed the "bourgeois" democracies found in other parts of the world. More to the point, proponents of liberal democracy have long disagreed among themselves about which institutional arrangements constitute the essence of a democratic system. Equally significant, some admirers of the advanced industrial democracies prefer to call such systems "polyarchies" and to treat democracy as a set of normative standards against which all political systems must be measured, in order not to gloss over the serious defects of contemporary liberal polities.[14]

For the purposes of this project, we have adopted a less stringent criterion for classifying a country as democratic. According to this standard, democracy is a political system in which the formal and actual leaders of the government are chosen within regular intervals through elections based on a comprehensive adult franchise with equally weighted voting, multiple candidacies, secret balloting, and other procedures, such as freedom of the press and assembly, that ensure real opportunities for electoral competition. Among the various attributes of democracy, competitive elections are the feature that is most easily identifiable and most widely recognized around the world. Competitive elections are arguably a precondition for the other political benefits that a democratic system may confer on its citizens, and they are a valuable yardstick for analyzing and distinguishing among postcommunist countries. One fundamental question is why some countries, such as Poland, have introduced fully competitive elections, while others, such as Uzbekistan, have not. Another question is why some postcommunist countries have continued to choose their governmental leaders through free elections, whereas other countries that initially introduced such elections, such as Armenia and Albania, have recently fallen victim to large-scale electoral fraud.

Although useful, our minimalist definition of democracy also involves potential pitfalls. Because it does not stipulate all the individual liberties that most Western observers consider an essential element of genuine democracy, it groups together the majoritarian and constitutionalist/libertarian traditions of democratic governance.[15] Under certain conditions, a competitively elected government is capable of behaving in a despotic fashion toward large numbers of its citizens or inhabitants, especially when those persons belong to a distinct ethnic or religious minority.[16] The behavior of the Croatian government toward many ethnic Serbian inhabitants of Croatia is a graphic example. Other postcommunist governments, such as those of Estonia and Latvia, have faced major dilemmas posed by the presence of sizable minorities, but they have dealt with these issues in a more humane though sometimes controversial manner. Confronted with ethnic mixes that pose less obvious risks to the state, still other governments have accorded full rights to citizens of minority extraction; Bulgaria is a case in point. In a fully functioning constitutional democracy, the rights of citizens and inhabitants are legally specified and protected by the government, no matter how sweeping a mandate it has received at the polls.

Another caveat concerns the application of the criterion of competitive elections. The project's case-studies show that in several countries postcommunist elections have been considerably more competitive than the typical stage-managed charades of the communist era, yet have not been entirely free by strict democratic standards. In the long run, however, this movement from communist-style to semidemocratic elections may constitute an important step in the process of liberalization and may lead, despite powerful resistance, to voting procedures that are fully democratic. One strand of the scholarly literature emphasizes that democracy is sometimes the unintended consequence of political struggles among antagonists who did not initially seek to create it. The political import of semi-competitive elections thus depends on whether they mark a national step forward from completely rigged elections or a regression from elections that were genuinely democratic. Semi-competitive elections in Turkmenistan would be a sign of dramatic democratic progress, whereas similar elections in the Czech Republic would not.

Care is also required in applying the notion of democratic transitions. Due to the astonishing cascade of events that brought about the collapse of communism and a Western victory in the Cold War, virtually all postcommunist leaders proclaimed their commitment to democratization – sometimes sincerely, sometimes not – and a considerable number of outside observers assumed that democracy would be the natural result of communism's demise. However, when thinking about the evolution of the postcommunist states it is important to maintain the distinction between transitions from communism and transitions to democracy. It may be true that liberal democracy has become the prevailing model of modern politics in much of the world.[17] But both historical experience and a priori reasoning suggest that a spectrum of possible postcommunist outcomes still exists. This spectrum includes variants of democracy, variants of authoritarianism, and some hybrids in between.

The consolidation of democracy is another important idea that warrants careful handling. To say that democracy has been consolidated in a country suggests, at a minimum, that the introduction of fully competitive elections has been completed and that the new political system has become stable. In this discussion, consolidation denotes the condition of a political system in which all major political actors and social groups expect that government leaders will be chosen through competitive elections and regard representative institutions and procedures as their main channel for pressing claims on the state.[18] A few scholarly critics have challenged the idea of consolidation, arguing that some democracies have demonstrated considerable staying-power without ever satisfying certain commonly accepted criteria of consolidation.[19] Nevertheless, the concept remains useful for differentiating democratic systems that have achieved internal stability from systems that have not, and for making probabilistic assessments of a particular democracy's political prospects. It calls attention to internal factors, such as fundamental divisions over national identity, constitutional structure, and criteria of citizenship, that can destroy a democratic polity. Because all systems are subject to political decay, consolidation does not guarantee that a democracy will survive, but does improve its chances. Although democratic consolidation typically required a long time in earlier eras, the contemporary ascendancy of liberal-democratic norms in many parts of the globe may accelerate the process. Since the 1970s the consolidation of new democratic systems has occurred quite quickly in some noncommunist countries, though not in others.[20]

Whether any of the postcommunist states have achieved democratic consolidation is a complex issue. A case can be made that the Czech Republic, Poland, and Lithuania have reached this political watershed, even though controversy persists over the shape of the Polish constitution. But most postcommunist states have not reached it. Some, such as Latvia and Estonia, have established representative institutions and political structures that work quite smoothly, but have not yet admitted large ethnic minorities to citizenship. Others, such as Russia, have made impressive progress in introducing competitive elections, but contain particular political parties and social groups whose loyalty to democratic principles remains highly questionable. Still others, such as Uzbekistan and Belarus, are plainly developing along authoritarian lines.

The spectrum of possible postcommunist outcomes includes such variants of democracy as parliamentary rule and presidential government. Each of these forms of government has been adopted by some postcommunist countries, and each has champions who argue that it is the least susceptible to political breakdown.[21] In addition, the spectrum of potential outcomes includes hybrid systems similar to the "delegative democracy" identified by students of comparative politics.[22] In a delegative democracy, the president is chosen through competitive elections. Once in office, however, he rules in the name of the whole nation, usually on the pretence that he transcends the petty concerns of particular parties and interest groups. Unconstrained by the legislature or the courts, the president governs without significant checks on his power, save for the constitutional requirement that regular presidential elections be held and the de facto power held by other officials, and he often seeks to change the constitution so as to prolong his time in power.[23] Several postcommunist countries, particularly some former Soviet republics, have concentrated governmental power in an executive president with the authority to issue decrees having the force of law. Depending on the future course of events, this hybrid arrangement has the potential to become either a constitutional democracy or a clear-cut form of authoritarianism.

The main potential forms of postcommunist authoritarianism are personal dictatorships, one-party states, and military regimes. The socioeconomic turmoil following the collapse of communism may make it hard to build stable versions of any of these types of authoritarianism, but oscillations among them may still preclude successful democratization. In countries where a substantial part of the population has already undergone sociopolitical mobilization, the lack of a well developed party structure makes a personal dictatorship vulnerable to sharp shifts in the public mood and to unbridled power-struggles when the dictator is incapacitated or dies.[24] Nonetheless, a few postcommunist countries are likely to come under the sway of such dictatorships. Contemporary Belarus fits this model, and Turkmenistan bears a significant resemblance to it.

Generally speaking, authoritarian states built around a single ruling party are more stable than personal dictatorships. A ramified party organization helps harness mass political participation to the leaders' objectives, reduces elite conflict, and smooths the process of succession. For postcommunist leaders set on following this path, the challenge is to create a party mechanism that can actually control mass participation and the behavior of any quasi-democratic governmental institutions that already have been set up. This stratagem is often more difficult to apply than it might seem. Once the old communist mechanisms of control have been weakened, building a stable new ruling party is a problematic undertaking, as developments in Kazakstan indicate. Success depends both on the top leader's willingness to assign high priority to building such a party and on the party's capacity to contain new socioeconomic forces within its structure. Absent these two conditions, leaders with a dictatorial bent may move toward a system of personal rule, eliminating quasi-democratic institutions and processes, such as elections, that they cannot effectively control.

As of the mid–1990s, direct military rule seemed the least likely postcommunist authoritarian outcome. Historically, one-party states have proven less susceptible to military coups than have other forms of authoritarianism.[25] Ruling communist parties exercised especially close civilian control over their military professionals, and this heritage of subordination appears to have shaped military behavior in most postcommunist countries. The rare episodes in which the armed forces have intervened collectively to affect the selection of national leaders have usually been precipitated by "demand pull" from feuding politicians eager to defeat their rivals rather than by any military desire to rule.[26] That said, it should be noted that irregular military forces and militias have played a sizable role in the politics of some postcommunist countries, especially those parts of the former Soviet Union and the former Yugoslavia that have become embroiled in warfare. In a number of countries the parlous economic and social condition of the regular military has facilitated transfers of weapons and personnel to irregular military forces. Although irregular forces have caused a change of government leadership in only a few cases, such as Georgia and Azerbaijan, they frequently have had a strong effect on the political balance inside their "host" states, whether those states are nominally democratic or authoritarian in character.[27]

The international environment and national historical legacies

The dynamics of postcommunist political change have been shaped by several major variables. One of the most important is the international environment, which includes geopolitical, institutional-normative, and cultural elements. Historically, the overall effect of the international environment on attempts to promote democratization has ranged from highly beneficial to extremely harmful.[28] By historical standards, the contemporary international setting has been relatively favorable to the creation and consolidation of new democracies, although there have been important regional variations in this respect. The generally propitious international environment has been shaped by a number of factors: the heightened Western commitment to human rights as a major aspect of interstate relations; the gradual absorption of liberal ideas into once-autarkic societies made increasingly permeable by competitive pressures from an open global economy; the decision of the Soviet leadership not to shore up communist regimes in Eastern Europe with military threats or intervention; the "gravitational pull" exerted by highly prosperous Western democracies and by multilateral institutions prepared to assist postcommunist liberalization; and the intensifying bandwagon effects exerted by leading exemplars of reform, such as Poland, on other former communist countries that initially dragged their feet.[29]

International conditions have not favored all postcommunist efforts at democratization in equal measure. The effects of the international setting have varied sharply by region and by the form of outside influence in question. For the most part, the Western powers have refused to intervene with decisive military force to suppress the savage ethnic violence that has undermined the chances for democratization in parts of the former Yugoslavia and the Transcaucasus.[30] In contrast to the situation after World War II, when the geostrategic interests of the Western Allies required the imposition of democratic institutions on the defeated Axis powers, the West has had no compelling strategic reason to impose liberal-democratic arrangements on such countries as Serbia.[31] Perhaps as significant, the West's political and economic impact on most European postcommunist states has exceeded its influence on the postcommunist states of the Transcaucasus and Central Asia. The scale of such influence is not determined solely by the receiving state's location or culture; witness the isolation of Belarus from the countries to its west. But the large cluster of established European democracies and the prospect of close political and economic ties with them have had a much stronger effect in Eastern Europe than in other postcommunist regions. In Eastern Europe, a desire to be admitted to NATO and the European Union has tempered the political conduct even of lagging states such as Romania.

Several factors account for this variation in Western influence: the greater physical and cultural distance between the West and most of the non-European postcommunist states; the lower level of Western strategic interest in these countries, coupled with a tendency to manifest less concern about their internal liberalization than about their potential as sources of energy and raw materials; the countries' greater vulnerability to pressures from a Russia preoccupied with ensuring the stability of its southern flank; and the substantial limits on the West's diplomatic leverage in Asia, where booming economies have emboldened some authoritarian regimes, such as China, to defy Western human-rights standards.[32]

In addition to being influenced by the international environment, the direction of postcommunist political development has been shaped by whether struggles over political change have taken place within the arena of a firmly established nation-state. In a handful of postcommunist countries, politics has unfolded within the boundaries and administrative framework of the old communist state. In most cases, however, the struggle over democratization has coincided with efforts to create the political scaffolding of a new state on a portion of the territory of the old communist regime. Due to the breakup of Czechoslovakia, Yugoslavia, and the Soviet Union, twenty-two of the twenty-seven postcommunist states are new sovereign entities. This is one of the main features that distinguishes postcommunist efforts to build democracy from comparable processes in Latin America and Southern Europe.[33]

The break-up of states severely complicates efforts to achieve democratization. The process frequently triggers incendiary controversies over the national identity of the new states, contested borders, and rival groups' competing claims to be the only indigenous inhabitants of their new country. In cases as diverse as Croatia, Azerbaijan, Georgia, Moldova, and

Russia, national declarations of independence from a larger communist regime have coincided with simultaneous attempts by local minorities to declare their own independence from the newly established states. Such centrifugal processes, which cannot be resolved by appealing to the principle of national self-determination, increase the probability of violent communal conflict and the emergence of ultranationalist sentiments harmful to democratization.[34] The conflicts between Serbia and Croatia and between Armenia and Azerbaijan provide examples. The collapse of an established state also accelerates the disintegration of the government bureaucracies that must function smoothly to ensure the administrative effectiveness of democratic institutions. This, in turn, may undermine the popular appeal of democracy as a political system.[35]

The creation of new states from old does not always preclude democratic development, however. The Czech Republic and Slovakia, Russia and the Baltic states, and the former Yugoslav republic of Slovenia are cases in point. Democratization is liable to fail when efforts to dismantle the old state interact with the mobilization of large internal ethnic "diasporas" and the emergence of ultranationalism in internal ethnic "homelands" to ignite large-scale violence. Democratization stands a greater chance of success when internal ethnic diasporas are small or are willing to be incorporated into successor states outside their "homeland," and when nationalist movements in the ethnic homelands are moderate rather than extremist.[36] In new, ethnically divided states, the political impact of ethnic differences depends on the actions both of the dominant group and of ethnic minorities and outside parties, as the contrasting internal political dynamics of Croatia and Estonia demonstrate.

Whether linked to the collapse of an established state or not, manifestations of nationalism and efforts to democratize can affect each other in very different ways. Careful observers have distinguished between two types of nationalism: inclusionary "civic" nationalism, which is compatible with the observance of individual rights, and exclusionary ethnic nationalism, which tends to subordinate such rights to the collectivist claims of the nation.[37] Rarely if ever do these two types of nationalism exist in pure form, but the weighting of the two tendencies in citizens' attitudes varies enormously from one country to another.[38] For example, Ukraine might be placed close to the "civic" end of the spectrum, Latvia nearer the middle, and Serbia near the "ethnic" end.[39] Before the final third of the nineteenth century, when nationhood in Europe became closely linked to ethnicity, nationalism was commonly understood to be a concomitant of democracy, and in postcommunist cases such as Poland, this connection can still be seen.[40] A modicum of nationalism is indispensable for the creation and cohesion of a modern state; without it many citizens will lack an incentive to participate actively in democratic politics, as the case of Belarus demonstrates. On the other hand, exclusionary nationalism can lead to the effective disenfranchisement of substantial segments of the population – witness the behavior of the Serbian and Croatian governments toward minorities within their borders – and undergird dictatorial practices.

In addition to examining the historical roots of national identity in each country, analysts of postcommunist political change must examine other effects of the country's precommunist political legacy. Studies of democratization in states lacking a communist past have shown that countries which have had a prior experience of democracy, even if the experience has been unsuccessful, have a better chance of democratizing successfully on their second attempt.[41] Prior democratic experience may promote current democratization in several ways. If fairly recent, it may provide "human capital" – that is, persons with a first-hand understanding of democratic institutions and practices who can help launch and maintain the new political arrangements. Even if historically remote, previous experience may provide instructive lessons in the design of democratic institutions matched to the particular features of the country in question. Finally, previous experience may help legitimize new democratic institutions by protecting them against the xenophobic charge that they are an alien cultural import.

By comparison with many democratizing countries that were never communist, the postcommunist countries have little prior democratic experience on which to draw, as Valerie Bunce has forcefully argued. This disadvantage is clearest with respect to human capital. Measured against Latin America and Southern Europe, where authoritarian and democratic rule frequently alternated with one another in the past, "Eastern Europe has no such democratic tradition. The so-called democratic experiments of the interwar period lasted less than a decade and are best understood, in any case, as authoritarian politics in democratic guise." Lacking "the 'feel' for democracy that Latin America and Southern Europe enjoyed," postcommunist states face special political obstacles.[42]

These obstacles are not insurmountable, however. Even if short-lived, a nation's previous attempts to build democracy can give reformers not only potential models for contemporary governmental arrangements but also lessons about constitutional flaws that have contributed to past democratic failures. Political learning of this kind has occurred, for example, in Estonia and Latvia. More broadly, national memories or even myths of a democratic past may facilitate popular acceptance of democratic political structures.[43] This sort of process has occurred in both the Czech Republic and Poland. Citizens of Slovakia, by contrast, tend to regard interwar Czechoslovakian history as a period of alien domination by the Czechs rather than as an integral part of their own national past, and countries such as Ukraine effectively lack any modern experience of independent statehood. But even in nations such as these, a strong popular aversion to decades of communist oppression may compensate for the absence of a "usable" democratic past. Due to the exceptional severity of most communist regimes, this kind of negative learning may be considerably stronger in postcommunist countries than in noncommunist countries that aspire to democratize.

Like the effects of the precommunist legacy, the effects of communist rule on the prospects for democratic political participation warrant careful scrutiny in each country. Exactly what constitutes political participation, it should be said, is a matter of some disagreement among Western scholars. Defining the concept narrowly, specialists on the "classic" democracies have tended to concentrate on citizen involvement in such activities as voting and contacting government officials, and have frequently excluded citizen involvement in such "unconventional" activities as peaceful protests and demonstrations.[44] This narrower definition may stem from an understandable concern, sharpened by the history of Fascism and Communism, that authoritarian elites bearing the standard of "direct democracy" can manipulate mass movements to destroy the institutions of representative democracy.[45] By contrast, scholars interested in comparative political development have tended to define participation more broadly and have sometimes classified nearly all politically motivated activities, including political violence, under this rubric.[46] Analysts also have differed over the importance of the distinction between voluntary and compulsory participation. Specialists on established democracies have generally treated the contrast between these two forms of political involvement as a key difference between democratic and non-democratic systems, whereas some students of political development have minimized its significance.[47]

Voluntary participation and compulsory participation can each be found in both authoritarian and democratic polities. However, the relative proportions of these types of participation differ dramatically in authoritarian and democratic systems and help explain the qualitative differences between the two.[48] Main-line communist regimes systematically excluded most kinds of voluntary participation – particularly competitive elections for high government office and the freedom to form independent associations – and introduced novel forms of compulsory mass participation directed from above. Mandatory participation reached its zenith in the stage of full-fledged totalitarianism. Communist totalitarianism rested on the discovery that under certain conditions the expansion of mass education and the creation of new social organizations could be joined with mass coercion to multiply rather than diminish the power of the state.[49]

The totalitarian approach to political participation was linked with a radical stance toward society. In the Stalin era, Marxist–Leninist regimes sought to create a political system that not only compelled every citizen to endorse a common sociopolitical program but excluded the very notion of a pluralist society with autonomous interests distinct from those of the ruling elite.[50] In essence, these regimes sought to obliterate the dividing-line between state and society. Although they never completely succeeded, some of them came quite close. For most of the twentieth century, communist systems remained the most stable form of dictatorship – a form so stable that their transformation into liberal polities was said by some observers to be impossible.[51]

The erosion of communism did, of course, pave the way for the expansion of autonomous political participation by citizens and groups acting outside the control of the political elite. To begin with, not all national societies went through so shattering a totalitarian experience as did the nations of the USSR, and this lent them greater political resilience. Poland, where the Catholic Church retained a substantial measure of autonomy and agriculture was never fully collectivized, is probably the best example. Moreover, although communist regimes went to unprecedented lengths to instill the official ideology, their simultaneous drive to transform the economy and raise educational levels gradually expanded the social groups whose members later found those ideological claims implausible or absurd. For example, during the early stages of Stalin's industrialization drive, citizen support for the Soviet regime was directly correlated with an individual's youth and level of education – no doubt partly because education served as an important vehicle of upward social mobility. During the next four or five decades, the stratum of persons with higher education grew dramatically, but at some point support for the regime became inversely correlated with youth and level of education.[52] In many communist countries a small group of citizens became the nucleus of a nascent civil society – that is, in the broadest sense, a society whose members insisted on a separation between state and society and on the moral primacy of societal interests – which ultimately contributed to the downfall of the political regime.[53]

Although communist regimes have generally pursued similar social and economic policies, the effects of communist rule have varied among countries and have contributed to different national patterns of postcommunist political change. At each stage in the transition from communism, the course of events has been shaped by the strength of the ruling elite vis-à-vis the political opposition, as well as by the relative strength within each camp of hard-line groups hostile to compromise and groups favoring compromise for the sake of peaceful change.[54] The overall disposition of the ruling communist elite for or against reform has thus had an important effect on the political development of individual countries. The dynamics of change have also been affected by the presence or absence of a vigorous dissent movement, which has sometimes exerted an indirect but powerful long-term influence on both elite and mass attitudes toward democratization. The influence of a generation of liberal Soviet dissenters on the policies of Mikhail Gorbachev contrasts strikingly with the absence of reformist currents among the intellectuals and communist party leaders of Belarus during the same period. In addition, disparate levels of social development and varying mass political cultures have affected the political evolution of individual countries. A case can be made, for instance, that Central Asia's comparatively low levels of urbanization and education have impeded efforts to democratize the states of the region. In such countries as Kyrgyzstan, these low levels have made it difficult to subordinate particularistic loyalties and local ties to a countrywide sense of political engagement and civic responsibility.

Ruling elites and opposition leaders have typically crafted their stances toward democratization with an eye to the shifting national constellation of political forces, and each group's successes and failures have been strongly influenced by its capacity to generate political power. In struggles over the postcommunist order, new forms of democratic participation, ranging from peaceful mass demonstrations to competitive elections, have frequently been pitted against antidemocratic forms of political action, ranging from attacks by hired thugs to mob violence or all-out civil war, as in Tajikistan and Georgia. Intermediate types of political action, such as organized boycotts of elections and general strikes, have been resorted to by both advocates and opponents of democracy. In cases where hostile camps of similar strength have confronted one other, the outcome has depended not only on elite objectives and tactics, but on the content of mass attitudes and the level of mass mobilization in behalf of democratic reforms.[55]

The impact of violence on struggles over the postcommunist order is complex. The prevalence of nonviolent and noncoercive forms of politics improves the chances for a democratic outcome but does not guarantee it. Under certain conditions, dictators and authoritarian parties may be voted into office and then roll back a political system's democratic features, as the example of Belarus shows. In authoritarian systems, many forms of voluntary participation regarded as normal in democratic systems are illegal, and "unconventional" forms of participation such as mass demonstrations and strikes may be indispensable for launching and sustaining the process of democratization. In these circumstances, eyeball-to-eyeball confrontations and the implicit threat of violent escalation may be a spur to reform.[56] Nor does limited violence necessarily eliminate the possibility of further democratic change; instead it may sharpen leaders' and citizens' awareness of the high risks of further violence, as it arguably did in the clash between Russian president Boris Yeltsin and his parliamentary opponents in the fall of 1993. The example of Georgia suggests that even civil war may not completely block a state's subsequent movement in a democratic direction.[57]

Nevertheless, the threshold between nonviolent and violent political action remains extremely important. Violence makes the political stakes a matter of life or death. It deepens grievances among the losers, intensifies fears of liberalization among the winners, and reduces the chances for political compromise. Often it creates armed camps that are prepared to resort to force and have a vested interest in the continued use of force to decide political conflicts, as in the countries of the Transcaucasus. Even if it sweeps away old communist structures, it may make noncommunist dictatorship more likely. Paradoxically, it also may extend the political life of established elites that are tied to the military or the security police but manage to shift the blame for past misdeeds onto the shoulders of a few fellow culprits – as the first phase of Romania's postcommunist development illustrates. The absence of violence does not guarantee a democratic outcome, but it improves the chances for substantial progress in this direction; witness the contrast between Georgia's first violence-laden years of postcommunist politics and Bulgaria's relatively peaceful transition to democracy.

Elections, parties, and political development

The introduction of competitive elections as a means of selecting a country's governmental leaders is a watershed in the transition to democracy. Because electoral rules can decisively affect the prospects for the survival of particular parties – and sometimes for the survival of an entire country – they generally become an object of intense struggle.[58] In transitions from communism, this struggle has been shaped both by the attitudes of established communist elites and by the power at the disposal of the proponents of full-fledged democratization. In a large number of cases, a combination of ideological erosion within the elite and vigorous public pressure for reform have led the elite to accept electoral procedures that are genuinely democratic by Western standards. In some instances the elite has accepted a major expansion of democratic participation partly because of doubts about the strength or reliability of the instruments of coercion needed to block it. Some major turning-points in the history of the "classic" democracies of North America and Western Europe were shaped by a similar calculus of power.[59] In contrast to most of the classic cases, however, the introduction of competitive elections at the close of the communist era generally entailed an extremely rapid expansion of voluntary political participation.[60]

Numerous postcommunist countries, of course, have experienced only a partial liberalization of electoral rules and conditions; a handful have experienced none at all. In Uzbekistan and Kazakstan, for example, where popular pressure for democratization was relatively weak, established elites managed to exert a large measure of influence over the quasi-competitive elections introduced near the close of the communist era, and thereby kept enough control over national politics to avoid comprehensive democratic reforms.[61] In lands such as Belarus, the postcommunist manipulation of electoral rules was initially more oblique, but led within a few years to flagrant violations of democratic electoral practices. Another graphic illustration of this trend is the refusal of the Serbian and Croatian regimes to recognize the victories of opposition parties in national rounds of urban elections conducted in 1995 and 1996.

In those transitions from communism in which the balance of political forces has favored the introduction of genuinely democratic elections, the choice of possible electoral systems has been wider than in most noncommunist countries. By comparison with cases of democratization in Latin America, far fewer preauthoritarian political parties have survived in the former communist states; this has reduced pressures to return to preauthoritarian electoral rules and has increased the scope for political maneuver in framing new rules.[62] Communist successor parties and nascent noncommunist parties have often altered their stance on the specifics of electoral reform according to apparent shifts in their chances under one or another electoral dispensation. However, by the mid-1990s it became clear that many of the postcommunist regimes that have introduced genuinely competitive elections have adopted rules for legislative elections that show certain broad similarities. These rules, which commonly distribute some or all legislative seats on the basis of proportional representation, have been tacitly designed to reduce the risk of extra-constitutional clashes by ensuring that all major groups will be represented in the legislature.[63]

Competitive elections have given rise to a host of postcommunist parties.[64] But just how these parties have affected the development of democracy remains an open question. Western observers have long debated the positive and negative consequences of parties for democracy and democratic values.[65] Political parties often fail to perform some functions deemed essential by democratic theorists, and in many established democracies the political salience of parties has diminished in recent decades.[66] Nonetheless, every contemporary political system that satisfies either the minimalist or a more rigorous definition of democracy has political parties. This fact indicates that the political mechanisms which enable citizens to replace governmental leaders through competitive elections cannot function effectively in the absence of parties. In this sense, parties are indispensable for the survival of democratic systems.

Party-formation in postcommunist countries has been subject to some influences that are distinctive and others that are common to postcommunist and noncommunist countries alike. As noted above, the industrial and social policies of communist regimes created many of the socioeconomic conditions – especially vastly expanded education and urbanization – that facilitate the emergence of voluntary associations and political parties. On the other hand, after seizing power communist regimes typically destroyed all noncommunist parties – with the occasional exception of one or two small "satellite" parties. Moreover, the high level of mandatory participation in communist party activities reportedly imbued the public in many countries with a distrust of parties of any kind. Also, the turbulence of postcommunist socioeconomic upheavals has hampered the efforts of voters to assess their short- and long-term interests and to pick a party that will represent those interests.[67]

Postcommunist party-formation thus appears to face an unusual array of structural obstacles. Unlike many post-authoritarian transitions in Latin America and other parts of the Third World, there are virtually no shadow-parties, independent trade unions, or other societal organizations that have roots in the pre-authoritarian period and that can quickly be reactivated to fight new elections.[68] This suggests that the rate at which postcommunist parties crystallize into reasonably stable institutions might be closer to the rates of party-formation during the nineteenth century than to the rates in other new democracies near the end of the twentieth.[69] Preliminary results of studies currently under way suggest that in several cases, postcommunist levels of electoral volatility – that is, the aggregate shift of voters among parties from one national election to the next – are unusually high by comparison with democratizing countries that lack a communist past.[70]

Other considerations, however, point in the opposite direction. Techniques of party-formation may be learned from abroad by ambitious political leaders and activists who have a large stake in party development. In addition, the proportional-representation features of the electoral systems hammered out in many postcommunist countries facilitate the formation of new parties. The sudden expansion of the scope of participation in meaningful elections also must be taken into account. In the nineteenth century, the step-by-step expansion of the franchise in most countries provided an incentive to create programmatic parties that appealed to the interests of each newly enfranchised segment of the population. By contrast, the simultaneous admission of all social strata and economic groups into postcommunist electoral systems has created an incentive to establish catch-all parties that appeal to many different constituencies.[71] Hence the low level of programmatic coherence in many postcommunist parties should not necessarily be equated with institutional weakness. Finally, the postcommunist states show major differences in the rate at which reasonably stable parties and competitive party systems are taking shape. For instance, parties in the Czech Republic and Poland appear to be fairly well institutionalized and to have established partisan attachments with a significant proportion of the citizenry. In Russia and Ukraine, by contrast, the level of party identification remains very low.[72]

In evaluating the relationship between party systems and democratization, it is important to remember that parties and party systems are overlapping but distinct concepts.[73] As used here, party system denotes all a country's politically significant parties – that is, those parties, small as well as large, whose behavior has a major impact on national politics – and the dominant characteristics of those parties taken as a constellation of political actors. Although the classification of party systems is a notoriously tricky matter, some of the relevant criteria are the number of significant parties, the strength of parties' linkages to particular social groups, the ideological range separating major parties on any given issue, and whether the strongest parties are situated near the extremes of the political spectrum or clustered near the center. Among polities lacking meaningful party competition, Giovanni Sartori has distinguished strictly one-party systems from systems dominated by a hegemonic party that permits but may not be challenged by "satellite" parties. Among polities with meaningful party competition, he has differentiated polarized multiparty systems, moderate multiparty systems, two-party systems, and systems characterized by one dominant party that is open to real electoral challenge. Sartori also has emphasized the importance of whether a particular party system promotes centripetal or centrifugal forms of competition among the parties.[74]

Scholars disagree about the effects of different types of party systems and electoral arrangements on democracy. In particular, these disagreements center on the effects of multiparty systems versus two-party systems and of proportional-representation versus winner-take-all electoral arrangements.[75] However, scholars generally agree that systems having a large number of significant parties with weak ties to a volatile electorate are harmful to democracy. They also agree that democracies with relatively strong extremist parties are vulnerable to authoritarian takeovers. Such anti-system parties may function under democratic conditions for an extended period without giving up their authoritarian orientation. This point is illustrated by the communist parties of Western Europe after World War II: most retained an anti-system orientation for many years, whereas socialist parties tended to undergo a gradual change of political ethos.[76] The largest anti-system parties, in France and Italy, appear to have been sustained by the political orientations of party activists and intellectuals, national levels of personal dissatisfaction among ordinary citizens that were unusually high by international standards, and the polarizing effects of the Cold War.[77]

Writing in 1990, Samuel Huntington observed that the international wave of democratization that began in the mid-1970s was characterized by a "virtual absence of major antidemocratic movements" that posed "an explicit authoritarian alternative" to new democratic regimes.[78] It is important to ascertain whether the same can be said of the postcommunist parties and political movements that have arisen since Huntington wrote these words. In a number of countries, such as Hungary and Lithuania, communist successor-parties have shed their hostility toward liberal democracy and accepted alternations in control of the government as the normal state of affairs. In cases such as Russia and Belarus, however, the main successor-party has not clearly disavowed its past authoritarian ethos.

As a rule, the postcommunist evolution of a party's goals and strategy depends on both elite and mass attitudes. Some observers have suggested that substantial rates of continuity between communist-era and postcommunist elites give members of the old guard a personal stake in the emerging democratic and economic system and reduce the incentive to try to restore authoritarianism. According to this analysis, extremely low or extremely high rates of elite continuity invite an antidemocratic backlash or a smothering of democratic reforms.[79] By themselves, quantitative measures of elite turnover cannot explain democratization's victories and defeats. But they may explain a great deal when combined with an analysis of elite values and the institutional structures through which elite members strive to advance their interests.[80] Taken together, these factors can help identify the point at which personal attitudes and the national political context "tip" old elites into acceptance of democratic political arrangements and practices.

Broadly speaking, the likely causes of moderating change among communist successor parties include the erosion of authoritarian ideas through the discrediting of Marxism–Leninism and generational turnover among top party leaders; a sense of "democratic inevitability" produced by shifts in the balance of organized political forces inside the country and by the seeming international triumph of liberal democracy; and widespread opportunities for personal enrichment through privatization and insider dealing.[81] In Hungary, for example, the path of political reform has been smoothed by elite opportunities for personal gain. Conversely, the factors that have facilitated the persistence of anti-democratic orientations in some successor parties include low leadership turnover; an exodus of moderate and liberal members who joined the party purely to advance their professional careers; the weakness of popular pressures for political liberalization; and a centripetal pattern of inter-party competition caused in part by deepening socioeconomic cleavages.

New anti-system parties based on ethnicity can also disrupt the process of democratization. The apparent explosion in the worldwide incidence of ethnic conflicts in the 1990s is largely a product of the increased public salience accorded such conflicts due to the end of the Cold War.[82] Still, extremist parties do pose a special danger to societies in which deep ethnic cleavages override or coincide with other socioeconomic divisions. Under these conditions, as Donald Horowitz has shown, the ethnicization of political parties and party competition for immobile blocs of ethnic supporters can lead to polarizing elections that preclude democratic alternations of government and pave the way for violence and an authoritarian seizure of power.[83] Whether postcommunist ethnic cleavages are as deep and unmitigated as the Third-World cleavages analyzed by Horowitz is a matter for careful consideration. In such countries or regions as Bosnia Herzegovina and the Transcaucasus, they often are. But in other countries, such as Kazakstan and the Baltic states, they appear to be more susceptible to political management and more compatible with democratization. Occasionally, ethnic cleavages are deeper among national elites than among ordinary citizens, and the competition to mobilize voters for electoral campaigns actually serves to reduce ethnic polarization, as in Moldova.

Anti-system parties that promote antidemocratic goals through nonviolent means should be differentiated from parties that are closely linked with paramilitary forces and are prepared to initiate large-scale violence. Although parties of both types constitute threats to democratization, the latter are probably a greater threat than the former. Nonviolent anti-system parties may gradually be coopted into the status of semi-loyal or even loyal supporters of a democratic system.[84] By contrast, parties predisposed to violence may trigger cycles of political conflict that spiral out of control. They also may precipitate military intervention in politics, either by design or as a result of the violent civil clashes that they set in motion, as some radical parties did in Latin America during the 1970s. To date, most postcommunist antidemocratic parties appear to fall in the nonviolent category. But there have been exceptions, as in Tajikistan, and under the stresses of prolonged social and economic turmoil, this broad pattern might change.[85]

A country's party system, it should be emphasized, can undercut democracy even in the absence of significant antidemocratic parties. One threat to the survival of democratic government is a widespread public perception that it is incapable of dealing with the numerous political and socioeconomic problems bequeathed by the collapse of communism. Such a perception may be fostered by feuding parliaments and inertial cabinets that seem unable to solve critical problems, or by frequent changes in governing coalitions that give the appearance of failing even to address the problems. Some types of multiparty systems are especially conducive to frequent changes of government; to the degree that they contribute to the formation of ineffectual coalition governments, they may erode the legitimacy of the whole democratic enterprise.

Such debilitating party systems may be less common than one might suppose, however. Certain types of coalition governments may last nearly as long as single-party ones, and turnover in the partisan make-up of governing coalitions does not always result in sharp changes of policy.[86] Much depends on the political longevity of individual cabinet ministers – which may considerably exceed the duration of a particular government coalition – and on the degree of public consensus or division over policy questions. Some postcommunist countries, such as Poland, Lithuania, and Hungary, have experienced several changes in the governing coalition but still have sustained quite consistent macroeconomic and social policies for several years. Moreover, a democratic government may experience several failures of performance in the economic and social realms without necessarily undermining the popular legitimacy of democratic institutions, as we shall see below.

Some postcommunist countries, of course, have remained in the grip of a single monopolistic party, or a hegemonic one. Sartori has distinguished totalitarian and authoritarian one-party systems from "one-party pragmatic systems" that have low levels of ideological intensity and are based primarily on political expediency.[87] This characterization bears a close resemblance to Turkmenistan and might become applicable to a few other postcommunist countries. The question is whether such parties have become effective instruments of authoritarian rule or have encountered serious challenges from other political forces. In addition, it is important to determine whether the satellite parties tolerated by hegemonic rulers have acquired real political influence or have become even more marginal since the cresting of pro-democratic symbolism and gestures immediately after the fall of communism. The experience of Kazakstan suggests that the role of these parties depends in part on whether elite factions seek to develop them as a means of defending their interests against attacks from other elite groups.

The effects of political culture and political society

As already noted, the political development of any postcommunist country is strongly influenced by the attitudes and strategies of elites and the character of the parties and other institutions through which they vie for power. Equally important to long-term postcommunist outcomes are the initial condition and subsequent evolution of the country's political culture and political society. Broadly speaking, a country's political culture reflects the inhabitants' basic attitudes toward such matters as the trustworthiness of their fellow citizens, the legitimacy of others citizens' rights and interests, the fashion in which conflicting interests ought to be reconciled, the ability of citizens to influence government policies, and the legitimacy of existing political institutions. A civic political culture embodies high levels of interpersonal trust, a readiness to deal with political conflict through compromise rather than coercion or violence, and acceptance of the legitimacy of democratic institutions.[88] It stands to reason that political culture affects whether citizens choose to support moderate or extreme political movements and parties, and whether they choose to engage in democratic or anti-democratic forms of political participation.[89]

Empirical evidence suggests that a country's political culture is neither fixed once and for all, nor completely malleable. It changes in response to new historical events and personal experiences, but with a considerable lag, and primarily through the generational turnover of citizens.[90] This makes political culture an important determinant of the way that political institutions evolve and operate. Over time political institutions and major sociopolitical events exert a reciprocal influence on the content of the country's political culture. But in any given period, the content of the political culture shapes the perceptions and actions of the political elite and the mass public.

A country's political culture and its political society are closely intertwined. The notion of political society is often defined broadly to include political parties, but here it is used to denote those nonparty, nongovernmental groups and associations that participate, directly or indirectly, in shaping a country's political life. The nature of these groups and associations varies widely according to the type of political society in question.[91] Civic associations, commercial enterprises, extended clans, and criminal organizations are examples of such groups. As some of these examples suggest, a political society may include a sizable number of organizational components but still not embody the values of a civic culture. In a statistical sense, social structure and the content of political culture are related; witness the widely accepted proposition that the rise of the middle class is a source of liberal democracy, and the more controversial notion that the working class is the main social basis of authoritarianism.[92] Analytically, however, social structure and political culture are distinct, and the relationship between them may vary from one country to the next. Taken in the aggregate, a country's political society generally reflects its prevailing political culture and significantly affects the operation of its governmental institutions.[93]

Civil society is a form of political society based on a dense network of nongovernmental associations and groups established for the autonomous pursuit of diverse socioeconomic interests and prepared to rebuff state efforts to seize control of these activities.[94] The components of a civil society may include such elements as independent media, religious confessions, charitable organizations, business lobbies, professional associations, labor unions, universities, and non-institutionalized movements for various social causes. The existence of a civil society depends not only on the presence of large numbers of associations and organized groups but on the spirit in which they act. The divergent fashions in which political thinkers have depicted civil society reflect the reality that relations among societal groups inevitably entail conflict as well as cooperation.[95] A society is civil only if its constituent groups demonstrate a substantial measure of self-restraint rooted in a recognition of the legitimacy of the interests of other groups – a recognition often reinforced by the existence of overlapping group memberships – and a commitment to forgo violence as means of deciding social conflicts. Because in the aggregate the structures of a civil society embody a civic culture, such a society is conducive to the consolidation of democratic governmental institutions. Under a democratic dispensation, the relationship of civil society to the state involves a large measure of cooperation as well as conflict.[96]

The application of the concepts of political culture and civil society to countries during their communist phase entails several difficulties. Until the late communist era, systematic survey data on citizens' political attitudes were generally unavailable for most communist countries; this created a risk that analysts would erroneously attempt to infer the characteristics of mass political culture from the history and structure of the regime rather than from the empirically measured values of the population.[97] Confusion also has arisen from the attribution of several disparate meanings to the concept of civil society: these range from the notion of small oppositional movements under communist regimes to the notion of the macrostructure of entire societies in noncommunist or postcommunist states.[98] Certainly the *idea* of a civil society with values and interests superior to those of the party–state apparatus was ardently embraced by many dissidents and played an important role in delegitimizing the quasi-totalitarian pretensions of a number of communist regimes. But how widely this idea was held by ordinary citizens in most countries is difficult to establish. During the communist era the notion of civil society was plainly not embodied in a ramified network of independent social organizations and associations, although elements of such a network began to crystallize during the late communist era in Poland.[99]

In addition, it is important to inquire whether all the activists who tenaciously championed the concept of civil society as a source of resistance to communism have been capable of making a postcommunist transition to tolerance and cooperation with groups whose central values and concerns differ from their own. Put differently, not all dissidents and anticommunist groups were liberals. Adamant opposition to communist rule was not necessarily equivalent to support for democracy or for compromise among conflicting societal groups, as the examples of Georgia's Zviad Gamsakhurdia and Croatia's Franjo Tudjman show. Nor do all autonomous social institutions find the transition from communism to liberal democracy easy; witness the controversies in Poland over the efforts of the Roman Catholic hierarchy to influence legislation on abortion and the curriculum of public schools.

Applying the concepts of political culture and civil society to postcommunist countries has proved easier but still entails some complexities. In many countries a wealth of survey data on popular attitudes and behavior has now become available. However, scholars have tended to disagree about the implications of political culture for postcommunist democratization.[100] Those who believe that it constitutes a serious obstacle have generally argued that the political culture which existed before the end of communism has considerable staying-power. The sources of this inertia may include enduring precommunist traditions of dictatorship and ultranationalism, as well as authoritarian attitudes absorbed by citizens from Marxist–Leninist propaganda and frequent contact with the party–state apparatus. According to this view, the content of mass political culture increases the possibility of a reversion to some form of authoritarian rule – or to its preservation in countries where the political hold of the old elite has never been broken.

Other scholars have taken a different approach that stresses the compatibility of postcommunist political culture with democratization in many countries. Research along these lines has revealed that major West European democracies and some East European countries show broad if incomplete similarities in political culture – and that some East European citizens exhibit greater acceptance of the rights of ethnic minorities than do most West Europeans.[101] Analysts of this school have often stressed the depth of the ideological erosion that occurred during the final decades of communist rule. Arguing that postcommunist political culture is more prodemocratic than Marxist–Leninist propaganda would lead one to expect, they have suggested that memories of the violence and repression experienced under communism have strengthened citizens' attachment to attitudes of tolerance and non-violence conducive to democratization.[102] Adherents of this school of thought also maintain that intergenerational turnover strongly favors democratization because younger citizens are more enthusiastic about a transition to democratic politics and market economies, partly because they can adapt more easily and have longer time-horizons in which to enjoy the personal benefits of reform.

Closely related to such issues is the question whether a particular country's postcommunist political society bears any resemblance to a civil society in the social-structural sense. Mapping the organizational density and value orientations of a whole society is an enormous intellectual task that scholars have only begun to attempt. Nonetheless, several things seem clear. Without key components of civil society, governmental structures that are formally democratic cannot be expected to operate in a fashion that is substantively democratic. This is particularly true of independent media, which serve not only as direct advocates for societal interests but as important channels through which the members of societal groups communicate with one another and voice demands on the government. In Poland, for instance, independent print and broadcast media have played a major part in the democratic process. In Serbia, by contrast, government manipulation of the media has been so extensive that opportunities for fair electoral competition at the national level have virtually been eliminated.

The character of political society varies sharply among postcommunist countries. Networks of nongovernmental organizations and voluntary associations are growing far more rapidly in states such as Poland and the Czech Republic than in states such as Belarus and Uzbekistan. But even in countries where this growth has been relatively rapid, the infrastructure of civil society has not yet approached the density and durability of such social networks in long-established democracies; in many countries the heavy dependence of the non-profit sector on funding from the state or foreign sources makes it particularly vulnerable.[103] Moreover, processes occurring after the collapse of communism may profoundly alter a country's political society and political culture – and not necessarily in a direction favorable to democracy. Of particular consequence are economic stabilization and liberalization, the privatization of state property, and changes in the levels of legality and public order.

Economic stabilization and liberalization hold out the promise of a long-term improvement in living standards, but at the cost of bruising economic hardships in the short run. When communism first collapsed, outside observers tended to adopt the pessimistic view that democratization and market reform were basically incompatible.[104] This outlook appears to have been shaped by a tendency to analyze the political behavior of economic groups schematically and to view the issue through the lens of a few dramatic but unrepresentative cases such as Chile.[105] With time it has become clear that the relationship between postcommunist democratization and economic reform varies from one phase to another and from one country to another. Economic elites and members of the working class are not monolithic blocs and do not pursue static goals. Moreover, the goals of more narrowly defined economic groups, including labor unions, encompass interests that are broadly political as well as strictly economic.[106] The citizens of many postcommunist countries do regard economic prosperity as a central feature of liberal democracy, but they seem prepared to endure material hardships so long as they believe that economic circumstances will ultimately improve.[107] On the other hand, the severe hardships inflicted on many persons by economic reform may ultimately sharpen disillusionment with democracy – especially if these hardships are accompanied by rapidly increasing disparities of income and extensive corruption.[108]

The effects of privatization on the prospects for democratization also are likely to vary. A wide distribution of private property has long been regarded by many political theorists as an essential check on the authoritarian tendencies that may arise even in popularly elected governments. In addition to this putative benefit, the privatization of state property may facilitate democratization by offering members of the old elite a means of personal aggrandizement more lucrative and far less risky than attempting to reinstate an authoritarian order. However, the insider dealings that help neutralize the former elite as a source of collective opposition also may give rise to mass sentiments that equate democracy with social injustice and rampant corruption. This is especially likely to occur if elite corruption and an equivocal elite attitude toward economic reform produce a protracted depression of popular living standards. Although national understandings of corruption and conflict of interest vary substantially from country to country, the process of economic transformation has made postcommunist countries susceptible to corruption on an unusually large scale.[109] Under these conditions, threats to democracy may come not so much from political and economic elites as from newly enfranchised citizens embittered by the emergence of a plutocracy. In Russia and several East Europe states, public disapproval of the privatization of state economic enterprises has grown substantially since 1991.[110] For most voters, political patience has thus far outweighed economic dissatisfaction, but a long-term economic downturn and an appearance of unchecked social injustice might alter their outlook.

This is one reason that changes in the level of legality and public order are significant. Economic liberalization may lead toward a civil society sustained by the growth of socioeconomic groups with a vested interest in further democratic change, predictable commercial laws, and vigorous civic associations. But the legacy of the totalitarian state may favor elements of an "uncivil" society rather than a civil one. Unless augmented by the growth of smaller civic associations, quasi-corporatist labor and industrial organizations like those in Slovakia and the Czech Republic may become the sort of large, impersonal entities that some Western political theorists view as endangering rather than embodying a civil society.[111] Similarly, deregulation of economic life in the absence of an adequate legal structure and a trustworthy state bureaucracy may lead to the domination of economic activity by predatory business and criminal groups indifferent or hostile to democracy, especially a democracy which blocks some highly profitable activities through effective laws and institutions.[112] At its worst, deregulation of this sort could generate not only citizen disillusionment with the elected leaders who set the process in motion, but also a widespread reaction against basic democratic values.

Perhaps the most fundamental question is whether most citizens in each country believe that democratization and economic reform are essential or that realistic alternatives exist. Comparing the initial phases of dual transitions – that is, the simultaneous liberalization of national political and economic systems – in selected countries of Latin America and Eastern Europe sheds light on this question. One striking difference between the two sets of countries is that elites and citizens were much more strongly convinced of the necessity for fundamental economic change in Eastern Europe than in Latin America.[113] This conviction, in turn, apparently has given greater impetus to the postcommunist drive for liberalization and has reduced the potential for a powerful political backlash against economic reforms. Evidence from some cases, such as Russia, shows that despite economic turmoil and dissatisfaction, public support for democratic political practices has grown substantially since 1991.[114]

In other words, the "deep beliefs" of the citizens of postcommunist countries – their most strongly held attitudes and values, as opposed to transient opinions about day-to-day politics – may be of decisive importance. In Western countries, disillusionment and cynicism about particular leaders and governmental institutions coexist with a continuing commitment to democratic principles.[115] The project's case studies suggest that similar split-level outlooks exist among the citizens of a number of postcommunist countries. The fact that significant proportions of citizens believe that their new governments are unresponsive or corrupt may be taken as a loss of faith in democracy. But it also may be interpreted quite differently – as an accurate assessment of current political realities, and as the social foundation for further efforts to achieve a full-fledged democratic order.

NOTES

I am grateful to Joan Nelson, Valerie Bunce, and Karen Dawisha for helpful comments on an earlier version of this chapter.

1   For a penetrating analysis of the global process of democratization, see Samuel Huntington, *The Third Wave: Democratization in the Late Twentieth Century* (Norman, OK: University of Oklahoma Press, 1991). For shifting Western views of communist systems, including the assertion that they could never be liberalized, see Abbott Gleason, *Totalitarianism: The Inner History of the Cold War* (New York: Oxford University Press, 1995), pp. 198–209.

2   The notion of the reinvention of politics is borrowed from Vladimir Tismaneanu, *Reinventing Politics: Eastern Europe from Stalin to Havel* (New York: Free Press, 1992).

3   See, among many possible examples, J. F. Brown, *Surge to Freedom: The End of Communist Rule in Eastern Europe* (Durham, NC: Duke University Press, 1991); Gale Stokes, *The Walls Came Tumbling Down: The Collapse of Communism in Eastern Europe* (New York: Oxford University Press, 1993); Sabrina Petra Ramet, *Social Currents in Eastern Europe: The Sources and Consequences of the Great Transformation*, 2d ed. (Durham, NC: Duke University Press, 1995); Tismaneanu, *Reinventing Politics*; Brendan Kiernan, *The End of Soviet Politics: Elections, Legislatures, and the Demise of the Communist Party* (Boulder, CO: Westview Press, 1993); Archie Brown, *The Gorbachev Factor* (Oxford: Oxford University Press, 1996); John Dunlop, *The Rise of Russia and*

the Fall of the Soviet Empire (Princeton: Princeton University Press, 1993); and M. Stephen Fish, *Democracy from Scratch: Opposition and Regime in the New Russian Revolution* (Princeton: Princeton University Press, 1995).

4   For example, *The Social Legacy of Communism*, ed. James R. Millar and Sharon L. Wolchik (Washington, DC and Cambridge: Woodrow Wilson Center Press and Cambridge University Press, 1994); *The Legacies of Communism in Eastern Europe*, ed. Zoltan Barany and Ivan Volgyes (Baltimore: Johns Hopkins University Press, 1995); J. F. Brown, *Hopes and Shadows: Eastern Europe after Communism* (Durham, NC: Duke University Press, 1994); Karen Dawisha and Bruce Parrott, *Russia and the New States of Eurasia: The Politics of Upheaval* (New York: Cambridge University Press, 1994); *New States, New Politics: Building the Post-Soviet Nations*, ed. Ian Bremmer and Ray Taras, 2d ed. (New York: Cambridge University Press, 1996); Anatol Lieven, *The Baltic Revolution: Estonia, Latvia, Lithuania and the Path to Independence*, 2d ed. (New Haven: Yale University Press, 1994); and *Central Asia and the Caucasus after the Soviet Union: Domestic and International Dynamics*, ed. Mohiaddin Mesbahi (Gainesville: University Press of Florida, 1994).

5   See, for instance, *Transition to Democracy in Poland*, ed. Richard F. Starr (New York: St. Martin's, 1993); Raymond Taras, *Consolidating Democracy in Poland* (Boulder, CO: Westview Press, 1995); Rudolf Tőkés, *Negotiated Revolution: Economic Reforms, Social Change, and Political Succession in Hungary, 1957–1990* (Cambridge: Cambridge University Press, 1996); Lenard J. Cohen, *Broken Bonds: Yugoslavia's Disintegration and Balkan Politics in Transition*, 2d ed. (Boulder, CO: Westview, 1995); Sabrina Petra Ramet, *Balkan Babel*, 2d ed. (Boulder, CO: Westview, 1996); Susan Woodward, *Balkan Tragedy: Chaos and Dissolution after the Cold War* (Washington, DC: Brookings Institution, 1995); Richard Sakwa, *Russian Politics and Society* (New York: Routledge, 1993); *Elections and Political Order in Russia*, ed. Peter Lentini (New York and Budapest: Central European University Press, 1995); *The New Russia: Troubled Transformation*, ed. Gail W. Lapidus (Boulder, CO: Westview Press, 1995); Stephen White, Richard Rose, and Ian McAllister, *How Russia Votes* (Chatham, NJ: Chatham House Publishers, 1997); *Independent Ukraine in the Contemporary World*, ed. Sharon Wolchik (Prague: Central European University Press, forthcoming); and Alexander Motyl, *Dilemmas of Independence: Ukraine after Totalitarianism* (New York: Council on Foreign Relations, 1993).

6   For example, Anders Åslund, *Post-Communist Economic Revolutions: How Big a Bang?* (Washington, DC: Center for Strategic and International Studies, 1992); Adam Przeworski, *Democracy and the Market: Political and Economic Reforms in Eastern Europe and Latin America* (Cambridge: Cambridge University Press, 1991); *A Precarious Balance: Democracy and Economic Reforms in Eastern Europe*, ed. Joan Nelson (Washington, DC: Overseas Development Council, 1994); Joan Nelson et al., *Intricate Links: Democratization and Market Reforms in Latin America and Eastern Europe* (Washington, DC: Overseas Development Council, 1994); *The Privatization Process in Central Europe*, ed. Roman Frydman et al. (Budapest and New York: Central European University Press, 1993); *The Privatization Process in Russia, Ukraine, and the Baltic States*, ed. Roman Frydman et al. (Budapest and New York: Central European University Press, 1993); Roman Frydman et al., *Corporate Governance in Central Europe*

and Russia, 2 vols. (Budapest and New York: Central European University Press, 1996); *Banking Reform in Central Europe and the Former Soviet Union*, ed. Jacek Rostowski (Budapest and New York: Central European University Press, 1995); Max Ernst et al., *Transforming the Core: Restructuring Industrial Enterprises in Russia and Central Europe* (Boulder, CO: Westview, 1996); and Anders Åslund, *How Russia Became a Market Economy* (Washington, DC: Brookings Institution, 1995).

7 Although the fullest coverage of democratization in the Third World has been devoted to Latin America, in the past few years more attention has been paid to democratization in other Third–World countries. See, for instance, *Politics in Developing Countries; Comparing Experiences with Democracy*, ed. Larry Diamond, Juan J. Linz, and Seymour Martin Lipset (Boulder, CO: Lynne Rienner, 1990).

8 For differing views on this question, see Kenneth Jowitt, *The New World Disorder: The Leninist Extinction* (Berkeley: University of California Press, 1992), pp. 284–305; Sarah Meiklejohn Terry, "Thinking about Post-Communist Transitions: How Different Are They?" *Slavic Review* 52, no. 2 (Summer 1993), 333–37; Philippe C. Schmitter and Terry Lynn Karl, "The Conceptual Travels of Transitologists and Consolidologists: How Far to the East Should They Attempt to Go?" *Slavic Review* 53, no. 1 (Spring 1994), 173–85; Valerie Bunce, "Should Transitologists Be Grounded?" *Slavic Review* 54, no. 1 (Spring 1995), 111–117; idem., "Comparing East and South," *Journal of Democracy* 6, no. 3 (July 1995), 87–100. See also Beverly Crawford and Arend Lijphart, "Explaining Political and Economic Change in Post-Communist Eastern Europe: Old Legacies, New Institutions, Hegemonic Norms, and International Pressures," *Comparative Political Studies* 28, no. 2 (July 1995), 171–99. The most comprehensive empirical examination of this issue is Juan J. Linz and Alfred Stepan, *Problems of Democratic Transition and Consolidation: Southern Europe, South America, and Post-Communist Europe* (Baltimore: Johns Hopkins University Press, 1996), which appeared just as this book was going to press.

9 *Developments in East European Politics*, ed. Stephen White, Judy Batt and Paul G. Lewis (Durham, NC: Duke University Press, 1993); *Developments in Russian and Post-Soviet Politics*, ed. Stephen White, Alex Pravda, and Zvi Gitelman (Durham, NC: Duke University Press, 1994); *The New Democracies in Eastern Europe: Party Systems and Political Cleavages*, 2d ed., ed. Sten Berglund and Jan Ake Dellenbrant (Brookfield, VT: Edward Elgar, 1994); *Party Formation in East-Central Europe*, ed. Gordon Wightman (Aldershot: Edward Elgar, 1995); *Public Opinion and Regime Change: The New Politics of Post-Soviet Societies*, ed. Arthur H. Miller et al. (Boulder, CO: Westview Press, 1993); *Political Culture and Civil Society in Russia and the New States of Eurasia*, ed. Vladimir Tismaneanu (Armonk, NY: M. E. Sharpe, 1995); Richard Rose, *What Is Europe?* (New York: HarperCollins, 1996); *Social Justice and Political Change: Public Opinion in Capitalist and Post-Communist States*, ed. James R. Kluegel, David S. Mason, and Bernd Wegener (New York: Aldine de Gruyter, 1995); *Stabilising Fragile Democracies: Comparing New Party Systems in Southern and Eastern Europe*, ed. G. Pridham and P. G. Lewis (London: Routledge, 1996).

10 As noted in the Preface, the term "Eastern Europe" is employed for the sake of conciseness; in this book it does not presuppose political or cultural uniformity among the countries that it encompasses.

11 The distinction between civil society and other forms of political society is discussed below.

12 Barbara Geddes, "Challenging the Conventional Wisdom," *Journal of Democracy* 5, no. 4 (October 1994), 117.

13 *Politics, Power, and the Struggle for Democracy in South-East Europe*, ed. Karen Dawisha and Bruce Parrott (New York: Cambridge University Press, 1997); *Democratic Changes and Authoritarian Reactions in Russia, Ukraine, Belarus, and Moldova*, ed. idem (New York: Cambridge University Press, 1997); and *Conflict, Cleavage, and Change in Central Asia and the Caucasus*, ed. idem (New York: Cambridge University Press, 1997).

14 See especially Robert Dahl, *Polyarchy: Participation and Opposition* (New Haven: Yale University Press, 1971), and Dahl, *Democracy and Its Critics* (New Haven: Yale University Press, 1989).

15 I am obliged to Sabrina Ramet for bringing this important point to my attention.

16 It is worth noting that such cases have not been confined to postcommunist democracies but have occurred in other democracies as well. India and Turkey, for example, have harshly suppressed some ethnic minorities among their citizens. (Samuel Huntington, "Democracy for the Long Haul," *Journal of Democracy* 7, no. 2 [April 1996], 10.)

17 Ghia Nodia, "How Different Are Postcommunist Transitions?" *Journal of Democracy* 7, no. 4 (October 1996), 15–17, 22–24.

18 This definition is derived from Joan Nelson, "How Market Reforms and Democratic Consolidation Affect Each Other," in Nelson et al., *Intricate Links*, pp. 5–6. For a similar but stricter definition designed to take direct account of military threats to democracy, see Juan J. Linz, "Transitions to Democracy," *Washington Quarterly*, 13 (1990), 156. For a more complex definition that deals also with the social and economic realms, see Juan J. Linz and Alfred Stepan, "Toward Consolidated Democracies," *Journal of Democracy* 7, no. 2 (April 1996), 34–51.

19 Guillermo O'Donnell, "Illusions about Consolidation," *Journal of Democracy* 7, no. 2 (April 1996), 38 and passim. Cf. Richard Guenther et al., "O'Donnell's 'Illusions': A Rejoinder," ibid. 7, no. 4 (October 1996), 151–59.

20 For example, a team of scholars has argued that consolidation was achieved within five years of the first democratic elections in Spain and within seven years of such elections in Greece. About a decade after the elections, elite and public acceptance of the superiority of democracy over all other forms of government in these two countries matched the average level in the countries of the European Union. By contrast, in Brazil, where the process of electoral democratization began at about the same time as in Spain, the level of elite and public acceptance of democracy remained far lower. Guenther et al., "O'Donnell's 'Illusions,'" 155-56.

21 For a sample of the Western debates over which form of democracy is more stable, see the chapters in Part II of *The Global Resurgence of Democracy*, ed. Larry Diamond and Marc F. Plattner (Baltimore: Johns Hopkins University Press, 1993).

22 Eugene Huskey discusses the applicability of this concept to Kyrgyzstan in his chapter in *Conflict, Cleavage, and Change*.

23 Guillermo O'Donnell, "Delegative Democracy," *Journal of Democracy* 5, no. 1 (1994), 59–60, 67.

24 Cf. Huntington, *Political Order in Changing Societies*, p. 177 f.

25 Huntington, *The Third Wave*, pp. 231–32.

26 On the other hand, the breakdown of communism has frequently been accompanied by a blurring of the line between civilian and military affairs and by the participation of some military men, as individuals, in civilian politics. See *State Building and Military Power in Russia and the New States of Eurasia*, ed. Bruce Parrott (Armonk, NY: M. E. Sharpe, 1995), esp. chs. 2, 8, and 13. Cf. Cohen, *Broken Bonds*, pp. 85–88, 183–88, 227–33, and Woodward, *Balkan Tragedy*, pp. 166–69, 255–62.

27 Charles Fairbanks, Jr., "The Postcommunist Wars," *Journal of Democracy* 6, no. 4 (October 1995), 18–34.

28 Assessing the character of the international environment leaves considerable room for disagreement among observers, especially where ideological and cultural currents are concerned. For example, Samuel Huntington has asserted that Marxist–Leninist regimes, Nazi Germany, and the advanced capitalist democracies shared some ultimate political values because they were all parts of the same Western civilization. In my view these three Western traditions were divided at least as fundamentally as are liberal democratic thought and the authoritarian strands of non-Western cultural traditions. See Huntington, "The Clash of Civilizations?" *Foreign Affairs* 72, no. 3 (Summer 1993), 23, 44, plus the reply from Fouad Ajami in ibid. 72, no. 4 (September-October 1993), 2-9.

29 Huntington, *The Third Wave*, pp. 86–100; see also the chapters by Geoffrey Pridham, Laurence Whitehead, John Pinder, and Margot Light in *Building Democracy? The International Dimension of Democratisation in Eastern Europe*, ed. Geoffrey Pridham et al. (New York: St. Martin's Press, 1994), pp. 7–59, 119–68; and Nodia, "How Different are Postcommunist Transitions?," 15–16, 20–23.

30 Richard Ullman, "The Wars in Yugoslavia and the International System after the Cold War," and Richard Sobel, "U.S. and European Attitudes toward Intervention in the Former Yugoslavia: *Mourir pour la Bosnie?*" in *The World and Yugoslavia's Wars*, ed. Richard H. Ullman (New York: Council on Foreign Relations, 1996), pp. 9–41, 145–81.

31 During the critical early phases of the Yugoslav civil war, NATO's member-states were preoccupied with managing the consequences of the unification of Germany, other major European-security problems thrown up by the collapse of the Soviet bloc, and the Persian Gulf War. See Ullman, "The Wars in Yugoslavia and the International System after the Cold War," Stanley Hoffman, "Yugoslavia: Implications for Europe and for European Institutions," and David C. Gombert, "The United States and Yugoslavia's Wars," in *The World and Yugoslavia's Wars*, pp. 14–15, 24–31, 36, 102–18, 122–30, 136–37.

32 Samuel Huntington, *The Clash of Civilizations and the Remaking of World Order* (New York: Simon and Schuster, 1996), pp. 192–98.

33 Bunce, "Comparing East and South," 91.

34 In such instances, democratic theory provides no reliable means of determining which proposed outcome is preferable. This, in turn, often spurs the advocates of each proposed outcome to argue their case in still more vehement and uncompromising terms. See Dahl, *Democracy and Its Critics*, pp. 32–33.

35 Linz and Stepan, "Toward Consolidated Democracies," 20–21; Jacek Kochanowicz, "Reforming Weak States and Deficient Bureaucracies," in *Intricate Links*, pp. 195–96.

36 For a fuller treatment of this question, see my "Analyzing the Transformation of the Soviet Union in Comparative Perspective," in *The End of Empire? The Transformation of the USSR in Comparative Perspective*, ed. Karen Dawisha and Bruce Parrott (Armonk, NY: M. E. Sharpe, 1996), pp. 13–14, 16–20.

37 Liah Greenfeld, *Nationalism: Five Roads to Modernity* (Cambridge: Harvard University Press, 1992), pp. 8–12. Cf. John Breuilly, *Nationalism and the State*, 2d ed. (Chicago: University of Chicago Press, 1993), pp. 404–24.

38 For a penetrating discussion of this issue, see Rogers Brubaker, *Citizenship and Nationhood in France and Germany* (Cambridge: Harvard University Press, 1992).

39 One set of opinion surveys suggests considerable variation in the levels of acceptance or hostility expressed by members of several East European nations toward other ethnic groups. The levels of hostility expressed by Serbs in 1992 appear to be unusually high, although this contrast may be due partly to the fact that Serbia was at war when the survey was conducted. Mary E. McIntosh and Martha Abele MacIver, *Transition to What? Publics Confront Change in Eastern Europe*, Occasional Paper No. 38, Woodrow Wilson International Center for Scholars, Washington, DC, 1993, pp. 15–17.

40 On these linkages in the nineteenth century, see E. J. Hobsbawm, *Nations and Nationalism since 1780: Programme, Myth, Reality*, paperback ed. (New York: Cambridge University Press, 1990), ch. 1.

41 Huntington, *The Third Wave*, p. 44.

42 Bunce, "Comparing East and South," 89. Bunce grants that interwar Czechoslovakia constitutes a partial exception to this generalization.

43 Note, too, that democratic experience is a matter not simply of kind but of degree; hence scholars may apply different chronological and substantive standards to assess whether a country has had prior national experience with democracy.

44 See, for example, Sidney Verba, Norman H. Nie, and Jae-on Kim, *Participation and Political Equality: A Seven-Nation Comparison* (Chicago: The University of Chicago Press, 1978).

45 For an analogous trend in historians' treatment of American populism, see Peter Novick, *That Noble Dream: The "Objectivity Question" and the American Historical Profession* (New York: Cambridge University Press, 1988), pp. 337–41.

46 See, for example, Samuel Huntington, *Political Order in Changing Societies* (New Haven: Yale University Press, 1968), chs. 1, 3; and Samuel Huntington and Joan Nelson, *No Easy Choice: Political Participation in Developing Countries* (Cambridge: Harvard University Press, 1976), p. 13.

47 In his classic study of political development, Huntington adopts a definition that conflates voluntary and compulsory forms of political participation and attaches little explanatory significance to the differences between the two. (*Political Order in Changing Societies*, chs. 1, 3; cf. Theodore H. Friedgut, *Political Participation in the USSR* [Princeton: Princeton University Press, 1979], ch. 5.) In a later book he and Joan Nelson do emphasize the distinction by differentiating "autonomous" from "mobilized" participation. (Huntington and Nelson, *No Easy Choice*, pp. 7–15.) In *The Third Wave*, Huntington sometimes employs the narrower definition favored by students of liberal democracy. For example, he states that one-party systems, among which he includes communist regimes, have "suppressed both competition and participation" (p. 111).

48 Huntington and Nelson, *No Easy Choice*, pp. 7–15.

49 In Russia, for example, the tsarist regime long feared the expansion of mass education as a threat to its legitimacy. The Soviet regime quickly recognized that the expansion of mass education would allow it to indoctrinate individuals during a stage of social and personal development when their capacities for abstract thought were weakly developed, making them highly susceptible to manipulation from above.

50 Gregory Grossman, "The USSR – A Solidary Society: A Philosophical Issue in Communist Economic Reform," in *Essays in Socialism and Planning in Honor of Carl Landauer*, ed. Gregory Grossman (Englewood Cliffs, NJ: Prentice Hall, 1970); Robert F. Miller, "Civil Society in Communist Systems: An Introduction," in *The Developments of Civil Society in Communist Systems*, ed. Robert F. Miller (New York: Allen and Unwin, 1992), p. 5.

51 Huntington, *Political Order in Changing Societies*, emphasizes the stability of communist dictatorships. See also Gleason, *Totalitarianism*, pp. 198–209.

52 Brian D. Silver, "Political Beliefs and the Soviet Citizen," and Donna Bahry, "Politics, Generations, and Change in the USSR," in *Politics, Work, and Daily Life in the USSR: A Survey of Former Soviet Citizens*, ed. James Millar (New York: Cambridge University Press, 1987), pp. 116–121; Donna Bahry, "Society Transformed? Rethinking the Social Roots of Perestroika," *Slavic Review* 52, no. 3 (Fall 1993), 514–17.

53 Miller, "Civil Society in Communist Systems: An Introduction," pp. 6–11; Moshe Lewin, *The Gorbachev Phenomenon* (Berkeley, CA: University of California Press, 1988). The concept of civil society as a separate sphere of social life superior to the state first emerged in the late eighteenth and early nineteenth centuries. See John Keane, "Introduction," and idem., "Despotism and Democracy," in *Civil Society and the State*, ed. John Keane (New York: Verso, 1988), pp. 22–25, 35–71.

54 For a general discussion of these factors, see Huntington, *The Third Wave*, ch. 3, and Guillermo O'Donnell and Philippe C. Schmitter, *Transitions from Authoritarian Rule: Tentative Conclusions about Uncertain Democracies*, paperback ed. (Baltimore: Johns Hopkins University Press, 1986), pp. 61–64.

55 For an illuminating analysis of this general issue based on noncommunist cases, see Sidney Tarrow, "Mass Mobilization and Regime Change: Pacts, Reform, and Popular Power in Italy (1918–1922) and Spain (1975–1978)," in *The Politics of Democratic Consolidation: Southern Europe in Comparative Perspective*, ed.

Richard Gunther et al. (Baltimore, MD: Johns Hopkins University Press, 1996), pp. 204–30.

56 For example, in the spring of 1991 the radical reform forces led by Boris Yeltsin staged a peaceful mass demonstration in Moscow, and Soviet miners launched a damaging strike that included demands for political reform and the resignation of President Mikhail Gorbachev. The sequence of events suggests that these public demonstrations of support for Yeltsin helped persuade Gorbachev to abandon his temporary reliance on conservative political forces and grant large concessions to the advocates of further reform. Brown, *The Gorbachev Factor*, pp. 283–88; Jonathan Aves, "The Russian Labour Movement, 1989–91: The Mirage of a Russian Solidarność," in Jeffrey Hosking et al., *The Road to Post-Communism: Independent Political Movements in the Soviet Union, 1985–1991*, paperback ed. (New York: St. Martin's Press, 1992), pp. 151–52.

57 In addition to the chapter by Darrell Slider in *Conflict, Cleavage, and Change*, see Jonathan Aves, *Georgia: From Chaos to Stability?* (London: Royal Institute of International Affairs, 1996).

58 In conditions of acute political tension, certain electoral rules can heighten the probability of civil war; and different electoral rules can lead to a legitimate victory of right–wing, centrist, or left–wing parties under the same distribution of popular votes. See Rein Taagepera and Matthew S. Shugart, *Seats & Votes: The Effects & Determinants of Electoral Systems* (New Haven: Yale University Press, 1989), ch. 1.

59 For example, the weakness of the US government's coercive capacities played a major role in the Federalists' reluctant decision to accept the creation of the Democratic–Republican party in the 1790s, when parties were still generally regarded as illegitimate factions harmful to democratic government. (Martin Shefter, *Political Parties and the State: The American Historical Experience*, paperback ed. [Princeton: Princeton University Press, 1994], pp. 9–10; James R. Sharp, *American Politics in the Early Republic: The New Nation in Crisis* [New Haven: Yale University Press, 1993], pp. 208–25).

60 One noteworthy historical exception is revolutionary France. For a concise historical description of the complex struggles over the scope and forms of electoral participation in several European countries, see Stein Rokkan, "Elections: Electoral Systems," *International Encyclopedia of the Social Sciences*, vol. 5 (London: Macmillan and the Free Press, 1968), pp. 7–13.

61 White et al., *How Russia Votes*, pp. 29–34; Dawisha and Parrott, *Russia and the New States of Eurasia*, pp. 148–53.

62 Barbara Geddes, "A Comparative Perspective on the Leninist Legacy in Eastern Europe," *Comparative Political Studies* 28, no. 2 (July 1995), 261–65.

63 Krzysztof Jasiewicz, "Sources of Representation," in *Developments in East European Politics*, pp. 137–46. Most of these new electoral systems also have established a minimum-vote threshold for party representation, meant to avoid a paralyzing proliferation of splinter parties in the legislature.

64 In this discussion a political party is defined as an organization that (a) is identified by an official label (b) seeks to place its representatives in government office or to change the governmental system and (c) employs methods that include mobilizing citizens and participating in free elections if the state allows such elections. This definition encompasses both political organizations that

pursue or exercise power solely through democratic methods and organizations that pursue or exercise power largely through non-democratic means. On the other hand, it excludes single-issue interest groups whose avowed purpose is not to place their representatives in government office. It also excludes organizations that pursue power solely through violent means.

65 For a brief historical account of American distrust of the impact of parties on democracy, see Alan Ware, *Citizens, Parties, and the State: A Reappraisal* (Princeton: Princeton University Press, 1987), ch. 1.

66 A list of important democratic functions includes (a) mobilizing a large proportion of the citizenry to participate in politics (b) ensuring the representation of all social groups (c) allowing citizens to select individual governmental leaders directly (d) promoting the optimal aggregation of social interests (e) ensuring that government officials fulfill their electoral promises and (f) punishing the originators of failed governmental policies. Note that not all these functions can be fulfilled simultaneously. For example, (b) and (c) are at odds, as are (b) and (d). (Ware, *Citizens, Parties, and the State*, pp. 23–29, 150–241; G. Bingham Powell, Jr., *Contemporary Democracies: Participation, Stability, and Violence*, paperback ed. [Cambridge: Harvard University Press, 1982], pp. 73–78.) The causes of party decline are attributable to such factors as media-based political campaigns, the "surrogate" effects of public opinion surveys, the displacement of some party activities by narrowly-focused interest groups, and a tendency for more citizens to regard themselves as political independents unwilling to vote automatically for any party's slate of candidates. (Robert D. Putnam, "Troubled Democracies: Trends in Citizenship in the Trilateral World," paper prepared for the planning workshop of the Project on Democratization and Political Participation in Postcommunist Societies, Washington, DC, April 1995; and Thomas Poguntke, "Explorations into a Minefield: Anti-Party Sentiment," *European Journal of Political Research* 29, no. 3 (April 1996), 319–44.)

67 Valerie Bunce, "Uncertainty in the Transition: Post-Communism in Hungary," *East European Politics and Societies* 7, no. 2 (Spring 1993), 240–75.

68 Nelson, "Introduction," in *A Precarious Balance*, pp. 4–5; Robert H. Dix, "Democratization and the Institutionalization of Latin American Political Parties," *Comparative Political Studies* 24, no. 4 (January 1992), 488–511.

69 In nineteenth-century democracies, most political parties crystallized and expanded gradually, as the suffrage was widened and as socioeconomic changes made more citizens susceptible to political mobilization. In England, for example, Liberal and Conservative elites took at least 20 years to build party structures capable of exploiting the widening of the suffrage that occurred in mid-century. Ware, *Citizens, Parties, and the State*, pp. 22–23.

70 Conference on Political Parties and Democracy, sponsored by the International Forum for Democratic Studies, National Endowment for Democracy, November 18–19, 1996, Washington, DC.

71 Geddes, "A Comparative Perspective," 253–57.

72 See the chapters by Andrew Michta and David Olson in this volume; the chapters by Michael Urban and Ilya Prizel in *Democratic Changes and Authoritarian Reactions in Russia*; Dawisha and Parrott, *Russia and the New States of Eurasia*, p. 131; and White et al., *How Russia Votes*, p. 135.

73 The pioneering scholarly writings on parties focused solely on individual parties rather than on party systems, and a tendency to blur the distinction has persisted in some more recent scholarly analyses. (Harry Eckstein, "Parties, Political: Party Systems," *International Encyclopedia of the Social Sciences*, vol. 11, pp. 436–53.) One weakness of Huntington's seminal treatise on political development is that it assigns great weight to parties but tends to conflate parties with party systems. See Huntington, *Political Order in Changing Societies*, ch. 7.

74 Giovanni Sartori, *Parties and Party Systems: A Framework for Analysis* (New York: Cambridge University Press, 1976); Powell, *Contemporary Democracies*, pp. 74–80. For a discussion of the problems of classifying party systems, particularly by numerical criteria alone, see Eckstein, "Party Systems."

75 See especially Powell, *Contemporary Democracies*, pp. 74–80.

76 Sartori, *Parties and Party Systems*, pp. 132–42.

77 For the correlation between levels of personal dissatisfaction and the strength of extreme parties of the Left or Right in these two countries, see Ronald Inglehart, *Culture Shift in Advanced Industrial Society*, paperback ed. (Princeton: Princeton University Press), pp. 36–40.

78 Huntington, *The Third Wave*, p. 263.

79 John Higley et al., "The Persistence of Postcommunist Elites," *Journal of Democracy* 7, no. 2 (April 1996), 133–47; Michael Burton and John Higley, "Elite Settlements," *American Sociological Review* 52 (June 1987), 295–307.

80 For a critique of past elite studies and comparative survey data showing unusually deep attitudinal cleavages within the Soviet/Russian political elite during both the Gorbachev and Yeltsin eras, see David Lane, "Transition under Eltsin: The Nomenklatura and Political Elite Circulation," forthcoming in *Political Studies*.

81 For data showing that the political attitudes of former communist party members and individuals who never belonged to the communist party are quite similar in Bulgaria, Romania, and several countries of East–Central Europe, see the table in Rose, *What Is Europe?* p. 142. (The table pools the national data sets, so that no conclusions for individual countries can be drawn from it.)

82 According to a careful study, in the past decade the number of ethnic conflicts has grown at approximately the same rate as in the 1960s and 1970s. See Ted Robert Gurr and Barbara Harff, *Ethnic Conflict in World Politics* (Boulder, CO: Westview, 1994), pp. 11, 13.

83 Horowitz, *Ethnic Groups in Conflict*, Part Three.

84 Juan Linz, *The Breakdown of Democratic Regimes: Crisis, Breakdown, & Reequilibration* (Baltimore: Johns Hopkins University Press, 1978), ch. 2.

85 For a general discussion of the connection between political parties and terrorism, see Leonard Weinberg, "Turning to Terror: The Conditions under Which Political Parties Turn to Terrorist Activities," *Comparative Politics* 23, no. 4 (July 1991), 423–38.

86 Arend Lijphart, *Democracies: Patterns of Majoritarian and Consensus Government in Twenty-One Countries*, paperback ed. (New Haven: Yale University Press, 1984), ch. 7; Powell, *Contemporary Democracies*, ch. 7.

87 Sartori, *Parties and Party Systems*, pp. 221–25.

88 My interpretation of these concepts, which have sparked vigorous scholarly debate, is derived from such works as Gabriel Almond and Sidney Verba, *The Civic Culture: Political Attitudes and Democracy in Five Nations*, paperback ed.

(Boston: Little, Brown and Co., 1965), and Inglehart, *Culture Shift in Advanced Industrial Societies*. Most of the controversial issues are well covered in *The Civic Culture Revisited*, ed. Gabriel Almond and Sidney Verba (Newbury Park, CA: Sage Publications, 1980). For reasons of space, my discussion omits several important distinctions, such as the existence of national political subcultures and differences between elite and mass political cultures.

89 However, scholars have disagreed about the particular cultural dispositions that actually support democracy. See especially Edward Muller and Mitchell Seligson, "Civic Culture and Democracy: The Question of Causal Relationships," *American Political Science Review* 88, no. 3 (September 1994), 635–52. Naturally, an important role is also played by non-cultural factors, such as the behavior of the state and major changes in citizens' socioeconomic circumstances.

90 Inglehart, *Culture Shift*, chs. 1–3. For evidence of dramatic increase in the democratic elements of German political culture and a decline in the civic elements of British and US political culture during the three decades following World War II, see the chapters by David Conradt, Dennis Kavanagh, and Alan Abramowitz in *The Civic Culture Revisited*.

91 For a discussion that relates civil society to other forms of political society, see Ernest Gellner, *Conditions of Liberty: Civil Society and Its Rivals* (New York: Allen Lane/The Penguin Press, 1994).

92 Seymour Martin Lipset, *Political Man: The Social Bases of Politics* (New York: Anchor Books, 1963), ch. 4.

93 Robert Putnam, *Making Democracy Work: Civic Traditions in Modern Italy* (Princeton: Princeton University Press, 1993). Cf. Sidney Tarrow, "Making Social Science Work Across Space and Time: A Critical Reflection on Robert Putnam's *Making Democracy Work*," *American Political Science Review* 90, no. 2 (June 1996), 389–98.

94 This paragraph is based on Dawisha and Parrott, *Russia and the New States of Eurasia*, pp. 123–25. For a nuanced discussion of the historical evolution of the concept of civil society, see Keane, "Despotism and Democracy," pp. 35–72.

95 For an exposition of these theoretical differences, which have centered especially on whether commercial organizations based on private property belong to civil society or undermine it, see Keane, "Introduction," pp. 13–14, and "Despotism and Democracy," esp. pp. 62–66. On the connection between civil society and relations within the family, see Carol Pateman, "The Fraternal Social Contract," pp. 101–28 in the same volume.

96 Larry Diamond, "Rethinking Civil Society: Toward Democratic Consolidation," *Journal of Democracy* 5, no. 3 (July 1994), 4–17.

97 For a discussion of this and other problems of analyzing political culture in the USSR and Russia, see Frederick J. Fleron, Jr., "Post-Soviet Political Culture in Russia: An Assessment of Recent Empirical Investigations," *Europe–Asia Studies* 48, no. 2 (March 1996), 225–60.

98 In keeping with prevailing usage before about 1800, the concept of civil society has sometimes been construed even more broadly to include both democratic governmental institutions and social structures conducive to democracy. However, this definition prevents analysis of the interactions between government and society that may fundamentally change the political system.

99   "Under whatever name – 'parallel *polis*,' 'independent culture,' or 'independent society' – the idea of civil society remained largely restricted to narrow circles of independent intellectuals in every East and Central European country save one. The exception . . . was Poland." Aleksander Smolar, "From Opposition to Atomization," *Journal of Democracy* 7, no. 1 (January 1996), 26.

100 Of necessity, this short excursus oversimplifies the analytical issues and omits discussion of the empirical variations among countries. For a general discussion of scholarly tendencies to explain postcommunist political development in terms of either "communist legacies" or "liberal institutional" determinants, see Crawford and Lijphart, "Explaining Political and Economic Change in Post-Communist Eastern Europe."

101 McIntosh and MacIver, *Transition to What? Publics Confront Change in Eastern Europe*, esp. pp. 6, 14.

102 For an insightful juxtaposition of survey data gathered from displaced Soviet citizens after World War II and data collected from Soviet emigrants during the late Brezhnev period, see Bahry, "Society Transformed? Rethinking the Social Roots of Perestroika." The data suggest that in the late Stalin years up to 50 percent of Soviet citizens may have favored a relaxation of intellectual controls, and that by the late Brezhnev period this percentage may have increased substantially (ibid., p. 539). On the role of authoritarian violence in strengthening the appeal of democracy, see Giuseppe di Palma, *To Craft Democracies: An Essay on Democratic Transitions*, paperback ed. (Berkeley: University of California Press, 1990), pp. 19–23, 150–51.

103 For a survey of the voluntary sector in advanced industrial democracies, see *Between States and Markets: The Voluntary Sector in Comparative Perspective*, ed. Robert Wuthnow (Princeton: Princeton University Press, 1991).

104 Geddes, "Challenging the Conventional Wisdom," 104; Jose Maria Maravali, "The Myth of the Authoritarian Advantage," *Journal of Democracy* 5, no. 4 (October 1994), 17–31; Joan Nelson, "Labor and Business Roles in Dual Transitions: Building Blocks or Stumbling Blocks?" in *Intricate Links*, p. 147. This issue was, of course, the subject of vigorous public debate in the West.

105 Geddes, "Challenging the Conventional Wisdom," 109–111.

106 In Eastern Europe, for example, labor unions have played a role in dislodging some government coalitions from power and have pressed governments to adopt their policy preferences. However, anti-democratic union violence and general strikes have been unusual and have tended to occur in countries, such as Romania, whose party systems have been least capable of representing workers' interests. Nelson, "Labor and Business Roles in Dual Transitions," pp. 154–63.

107 Linz and Stepan, "Toward Consolidated Democracies." For example, in Russia's 1996 presidential run-off, Boris Yeltsin won the votes of more than two-thirds of the persons who believed the government would solve the economy's problems in 10 years or less. By contrast, Genadii Zyuganov, the communist party candidate, won the support of 70 percent of those who thought the government would never be able to solve these problems. (*New Russia Barometer VI: After the Presidential Election*, Centre for the Study of Public Policy, University of Strathclyde, Glasgow, 1996, p. 13.) Considerable evidence also suggests that many categories of workers, though hard-hit by economic reform, have devised unofficial sources of income that are not reflected in

gloomy official estimates of declining output. See Daniel Kaufman and Aleksander Kaliberda, "Integrating the Unofficial Economy into the Dynamics of Post-Socialist Economies: A Framework of Analysis and Evidence," in *Economic Transition in Russia and the New States of Eurasia*, ed. Bartlomiej Kaminski (Armonk, NY: M. E. Sharpe, 1996), pp. 81–120.

108 In Russia and several democracies of Eastern Europe, public opinion has shifted since 1991 toward more support for government involvement in the economy, although acceptance of economic inequalities has simultaneously grown in most of the same countries. A recent survey of several postcommunist countries found that the only one in which public attitudes have moved toward greater support for egalitarianism is Russia. (James Kluegel and David S. Mason, "Social Justice in Transition? Attitudinal Change in Russia and East-Central Europe," paper presented at the annual convention of the American Association for the Advancement of Slavic Studies, Boston, November 1996.) In the early 1990s, measurable economic inequalities in postcommunist countries generally remained smaller or no larger than than those in Western democracies. (Branko Milanovic, "Poverty and Inequality in Transition Economies: What Has Actually Happened," in *Economic Transition in Russia and the New States of Eurasia*, pp. 180–81.)

109 For a discussion of national variations in the understanding of corruption, see Michael Johnston, "Historical Conflict and the Rise of Standards," in *The Global Resurgence of Democracy*, pp. 193–205.

110 Kluegel and Mason, "Justice Perceptions in Russia and Eastern Europe, 1991–1995"; Richard Dobson, "Is Russia Turning the Corner? Changing Russian Public Opinion, 1991–1996," *Research Report*, Office of Research and Media Reaction, US Information Agency, September 1996, pp. 11–13.

111 Miller, "Civil Society in Communist Systems," p. 9; Keane, "Despotism and Democracy," pp. 64–66.

112 Richard Rose, "Toward a Civil Economy," *Journal of Democracy* 3, no. 2 (1992), 13–25, and Kochanowicz, "Reforming Weak States and Deficient Bureaucracies," pp. 195–204, 214–22. The fullest account of the criminalization of economic activities in Russia is Stephen Handelman, *Comrade Criminal* (New Haven: Yale University Press, 1995).

113 Nelson, "How Market Reforms and Democratic Consolidation Affect Each Other," pp. 11–13.

114 Dobson, "Is Russia Turning the Corner?" pp. 8–9.

115 For example, surveys of citizens in the European Community's member-countries show that the average percentage of respondents saying they were "very satisfied" or "fairly satisfied" with the way democracy works ranged between 66 and 41 percent in 1985–1993. Leonardo Morlino and Jose R. Montero, "Legitimacy and Democracy in Southern Europe," in *The Politics of Democratic Consolidation: Southern Europe in Comparative Perspective*, p. 239.

2 Democratization and political participation: research concepts and methodologies

Karen Dawisha

The primary objectives of the Project on Democratization and Political Participation have been to gauge the prospects for democratization in Eastern Europe and the former Soviet Union by systematically examining and comparing trends in the organized political activities of society in each country and to contribute to the theoretical discussion about the determinants of these trends. This chapter has several objectives. It begins with an discussion of how the concepts of democracy, democratization, and democratic consolidation are defined and operationalized in this project. Three sections then follow in which the research questions which have guided the project are discussed (the questions themselves are presented in the Appendix), along with propositions and hypotheses derived from the existing literature on democratization. The sections substantively address three disparate parts of the democratization process: two sections on inputs to the process, namely factors influencing the formation of political groups and parties, and the political evolution of society, and one section on outcomes, namely the factors affecting the possible emergence of party systems in postcommunist states.

Conceptualizing democracy and democratization

What is meant by democracy, and how is the process of democratization understood in this project? In line with recent research,[1] a procedural or minimalist conception of democracy was employed. Democracy is defined as a political system in which the formal and actual leaders of the government are chosen through regular elections based on multiple candidacies and secret balloting, with the right of all adult citizens to vote. It is assumed that leaders chosen via free and fair elections, using universal adult suffrage, will be induced to modify their behavior to be more responsive to popular wishes and demands than leaders in authoritarian states.

There remains, however, the crucial task of making the transition from the conceptual level to the empirical-observational level. Even if the features of the conception can be elaborated, how does one determine their presence or their absence over time, within individual countries or across the postcommunist world? Simply put, how does one know when the level of democracy is high, or when it is low or non-existent? Over the past thirty years or so, there have been numerous attempts at objectively measuring democracies.[2] Some of the more recent efforts such as those of Kenneth Bollen have, arguably, resulted in more finely calibrated instruments.[3] These measures are most useful as indicators of the extent to which democracy exists in a country at a specific time. In and of themselves, they are not useful for explaining democratic change. As noted recently, "with these scores, one can only estimate the extent to which democracy has advanced or regressed in that given country over a very long period of time or compare the country with others similarly scored."[4] Indeed most analysts who draw up such indicators would be the first to recognize that their contribution has been in measuring democracy, not explaining its underlying dynamics.

Civil liberties and political rights can be viewed as two distinct conceptual dimensions of democracy. The dimension of political rights can be, more or less, directly observed. The degree to which adult suffrage is universal, elections are fairly conducted, and all persons are eligible for public office can be directly observed through objective analysis of electoral laws and practices. The degree to which leaders freely compete for votes can be ascertained in a similar manner. An analysis of political rights allows one to draw conclusions about the level of democracy, since it can reasonably be hypothesized that the higher the number of rights universally enjoyed by the population, the greater will be the level of democratization.

Democracy is also dependent upon the provision of civil liberties, specifically: (1) freedom to form and join organizations; (2) freedom of expression; and (3) access to multiple and competing sources of information. Empirical data can be garnered to support a judgment about the extent to which the three components of civil liberties exist. It is assumed that the more the number and level of civil liberties enjoyed by a country's population, the greater will be the level of democratization. Thus, political rights and civil liberties serve as indicators of democracy and both must be present in order for a country to be classified as democratic. Through the assignment of numerical values to the empirical properties representing political rights and civil liberties, according to consistent rules, one could draw up a representation of the level of democracy existing within a country at any given time.

Such a measure, however, would not necessarily allow one to conclude that any given democracy was likely to be both stable and durable. Indeed, the free and unfettered exercise of political rights and liberties has been seen on occasions as negatively affecting the durability of democracies, sometimes obliging leaders and populations to accept various trade-offs which would limit the degree of representation of societal groups in return for sustaining democratic institutions over time. A good example is the tendency of democracies to introduce measures which effectively limit the number of parties that can be represented in the legislature to those which gain above a certain percentage threshold of the popular vote, so as to lessen the impact of minority opinion and of groups at the left and right of the political spectrum and magnify the influence of majoritarian views and centrist groups. Such measures, while in fact denying some voters the right to have their votes have an equal impact upon outcomes, are justified by reference to the universal interests of all voters in ensuring the long-term durability of democratic institutions.

Equally, democracies vary in their protection of civil liberties such as freedom of speech and assembly. Many established democracies curtail the rights of groups which have in the past shown their intent to overthrow the democratically elected order. These actions, too, are justified by reference to the right of the state to limit the liberties of some in the short term in order to ensure the liberty of all in the long-term.

Finally, one must distinguish between democracy and democratization. To a certain extent, all states, even those that call themselves, and are recognized by others as, democratic are still evolving, either towards or away from more democracy. The perennial debates in even the most stable democracies about justice, liberty, equity, rights, and governability reflect this continuing concern. But more problematic is drawing the line between an authoritarian polity which is breaking down and a democratic entity which is emerging. When can one say that the process of democratization actually begins? For the purposes of this project, democratization is said to begin when the first set of free and fair elections for national-level office takes place. This first set of elections must be accompanied in short order by the granting of civil liberties and political rights and the establishment of both state institutions that operate according to the rule of law and intermediate organizations that mediate between the citizen and the state. If these events do not take place, then it is likely that the process of democratization will not be fully consolidated.

Measuring democratic consolidation

Unlike the numerous efforts to measure democracy systematically, relatively few attempts have been made to measure democratic consolidation. Central to this notion is acceptance that not all states that start out on the road to democracy will complete the transition. Some will fall back into authoritarianism, others might regress into civil war, others will maintain a low equilibrium democracy for decades, verging constantly on the brink of collapse.[5] And all transitions will differ, combining as they do on the one hand individual historical legacies, leaders, socioeconomic foundations and international interactions and on the other hand the policies pursued by elites and their varied impact on individual societies at any given time.

A consolidated democracy is one in which most major social groups expect that government leaders will be chosen through competitive elections and regard representative institutions and procedures as their main channel for processing claims on the state. One way of measuring consolidation is to apply a "two-turnover test," in which a democracy "may be viewed as consolidated if the party or group that takes power in the initial election at the time of the transition loses a subsequent election and turns over power to those election winners, and if those election winners then peacefully turn over power to winners of a later election.[6] Thus, for example, when communism fell, a first round of elections was held. Typically two to four years later, a second round was held: if the group in power since the fall of communism was displaced, this would count as the first turnover. Only after this group or party was displaced by a second round of elections could one then speak of a country having passed the 'two turn-over test.' Of the postcommunist states, only postcommunist Lithuania had by the end of 1996 passed such a test: the Lithuanian Democratic Labor Party, the renamed Communist Party, took power from the conservative Sajudis led by Vytautas Landsbergis in 1992, and then surrendered it back to Landsbergis' party (the renamed Homeland Union) when they lost parliamentary elections in November 1996. However, such a test has been criticized on the grounds that it would fail to classify either interwar Eastern Europe or postwar Italy or Japan as democracies. Moreover, if used alone, it does not provide levels of calibration and gradation adequate for the comparative scope of the project. Also while a determination could be made if a democracy were consolidated or not using a two-turnover test, it would not be possible to answer the questions "why?" or "why not?" using the test.

In measuring democratic consolidation over time within a given country or across nations, it may prove more theoretically informative to treat it as a continuum, rather than a two-step process. There are at least four distinct conceptual aspects of democratic consolidation, each of which could be observed by various measures: the two-turnover test, low public support for anti-system parties or groups, high public commitment to the fundamental values and procedural norms of democratic politics, and elite consensus about the desirability of institutionizing and legitimizing democratic norms and values.[7]

An index could be constructed by combining the latter three indicators if the criteria for the two-turnover test are not met. This would serve at least three purposes. First, several variables relating to democratic consolidation could be represented by a single score, thereby reducing the complexity of the data and facilitating comparison. Second, such an index could provide a quantitative measure of democratic consolidation amenable to statistical manipulation. Finally, because it measures several properties, the index is inherently more reliable than a measure based on a single factor.

Clearly, democratic consolidation is still a goal in almost all of the postcommunist countries, yet significant strides have been made. Autonomous societal action has largely replaced communist dictatorship in most countries; and the notions of choice, competition, and tolerance are increasingly salient. As emphasized in the working definition of democracy, elections should be based on multiple candidacies that ensure real opportunities for electoral competition. Informal alliances rapidly evolved into political parties in the wake of the communist collapse: these parties are gradually becoming rooted and stable. The following section examines some of the factors influencing the formation of political groups and parties across the countries under investigation. In each of the following sections, the research questions (as presented in the Appendix) which were given to the authors are used as the basis for deriving hypotheses and propositions, and a consideration is made of the range of results which might be expected from the various hypotheses. This section is followed by sections on the political evolution of society and on the emergence of political parties and party systems.

Factors influencing the formation of parties

Authors were presented with a number of questions, listed in the Appendix, which addressed the factors influential in forming the political groups and parties, considered as a cornerstone in any country's move toward democracy. The comparative literature is deeply divided over the relative influence of historical, ethnic, social, cultural, institutional, and economic factors in determining the success of a country's move toward democracy. This section was intended to elicit the panel's responses to these various issues.

In the literature on transitions, it is generally assumed that those countries which have to establish a national identity before going on to build the institutions of the state and inculcate civic virtues in the populace will face the greatest challenge.[8] In doing so they will have to replace other national identities which may command popular support if the new state was carved out of old ones and strive to surpass and mobilize the other nested identities of family, clan, region, and ethnicity in the service of a new civic mindedness.

Authors were asked to elaborate the key elements of the precommunist historical legacy of each country. They were additionally asked to focus on any precommunist experience of democracy, and whether elements of the postcommunist polity, such as particular government structures, intermediary associations, and political parties have been modeled on precommunist patterns.

The literature would appear to support three interrelated hypotheses: polities with a strong, unified national identity based on a precommunist legacy of independence will be able to make the most rapid and peaceful transition to sovereign independence; those polities with a precommunist tradition of exclusivist nationalism will have more difficulty in making the transition to democracy; and those polities with a precommunist tradition of competitive multiparty systems are most likely to be successful in establishing stable multiparty democracies.

It could reasonably be assumed that those countries which are being "reborn" after a period of communist suppression would have an enormous advantage over states being established for the first time. One would expect a shorter time in putting basic institutions in place, in passing a constitution and other basic laws, and in regularizing state-society relations on the basis of a national accord. States coming into existence for the first time are not able to operate on the basis of historical trust or on a shared remembrance of the role the state played in the past in forging a partnership between state and society to nourish and sustain the nation. On the contrary, given the role of the state in the communist period in suppressing both nation and society (although to be sure the nation was often harnessed to the needs of the state during times of crisis in all the communist states and was symbiotically allied to the state in Yugoslavia, Hungary, and Romania in particular), any state without a precommunist legacy of trust might reasonably be expected to falter in the project of legitimization.

There are, however, two related dilemmas: first, countries that are resurrecting states which, in the precommunist era, had an authoritarian character may have more difficulty overcoming the burden of this legacy than countries that are creating state institutions anew. Secondly, while a regeneration of a previous national identity is expected to facilitate the process of state-building, if the national identity was exclusivist, then its renaissance might promote state-building but impede democratization. This tendency is underscored by Beverly Crawford and Arendt Lijphart, who address the problem that unlike in France or England, where nationalism had its origins in the Enlightenment, in Eastern Europe and the former Soviet Union, it had its roots "in the Russian and German tradition of *Volk*, blood, *narod*, and race as the basis for membership in the nation."[9] To be sure, the distinctions between the historical origins of the national identities of the Germans and Russians on the one hand and the British and the French on the other are clear. Yet this view does not account sufficiently for the fact that even in England, the process of transforming narrow English identity centered in the Home Counties into a greater United Kingdom entailed the forcible suppression of independent national aspirations in Wales and Scotland, as we;; asa lengthy and continuing struggle with Northern Ireland. And despite this, democratization proceeded apace in Great Britain, suggesting that the connections between a state's formative national identity and the identity which underpins its institutions is not fixed for all time.

It is also posited in the transitions literature that those states with precommunist traditions of multiparty elections and capitalist development are more likely to be able to reestablish these institutions. There are two reasons: one is that to the extent that a state had already adopted a multiparty system and/or capitalism in the past, protracted and often divisive national debates on paths of development could be avoided. Additionally many of the actual laws governing political and economic life can be resuscitated with only minor amendments. Of course, given the number of ultra-nationalist parties that inhabited the landscape of interwar Eastern Europe, the resuscitation of these parties has not necessarily promoted simultaneous liberalization.

Postcommunist states have had to sift through, resurrect, and overcome elements not only of their precommunist heritage, but also of their communist past. Authors were asked to identify key elements of the legacy of the communist era. In addition, they were asked to speculate on how the political and social evolution of each country in the late communist era (e.g., the emergence or nonemergence of a significant dissent movement) affected the postcommunist formation of societal interest groups and parties.

Prevalent in the field are two core assumptions that require some systematic elaboration: first, the assumption that the more and the longer a country was subjected to the antidemocratic and totalitarian features of Stalinism, the less likely will be the chances of democracy succeeding, and secondly, if there is a prior history of democracy and civil society, and a communist legacy of reform and openness, then the chances of a successful transition to democracy will be greater and the speed of transition will be quicker.

The literature on the legacy of the communist era is vast, growing, and divided. Most would agree that communism left a "poisonous residue"[10] on virtually all aspects of society, but whether that residue can easily be washed away is open to controversy. Those who subscribe to the view that the legacy of communism will be significant and abiding look at its effect in several areas.[11] Politically, the fact that there essentially were no public politics in the communist era is presumed to have left a deep legacy: there were no self-governing institutions, no interest groups or rival parties operating independent of the state, and no competing sources of information. At the same time, Soviet systems were characterized by a single elite which, while capable of being split into factions, did not regularly or routinely circulate into and out of power. These elites, it was assumed by some, would resist the construction of new institutions which would limit the reach of their authority.[12] Some would see these features as a significant barrier to the emergence of democracy and civil society.[13] Other authors also assume that the Soviet-era largely succeeded in one of its aims, namely to destroy the pre-Leninist past, thus robbing these societies of their ability to resurrect precommunist identities, parties, and institutions.[14]

Soviet-style systems, in addition, were command economies controlled from the center, without private ownership of the means of production or market relations. As the sector ideologically most suited to the Stalinist world view and economically most capable of thriving under command conditions, the military-industrial complex grew to become not only the dominant sector of the economy but also the only sector which functioned more or less according to plan. The performance of this sector in most communist countries (most notably the USSR, Yugoslavia, and the Slovak sector of Czechoslovakia) not only gave central planning whatever credibility it enjoyed but also was designed to form the protective outer shell for the entire system, leading analysts inside and outside the country to attribute far more capability to the economy and the system as a whole than ultimately it possessed.[15] This sector bequeathed to the successor states industries which could produce high quality goods but which required both continued subsidies and a Cold War-style mission concomitant with its size and orientation. Additionally, it is believed by some that sectors of the military-industrial complex in Russia, in support of like-minded groups within the Ministry of Interior, the revamped KGB, and the Ministry of Defense, have been a major buttress of a strong but not necessarily democratic or non-imperial state.[16]

Underneath this strong outer shell resided the light industrial and consumer sectors of the economy which were denied funds, resources, initiative, and personnel – virtually everything except planning targets; and after de-Stalinization ended the use of terror to force compliance, these could be met only by bribery, corruption, distortion, and the formation of informal and illegal production networks. The fact that such a high percentage of total state economic interactions took place outside the plan meant that whatever performance the economy achieved was bought at the expense of the integrity of the planning mechanism of the state and the trust, loyalty, and ultimately the compliance of the population. These socioeconomic and political failures weakened central control, but also left a legacy of cynicism and disrespect for the state, to say nothing of the vast array of informal economic networks which fell out of the state and beyond the law when the regimes collapsed.[17] In *New World Disorder*, Ken Jowitt predicted that the combined legacy of bureaucracy, corruption, and interpersonal distrust would hinder the implementation of democratic reforms, although it is unclear from his analysis whether and why this legacy might vary across countries and whether and why it might be relatively transient.[18]

The great difficulty of establishing political and economic institutions from the bottom up cannot be overstated: Samuel Huntington found that twenty-three of the twenty-nine countries that democratized during the so-called "third wave" (between 1974 and 1990) had previous democratic experience. Equally, those that had not democratized by 1990 had no democratic past. So while states are not condemned necessarily to relive their past, clearly the results of Huntington's study would support the thesis that all other factors being equal, previous democratic experience greatly facilitates the transition to democracy.[19]

The hypotheses generated in the remainder of the section are designed to address not the legacy of the precommunist or communist era, but the nature of the transition and the actual social situation inherited by the first postcommunist leaders. In particular, questions focus on the possibility of overcoming the Leninist legacy through what Crawford and Lijphart call "the imperatives of liberalization." As they state, this approach "suggests that new institutions can be crafted and new international pressures can be brought to bear that shut out the negative influences of the past."[20] Even those authors like Samuel Huntington who favor a strong political cultural argument are supportive of the view that the success of one country or region in introducing democratic reforms can have a snowballing effect in encouraging democratization elsewhere. The economic, political, and cultural policies pursued by actors in the external environment also are seen as extremely consequential for stimulating and supporting movement toward liberalization, particularly in an era when communication is global and international norms favor human rights and democracy.[21]

From this discussion and the literature on transition, it is possible to generate a number of propositions and hypotheses: the following are among the most salient. In those countries whose transition was non-violent and pacted between the elites and the opposition, a party system is most likely to be quickly established.[22] In those countries whose transition was non-violent and pacted between different groups of elites, the ruling party or group will be most able to maintain their elite status, if not their monopoly.[23] In those countries where the new elites moved most quickly to impose rapid liberalization, privatization, and democratization, extremist opposition parties will be less likely to gain a foothold amongst the populace.[24] In those transitions marked by violence, the elites are most likely to attempt to preempt the emergence of independent associations and parties.[25]

Another crucial aspect of transition is the assertion of civilian control over violent coercion in society. Many theorists, most notably Robert Dahl, have underlined the civilian control of the military as a crucial requirement for successful democratization,[26] leading one to suppose that it should be possible to demonstrate the validity of the following propositions: the greater the popular support for democracy as opposed to other political systems or of democratic values as opposed to other political ends (for example, stability, social justice, and so forth), the lower the levels of military intervention in domestic politics;[27] the greater the participation of the citizenry in electoral politics, the lower the levels of military intervention in politics;[28] and the greater the tradition of civilian control of the military within a country, the less will be the tendency of the military to intervene in politics.[29]

Also of concern is the need to analyze the impact on democratization of the political balances among the transitional groups, since much has been made by Adam Przeworski, Mancur Olson, and others of the likelihood that transitional elites would attempt to shape new institutions to maximize their interests. Thus it could be hypothesized that the more that the transition is coopted by hard-liners on the ruling side and radical factions amongst the opponents, the greater will be the prospect for failure of talks to produce a workable and democratic electoral system.[30] And conversely, the more evenly balanced the power amongst diverse elite groups at the time of transition, the more will be the tendency to design electoral legislation which does not favor any particular electoral constituency.[31]

Social and ethnic cleavages suppressed under communism are likely to emerge in the transition and are often intensified by economic changes and political and personal uncertainty. The challenge facing authors is both to identify these cleavages and to analyze the extent to which they have shaped the formation of parties and other political groups. The literature suggests the following relationships exist between social and ethnic cleavages and the prospects for democratization: the more that societies are characterized by spatial distances between mutually reinforcing and exclusivist ethnic, social, economic, and religious groups, the greater will be the tendency for parties to be formed reflecting these divisions;[32] the larger the size of ethnic minorities as a proportion of the total population, the greater is the probability that democratization using majoritarian formulas will fail to contain communal violence if it breaks out;[33] as long as no group has a monopoly over control of resources, then social divisions and unequal access to those resources can be mitigated within a democratic regime;[34] and to the extent that parties and associations promote and facilitate social mobility and civic awareness, then their aggregative function will assist democratization.

The pattern and pace of postcommunist economic change is another independent variable seen as having an impact on democratic outcomes, affecting the emergence of political parties, and increasing the stakes of winning and losing in the political arena. On the whole, it is accepted that the pattern and pace of economic change is a function of the political will of the ruling elites, but that both elites and social groups interact to maximize their access to resources. Thus, political elites will structure economic reforms to maximize their political and economic interests, while setting the pace of change in order to minimize the chances of systematic and widespread social unrest.[35]

Among the greatest challenges to successful democratization is the existence of violent conflict either inside the country or with other states. Indeed, it would appear that the greater the level of violent conflict within a society, the more democratic institutions will be undermined.[36] But its actual impact, upon observation, is diverse, depending on the level and direction of conflict, elite reaction, state capacity to terminate, suppress, resolve, or withstand the violence, and the impact of the violence on the attitude of core social groups toward the process of democratization. Violence may weaken existing institutions in an emerging democracy, but it can also increase pressure toward the adoption of changed institutional arrangements which maintain democracy, ranging from the introduction of nonmajoritarian consociational arrangements to widen the representation of marginalized and alienated minorities[37] to the adoption of corporatist forms of democracy in which large interest-based groups mediate between the state and the citizenry, to a certain degree suppressing citizens' direct involvement in policy making and aggregating overlapping and pluralistic intermediate groups into larger and more monopolistic associations.[38]

The political evolution of society

Central to the questions in this section is the assumption that citizens' attitudes matter. Gabriel Almond and Sidney Verba's theory of civic culture[39] postulates that the viability of democratic institutions is significantly affected by attitudes such as belief in one's ability to influence political decisions, feelings of positive affect for the political system, and the belief that fellow citizens are trustworthy. Challenges to political culture theory have taken place primarily on two levels and have emerged from two intellectual camps.

One challenge emerged in the 1960s and lasted throughout the 1970s as radical scholars polemicized against political culture theory. These scholars, many of them Marxist or neo-Marxist, argued that the dominant political culture in any society was a necessary reflection of the relationships between the ruling and subordinate classes. As Almond later wrote, political culture theory, in particular, "was challenged on the grounds that political and social attitudes were reflections of class and/or ethnic status or else were the 'false consciousness' implanted by such institutions as schools, universities and media."[40]

Also in the 1960s another challenge to political culture theory emerged with the ascension of rational choice models, which asserted that all individuals and institutions in a political system – whether ordinary members of society or politicians or parties, coalitions, intermediate organizations, and governmental institutions comprised of or representing those individuals – would act efficiently to maximize interests, often defined in economic terms.[41] By the late 1960s models based on rational choice and game theoretic approaches had become a dominant mode of social analysis. This emergence of "rational choice," "public choice," and "positive political theory" challenged the very premise of political culture theory. From within this perspective, examining political culture amounted to little more than a superfluous exercise. It was widely held that sufficient explanatory power could be generated by assuming self-interested, short-run rationality. Contributing to the ascension of this mode of analysis, especially within comparative political science, were the availability of economic data and the lack of sufficient cross-national data on political attitudes.

This paucity of aggregate data or large-N studies that would allow researchers to go beyond individual country or region case-studies and draw broader conclusions about factors outside the economic realm hampered efforts by those interested in political culture to reach generalizable conclusions. However, by 1988, Ronald Inglehart[42] had compiled data on attitudes of the general public for a sample of countries large enough to permit multivariate statistical analysis of the relative influence of mass political attitudes as compared with macro-socioeconomic variables on democratization. The accumulation of cross-national data on attitudes of the general public combined with the collapse of Marxism as an alternative explanatory system and the reorientation of some public choice theorists toward a "new institutionalism" has led to a resurgence of interest in political culture as an explanatory variable.

It is now more generally accepted that democracy requires a supportive culture, even if it is agreed that this culture can be strongly shaped both by transient and short-term factors including economic performance and by more underlying variables, including the institutional setting in which this culture is set. Democratic institutions both promote and are promoted by a democratic political culture. In a democracy, popular support for the creation of an independent civil society embodying intermediate groups and associations which feed into the political process and aggregate different societal interests is also required. Because freedom of speech, media, religion, assembly and the right to form independent groups and opposition parties were all suppressed in the communist era, the norms associated with a civic culture cannot be expected to emerge overnight. The legacy of mistrust must first be overcome in order for a previously atomized society to establish the basic level of tolerance and civic responsibility required to sustain even the most basic levels of freedom.[43] Even then, clearly, underlying cultural factors independent of the communist legacy could accelerate or impede the emergence of the kind of civil society associated with liberal democracy.[44]

When examining the emergence of political associations in early transitional societies, authors were asked to collect data on the types of political associations or actors that have become most prominent in each country's political life, that is, political parties, state sector managerial lobbies, trade unions, business organizations, professional associations, religious organizations, clans, paramilitary units, criminal groups, and so forth. In addition, data was collected on how the public perception of political parties and what they claim to represent has affected citizens' attitudes to the political system. Authors were asked to comment on the relative importance of parties as vehicles for new elites intent on accumulating political power and wealth, as opposed to alternative vehicles, such as associations, informal groupings, and the like.

The assumptions in the comparative politics literature that underlie the section on the emergence of political parties are several, including: the higher the level of citizen distrust of political institutions, the greater will be the difficulty of establishing a viable party system; parties will gain preeminence as intermediary institutions only if elections are regular, free, and fair; and the holding of regular, and free and fair elections will increase civic trust over time.[45]

Also central to an understanding of the evolution of societies in transition is the extent to which attempted marketization and privatization have affected the political strength and behavior of various economic groups in society. Operating at the level of abstraction, one could envision distinct responses from economic groups along a continuum ranging from strategies of intransigent resistance to reforms which directly (and in the short-term, negatively) impact their respective economic interests to strategies of ready accommodation with the reforms based on the assumption that these individuals are, or could easily become, aware of the long-term benefits of marketization and privatization which are readily observable throughout the West. With this continuum in mind, authors were asked to analyze the extent to which attempted marketization and privatization have affected the political strength and behavior of business and managerial groups, agricultural groups, and organized industrial labor. Authors were asked to gather information on whether these groups had formed or formally affiliated themselves with political parties and what role they had assumed in the financing of elections and the control of the media.

Monitoring of the emergence of new economic strata in transitional polities is important because of the assumptions about the relationship between marketization and democratization which underpin the literature. The transition to democracy has previously been thought to occur as a result of a long period of capitalist development in which previously subordinate classes – the middle class, most notably, but also the urban working class and small and medium-sized farming interests – evolved an economic interest in the promotion of democracy as a way of balancing class power. Thus, a strong middle class allied with commercial and industrial elites in the private sector is generally seen as a necessary but not sufficient condition for successful democratization.[46] Economic winners are thought to support democracy to the extent they feel it legitimizes and sustains their dominant economic position, whereas economic losers are seen as supporting democracy to the extent they feel the existence of democratic state autonomous of dominant economic classes erodes economic inequality.[47]

This obviously raises the question of whether an economy which liberalizes before the rule of law is in place can prevent the rise of organized criminal activity which in turn can disrupt, impede, and even capture the process of democratization itself. Authors were asked to analyze the political impact of organized criminal groups in the respective countries under review and to discuss the extent to which associations or political parties have become linked with organized crime. In general, it can be assumed that the emergence of organized crime will not be welcomed by the population, and authors were asked to gather data on how the public perception of the role of organized crime has affected citizens' attitudes toward the political system. But studies done in economic theory suggest that to the extent that organized crime provides stability and economic security and benefits, the population will be more likely to acquiesce in its existence.[48] And further, it is postulated that the existence of widespread random criminality will predispose the population to allow organized crime to establish rules and norms over geographic regions.[49] The public's predisposition to prefer organized criminal activity to large-scale inchoate activity does not necessarily translate into greater support for democracy, however, and indeed one could suppose that the existence of connections between elected officials and organized crime would erode public confidence in democracy and increase public support for a "strong hand" to end corruption, even if democracy is put on hold for a time.[50]

The redistribution of wealth, the emergence of political parties tied to diverse societal interests, the struggle to control marketization – all have an impact on citizen attitudes toward the democratic process. The collapse of communism has allowed researchers to conduct public opinion surveys and collect data on the changes over time in the level of public support for democratization. Many of these countries have had declines in economic performance which have matched or even exceeded rates seen in the West during the Great Depression, a depression in which democracy endured the test in most of Western Europe and North America, but was wiped out in Germany, Austria, and Italy by the rise of fascism. Based on past trends, it can obviously be expected that the impact of poor economic performance can and will erode support for government leaders, but it is not clear that such performance will necessarily also diminish popular support for democracy as a whole; and authors were asked to collect data on this where it exists.[51]

Surveys also exist which measure a number of factors – such as attitudes toward specific institutions, levels of tolerance in the society, the likelihood of participation in elections, and membership in political parties and intermediary associations – as among different sectors of the society: specifically, authors were asked to gather data which surveyed attitudes by various groups. As with other democratic countries, one would expect attitudes toward democratization to vary across generations, ethnic identification, region, class, and gender.[52]

Popular attitudes are in constant interaction with a free media, which both reflects those attitudes and helps to shape them. What is at stake in postcommunist countries is the establishment of a media which is a channel for the expression of a range of societal interests independent of the preferences of the government. And while the media in all countries are subject to some regulation, what is vital to examine is whether control of the media has affected the conduct of elections and other forms of political participation. It can generally be assumed that the greater the independence and pluralism of the media from the outset of the democratization process, the greater will be the level of civic trust and civic involvement.

Political parties and the party system

With the political evolution of society and increases both in levels of tolerance and in civic involvement, it is assumed in a democracy that a system which promotes parties' sustained competition and pluralism over time will enhance the possibility that political parties will develop and become rooted. Clearly, the comparative literature supports the proposition that a strong civil society is a necessary but not sufficient condition for a strong party system, and it is difficult to find examples where party systems have been established in states with weak civic cultures.[53] Authors were presented with a number of questions addressing the actual emergence of party systems in postcommunist states. They were asked to assess the strength and durability of political parties and the impact of electoral laws, electoral competition, and the type of government on the development of a party system. Particular attention was paid to the renamed communist parties and extremist anti-democratic parties and social movements. Finally, the effect of the party system on the strength of government itself was studied.

Literature in the field traditionally has been divided over the prerequisites for the creation of a strong party system between those who assess the strength of political parties by reference to their intrinsic qualities (internal structure, leadership, platform) and those who emphasize their strength in terms of their ability to perform effectively as a channel for, and reinforcement of, citizens' interests. The former view minimizes the relationship between civil society and political parties; the latter sees that relationship as intrinsic to, and the *raison d'etre* for, a party system. Thus, the former would see a strong party system existing without civic engagement as unproblematic for democracy: the latter would see such a situation as inimicable to the very aims of democracy.

Authors were also asked to comment on the type of electoral system introduced in the postcommunist states and the results. Electoral laws provide the method for the conversion of votes into the selection of leaders for electoral office. There are two major types of electoral systems – majoritarian and proportional representation (or PR). Plurality and majority systems reflect a majoritarian philosophy – the candidate who garners the largest number of votes wins. These formulas can be used to elect both individual leaders, as with presidential elections, and multimember bodies, as with parliaments and legislatures. The PR model, which can be used only for multimember bodies, provides proportional allocation of seats according to the percentage of votes parties received. These differences in electoral systems have an impact on party evolution, with parties in majoritarian systems tending to move toward the center of the political spectrum (median voter theorem), and parties in PR systems likely to be more diverse and more extreme in their approach.[54] The desire to favor majoritarian rule while not disenfranchising minorities has also produced a large number of mixed systems, including in the postcommunist states. Mixed systems typically utilize a version of PR to elect the legislature, and one of several majoritarian formulas to select the chief executive, thereby balancing the benefit of governability produced by majoritarian results with the value of representativeness exhibited by PR formulas.[55]

The strength and structure of the party system is also affected by the structure of government, especially whether the system is parliamentary or presidential. Studying the failures of presidential regimes in Latin America, Juan Linz has concluded that parliamentarism imparts greater flexibility to the political process, promotes consensus-building, and reconciles the interests of multiple political parties. Presidentialism, by focusing on the election of a single individual to an all-powerful post, diminishes the influence of the party system. Political parties tend to be less cohesive in presidential than in parliamentary systems. Presidential systems foster the creation of a two-party or two-bloc system.[56] It has also been shown that presidentialism favors the emergence of two large parties and reduces their distinctiveness and internal cohesion. Party discipline is stronger in parliamentary systems where the prime minister or chancellor belongs to the legislative branch and depends on disciplined and cohesive parties for the survival of government. It is possible for presidential systems to maintain a strong party system and better represent minorities by encouraging federalism and separation of powers, but one cannot ignore findings which point to the tendency of presidentialism to overrepresent the majority, thereby increasing the chance that an alienated and mobilized minority might drop out of party life and pursue political objectives by other, often violent, means.[57]

The attitudes and activities of extremist and communist parties and movements are central to an analysis of the future stability and cohesiveness of party systems in postcommunist countries. The impact of all these parties will depend on their leadership, the institutional and legal setting, constituency, and organization. But postcommunist regimes are challenged to build consensus at the center at the same time they are trying to overcome the institutional and bureaucratic inheritance of a one-party system which still has many well-organized adherents at the political extreme. Trying to construct an electoral and legal system which favors a shift to the center while these groups remain powerful is, therefore, a significant and indeed unprecedented challenge.

Turning to parties of the left and the right, authors were asked to examine the extent to which the renamed communist parties have actually changed (a) their attitudes toward liberal democracy (b) their political leadership, and (c) the interests that they represent as a result of their experience in the emerging democracies. On the other side of the political spectrum, anti-democratic parties and social movements based on clericalism, fascistic traditions, or radical nationalism have arisen in some countries, and authors were asked to determine, among other things, the number and importance of such parties, their willingness to endorse political violence, and their links with paramilitary forces. The literature is split between those who maintain that when electoral systems provide the possibility of coming to power by legal means, the tendency of communist and extremist parties to support the overthrow of the current elected government will subside and those who assert that extremist parties become most destructive to the democratic process when they win elections. These two views are reconciled by the notion that extremist groups will become less extreme through participation in the democratic process, that they will lose their authoritarian and anti-democratic impulse and cease to be a threat to the democratic order. This assumption works best when there is a strong and stable center, fairly good economic conditions, and low levels of social mobilization. However, as the example of Weimar Germany demonstrated, both the Nazis and the Communists won seats in the legislature; and the violent fighting between them paralysed the body in the face of Hitler's rise to power. Concern about the possibility of a repeat of the Weimar example has been widespread in postcommunist countries, most notably Russia, with many analysts concerned about the growth of extremist groups. It is assumed that such groups have the best chance of coming to power without a significant moderation of their political platform when poverty is on the rise, when elected officials are perceived as unable or unwilling to take steps to ameliorate the situation, and when the electoral system is so structured in favor of a pure PR formula as to give parties little incentive to moderate their stand.[58]

Authors were asked to assess the strength of the countries' political parties and party system, including whether emerging party systems are characterized only by the creation of ephemeral parties, or by more stable parties, as indicated by patterns of leadership, electoral results, and survey data. Studies have shown that the more a party exhibits a stable constituency, a consistent party platform, and internal consensus, the greater its durability over time.[59] In looking at parties, authors were also asked to speculate on how the structure and durability of political parties has been affected by any laws on campaign finance and by the timing of elections – including regional versus countrywide elections. Additionally, the literature suggests many propositions which deserve analysis in light of results from postcommunist elections: that the number of coalitions amongst parties will be lower in countries with a proportional representation system than in a majoritarian electoral system; that parties representing women and minorities will fare better in proportional representation systems than in majoritarian systems; that voter turnout will be less among women and minorities in majoritarian systems; that majoritarian systems produce moderate parties, weak in ideological and social class definition, whereas proportional representation systems encourage parties defined along class, ethnic, and regional lines, including extreme right-wing and left-wing parties. All of these propositions can be tested in the new environment provided by postcommunist transitions. Elsewhere, it has been shown that even in a mixed presidential/parliamentary system with proportional representation used for the legislative elections, the large parties which are favored in a winner-take-all presidential election continue to be favored in elections to the legislature, particularly if they are held at the same time, thereby reducing the bias of proportional representation toward greater inclusion of minorities, regional elites, and women.[60]

The party system as it has emerged in postcommunist countries has sometimes facilitated and sometimes obstructed the creation of governments able to formulate and carry through reasonably coherent policies. And conversely the capacity of postcommunist regimes to formulate and implement policies has affected citizen support of democratization and marketization processes. This interaction and essential circularity makes the identification and isolation of variables responsible for shaping the process of democratization difficult. Yet the reasons for undertaking the attempt go beyond the normal intellectual curiosity of academe: never before have so many countries which cover such a large percentage of the world's surface started at the same time along the path of transition from one single kind of regime to another; never before have populations embarking upon a democratic path been so educated, urban, and mobile; and never before has the international system been so clear and unequivocal (if not unanimous) in its support for democracy and marketization as the dominant paradigm. This unique opportunity essentially to control for so many variables makes it all the more likely that observers will be able to judge whether differential strategies for democratic development will also have predictable outcomes. Democracy may be the "only game in town" but as with any game there can be winners and losers, and the winners will be those countries where social, economic, and institutional engineering has received the most attention by elites, parties, and citizens alike.

NOTES

For their generous and insightful comments on an earlier draft of the chapter, the author wishes to thank Valerie Bunce, Joan Nelson, Bruce Parrott, Darya Pushkina, Melissa Rosser, and DelGreco Wilson.

1 *Politics in Developing Countries: Comparing Experiences with Democracy*, ed. Larry Diamond, Juan Linz, and Seymour M. Lipset (Boulder, CO: Lynne Rienner, 1990); *Elites and Democratic Consolidation in Latin America and Southern Europe*, ed. John Higley and Richard Gunther (Cambridge: Cambridge University Press, 1992); Samuel Huntington, *The Third Wave: Democratization in the Late Twentieth Century* (Norman, OK: University of Oklahoma Press, 1992); Stephanie Lawson, "Conceptual Issues in the Comparative Study of Regime

Change and Democratization," *Comparative Politics* 25 (January 1993), 88–92; Scott Mainwaring, "Transition to Democracy and Democratic Consolidation: Theoretical and Comparative Issues," in *Issues in Democratic Consolidation*, ed. Scott Mainwaring, Guillermo O'Donnell, and J. Samuel Valenzuela (Notre Dame, IN: University of Notre Dame Press, 1992).

2 Among the more pioneering works are Daniel Lerner, *The Passing of Traditional Society* (Glencoe, NY: Free Press, 1958); Seymour M. Lipset, "The Social Requisites of Democracy," *American Political Science Review* 53 (1959), 69–105; James P. Coleman, "Conclusion: The Political Systems of the Developing Areas," in *The Politics of Developing Areas*, ed. Gabriel A. Almond and J. S. Coleman (Princeton: Princeton University Press, 1960); Phillips Cutright, "National Political Development: Its Measures and Analysis," *American Sociological Review* 28 (1963), 253–64; *On Measuring Democracy*, ed. Alex Inkeles (New Brunswick, NJ: Transaction Publisher, 1991); and Arthur S. Banks and R. B. Textor, *A Cross Polity Survey* (Cambridge, MA: MIT Press, 1963).

3 For example, see Kenneth Bollen, "Issues in the Comparative Measurement of Political Democracy," *American Sociological Review* 45 (1980), 370–90; Kenneth Bollen, "Political Democracy: Validity and Method Factors in Cross-National Measures," *American Journal of Political Science* 37 (November 1993), 1207–30; Raymond D. Gastil and Freedom House, *Freedom in the World* (New York: Freedom House, annual); and Ted Robert Gurr, et al., Polity I, II and III data sets, Inter-University Consortium for Political and Social Research.

4 Doh Chull Shin, "On the Third Wave of Democratization," *World Politics* 47 (October 1994), 148.

5 See Valerie Bunce, "It's the Economy, Stupid . . . Or Is It?" Paper presented for the Workshop on Economic Transformation, Institutional Change and Social Sector Reform, National Academy of Sciences/National Research Council, Task Force on Economies in Transition, Washington, DC, September 19-20, 1996.

6 Huntington, *The Third Wave*, 266–67.

7 Peter McDonough, Samuel Barnes, and Antonio Lopez Pina, "The Growth of Democratic Legitimacy in Spain," *American Political Science Review* 80, no. 3 (September 1986), 735–60. While focusing on the prerequisites and indicators of democratic legitimacy they nevertheless are concerned with consolidation more broadly. Also see *Transitions from Authoritarian Rule: Prospects for Democracy*, ed. Guillermo O'Donnell, Philippe C. Schmitter, and Laurence Whitehead (Baltimore, MD: Johns Hopkins University Press, 1986).

8 For a classic statement of this view and the corollary that factors other than a country's level of economic development were crucial to the explanation of why some countries embarked upon democratization and others did not, see Dankwart Rustow, "Transitions to Democracy," *Comparative Politics* 2 (April 1970), 337–63.

9 Beverly Crawford and Arend Lijphart, "Explaining Political and Economic Change in Post-Communist Eastern Europe: Old Legacies, New Institutions, Hegemonic Norms, and International Pressures," *Comparative Political Studies* 28, no. 2 (1995), 187.

10 Tina Rosenberg, "Overcoming the Legacies of Dictatorship," *Foreign Affairs* 74, no. 3 (May–June 1995), 134.

11 There are many articles and books in the literature, but one which approaches the subject thematically is *The Legacies of Communism in Eastern Europe*, ed. Ivan Volgyes (Baltimore, MD: Johns Hopkins University Press, 1995).

12 The best case is made by Ken Jowitt, *New World Disorder: The Leninist Extinction* (Berkeley, CA: University of California Press, 1992).

13 See Jacques Rupnik, *The Other Europe: The Rise and Fall of Communism in East Central Europe* (London: Pantheon, 1989); Roy Medvedev, *Let History Judge: The Origins and Consequences of Stalinism* (Oxford: Oxford University Press, 1989); Jeffrey Goldfarb, *After the Fall: The Pursuit of Democracy in Central Europe* (New York: Basic Books, 1992); Timothy Garton Ash, *The Uses of Adversity: Essays on the Fate of Central Europe* (New York: Vintage Books, 1989); Milovan Djilas, *The New Class: An Analysis of the Communist System* (New York: Praeger, 1957); and Vladimir Tismaneanu, *Reinventing Politics: Eastern Europe from Stalin to Havel* (New York: The Free Press, 1992).

14 Richard Rose in doing cross-national surveys found support for the hypothesis that "if the common historical experience of Sovietization has had a decisive influence, generational differences in attitudes should be similar from one former Communist country to another." "Generational Effects on Attitudes to Communist Regimes: A Comparative Analysis," *Post-Soviet Affairs* 11, no. 1 (January–March 1995), 37. Also see Ellen Comisso, "Legacies of the Past or New Institutions?" *Comparative Political Studies* 28, no. 2 (July 1995), 200–38; and Barbara Geddes, "A Comparative Perspective on the Leninist Legacy in Eastern Europe," ibid., 239–74. Both maintain that the Soviet era destroyed popular support for pre-Leninist parties and traditions in most countries.

15 See, for example, Anders Åslund, *Gorbachev's Struggle for Economic Reform* (Ithaca, NY: Cornell University Press, 1989); and Ed A. Hewett, *Reforming the Soviet Economy* (Washington, DC: Brookings Institution Press, 1988).

16 The varied political views and splits within the military/security services are discussed in Karen Dawisha and Bruce Parrott, *Russia and the New States of Eurasia* (Cambridge: Cambridge University Press, 1993), ch. 6. Although she is dealing only with the security service, the role and political attitudes of this service are discussed by Amy Knight, *Spies without Cloaks* (Princeton, NJ: Princeton University Press, 1996).

17 Janos Kornai, *The Socialist System: The Political Economy of Communism* (Princeton, NJ: Princeton University Press, 1992). See also Peter Wiles, *The Political Economy of Communism* (Cambridge, MA: Harvard University Press, 1962).

18 Jowitt, *New World Disorder*. Also see Sten Berglund and Jan Dellenbrant, "Prospects for the New Democracies in Eastern Europe," in *The New Democracies in Eastern Europe*, ed. Sten Berglund and Jan Dellenbrant (Brookfield, VT: Edward Elgar Publishing Company, 1991).

19 Huntington, *The Third Wave*, pp. 40–6; also see Valerie Bunce and Maria Csanadi, "Uncertainty in the Transition: Post-Communism in Hungary," *East European Politics and Societies* 7 (Spring 1993), 240–75.

20 Crawford and Lijphart, "Explaining Political and Economic Change," p. 172.

21 Huntington, *The Third Wave*, pp. 85–108.

22 For a consideration of the impact of previous regime type on transition success and of transition type on prospects for consolidation, see Juan J. Linz and Alfred Stepan, *Problems of Democratic Transition and Consolidation: Southern Europe, South America, and Post-Communist Europe* (Baltimore, MD: Johns Hopkins University Press, 1996), ch. 4.

23 For a discussion of pacted transitions, see Arend Lijphart, *Democracy in Plural Societies: A Comparative Perspective* (New Haven: Yale University Press, 1977); and in the Arab world, see *Democracy without Democrats? The Renewal of Politics in the Muslim World*, ed. Ghassan Salame (New York: I. B. Taurus, 1994).

24 This hypothesis is drawn from Joan Nelson, "How Market Reforms and Democratic Consolidation Affect Each Other," in *Intricate Links*, ed. Joan Nelson (New Brunswick, NJ: Transaction Publishers, 1994).

25 See Alfred Stepan, "Paths toward Redemocratization: Theoretical and Comparative Considerations," in *Transitions from Authoritarian Rule*, ed. O'Donnell, Schmitter, and Whitehead, pp. 79–81.

26 Robert A. Dahl, *Democracy and Its Critics* (New Haven: Yale University Press, 1989).

27 The idea that a state's movement toward democracy is conditioned by its ability to exercise civilian control of violent coercion is most fully developed by Dahl in *Democracy and Its Critics*.

28 See, for example, Jendayi Frazer, "Conceptualizing Civil–Military Relations during Democratic Transition," in *Africa Today*, Quarters 1 & 2 (1995), 39–48; Philippe Schmitter, "Dangers and Dilemmas of Democracy," *Journal of Democracy* 5, no. 2 (April 1994); and *Civil–Military Relations in the Soviet and Yugoslav Successor States*, ed. Constantine Danopoulos and Daniel Zirker (Boulder, CO: Westview, 1996).

29 S. E. Finer, *The Man on Horseback: The Role of the Military in Politics*, 2d ed. (Boulder, CO: Westview Press, 1988); and Morris Janowitz, *The Military in the Political Development of New Nations* (Chicago: University of Chicago Press, 1964).

30 This proposition is derived from Adam Przeworski, *Democracy and the Market: Political and Economic Reforms in Eastern Europe and Latin America* (Cambridge: Cambridge University Press, 1991). It largely coalesces with the view promoted by rational choice theorists such as Douglass C. North, *Institutions, Institutional Change, and Economic Performance* (Cambridge: Cambridge University Press, 1990); Anthony Downs, *An Economic Theory of Democracy* (New York: Harper and Row, 1957); and Mancur Olson, "Dictatorship, Democracy, and Development," *American Political Science Review* 87 (September 1993), 567–76.

31 G. Bingham Powell, Jr., *Contemporary Democracies: Participation, Stability and Violence* (Cambridge, MA: Harvard University Press, 1982); Larry Diamond and Marc F. Plattner, *The Global Resurgence of Democracy* (Baltimore, MD: Johns Hopkins University Press, 1993).

32 See, for example, Phillippe C. Schmitter, "The Consolidation of Democracy and Representation of Social Groups," *American Behavioral Scientist* 35 (March–June 1992), 422–49.

33 See Ted Robert Gurr, *Minorities at Risk: A Global View of Ethnopolitical Conflict* (Washington, DC: US Institute of Peace, 1993). Also Linz and Stepan, *Problems of Democratic Transition and Consolidation: Southern Europe, South America and Post-Communist Europe*.

34 This problematic relationship between capitalism and democracy is most fully explored in Przeworski, *Democracy and the Market*.

35 The debate over whether shock therapy or gradualism is the best policy is extensive and is well analyzed in *The Postcommunist Economic Transformation: Essays in Honor of Gregory Grossman*, ed. Robert W. Campbell (Boulder, CO: Westview Press, 1994); and in articles by Anders Åslund and Bela Kadar in *Overcoming the Transformation Crisis: Lessons for the Successor States of the Soviet Union* (Tubingen, 1993). Public choice literature has contributed most to a discussion of rational calculations in polities which are already established, not in those being formed, so its contribution has been more limited, but is discussed in Dennis Mueller, "Public Choice: A Survey," in *The Public Choice Approach to Politics*, ed. Dennis Mueller (Brookfield, VT: Edward Elgar, 1993), pp. 447–89.

36 Donald L. Horowitz, *Ethnic Groups in Conflict* (Berkeley, CA: University of California Press, 1985); Juan Linz, *The Breakdown of Democratic Regimes: Crisis, Breakdown, and Reequilibration* (Baltimore, MD: Johns Hopkins University Press, 1978).

37 See especially Arendt Lijphart, "Consociational Democracy," *World Politics* 21 (January 1969), 207–25.

38 Charles Tilly, *Coercion, Capital, and European States*, rev. ed. (Oxford: Blackwell, 1992); Harry Eckstein, ed., *Internal War: Problems and Approaches* (Glencoe, IL: Free Press, 1963); and *Organizing Interests in Western Europe: Pluralism, Corporatism, and the Transformation of Politics*, ed. Suzanne Berger (Cambridge University Press, 1981).

39 Gabriel Almond and Sidney Verba, *The Civic Culture: Political Attitudes and Democracy in Five Nations* (Princeton: Princeton University Press, 1963).

40 Gabriel Almond, "Foreword: The Return to Political Culture," in *Political Culture and Democracy in Developing Countries*, ed. Larry Diamond, ix–xii. Among the more important critiques lodged against mainstream comparative politics during this era were the following: Mark Kesselman, "Order or Movement? The Literature of Political Development as Ideology," *World Politics* 26, no. 1 (1973); Fernando H. Cardoso and Enzo Faleto, *Dependency and Development in Latin America* (Berkeley: University of California Press, 1979); and André Gunder Frank, *Latin America: Underdevelopment or Revolution* (New York: Monthly Review Press, 1969).

41 Among the seminal works are Downs, *Economic Theory of Democracy*, and William Riker, *The Theory of Political Coalitions* (New Haven: Yale University Press, 1962).

42 Ronald Inglehart, "The Renaissance of Political Culture," *American Political Science Review* 82, no. 4 (December 1988), 1203–30; and idem., *Culture Shift in Advanced Industrial Society* (Princeton: Princeton University Press, 1990).

43 This requirement is explored most fully by Ernest Gellner, *Conditions of Liberty: Civil Society and Its Rivals* (New York: Allen Lane, The Penguin Press, 1994).

44 The debate about this possibility was begun by the publication of Samuel P. Huntington, "The Clash of Civilizations," *Foreign Affairs* 72 (Summer 1993), 22–49.

45 See Seymour M. Lipset, "The Social Requisites of Democracy Revisited," *American Sociological Review* 59 (February 1994), 1–22; Inglehart, "The Renaissance of Political Culture"; and Inglehart, *Culture Shift in Advanced Industrial Society*; Almond and Verba, *The Civic Culture*. The dilemma of how to build trust in societies where the state had systematically gone about its destruction is deftly argued in Richard Rose, "Postcommunism and the Problem of Trust," in Diamond and Plattner, *The Global Resurgence of Democracy*, 2d ed., pp. 251–63.

46 Barrington Moore, *Social Origins of Dictatorship and Democracy* (Boston: Beacon Press, 1966); and Charles Lindblom, *Politics and Markets: The World's Political-Economic Systems* (New York: Basic Books, 1977). They were among the first to assert the connection between a strong bourgeoisie and democracy. This view has been challenged only rarely, including by Dietrich Reuschemeyer, Evelyne Huber Stephens, and John D. Stephens in *Capitalist Development and Democracy* (Chicago, IL: University of Chicago Press, 1993) who argued that it was the working class that had proved over time to have been the greatest supporter of democracy.

47 Mancur Olson, "Dictatorship, Democracy, and Development," *American Political Science Review* 87, no. 3 (September 1993), 567–76; Rueschemeyer, Stephens, and Stephens, *Capitalist Development and Democracy*; and Edward N. Muller, "Democracy, Economic Development and Income Inequality," *American Sociological Review* 53 (1988), 50–68.

48 Louise Shelley, "The Internalization of Crime: The Changing Relationship Between Crime and Development," in *Essays on Crime and Development*, ed. Ugljesa Zvekic (Rome: UN Interregional Crime and Justice Research Institute, 1990); J. S. Nye, "Corruption and Political Development: A Cost-benefit Analysis," *American Political Science Review* 61, no. 2 (1967), 417–27.

49 This is a central tenet of Olson, "Dictatorship, Democracy and Development."

50 James Walston, *The Mafia and Clientism* (London: Routledge, 1988); Rensselaer W. Lee III, *The White Labyrinth* (New Brunswick, NJ: Transaction Publishers, 1989).

51 Studies done in six Central European countries suggest that respondents continue to have a very positive perception of the political benefits of democracy even as they hold a very negative perception of the economic benefits of marketization. See Richard Rose and Christian Haerpfer, "New Democracies Barometer III: Learning from What is Happening," *Studies in Public Policy* 230 (1994), questions 26,35,36,39,40,42, as presented in Linz and Stepan, *Problems in Democratic Transition and Consolidation*, 443.

52 The first attempt to see democracy as strongly affected by culture was Almond and Verba, *The Civic Culture*. Page and Shapiro have argued that irrespective of cleavages within public opinion, overall the public in aggregate is able to make rational and informed judgments (Benjamin Page and Robert Shapiro, *The Rational Public: Fifty Years of Trends in Americans' Policy Preferences* [Chicago: University of Chicago Press, 1992]). One of the first attempts to gauge public opinion and attitudinal shifts in the Soviet Union was Ada W. Finitfer and Ellen

Mickiewicz, "Redefining the Political System of the USSR: Mass Support for Political Change," *American Political Science Review* 86 (1992), 857-74. More recently, a wide array of authors have examined changes in public opinion and political culture in postcommunist states: see, for example, James L. Gibson, "The Resilience of Mass Support for Democratic Institutions and Processes in the Nascent Russian and Ukrainian Democracies," and Jeffrey W. Hahn, "Changes in Contemporary Political Culture," in *Political Culture and Civil Society in Russia and the New States of Eurasia*, ed. Vladimir Tismaneanu (Armonk, NY: M. E. Sharpe, 1995).

53 In *Making Democracy Work: Civic Traditions in Modern Italy* (Princeton, NJ: Princeton University Press, 1993), Robert Putnam argues that a strong party system can operate within a weak civic culture; also see Robert Putnam, "Troubled Democracies," paper prepared for the University of Maryland/Johns Hopkins University Workshop on Democratization and Political Participation in Postcommunist Societies, US Department of State, May 1995; and Robert Putnam, "Bowling Alone: America's Declining Social Capital," in Diamond and Plattner, *The Global Resurgence of Democracy*, 2d ed., pp. 290-307.

54 Connections between electoral laws and political parties are the subject of many works, of which some of the best are Arend Lijphart, *Democracies* (New Haven, CN: Yale University Press, 1984); Arend Lijphart, *Electoral Systems and Party Systems: A Study of Twenty-seven Democracies, 1945-1990* (Oxford: Oxford University Press, 1994); Richard S. Katz, *A Theory of Parties and Electoral Systems* (Baltimore, MD: Johns Hopkins University Press, 1980); and *Electoral Laws and Their Political Consequences*, ed. Bernard Grofman and Arend Lijphart (New York: Agathon Press, Inc., 1986). Also see Part II of Dennis Mueller, *The Public Choice Approach to Politics* (Brookfield, VT: Edward Elgar, 1993).

55 On the effects of different varieties of electoral systems, see Douglas W. Rae, *The Political Consequences of Electoral Laws*, 2d ed. (New Haven: Yale University Press, 1971); and Rein Taagapera and Matthew Soberg Shugart, *Seats and Votes: The Effects and Determinants of Electoral Systems* (New Haven: Yale University Press, 1989).

56 See Juan Linz and Arturo Valenzuela, *The Failure of Presidential Democracy* (Baltimore, MD: Johns Hopkins University Press, 1994), for an argument in support of this hypothesis. By contrast, see Donald Horowitz, *A Democratic South Africa? Constitutional Engineering in a Divided Society* (Berkeley: University of California Press, 1991), who finds no necessary link, and W. H. Riker, who theorizes that all party systems converge to two coalitions of equal size (*The Theory of Political Coalitions* [New Haven, CN: Yale University Press, 1962]).

57 Juan Linz, "Presidential or Parliamentary Democracy: Does it Make a Difference?" in Linz and Valenzuela, *The Failure of Presidential Democracy: Comparative Perspectives*, 3-91; and Arend Lijphart, "Democracy in Plural Societies: A Comparative Exploration," in *The Failure of Presidential Democracy*, 91-105. Also see Vladimir Tismaneanu, *Fantasies of Salvation: Post-Communist Political Mythologies* (Princeton, NJ: Princeton University Press, forthcoming).

58 Quentin L. Quade examines the impact of an unmodified proportional representation system on the potential for takeover by extremist groups in "PR and Democratic Statecraft," in Diamond and Plattner, *The Global Resurgence of*

Democracy, 2d ed., pp. 181–7. The case for the likely rise in extremist politics was first and most forcefully made in Jowitt, *The New World Disorder*.

59 Giovanni Sartori, *Parties and Party Systems* (Cambridge: Cambridge University Press, 1976), 6; and Lijphart, *Democracies;* in opposition to Robert Michels (*Political Parties* [Glencoe, IL: The Free Press, 1958]) who dismissed the need for constituency support, focusing instead on the centrality of elites and their ability to instill beliefs in the masses. On the need for a party to show internal consensus, see Katz, *A Theory of Parties and Electoral Systems*.

60 The seminal work on the relationship between party and electoral systems is Maurice Duverger, *Political Parties: Their Organization and Activity in the Modern State* (New York: Wiley, 1954); see also Douglas J. Amy, *Real Choices/New Voices: The Case for Proportional Representation in the United States* (New York: Columbia University Press, 1993); and Michel L. Balinski and H. Peyton Young, *Fair Representation: Meeting the Ideal of One Man, One Vote* (New Haven, CN: Yale University Press, 1982).

3   Democratic consolidation in Poland after 1989

Andrew A. Michta

> Our democracy is like a reed – it sways in the wind and a strong gust can hurt it. It was almost never used before, and that is why we lack experience on how to use it now.
> Dariusz Fikus, "Demokracja jak trzcina," *Rzeczpospolita*, May 22, 1995.

Overview

The Republic of Poland, or the "Third Republic" as the Poles refer to it to emphasize continuity with the interwar "Second Republic," is a medium-size country with a population of 38.5 million and an estimated per capita GDP of about US$5,000.[1] Located between Germany and the former Soviet Union, Poland is a pivotal state for the future stability and security in postcommunist Central Europe. After six years of radical political and economic reform, by 1996 Poland has established an institutional framework for democracy and a free market economy. The country has developed a parliamentary-presidential system of government, codified in the 1992 "Little Constitution." In 1990 Poland opened its economic system to market competition by introducing a radical reform package, the so-called "Balcerowicz program" named after the country's finance minister in the first Solidarity government; two years later the country began to see the benefits of the economic "shock therapy." The economic basket case of Eastern Europe in the 1980s, after 1992 Poland began to recover, posting 5.0 and 5.5 percent GDP growth rates in 1994 and 1995, respectively, and reducing the inflation rate to under 30 percent by 1995. Increasingly confident about the economy, in January 1995 the government introduced a new currency; the exchange rate for the new Polish złoty was set by the market at US$1.00 to Pzl 2.40.

Political reform in Poland after 1989 has included free elections, the abolishing of censorship, and the privatization of the media. Poland changed the structure of its parliament by reestablishing the 100-member Senate in addition to the 460-member Sejm (lower house). The country's nascent party system has been gaining strength and by 1996 the political scene was dominated by five parties. Twice over the past six years the Polish society elected the parliament and the president, with an orderly transition of power accepted by all the parties and candidates as a matter of principle. While disputes as to the final shape of the new constitution to replace the 1992 basic law have persisted into 1996, especially in the areas of parliamentary versus presidential authority and the role of the Catholic Church, none of the political players has advocated non-democratic programmatic solutions.

Poland has also reestablished an independent judiciary, with Supreme Court justices appointed by the Sejm to life terms as the nation's highest judicial body. The Tribunal of State, chaired by the president of the Supreme Court, adjudicates on the responsibility of persons holding high state office for violation of the Constitution and the laws. The Constitutional Tribunal, another independent body, renders judgment on the consistency of all legislation with the Constitution; it has already done so effectively in several instances.

In the international arena, Poland has established good relations with Germany, thereby moving to eliminate the historical source of tension in the region. The two countries signed a border treaty and a good neighborly relations treaty in 1991 – the first steps on the road to Polish–German reconciliation. With German support, Warsaw has worked to gain entrance into the European Union and NATO, although the latter policy put it on a collision course with Russia. In contrast to the relations with the West, in 1996 Poland's relations with its neighbors to the East were strained, while uncertainty about the direction Russia would ultimately take remained a paramount concern.

Overall, six years into reform the record of political and economic change in Poland has been encouraging, even though Poland's postcommunist transition remains work in progress. The economy has performed above expectations, but Poland has yet to complete the large-scale privatization program, to address the problem of persistently high double-digit unemployment and to deal effectively with the potential for social unrest caused by the current rapid class stratification. In addition, the political division between those with roots in the anti-communist opposition movement and those who had ties to the power structure of communist Poland has become more pronounced. The 1996 resignation of Prime Minister Józef Oleksy, amidst allegations that he was an agent of the Russian intelligence service, has deepened the political cleavages in Polish society and once more raised concern about Russian interference in Polish domestic affairs. Other issues, such as the question of church–state relations, civilian control over the military, and especially the new constitution often led to acrimony and political infighting at the highest levels of the government.

The analysis of democratic consolidation in Poland presented here is organized around several themes central to Polish postcommunist transition, including (1) the legacy of the Commonwealth of Poland–Lithuania and the Second Republic between the two world wars; (2) the legacy of the second world war; (3) the experience of communism and anti-communist dissent; (4) the character of the 1989 revolution and the 1990 fragmentation of the Solidarity movement; (5) the impact of the parliamentary and presidential elections; (6) systemic constitutional issues with an emphasis on the power of the presidency; (7) the evolution of political parties after 1989; (8) Polish attitudes to democracy; (9) the economic reform; and (10) the evolution of civil society and the role of the media. The chapter concludes with an assessment of Poland's long-term prospects, as well as problems that are likely to confront the Third Republic in the remainder of the decade.

The role of predemocratic experience

The development of a democratic culture depends not only on the presence of democratic institutions and the rise of civil society, but also on the willingness of the citizenry to view the emerging democratic framework as historically legitimate. In that regard, democratic consolidation is affected by the society's predemocratic experience. This is not to suggest that societies with no history of democracy will necessarily fail to democratize, but rather that democratic consolidation has a greater chance for success if the postcommunist society considers its current systemic transformation as a necessary extension of its past. This "historical legitimacy," that is, whether a nation sees itself as sharing in the Western liberal democratic tradition, is particularly important when considered against the relative weakness of political parties and of civil society at the early stages of reform. In Poland democracy has been viewed as part of the country's historical legacy dating back to the Commonwealth of Poland–Lithuania of the sixteenth to eighteenth centuries and to the experience of the Second Republic between the two world wars. It has often been synonymous with the Polish aspirations to rejoin the West.

In contrast to Latin America and southern Europe, transition to democracy in postcommunist Europe has occurred under conditions of a deepening economic crisis, a disintegration of regional security and economic institutions, and political instability across the region. Poland was hit especially hard by the economic crisis of the 1980s, with an inflation rate reaching close to 600 percent by 1990, a crushing foreign debt, persistent food shortages, and the collapse of the manufacturing sector. As Poland moved to develop and consolidate its new political institutions after 1989, it confronted both a deeply dysfunctional economy and a discredited political system. Moreover, the imperative simultaneously to build democratic institutions and to implement economic reform was unprecedented.[2] It is in this context that the Polish acceptance of the general idea of democracy as a historically legitimate systemic solution has contributed to political reform. For the majority of the Poles, economic prosperity was also associated with democratic institutions. Six years into postcommunist reform those who believed that democracy has made economic reform possible in Poland outnumbered the opponents two-to-one (57 percent for, 23 percent against, with 20 percent undecided).[3]

Considered against the initial weakness of the political institutions and the lingering communist legacy, the "historical legitimacy" of democratic change in Poland has been important to democratic consolidation. The lessons learned by the Poles from the tortuous evolution of their state may prove to be the ultimate source of Polish democracy's enduring strength. The Poles have regarded democracy as the culmination of their historical struggle for self-determination and independence. The Third Republic has been seen as the direct progeny of the sixteenth to eighteenth century Polish-Lithuanian Commonwealth and the Second Republic of 1918–39, though in fact it is quite different from both. Even more importantly, the Poles have regarded the establishment of democracy as the prerequisite for becoming a "normal state," that is, one built on the systemic principles derived from the West, and as the necessary precondition for joining Western political, economic and security institutions.

The historical roots of Polish democracy

During the fifty years of communism Poland was the most unpredictable among Moscow's satellites. The Poles saw themselves as a Catholic Western nation, which although dominated by Russia, would not shed its distinct national identity. The national "collective memory" of the Poles emphasized their uniqueness and their alienation from foreign rulers, as embodied in the history of the Commonwealth of Poland–Lithuania and the Second Republic. The legacy of the Commonwealth of Poland–Lithuania, a multi-ethnic and multi-cultural Polish-dominated state, blended Roman Catholicism with the tradition of an "aristocratic democracy." In its tortuous history, the country had risen as the region's hegemonic power in the sixteenth century and disappeared from the map of Europe two centuries later. The legacy of the Second Republic of 1918–39 has given the Poles the experience of regained national sovereignty, parliamentarism, and a pro-Western foreign policy.

Polish history has informed the myth of a unique Polish democratic tradition rooted in individual liberties and civil disobedience to state authority. Anarchic at the core, the aristocratic ideal of "golden freedom" propagated by the nobility (*szlachta*) became fused with the suspicion and rejection of organized state authority and, after the absorption of the Commonwealth by the neighboring great powers in 1795,[4] with a sense that the Polish cultural bond transcended narrowly defined ethnicity.[5]

Polish culture has been formed by influences both from the West and the East. Historical Poland straddled the juncture where Roman Catholicism, Lutheranism, and Eastern Orthodoxy met. Still, Polish national and political aspirations looked to the West. Historically, Poland saw itself as a bastion of Latin civilization against Byzantine Russia.

Between 1795 and 1918 Poland disappeared from the map of Europe. Outside domination became a formative experience for the emerging modern Polish national identity. The majority peasant population remained excluded from politics, while the nobility and the emerging intelligentsia partook in national uprisings and absorbed the revolutionary trends of the time. The Polish insurrectionary tradition grew out of the succession of failed armed uprisings against Russia, in 1794, 1830, and 1863. It has remained a powerful influence in the Polish political culture often invoked with pride by the citizens and politicians alike. Reinforced by the perceived success of Józef Piłsudski's legions in 1918 and by Polish victory in the 1919–20 war with Soviet Russia, it has been a constitutive element of Polish national identity.

The Polish experience of a working democratic system during the Second Republic of 1918–39 was brief and its institutions were never sufficiently consolidated. The military coup of 1926 launched by Piłsudski in the name of saving the country from chaos and preserving its independence placed Poland squarely on an authoritarian path. Nevertheless, during the fifty years of communism after the Second World War the legacy of the Second Republic would sustain the ideal of a sovereign Polish state. Despite the host of economic and political problems, the twenty years of independence would also give the Poles an experience of a nascent party system, a state administration, an independent foreign policy, and a market economy. It passed on to the post-World War II generation a memory of political participation, parliamentarism (albeit limited by the consequences of the 1926 coup), and party politics.

The vastness of the task of nation building prevented the consolidation of democracy in the Second Republic. The interwar Polish state was put together from territories formerly controlled by three neighboring powers, with disparate administrative systems and economic infrastructures. The problem was compounded by the devastation brought about by the war, the overall economic underdevelopment, and low literacy rates. The Second Republic sought to establish a democratic system in exceedingly unfavorable geopolitical circumstances, with its great power neighbors, Russia and

Germany, determined to lay irredentist claims against it, and its principal ally, France, too weak to guarantee its security. Finally, the multi-ethnic character of resurrected Poland, with ethnic Poles constituting 68 percent of the population,[6] meant that to a large degree Polish national identity would remain class based, especially in the Eastern borderlands (*kresy*) where the Poles were a minority and where the ethnically Ukrainian or Lithuanian nobility would often regard itself as Polish, but the majority peasant population would not. In the end, the infant Second Republic succumbed to forces by far exceeding the resources available to it; still, it raised a generation that would preserve the idea of Polish sovereignty and statehood through the trauma of the Second World War.

The impact of World War II

For Poland, the end of World War II ushered in over four decades of Soviet domination and communist rule. Three enduring direct consequences of the Second World War relevant to the process of postcommunist political consolidation in Poland are (1) a change in the ethnic composition of Polish society; (2) a change in the class stratification; (3) a territorial adjustment.

Poland lost six million of its citizens in the course of World War II, including almost all of its three million Jews. This tragic legacy of the war resulted in a historically unprecedented ethnic consolidation in Poland. While the Second Republic was a multi-ethnic state, the Holocaust, the postwar expulsion of the Germans from the newly acquired Western territories, and the repatriation of ethnic Poles from the Eastern territories lost to the Soviet Union transformed the postwar Polish People's Republic into an ethnically homogeneous state. This change shifted ethnic relations to the periphery of national concerns, residual anti-semitism and friction between ethnic Poles and the small remaining Ukrainian and Byelorussian minorities notwithstanding.

The ravages of the Second World War brought about the implosion of the Polish class structure. Nazi extermination policies directed against the Jews and the Polish intelligentsia hit hardest at the country's elite, decimating the professional class. Soviet policies, including the Katyń massacre of Polish officers and the elimination of the pro-London resistance during and immediately after the war, aggravated the problem. In terms of its class structure, the Polish People's Republic began the postwar reconstruction as a predominantly peasant nation with the overall levels of education lower than the Second Republic's.

In 1945 Poland lost 30 percent of its territory in the East for which it was compensated with territory taken from Germany. In addition to the lasting political consequences of the country's shift to the West, especially simmering German irredentism and concomitant Polish insecurity that would become an obstacle to the normalization of relations between Poland and Germany, the shift marked a break in the country's cultural heritage. Historically, Poland had seen its destiny in the *kresy*, where for centuries it confronted the Orthodox East. The loss of the *kresy* after 1945 transformed Poland into a central European nation-state. Polish national identity shifted away from the class to the ethnic, linguistic, and cultural bases. It became consolidated in the course of communist domination. Increasingly, the Poles have come to think of themselves as an ethnically homogeneous nation.

Communism and dissent: to and from Solidarity

Historically, the primacy of the struggle for national independence and statehood placed the question of preferred systemic solutions in the background of Polish politics. In that sense, Polish nationalism was quintessentially a culture in search of a state.[7] More than forty years of communist rule reinforced this paradigm. Within its broad parameters, the Polish United Workers' (Communist) Party (PUWP, Polska Zjednoczona Partia Robotnicza), the Roman Catholic Church, and the dissident movement interacted and defined the country's political scene. Communism was perceived by the majority of the Poles as synonymous with the loss of independence to Russia. To the dissident movement liberation from outside domination and oppression meant also the restoration of Poland to its rightful place among the community of Western nations. The dissidents identified national independence with reclaiming Western values (becoming a "normal state"), as they reached across the centuries of the nation's history to the formative experiences of Polish politics. The dissident elite viewed the Polish nation-state as historically democratic, Western, and majority Roman Catholic.

Communism remade the class structure of the Polish society. It created a large industrial working class and shifted the majority of the people from the countryside to the cities. In the process, the rural population was reduced from being a clear majority to being a little over a third of the total. Even more significant was a shift in education levels, especially the almost three-fold increase in the number of people with secondary education and the more than two-fold increase in the number of people with higher education (table 3.1). Communism also raised popular expectations about the level of social security and the state's responsibility to provide it.

Although the Poles rejected communist ideology, the socialist mindset on social welfare issues formed in the communist era would remain a potent force in postcommunist politics. It would be reflected in the voters' choice

Table 3.1 *Demographic trends in Poland since the 1950s*

	1950s	1970s	1980s
Percentage of population	(1956)	(1970)	(1990)
Rural	57.2	47.7	38.3
Urban	42.8	52.3	61.7
Average annual rates of	(1953-59)	(1970-74)	(1980-90)
population growth (%)	1.8	0.9	0.7
Age distribution (%)	(1956)	(1977)	(1988)
15–24	16.6	19.2	13.7
25–49	33.6	33.7	35.7
50–59	9.8	9.8	10.6
Over 60	8.6	13.5	14.6
Levels of education[a] (%)	(1960)	(1970)	(1988)
Primary	80.3	73.9	44.3
Secondary	16.6	20.7	47.8
Post-secondary	3.2	5.4	7.9

Note: [a]Among persons over 25 years of age. Indicates attainment of completed or partial education at each level.

Sources: US Department of Commerce, *Statistical Abstracts of the United States*; Paul S. Shoup, *The East European and Soviet Data Handbook*; UNESCO, *Statistical Yearbooks*; United Nations, *Demographic Yearbooks*.

in the 1993 parliamentary election, which gave the parties with roots in the communist system a dominant position in the parliament. It would undergird the continued social discontent with the government. It would drive Solidarity to challenge the government in the streets after 1989 when the union became committed to resisting market reform in the name of protecting the vested interests of the occupational groups it represented.[8]

The loss of sovereignty and the communist takeover in Poland after the second world war revitalized the Catholic Church. While in the interwar period the overall political influence of the Church hierarchy on the country's politics had declined in relative terms, the direct assault on religious freedom in Poland by the communist regime transformed the Church in the eyes of society into a standard bearer for the cause of national independence and a sole legal form of opposition to the regime.

During the communist period the Catholic Church remained independent of the state despite the early attempts by the government to assert control over it. The church served as a critical focal point of anti-communist resistance; the PUWP recognized its autonomy after the crisis in 1956 that brought about a truce between the party and the Church hierarchy. The institution of the Catholic Church in Poland provided an ideological alternative to the regime, while its history and its roots in Polish culture gave it its vitality to become a counterforce against the policies of the state.

The PUWP played the role of a hegemonic party, rather than being the sole party organization in the country. Established in 1948 after a rigged merger by the Polish Workers Party (PWP, Polska Partia Robotnicza), and the left wing of the Polish Socialist Party (PSP, Polska Partia Socjalistyczna), the PUWP led a "bloc" that also included the United Peasant Party (UPP, Zjednoczone Stronnictwo Ludowe), and the Democratic Party (DP, Stronnictwo Demokratyczne). While the UPP and DP were only nominally independent, they did establish an institutional presence in Polish politics. The UPP in particular as the only peasant party tolerated for fifty years by the communist regime provided for a modicum of continuity with the prewar peasant movement and, more importantly, developed an administrative structure and leadership that would be crucial in its re-emergence after 1989 as one of the better organized political parties in postcommunist Poland.

Two other factors played a role in shaping political dissent in Poland. One was the resistance of the peasantry, who had managed to sustain private land ownership despite the government's early efforts at collectivization. Another was the relative success of the media and the universities in expanding the limits of permissible political debate. By the 1960s popular dissent gave rise to independent intellectual activities outside the party's control. The 1970s saw the emerging alliance of the dissident elite and the industrial working class in the form of the Committee for the Workers' Defense (CWD, Komitet Obrony Robotników), established after the 1976 workers' protest in Radom and Ursus.[9] In the 1970s the nationalist independence movement was channelled into the ranks of the Confederation for an Independent Poland (CIP, Konfederacja Polski Niepodległej). Human rights issues raised by the Helsinki conference were at the center of the Movement for the Defense of Human and Civil Rights (MDHCR, Ruch Obrony Praw Człowieka i Obywatela). Dissent among the intelligentsia fanned the network of "flying universities" which taught subjects deemed subversive by the regime. In the 1980s the spontaneous strikes by shipyard workers at the Baltic Coast fused the various dissident strands into an alliance of all anti-communist forces in Poland. The Solidarity Trade Union movement of 1980–81 was the beginning of the Polish anti-communist revolution. It would endure the 1981 military crackdown and would eventually bring down communist power.

In retrospect, dissent defined the phases of Polish communism. Popular resistance to communist rule gained its first impetus from the 1956 Poznań demonstrations, which brought to power the "national communists" led by Władysław Gomułka and marked the end of Stalinist repression. The subsequent landmarks of Polish anti-communist resistance were the 1968 student riots in Warsaw, the 1970 December bloody shipyard strikes at the Baltic Coast, the 1976 strikes in Radom and Ursus, and the 1980 August strikes at the Baltic Coast that finally broke the PUWP's monopoly on political power. With each of the successive crises, the area of collective and individual freedom in communist Poland rose incrementally as forced collectivization ended, censorship weakened, church-state relations became normalized, economic concessions were won, and finally the state recognized the citizens' right to independent political organization.

In 1980–81, during its sixteen months of legal existence under communism, Solidarity became a movement for national independence. Numbering close to ten million, it cut across the entire political and social spectrum. More significantly, Solidarity brought to the fore grass roots organizations and allowed the Poles to engage in politics outside of state-controlled channels, laying the foundations for a civil society. This was greatly aided by the union's regional organizational structure. Even after the December 1981 imposition of martial law, Solidarity survived underground as an ideal of community and a formula for collective resistance to the regime. The communist decision, in 1989, to open round-table negotiations with Solidarity was a testimony to the strength of the nascent civil society in Poland, as well as to the extent to which communist power had by then decomposed.

The legacy of Solidarity as a movement for national rebirth remains a formative influence in Polish transition to democracy. It sets the Polish postcommunist experience apart from the other countries in the region in several ways. First, Solidarity gave the Polish revolution and the attendant transformation of society an early start. The experience of 1980–81 established the foundations of a civil society and created a sense of community indispensable to the growth of democratic institutions. Second, Solidarity became the formative experience for the new governing elite that would take over in 1989 and would steer Poland through the critical first four years of economic and political reform. The "Solidarity ethos," which emphasized the moral and ethical values of a "normal," that is Western democratic society, was shared by the first four cabinets as well as President Lech Wałęsa. Third, Solidarity gave rise to Poland's center and center-right political parties of today.

The legacy of the 1989 revolution

The collapse of the communist system in Poland was pacted in that it began in 1989 with a round-table political compromise agreement between the opposition and the communists. However, it occurred against the background of an overwhelming popular demand for change. It was a two-stage negotiated revolution, including (1) the round-table agreement which relegalized Solidarity, and (2) the subsequent elections to the "contract parliament" which destroyed the communists' ability to govern.

The pacted character of the 1989 revolution blunted the Solidarity leadership's desire for retribution. The policy of the so-called "thick line," pursued by the first Solidarity government of Tadeusz Mazowiecki placed clear limitations on de-communization after 1989. Mazowiecki's decision to concentrate instead on the issue of economic reform subsequently became the target of intense criticism from the right, which blamed it for the return of former communists to power in 1993 and for the nation's inability to come to terms with past abuses. The policy generated the initial popular dissatisfaction with the process through which democracy was being implemented in Poland. The successful presidential campaign of Lech Wałęsa in 1990 was built around the theme of "accelerating" change and cleaning house. The populist tone of that campaign remains a strong undercurrent in Polish politics.

Prior to 1989 Polish opposition to the regime was unified around a single issue, that is, the quest for national emancipation. The social aspirations were manifested by cyclical crises that exposed progressively ever-deeper fissures in the facade of Polish communism. The unity of national purpose came at a price, however, in that the diverse groups and classes that made up the movement failed to articulate political programs of their own; instead, in the 1980s they shared the "Solidarity ethos," with its emphasis on the ethical values of Western democratic society. In 1989 during the early stage of Polish transition to democracy the "contract" parliament that emerged from the round-table negotiations between the communists and the opposition became a forum for program and party-formation, with fissures appearing early on among the organizations with roots in Solidarity. The 1989 round-table agreement was intended by the communists to ensure their continued control over the key levers of state power through a guaranteed 65 percent majority in the lower house (the Sejm) and the ministerial portfolios of defense, internal affairs, and foreign affairs. In return, the PUWP accepted the principle of free competition for the remainder of the seats in the Sejm and for all 100 seats in the restored Senate. The 1989 election to the "contract parliament" opened the floodgates of genuine political competition. While the new parliament functioned as a legislative body – that is it appointed the government, passed laws, and so on – it also became a vehicle for party-formation by providing a testing ground for political programs and leaders.[10]

The Polish revolution of 1989 lacked the symbols of a sudden break with the past. The final decomposition of communist power in Poland took a decade to reach the breaking point. In 1989 the transition of power occurred in a carefully negotiated manner, with the Solidarity leadership well aware of its pioneering role in Eastern Europe and of the danger inherent therein. The experience of the 1981 martial law and the continued treat of direct Soviet intervention in Polish politics were foremost in the minds of the Solidarity leadership in 1989, while the disintegration of the country's economy was the most urgent concern. The Polish revolution of 1989 was contained by the perimeter drawn by the experience of Solidarity during the 1980s and by the fact that in the early stages the Mazowiecki reform government stood alone among Soviet dominated regimes. The Poles were very much aware that they had entered an uncharted territory. Until the 1990 Zheleznovodsk agreement between Germany and the USSR, which facilitated German reunification, the Mazowiecki government could not foresee that a radical restructuring of the entire region would follow.

Another important development of 1989, one with far-reaching consequences for the formation of political parties in Poland, was the fragmentation within the Solidarity elite, especially the rift between Solidarity chairman Lech Wałęsa and the dissident intelligentsia led by Tadeusz Mazowiecki. The schism within Solidarity came into sharp focus at the time of Poland's first free and direct presidential election campaign in 1990, which pitted Wałęsa against Mazowiecki, with Stanisław Tymiński, a dark horse populist candidate challenging both (table 3.2). In December 1990 Lech Wałęsa was elected by a landslide in a run-off against Tymiński by getting close to 75 percent of the vote.[11] This constituted a powerful popular mandate for the president, and it put Wałęsa in a strong position *vis-à-vis* the Sejm, which was still composed of deputies elected at the end of the communist period. However, the damage to Solidarity's cohesion done by the bitter acrimony of the presidential campaign and the subsequent "war at the top" could not be repaired. The experience of the presidential election polarized Solidarity between those who supported Wałęsa's traditional workers power base against the intelligentsia centered around Mazowiecki's candidacy. Wałęsa's victory tilted the balance of power in the country away from the parliament. The imbalance was underscored by the constitutional provisions dating back to the presidency of General Wojciech Jaruzelski, which gave the president broad powers, including control over the armed forces through the National Defense Committee (NDC, Komitet Obrony Kraju).

The 1990 presidential election was a milestone in Polish transition to democracy in that it broke the unity of the dissident movement at the time when the fundamental question of the constitutional framework was first being addressed. The fragmentation of Solidarity would become the immediate cause of the compromise formula of presidential-parliamentarism, adopted in 1992 in the "Little Constitution," that has bedeviled the country's political scene since. The new Polish basic law reflected the struggle for power between President Lech Wałęsa and his former Solidarity allies in the

Table 3.2 *Presidential elections in Poland, 1990*

	First ballot	% first ballot[a]	Second ballot	% second ballot
Lech Wałęsa	6,569,889	39.96	10,622,696	74.25
Stanisław Tymiński	3,797,605	23.10	3,683,098	25.75
Tadeusz Mazowiecki	2,973,264	18.08		
Włodzimierz Cimoszewicz	1,514,025	9.21		
Roman Bartoszcze	1,176,175	7.15		
Leszek Moczulski	411,516	1.49		
Total votes	16,422,474		14,305,794	
Voter turnout (%)		61		54
Total eligible to vote	27,600,000			

Note: [a]1.01 percent of the ballots for the first round were invalidated.

Source: *The Europa World Year Book 1995* (London: Europa Publications Ltd, 1995), p. 2,492, and author's calculations.

parliament. It put off the decision on the final shape of Polish democracy, while it reflected the fault lines in the country's politics at the time.

The 1991 and 1993 parliamentary elections

The parliamentary election of October 1991 demonstrated how divided the original Solidarity movement and the electorate had become in the course of two years. On the eve of the Sejm election Poland had over 100 registered political parties.[12] Some of the fringe organizations among them would have an impact on the nation's political scene; for example, the Polish Friends of Beer Party would capture sixteen seats in the 1991 parliament.

A new electoral law was passed on June 28, 1991. It provided for the election of 460 deputies to the Sejm (lower house) and 100 deputies to the Senate. The draft law had been vetoed twice by Wałęsa before the final version was agreed upon after several protracted debates in the Sejm and the Senate[13] At issue was the concern of small political parties that feared they would be left out of the parliament if stringent thresholds for representation were adopted.[14] The law for the 1991 election to the Sejm was based on the principle of proportional representation, with the stipulation that 391 deputies would be chosen from regional lists and 69 deputies would be chosen from national lists tied to the regional lists (Article 2). All Polish citizens 18 years or older were eligible to vote; candidates to the Sejm had to be 21 years of age and had to have resided in Poland for at least five years (Articles 6 and 8).[15]

The voter turnout on October 27 was disappointingly low, estimated on the election day at about 40 percent of the 27.6 million of the Polish electorate.[16] Almost two-thirds of the electorate did not vote. The voters chose from among some 7,000 candidates for the 460 seats in the Sejm and from among 612 candidates for the 100 seats in the Senate. In an indication of the weakness of the nascent political parties, no party received more than 13 percent of the vote in the Sejm election. Final election results, published on October 31 by the State Electoral Commission, set the voter turnout at 43.2 percent. Of the sixty nine political groups contesting the elections, twenty-nine won seats in the parliament. The scope of the fragmentation was best symbolized by the fact that eleven of the twenty nine political parties represented won only one seat in the parliament each. The top ten parties in the 1991 Sejm were: (1) Democratic Union (DU, Unia Demokratyczna) – 62 seats; Democratic Left Alliance (DLA, Sojusz Lewicy Demokratycznej) – 60 seats; Catholic Electoral Action (CEA, Wyborcza Akcja Katolicka) – 49 seats; Polish Peasant Party (PPP, Polskie Stronnictwo Ludowe) – 48 seats; Confederation for an Independent Poland (CIP, Konfederacja Polski Niepodległej) – 46 seats; Center Alliance (CA, Porozumienie Centrum) – 44 seats; Liberal-Democratic Congress (LDC, Kongres Liberalno-Demokratyczny) – 37 seats; Peasant Alliance (PA, Porozumienie Ludowe) – 28 seats; Solidarity Trade Union – 27 seats; and Polish Friends of Beer Party (PFBP, Polska Partia Przyjaciół Piwa) – 16 seats (table 3.3).[17] From among the 200 deputies who ran for reelection, the voters returned to the Sejm only 115.[18]

The Democratic Left Alliance carried eleven of Poland's 37 electoral districts; the Democratic Union carried ten; the peasant parties jointly carried nine; the Catholic Electoral Action and the Center Alliance carried two districts each; the Confederation for an Independent Poland, the Liberal-Democratic Congress and the German Minority Party carried one district each. The two biggest winners, the Democratic Union and the Democratic Left Alliance represented two different regions of the country. Most of the electoral support for Mazowiecki's Democratic Union was concentrated in large cities in central and southern Poland; the Democratic Left Alliance was the strongest in the northern and northwestern regions of Poland, in the formerly German areas settled after World War II.[19]

The 100 Senate seats were divided up as follows: the Democratic Union won 21 seats, Solidarity – 11, the Center Alliance and the Catholic Electoral Action – 9 each, the Polish Peasant Party – 8, Rural Solidarity – 7, the Liberal-Democratic Congress – 6, and the Democratic Left Alliance – 4.[20]

The most important result of the October election was the fragmentation of the Sejm. With twenty-nine political parties represented, none had the

Table 3.3 *Parliamentary elections in Poland, 1991 (Sejm)*

	No. of votes (approx.)	% of votes	No. of seats	% of seats
Democratic Union (DU)	1,467,000	12.31	62	13
Democratic Left Alliance (DLA)	1,368,000	11.48	60	13
Catholic Election Action (CEA)	1,040,000	8.73	49	11
Polish Peasant Party (PPP)	1,033,000	8.67	48	10
Confederation for an Independent Poland (CIP)	894,000	7.50	46	10
Center Alliance (CA)	1,038,000	8.71	44	10
Liberal-Democratic Congress (LDC)	891,000	7.48	37	8
Peasant Alliance (PA)	651,000	5.46	28	6
Solidarity Trade Union	602,000	5.05	27	6
Polish Friends of Beer Party (PFBP)	389,000	3.27	16	3
Others	2,484,000	20.84	43	9
Total	11,900,000	100	460	100

Voter turnout (%): 43.2
Total eligible to vote: 27,600,000

Sources: *RFE/RL Daily Report*, November 4, 1991, *The Europa World Year Book 1993* (London: Europa Publications Ltd., 1993), p. 2329, and author's calculations.

prospects of building a strong government. Furthermore, the fragmentation of the parliament reflected the ideological polarization of the Polish electorate, making the passage of a new constitution (including the bill of rights) a truly formidable task.[21] The two years after the 1991 election were marked by a succession of weak coalition governments on the one hand, and Wałęsa's increased pressure for greater political powers for the presidency.

In 1993 a new election was forced by the parliamentary vote of no-confidence in the coalition government of Hanna Suchocka, and by the subsequent decision by President Wałęsa to dissolve the parliament. The 1993 vote marked a dramatic shift in Polish politics by removing from power the Solidarity elite and by legitimizing the postcommunist DLA. The election reduced the number of parties represented in the parliament from twenty-nine to seven (table 3.4) and gave the post-Solidarity parties only 157 seats out of 460 seats. In 1993 the voter turnout of about 52 percent was about 10 percent higher than in 1991.

The dramatic setback to the post-Solidarity parties was largely caused by the new electoral law, passed on May 28, 1993 and signed by President Wałęsa on June 1, 1993. The new law aimed at curbing the excessive parliamentary fragmentation blamed at the "hyperproportional" regulations of 1991. The most significant provision of the law was the augmentation of the proportional representation principle with thresholds for representation set at

Table 3.4 *Parliamentary elections in Poland, 1993 (Sejm)*

	No. of votes (approx.)	% of votes	No. of seats	% of seats
Democratic Left Alliance (DLA)	2,815,000	20.4	171	37
Polish Peasant Party (PPP)	2,124,000	15.4	132	29
Democratic Union (DU)	1,461,000	10.6	74	16
Union of Labor (UL)	1,005,000	7.3	41	9
Confederation for an Independent Poland (CIP)	795,000	5.8	22	5
Non-Party Bloc in Support of Reform (NPBSR)	746,000	5.4	16	3
German ethnic minority	84,000	0.6	4	1
Others (did not clear the threshold)	4,764,000	34.5	—	—
Total	13,796,000	100	460	100

Voter turnout (%): 52
Total eligible to vote: 27,000,000

Sources: *The Europa World Year Book 1995* (London: Europa Publications Ltd., 1995), p. 2,492, *Rzeczpospolita*, September 27, 1993, and author's calculations.

5 percent for political parties and 8 percent for coalitions (Article 3).[22] The law put 391 seats up for competitive election, leaving the remaining 69 seats to be awarded as additional bonus seats to parties that cleared at least 7 percent of the popular vote to be distributed to candidates from the so-called "national lists" of the most prominent party candidates (Article 4). The new law also raised the number of electoral districts from 37 to 52, to correspond to the provinces (*wojewódstwa*) and the two metropolitan areas of Warsaw and Katowice. The 1993 law kept the proportional representation principle, while favoring the largest winners in order to limit as much as possible the political fragmentation of the legislature. By doing so it generated another problem – under-representation. The new parliament left outside the legislative process all of the conservative, nationalist, free-market and Catholic parties. By favoring the biggest vote getters, the election law eliminated political parties that jointly polled 26.4 percent of the popular vote but failed to clear the threshold by a narrow margin, as opposed to 20.4 percent of the popular vote going to the DLA. The most dramatic in its symbolism of change in Polish politics was the inability of Solidarity and the Liberal-Democratic Congress (the latter the greatest champion of Polish market reform) to clear the 5 percent threshold in the Sejm. The PPP and the DLA won jointly only 36 percent of the popular vote; however, the high threshold requirement in the law and the additional bonus seats it gave to the

largest winner doubled the actual number of seats in the Sejm awarded to the PPP and the DLA to 66 percent of the total. Since the DLA and the PPP also won 76 of the 100 seats in the Senate, with a two-third control of the Sejm and over three-fourth control of the Senate they now had an effective majority in both houses sufficient to pass a new constitution.[23]

The 100 seats in the 1993 Senate were divided up as follows: the Democratic Left Alliance – 37; the Polish Peasant Party – 36; Solidarity – 10; the Democratic Union – 4; the Non-Party Bloc in Support of Reform – 2; the Union of Labor-2; the Liberal-Democratic Congress – 1; the German Minority – 1; others – 7; the Liberal-Democratic Congress lost representation after its 1994 merger with the Democratic Union into the Union of Freedom.[24]

After the 1993 election the question whether the parliament was representative enough to adopt a new constitution ranked among the most important questions for the future of democratic transition in Poland. According to polls conducted by the Center for Social Opinion Research (Centrum Badania Opinii Społecznej, CBOS) before the 1995 presidential election, 53 percent of the voters who identified themselves with the right wing parties that in 1993 had been left outside the parliament believed that upon taking office the new president should dissolve the legislature and call a new election.[25]

The scope of the DLA and PPP electoral victory in 1993 set the stage for further polarization of the Polish political scene, as the extra-parliamentary opposition framed its programs in terms of renewed struggle against the "reds." The polarization was underscored by charges coming from Cardinal Józef Glemp, the primate of the Catholic Church, that the DLA's 1993 electoral victory marked the re-emergence of communist Poland, the "PRL-bis." The election outcome placed the presidency and the parliament firmly on a collision course, with the ruling coalition claiming to act within the limits of the constitutional framework, and Wałęsa assuming the role of the sole defender of the Polish revolution and the legacy of Solidarity against the entrenched former nomenklatura.

The constitution and the powers of the presidency

The first stage of postcommunist transformation took place under conditions of only partial parliamentary legitimacy. Even more importantly, the "contract parliament" of 1989 was in no position to draft a new constitution. Poland had to wait until 1992 to approve an interim basic law, and as of late 1996 it still awaits a new constitution. During Lech Wałęsa's presidency, 1991–95, the provisional nature of the basic law and its occasional deliberate vagueness on the issue of presidential versus parliamentary authority resulted in tense and often confrontational relations between the president and the legislature, as both sought to assert their power position.

Polls conducted on the eve and immediately after the first parliamentary election showed general confusion over the division of governmental authority in the country. According to a November 1991 poll by the Center for Public Opinion Research (Ośrodek Badania Opinii Publicznej, OBOP) the dominant popular perception was that the country was in chaos. When asked who in their view was in charge in Poland, 24 percent of the respondents named President Lech Wałęsa, 15 percent named the government, 11 percent named the Catholic Church, and 6 percent named the Sejm; 13 percent of the respondents stated that they did not know who was in charge, and 9 percent responded that nobody was in control.[26]

After the October 1991 parliamentary election the Sejm moved to bring about constitutional reform. It set up an Extraordinary Commission to recommend revisions to the Constitution. President Wałęsa submitted to the Sejm a draft proposal for the so-called "Little Constitution" (*Mała Konstytucja*), which would strengthen the presidency and to some extent the government (Wałęsa's version of the "Little Constitution" would have given the government the authority to issue decrees with the force of law). Wałęsa's goal was to create a strong presidency modelled after the French system, and as such it faced strong opposition in the Sejm.[27] In addition to Wałęsa's proposal, three more drafts were reviewed in 1991–92. They were submitted by the Sejm, the Senate, and a group of lawyers from the University of Warsaw. The principal differences among them concerned the authority to form and dismiss the government (Wałęsa had insisted that this should be the president's prerogative), the procedures for the no-confidence vote in the Sejm, and the scope of the special legislative prerogatives of the government.[28]

The "Little Constitution" that was finally adopted by the Sejm on August 1, 1992 describes a hybrid presidential-parliamentary system, a compromise solution that accommodated the current political reality in Poland. It was a compromise between the Sejm's insistence on its overall supervision of the government and Wałęsa's demand for greater presidential powers, while it also attempted to strengthen the government.

The "Little Constitution" established a division between the three branches of government: the legislature (the Sejm and the Senate), the executive (the president and the Council of Ministers), and the independent judiciary. The compromise reached on a number of issues, especially the question of who controls the nation's security policy, foreign policy, and internal affairs reflected the relative strength of Wałęsa *vis-à-vis* the fragmented parliament.

The parliament may be dissolved by the president if it fails for three months to pass the budget or approve the cabinet (Articles 4 and 21); however, the president cannot dissolve the parliament on other grounds even if the Sejm passes a law which limits his powers. The constitution gives the parliament the right to dissolve itself by a two-third majority vote.

All legislation and decrees require the president's signature. The Sejm, the Senate, the president, and the Council of Ministers can initiate legislation (Article 15). The Sejm can accelerate parliamentary procedure if it decides that a bill qualifies for the "fast track" review (Article 16). The constitution tries to control deficit spending by requiring that all amendments to legislation introduced in the Senate should be accompanied by a clear statement as to how they will be paid for without adding to the budget (Article 17). Most importantly, the Sejm will entrust the government to issue decrees with the power of law, except in the areas of constitutional change, presidential and parliamentary election laws, regional government, budget, civil rights, and the ratification of international treaties (Article 23).

The president is elected through direct popular vote to a five-year term (Article 30). The president is the head of state and the commander-in-chief of the armed forces (Articles 29 and 36). Upon consultation with the minister of defense, the president appoints the chief of the general staff of the armed forces, the chiefs of the different services, the commanders of the military districts, as well as the chief commander of the armed forces. The president can introduce martial law for a period of up to three months, with one three-month extension permitted provided it has been authorized by the Sejm (Article 38). The Sejm cannot be dissolved while martial law is in place nor can the constitution be amended during that time. In one of the most controversial provisions of the constitution, the president has the "leading role" on matters of foreign policy and national security (Articles 33 and 35). This provision became a focus of an intense power struggle between Wałęsa and the parliament, as he subsequently insisted that the military should be subordinated directly to the president.

The lengthy and complicated process through which a government is selected and approved pits the president and the parliament against one another. As outlined in the "Little Constitution," the president appoints the prime minister, and upon his recommendation, his cabinet (Article 58). (In the past, the government was appointed by the parliament upon the president's nomination). The government must present its program to the Sejm within fourteen days of appointment and it must win an absolute majority vote of confidence. If the cabinet fails to win the confidence vote, the Sejm has twenty one days to appoint a government of its own choosing, which then again has to win an absolute majority vote of confidence (Article 59). Should this attempt to form the government fail, the president again appoints a government, which has to win only a simple majority vote of confidence in the Sejm (Article 60); should this fail, the Sejm gets another twenty one days to appoint yet another cabinet, and must back it up with a simple majority vote. If all four attempts to put together a government fail, the president can either dissolve the parliament or appoint within two weeks a government of his own choice which must win a vote of confidence within the next six months; if it does not, the president must dissolve the parliament and call a new election (Article 63).

A new constraint on presidential powers in the "Little Constitution" is the requirement of the prime minister's or a minister's counter-signature on presidential decisions other than the dissolution of the parliament, calling a new parliamentary election, submitting new legislation, presidential legislative veto, nominating the prime minister, calling a meeting of the Council of Ministers, initiating a referendum (provided the Senate approves the decision), judicial appointments, nominating the president of the Polish National Bank, and calling for an investigation by the Constitutional Tribunal (Articles 47 and 48). This provision was put in place to prevent the president from direct interference in the day-to-day operation of the government. The president can be impeached for violating the constitution or other crimes by a two-third majority in both the Sejm and the Senate and can then be tried by the Constitutional Tribunal (Article 51).

Another limitation on presidential powers is the requirement that the prime minister win the president's approval only for the appointments of the minister of internal affairs, the minister of national defense, and the minister of foreign affairs, regardless of whether the government is being formed based on the presidential or the parliamentary appointments. The government can be dismissed by the Sejm which then can present a new cabinet. The president can no longer dismiss the government although he can change individual cabinet ministers upon the prime minister's request (Article 69).

The relative weakness of Polish political parties in the early 1990s opened the door to Lech Wałęsa's assertive presidency. The president insisted on maintaining control over foreign policy, internal affairs, and national security affairs, while he also tried to influence the National Broadcasting Council, which supervises both public and private broadcasting in Poland. Among the most contentious issues was the question of civil-military relations, specifically whether the Polish general staff would be controlled by the defense ministry or subordinated directly to the president. In 1992 the conflict resulted in the removal of the defense minister after he had accused Wałęsa of politicizing the military. In 1994 another defense minister was fired, this time after the senior army officers expressed to Wałęsa their lack of confidence in the minister's leadership. Both the 1992 "Parys Affair" and the

1994 "Drawsko Affair" led to accusations in the parliament that Wałęsa was trying to make the army into his base of political support.[29]

In February 1995, Wałęsa forced PPP's Waldemar Pawlak to relinquish the office of the prime minister, charging that the government was responsible for slowing down economic and political change. Amidst implied threats that he might dissolve the parliament, Wałęsa took Poland to the edge of a constitutional crisis, demonstrating that he could destabilize the country's political situation. This all-out confrontation between the parliament and the president reinforced the popular frustration with the apparent gridlock in the system, for which the Poles would blame power-hungry politicians. According to a survey conducted by the CBOS in January 1995, 64 percent of the Poles believed that the war between the highest levels of the government was driven by power considerations alone. Only 19 percent conceded that real differences on issues were indeed at stake, and 13 percent thought that the different political biographies of Wałęsa and the ruling coalition were the real cause of the crisis.[30]

Debate over the new constitution has dominated Polish politics since the 1993 electoral victory of the postcommunists. On paper the DLA/PPP coalition has had a sufficient margin in the parliament to pass a new basic law. In practice, divisive social issues, such as church-state relations or abortion rights, have prevented the drafting of the new constitution from moving forward. The Constitutional Commission of the National Assembly has gone on record with its intention to limit substantially the powers of the presidency contained in the "Little Constitution." In the DLA proposal, the Polish presidency would become, much like its German counterpart, limited primarily to representative functions.[31] The DLA position is a minority view, and in 1995 the party itself showed ambivalence about the plan, as it appeared that its leader Aleksander Kwaśniewski stood a good chance to be elected president. Still, the majority of the Constitutional Commission wants to weaken the president's powers by taking away the contentious "presidential ministries," that is Defense, Internal Affairs, and Foreign Affairs. The shift would move the Polish system closer to the classical parliamentary system, whereby the executive power is concentrated in the hands of the government overseen by the legislature.

A new "big constitution" has been in the works virtually since the collapse of communism in Poland. It is unlikely that it will be passed in 1996, despite the victory of DLA's Kwaśniewski in the 1995 presidential election. An important stumbling bloc to constitutional reform are the questions of the relationship between the Catholic Church and the state, and the extent to which religion is to be reflected in the new document. Issues such as abortion, religious instruction in schools, and the reflection of religious values in the media have polarized the society and made the Church a powerful broker in the constitutional debate. In the spring of 1995 the Catholic bishops devoted a special three-day plenary session to the discussion of constitutional issues. The meeting rejected the proposed draft of the constitution as "nihilistic" and "directed against morality." Even before the plenary meeting, the bishops insisted that the constitution should include guarantees of religious instruction in schools, "protection of life from the time of conception," and that it should define the state as "neither secular, nor neutral" on the issue of faith.[32]

As time passes, ideological differences have crystallized and positions have hardened, making it more difficult to reach a workable compromise on the bill of rights.[33] It may be that Poland will have to wait for the next parliament to take up the issue of the new constitution, or that in fact the provisionary "Little Constitution" will prove to be much more permanent than it was originally intended.

The constitutional debate will no doubt be affected by the outcome of the 1995 presidential election, in which DLA's leader Aleksander Kwaśniewski narrowly defeated the incumbent president Lech Wałęsa. Kwaśniewski's victory in the runoff election on November 19, 1995, gave the DLA a dominant position on the country's political scene by placing both the government and the presidency in the DLA's hands.

The 1995 presidential campaign demonstrated once more how disorganized and fragmented the country's post-Solidarity center and right had become. Lech Wałęsa, whose popularity among the electorate was low compared to the ratings given his young and articulate opponent, was also challenged by candidates from within Solidarity's power base. Although ultimately he received an endorsement from the Solidarity Trade Union, the Catholic Church favored Hanna Gronkiewicz-Waltz, the president of the Polish National Bank almost to the very end of the campaign, switching its support to Wałęsa only after it had become clear that Gronkiewicz-Waltz would lose in the first round. Likewise, the Union of Freedom, (UF, Unia Wolności) the largest post-Solidarity party since the 1993 parliamentary election, did not endorse Wałęsa at first and instead nominated Jacek Kuroń as its candidate for president. CBOS polls conducted between October 13–17, 1995, identified Kwaśniewski as the favorite to win the first round, giving him about 27 percent of the popular vote, with Wałęsa coming in second with 22 percent and the other candidates trailing far behind.[34] In fact, both Kwaśniewski and Wałęsa did significantly better during the first round on November 5 than had been projected. The early exit polls gave Kwaśniewski 34.8 percent of the vote to Wałęsa's 33.3 percent. They were followed by Jan Olszewski with 7 percent, Waldemar Pawlak with 4.8 percent and Hanna Gronkiewicz-Waltz with 2.7 percent.[35] These numbers were subsequently revised slightly upward for both leading contenders, with Kwaśniewski getting 35.11 percent of the vote and Wałęsa 33.11 percent. The voter turnout of 64.79 percent was larger than at any presidential or parliamentary election since 1989.[36]

The results of the first round eliminated fringe candidates and suggested clear voter preferences. The especially poor performance of Hanna Gronkiewicz-Waltz was a powerful message to the Catholic Church, her strongest support base, that the electorate wanted to impose limits on its involvement in the country's political life. The two weeks leading up to the run-off were filled with intense negative campaigning by both sides. The Wałęsa camp accused Kwaśniewski of falsifying his resume by claiming a degree in economics although he had not actually received the diploma. Kwaśniewski retaliated by calling on Wałęsa to make his income tax declarations public, suggesting that Wałęsa was hiding the extent of his assets. In turn Wałęsa pointed out that Kwaśniewski failed to report on his income tax return his wife's stock in the Polisa insurance company worth some $20,000.[37] Two nationally televised debates between the candidates revisited the issues that had defined Solidarity in the past. Wałęsa argued that Kwaśniewski was a communist masquerading as a social-democrat, while Kwaśniewski accused Wałęsa of trying to capitalize on the political divisions of the past, instead of "choosing the future," Kwaśniewski's campaign slogan.

The November 19 run-off gave Kwaśniewski a narrow margin of victory over Wałęsa. The DLA candidate received 51.72 percent of the vote to Wałęsa's 48.28 percent; voter turnout was put at 68.23 percent (table 3.5). Kwaśniewski won in thirty-four provinces, mostly in northern and western Poland, while Wałęsa took fifteen provinces, mostly in the southeast.[38] Immediately after the election Wałęsa's camp launched a petition drive to ask the Supreme Court to declare the election invalid on the grounds that Kwaśniewski misrepresented his credentials to the voters; the petition collected approximately 600,000 signatures. In early December 1995, the Supreme Court reviewed the case and pronounced Kwaśniewski's election legally valid.[39] Shortly after the election the three "presidential ministers," that is defense, internal affairs, and foreign affairs submitted their resignation.

Although the new president reaffirmed upon taking office in 1996 his commitment to the principal tenets of the economic, security, and foreign policy of his predecessor, emphasizing the necessity for Poland's integration with the European Union and NATO, the opposition remained skeptical. The situation was further aggravated by the resignation in early 1996, shortly after Kwaśniewski's inauguration, of Prime Minister Józef Oleksy, a prominent member of the DLA, amid allegations and a subsequent investigation of charges that he had spied for the Russians.

Table 3.5 *Presidential elections in Poland, 1995*

	First ballot	% first ballot[a]	Second ballot	% second ballot
Aleksander Kwaśniewski	6,275,670	35.11	9,704,439	51.72
Lech Wałęsa	5,917,328	33.11	9,058,176	48.28
Jacek Kuroń	1,646,946	9.22		
Jan Olszewski	1,275,670	6.86		
Waldemar Pawlak	770,419	4.31		
Tadeusz Zieliński	631,432	3.53		
Hanna Gronkiewicz-Waltz	492,628	2.76		
Janusz Ryszard Korwin-Mikke	428,969	2.40		
Andrzej Lepper	235,797	1.32		
Jan Pietrzak	201,033	1.12		
Tadeusz Koźluk	27,259	0.15		
Kazimierz Wojciech Piotrowicz	12,591	0.07		
Leszek Bubel	6,825	0.04		
Total votes[a]	17,872,350		18,762,615	
Voter turnout (%)		64.79		68.23
Total eligible to vote: 28,100,000				

Notes: [a]The State Election Commission invalidated 330,868 ballots of the first ballot; the total number of votes on the first ballot including the invalidated ballots was 18,203,218. On the second ballot the Commission invalidated 383,881 votes, which would have put the total number of voters on the second ballot at 19,146,496.

Sources: *Polska Agencja Prasowa*, November 7 and 21, 1995, and author's calculations.

Political parties

Historically, Polish political culture has favored splintering over compromise. Turmoil within the post-Solidarity camp after 1989, as opposed to consolidation on the left, reflected that pattern. In addition to the impact of the Polish anarchic democratic tradition, the fragmentation of the center and right political parties has been a result of the negotiated 1989 revolution. On the other hand, on the left of the Polish political spectrum the revolution of 1989 left the old PUWP and UPP grass roots organizations and the local cadres largely untouched, despite the official dissolution of the PUWP and a schism within the communist-controlled UPP. The gravity of the economic crisis and the need to concentrate on the implementation of the IMF-recommended Balcerowicz austerity program dominated the agenda of the first Solidarity government, pushing aside ideological considerations and making the "thick line" policy a lasting feature of Polish politics. Another formative factor in the emergence of the Polish party system was the bitterly fought presidential election of 1990 and the subsequent "war at the top" that accompanied it, which polarized the Solidarity movement and made party allegiance a function of personal loyalty.

As both the left and the right in Poland agreed on the need for economic change, ideology entered the process of party formation first outside the area of economic policy, focusing instead on ethics, morality, and church–state relations, as debates on abortion and the role of the church were joined in the presidential and parliamentary elections. Subsequently, however, differences in the approach to economic reform manifested themselves, helping define the parties on economic policy as well as other issues. By 1993 the DLA and the PPP, both with roots in their communist predecessors, emerged as an alternative to the parties with their roots in the Solidarity ethos, because the Polish left was able to capitalize on the social costs of the Balcerowicz program. While parties derived from Solidarity maintained a hard line on economic reform, between 1989 and 1993 the PPP and the DLA defined themselves as the proponents of greater state intervention in the economy, including higher subsidies for the enterprises, protective tariffs for agriculture, and greater spending on social services. Although the left supported the overall direction of market reform, it argued that its social cost was unjustifiably high and could have been made lower through government policy.

In early 1996 the strongest parties of the Polish party system were the DLA, the PPP, and the Union of Freedom (UF), the latter created after a 1994 merger of the Liberal-Democratic Congress and the Democratic Union. These together with the Union of Labor (UL, Unia Pracy), covered the left and center of the political spectrum, with some overlap with the Solidarity Trade Union, the principal labor organization in the country. The right remained fragmented into a number of small parties which drew on religion, national tradition, and radical market reform ideas for their political programs; parties with a strong populist appeal, such as the Confederation for an Independent Poland (CIP, Konfederacja Polski Niepodległej) and the Center Alliance (CA, Porozumienie Centrum) also commanded a small support base.

Democratic Left Alliance (DLA)

The composition of the DLA reflects the party's roots. The DLA was created as a broad coalition of left-wing forces organizing for the 1993 parliamentary elections, but it has its roots in the January 1990 breakup of the Polish United Workers' Party (PUWP) into two competing organizations, the Social Democracy of the Republic of Poland (SDRP, Socjaldemokracja Rzeczpospolitej Polskiej) led by Aleksander Kwaśniewski, and the Social Democratic Union of the Republic of Poland (SDURP, Unia Socjaldemokratyczna

Rzeczpospolitej Polskiej), led by Tadeusz Fiszbach. The DLA became an umbrella coalition of all the forces associated with the former communist establishment. Under Kwaśniewski's leadership, the SDRP has become a dominant voice within the DLA, which also includes the former official National Alliance of Trade Unions, (NATU, or Ogólnopolskie Porozumienie Związków Zawodowych) and some two dozen other groups and organizations. The SDRP membership is estimated at 65,000.

The DLA program supports the system of parliamentary democracy, the rule of law, local and employee self-government, and the rights of minorities. It emphasizes the separation of church and state. From the start Kwaśniewski focused his efforts on building a party with a Social-Democratic image among the population. The DLA has attacked the excesses of market privatization, but did not repudiate the reform itself. It became a voice against the growing involvement of the Catholic Church in national politics. In contrast to the PPP, the DLA is a relatively loose coalition of often competing groups. The liberal pro-market policy line propounded by Kwaśniewski is strongly opposed by the older hard-line communists who demand the restoration of state subsidies and the slowing down of market reform. That faction within DLA, led after 1993 by Labor Minister Leszek Miller, is closer in spirit (if not policy) to the core electorate of the PPP. The more liberal elements of the DLA, led by Kwaśniewski, look to the UF as their potential coalition partner.

Polish Peasant Party (PPP)

The PPP is unique among the Polish parties in that it represents a relatively uniform constituency with a clearly articulated set of political interests. The peasants want agricultural subsidies, subsidized credits, and the protection of Poland's agricultural market.[40] With an estimated membership of 170,000 (some earlier estimates placed it even at close to 500,000), the PPP has succeeded in making the transition from the communist-era UPP.

In 1990 the Polish Peasant Party – "Renewal" (the successor to UPP) merged with the Polish Peasant Party "Wilanów," reestablished in 1989 to continue the traditions of the prewar peasant movement, and with elements of the peasant "Solidarity" movement.[41] The PPP's "neo-agrarian" program emphasizes agriculture as a critical branch of the national economy and demands that the government guarantee an "equitable exchange" between the cities and the countryside.[42] In practice, the PPP has pushed vigorously for government subsidies and protective tariffs. Under the leadership of young Waldemar Pawlak, the PPP became a key player in Polish politics after 1993 by entering a coalition with the DLA and claiming the premiership for the party's chairman from 1993 until his ouster engineered by President Wałęsa in early 1995.

Although it presents a unified front, the PPP is internally divided between two factions representing on the one hand the interests of big agricultural producers and food-processing companies, and on the other hand the small farmers and agricultural laborers. The division has broader national implications, as it forces the peasants to confront the question of the terms on which Polish agriculture has to become consolidated if in the future the country is to join the European Union.

Union of Freedom (UF)

The UF became the largest opposition party in the Polish parliament after the 1993 election. It was created in April 1994 through a merger of the Democratic Union (DU, Unia Demokratyczna), led since his failed 1990 presidential campaign by Tadeusz Mazowiecki, and the Liberal-Democratic Congress (LDC, Kongres Liberalno-Demokratyczny), led by Donald Tusk. In 1993 the LDC found itself outside the parliament, while the DU's position in the Sejm imploded. The UF, which has about 17,000 members drawn mostly from the Solidarity movement has remained divided between a center-left faction, led by Jacek Kuroń, and a center-right faction, led by Mazowiecki, Hanna Suchocka, and Jan Rokita. An attempt at healing the rift within the party was made in the spring of 1995 with the selection of Leszek Balcerowicz, the founding father of Polish economic reform, as the party's new chairman in place of Mazowiecki. However, the subsequent fight over the selection of Kuroń as the party's presidential candidate deepened the internal divisions within the UF. In 1996 the UF remained the best known and largest opposition party, counting among its membership some of the best known Polish intellectuals.

Union of Labor (UL)

The Union of Labor (UL), led by Ryszard Bugaj, is a left-wing party close in its program to the DLA but without the baggage of communist past. It was established in 1992 by a merger of a number of left-wing groups. It has advocated state intervention in the economy, has criticized privatization, and has demanded continued state protection of large enterprises. The UL political program draws upon the cooperative movement traditions of the Polish left. It emphasizes the redistributive role of the income tax code as a means to limit social inequalities. The party opposes the involvement of the church in Polish politics. The UL as a minority center-socialist party has asserted its role as a swing voter in the 1993 parliament.

Solidarity Trade Union

Solidarity, led by young and charismatic Marian Krzaklewski, has been transformed over the last six years into an organization fiercely committed to the defense of the class interests of the workers. It has demanded government support for the state enterprises and has frequently attacked privatization.

Right-wing parties

The right in Poland is weak and fragmented. Right wing parties seem riven by battles over personalities, and are often described as "sofa parties" in an unflattering suggestion that for some their entire membership would fit on a couch in the leader's living room. Attempts at unity, such as the church-sponsored "Convent of St. Katherine" have so far failed. The Concord for Poland (CfP, Przymierze dla Polski) that had brought together in 1993 the Center Alliance (CA, Porozumienie Centrum), the Conservative Coalition (CC, Konserwatywna Koalicja), Movement for the Republic (MfR, Ruch dla Rzeczpospolitej), PPP-Peasant Alliance (PPP-PA, PSL-Porozumienie Ludowe), and the Christian National Union (CNU, Zjednoczenie Chrześcijańsko-Narodowe) disintegrated within months after the election. The same fate befell the "Coalition of November 11" (Koalicja 11 Listopada) that consisted of the Union of Real Politics (URP, Unia Polityki Realnej), the Christian Democratic Party (CDP, Partia Chrześcijańskich Demokratów), the Conservative Party (CP, Partia Konserwatywna), the Christian Peasant Party (CPP, Stronnictwo Ludowo-Chrześcijańskie), and the National Democratic Party (NDP, Stronnictwo Narodowo-Demokratyczne), which even failed to compete in the 1993 election as a group.[43]

The Christian-National Union (CNU, Zjednoczenie Chrześcijańsko-Narodowe), founded in 1989 after a merger between the political clubs Order and Freedom (Klub Polityczny "Ład i Wolność") and Order and Solidarity (Klub Polityczny "Ład i Solidarność"), is probably the closest Poland has to a proto-Christian Democratic party. The CNU's electorate is drawn from among Catholics who emphasize moral issues, such as abortion or teaching catechism in schools over other issues.[44]

Populist parties

Poland also has parties that propound a radical populist agenda. The Confederation for an Independent Poland (CIP, Konfederacja Polski Niepodległej), founded in 1979 by Leszek Moczulski is the oldest political party with roots in the dissident movement and a radical populist appeal and ties to the traditions of the prewar left. The CIP, whose membership is less than 15,000, declares itself to be a successor to the legacy of Józef Piłsudski, the founding father and leader of the interwar Second Republic. The CIP and the Center Alliance (CA, Porozumienie Centrum), led by Jaroslaw Kaczyński, stand apart from the rest of the right in that although they recognize the importance of the Catholic Church in Polish politics, they do not make Christian moral issues and values critical to their programs and they maintain some distance from the church hierarchy. The Center Alliance has roots in the Solidarity faction that supported Lech Wałęsa against Tadeusz Mazowiecki during the 1990 presidential election, but it did not work with the president afterwards. A different sort of populism is represented by the Non-Party Bloc in Support of Reform (NPBSR, Bezpartyjny Blok Wspierania Reform), Wałęsa's proto-party set up on the eve on the 1993 election and represented in the 1993 parliament. After Wałęsa's loss to Kwaśniewski in the 1995 presidential election, the NPBSR has remained the voice for Wałęsa's camp in the legislature. It has harkened back to the interwar Non-Party Bloc in Cooperation with the Government, as it has sought to appeal to the segment of the electorate most frustrated with the existing political parties.

Party support

Support for political parties in Poland after 1989 has remained fragmented, especially for parties with roots in the Solidarity ethos, but there are signs that the party system has matured. In the 1991 election none of the political parties got more than 13 percent of popular vote; in the 1993 election none got more than 20 percent of the popular vote. However, polling data obtained on the eve of the election by the OBOP showed that five parties had more supporters than opponents, an indication that these parties were consolidating their support base.[45]

A June 1995 poll by the CBOS showed that the greatest level of support among the electorate was still enjoyed by the DLA (21 percent), which far exceeded support for the PPP (13 percent), Solidarity (13 percent), the UF (11 percent), the UL (10 percent), the right-wing parties not represented in the parliament (10 percent), the NPBSR (5 percent) and the CIP (4 percent).[46]

The level of support for different political parties in Poland appears to have stabilized. Polls conducted in 1995 show that fluctuations in the size of support for a given party remain well within the margin of error. The PPP clearly dominates the Polish countryside as the party representing the peasant interests. The DLA has the greatest support in small and medium-size cities (between 20,000-100,000 inhabitants), while in the largest cities (200,000 and up) the DLA competes for support against Solidarity, the UF, and the UL.

The cleavages cut across different educational levels, with college educated Poles supporting mainly either the DLA or the UF, high school graduates supporting the DLA, and those with elementary education supporting the PPP and the Solidarity Trade Union. In terms of income disparity, supporters of the UF and the DLA declare the highest levels of income, while the PPP electorate is drawn predominantly from among those declaring the lowest income levels.[47]

Polling conducted in 1995 by the CBOS suggests that the process of party consolidation in Poland is moving in two general directions, reflecting the overall polarization of the electorate between those who support (1) the "independence" parties and those who choose (2) the "social justice" parties (table 3.6). The polling data suggests that in 1995 the majority of the support base for the NPBSR, the UF, and of the right-wing parties unrepresented in the parliament came from among those in Polish society who considered freedom as the highest value. On the other hand, the supporters of the UL, the CIP, the Solidarity Trade Union, and the PPP considered social justice as their most important value, with the UL commanding the most radically pro-socialist segment of society, and the PPP and Solidarity being overall the most radical among them.

The most interesting result of the 1995 poll was the support base of the DLA, whose electorate, while it still chose in greater numbers social justice over freedom, nevertheless also placed freedom at the top of its values.[48] The data on the DLA electorate suggest that while in 1995 the DLA was identified with the left it also appealed to a large segment of the centrist vote. In general, with the exception of the UL and the CIP, freedom was the organizing principle for political parties with their roots in the former anti-communist opposition, while the issue of social justice was the organizing principle of the Polish left whose electorate included the former communists as well as those responding to the growing social stratification; on this score, the DLA found itself alongside the Solidarity Trade Union. The 1995 polling of voter party identification suggests that egalitarian socialist values have been internalized by Polish society to a much greater extent than the anti-communist opposition believed and that those have become an integral part of the party consolidation process.

Public attitudes toward democracy

In 1996 Polish transition to democracy remained a work in progress, but there were encouraging signs suggesting that democratic consolidation was taking place and that Polish civil society was maturing. There were still questions about the ultimate staying power of the current political parties,

Table 3.6 *Principal values of the electorate in Poland (by party identification), 1995*

	Freedom		Prosperity		Equality under the law		Social justice	
	A	B	A	B	A	B	A	B
NPBSR	67	81	11	22	9	44	13	50
UF	51	66	15	41	19	48	15	46
Right-wing parties	51	69	11	24	10	44	28	63
Solidarity Trade Union	41	62	9	37	10	24	39	75
PPP	34	60	10	28	18	41	35	70
DLA	34	50	17	36	19	51	30	62
CIP	28	46	11	38	16	32	44	84
UL	25	39	13	38	16	47	47	77

Notes: A – percentage of respondents indicating as the most important value. B – percentage of respondents indicating as one of the two most important values.

Source: *Społeczna wizja ustroju demokratycznego* (Warsaw: CBOS, 1995), p. 3.

especially on the right, as well as uncertainty about the shape of the "big constitution," but overall the Poles seemed to have accepted democracy as a preferred political system. In 1995 Polish media commentators often remarked that while generally the society was familiar with democratic rules and procedures, it also lacked democratic experience.[49] In addition, a generational gap appeared to have opened between those who had experienced both the communist system and Solidarity as their formative political experience, and the generation that matured after 1989. While the economic transformation in Poland has been widely accepted by the majority of young people, the experience of the six years of transition has generated considerable alienation from politics among the young. However, according to a CBOS study published in June 1995, the majority of the Polish youth rejected politics not because it considered the system deficient, but because it did not understand it.[50] The results obtained were disturbing in one respect, however, in that in contrast to the Solidarity generation, the young respondents expressed no objection to replacing democracy with a competent autocrat. According to the poll, 76 percent of the young agreed with the statement: "It would be better if instead of political parties Poland were governed by a decisive and competent man," while 77 percent agreed with the statement that "a bit of dictatorship would not harm anyone," and that "some strong hand should take charge of the bureaucrats and those arguing political parties."[51]

The views of the Polish youth, however, constituted a minority position. In 1995 there was a clear generational cleavage in Poland on the issue of democracy versus authoritarianism. While there was also some support for the "government of the strong-hand" among the retirees, these views were more than offset by the majority public opinion in the country. Close to 75 percent of Polish society regarded transition to democracy over the last six years as a positive change. The majority identified democracy with human freedom and new possibilities for individual and social growth, even if it bemoaned the unruly character of the Polish political scene. Moreover, the percentage of those who supported democracy as the best political system for the country had slightly increased over the 1994–95 period. The overall number of those who considered democracy superior to all other forms of government grew from 52 percent in 1992 to 62 percent in 1993 to 67 percent in 1995.[52]

The overall level of education seems to constitute another cleavage between those who have favored democracy and those who would support authoritarian solutions: the lower the education level the greater the preference for a "strongman" to solve Poland's problems. Interestingly, in 1995 the greatest level of support for democracy and the most powerful rejection of authoritarian solutions was represented not only among the electorate of the UF (69 percent for democracy and 23 percent for authoritarianism) but also among voters for the DLA, which comes in second (65 percent for democracy and 27 for authoritarianism) (table 3.7).[53]

Support for democracy in Poland has coexisted with a strong sense of frustration with the actual workings of the system. In the 1993 polls 50 percent of the respondents rejected the current political and media elites for failing to speak to their concerns, but they also accepted the general principles of democracy. Asked to identify "us vs. them," the respondents did note include anyone connected to the government, the presidency, or the parliament in the "us" category.[54] The polls showed that while the majority expressed acceptance of the principles of democratic government in the abstract, they remained disenchanted by the practical experience of democracy, especially the ineffectiveness and incompetence of the elites. While the Poles continue to view democracy as "historically legitimate," the growing popular frustration seems to have focused on the perceived irresponsiveness of the political process. However, the overall popular dissatisfaction with the practice of democracy ought to be weighed against the apparent rising appreciation of democratic values in Polish society and the fact that the Poles associate democracy with successful economic reform.[55] Although in the polls conducted in 1995 the respondents chose most frequently social justice as an important value, they also placed the greatest emphasis on individual freedom; equality under the law and prosperity come a distant second (table 3.8). The choice of either of the two principal values indicated by the 1995

Table 3.7 *Support for democracy among the electorate in Poland (by party identification), 1995*

Voter party identification	Pro democracy (%)	Pro "strongman" (%)
Union of Labor (UL)	48	47
Confederation for an Independent Poland (CIP)	61	39
Non-Party Bloc in Support of Reform (NPBSR)	60	38
Solidarity Trade Union	55	35
Right-wing parties outside parliament	57	35
Polish Peasant Party (PPP)	57	29
Democratic Left Alliance (DLA)	65	27
Union of Freedom (UF)	69	23

Source: *Społeczna wizja ustroju demokratycznego* (Warsaw: CBOS, 1995), p. 12.

Table 3.8 *Principal values of the electorate in Poland, 1995*

	Most important value (%)	Second most important value (%)
Freedom	37	19
Prosperity	16	22
Equality under the Law	14	25
Social Justice	33	33

Source: *Społeczna wizja ustroju demokratycznego* (Warsaw: CBOS, 1995), p. 1.

polls seems to reflect the new class cleavages in Poland, whereby freedom was most often selected by businessmen, professionals, members of intelligentsia, managers, and students while social justice dominated the preferences of the workers, employees of the state sector, the unemployed and those among the professional classes who identified their political orientation as left-wing. In general in 1995 the higher income levels opted for freedom, while those at the bottom of the social ladder identified social justice as their principal concern. Another interesting result of the 1995 CBOS polling was a pronounced difference in values between Polish men and women, which seemed to cut across the class divide. In contrast to men, who generally chose freedom as the most important value, the majority of women selected social justice as their principal concern, suggesting that women might have felt discriminated against in the new economic order and were therefore more sensitive to the issue of income disparity. The relatively low recognition of the importance of equality under the law, as well as the fact that those who chose it as an important value in the 1995 polls tended to come from among university graduates, suggests that Polish society as a whole still had a relatively low awareness of the importance of law in a democratic society.

Civil society and the media

There are signs that civil society has taken hold in Poland since 1989, as evidenced by the proliferation of nongovernmental organizations and grass-roots activism. The American Committee of Aid to Poland and the Civicus organization estimated in 1995 that since 1988 there might be close to 20,000 nongovernmental organizations operating in Poland. These included political, professional, cultural, ecological, and single-issue groups and associations, women's groups, think tanks, and student organizations.[56] In addition to the Catholic Church which operated shelters for the homeless, soup kitchens, and the like, a number of small voluntary charities worked closely with the Church and local welfare offices. In 1995 Poland had four national interbranch industrial unions; in addition, there were seventeen major independent industrial branch unions and three agricultural unions. Poland's 2.1 million peasants and agricultural workers were organized in a number of local and regional associations and cooperatives.

Overall, there were over 200 national unions registered in Poland in 1995, the largest among them being the Solidarity Trade Union, the successor to the original "Solidarity" movement, which claimed over two million members, and the National Alliance of Trade Unions (NATU), the successor to the communist-era official trade union, whose membership was estimated at approximately three million. Estimates of union participation in Poland in 1995 ranged from 30 to 40 percent of the country's twenty-one million workers, although the rate of unionization was low in the rapidly growing private sector.

Another area of considerable progress toward democratic consolidation in Poland has been the explosive growth of the free press and broadcast media. In 1990 the Solidarity government abolished censorship and eliminated the state-controlled press distribution network RSW "Prasa Książka Ruch." In December 1991 a new broadcasting law terminated the state's monopoly on radio and television broadcasting. By 1996 Poland had both public sector broadcast media in the form of public radio and television and a rapidly growing network of private and public television stations. The law limited to 33 percent foreign capital in the private radio and television stations.

Privatization has been especially successful in the broadcast media at the local level. Reportedly, in 1995 65 percent of local radio stations in Poland were in private hands, as opposed to only 15 percent of national radio stations. Private ownership of local television stations stood at 25 percent, while only 15 percent accounted for privately owned national broadcasters.

The question of licensing private commercial television stations has remained a hotly debated issue.

The print media in Poland have been quickly transformed by the market forces by drawing its resources from advertising fees. In 1995 it was estimated that foreign stakes in all national publications stood at 56 percent and 50 percent in regional ones. German publishers were the greatest share-holders in the Polish press with 18 percent of national and provincial titles. In 1995 almost all of Poland's print publications were privately owned, with a substantial foreign capital stake in them. The newspapers editorial policies ran the entire political gamut from left to right, reflecting the diversity of Polish politics. In 1995 the overwhelming majority of the Poles (82 percent) believed that freedom of the press was the best guarantor of continued political pluralism.[57]

Broadcasting in Poland has been controlled since March 1993 by the National Broadcasting Council consisting of nine members are nominated by the Sejm, the Senate, and the president, the latter also appointing its chairman. Although nominally independent of the government, the Council has been subject to political pressure, as reflected in the 1993 media law which stipulated that radio and television programs should respect Christian values.

Economic transformation

In 1990 and 1991 the Polish government implemented an economic stabili-zation program developed with the assistance from Western economists and the International Monetary Fund (IMF). Introduced on January 1, 1990, the so-called "Balcerowicz Plan" named after the country's finance minister Leszek Balcerowicz, concentrated on fighting hyperinflation, making the Polish złoty convertible, and beginning the process of privatizing the economy. In January 1990 Warsaw freed prices, imposed taxes on excess wages at state enterprises, and all but eliminated government subsidies; by the end of 1991 the subsidies constituted less than 5 percent of the govern-ment's budget.

The Balcerowicz program has been a success. The inflation rate went down from 585.8 percent in 1990 to 27 percent in 1995. Today, the Polish złoty is fully convertible internally, with an exchange rate reflecting the currency's real value against principal Western currencies. The transition to the convertible złoty was achieved without the government having to draw upon the $1 billion currency stabilization fund set aside by the International Monetary Fund. The Balcerowicz program also contributed to the revitaliza-tion of Polish trade with the West. Already in 1990 Poland achieved a surplus from its convertible currencies exports.[58]

Since the implementation of the Balcerowicz plan, the private sector doubled from 28.6 percent of the GDP in 1989 to 56 percent of the GDP in 1994. In 1992 Poland reversed the decline of the GDP when it posted a 2.6 percent growth; in 1994 and 1995 Poland posted 5.0 percent and 5.5 percent GDP grown rates, respectively, making it the fasted growing economy in Europe. In 1991 the Warsaw Stock Exchange was reopened; by 1994 it listed 44 companies, up from 9 in 1991 (table 3.9).

In 1990 the Polish government passed a Privatization Law to augment small-scale privatization initiated early in the Balcerowicz program. The new law resulted by the end of 1993 in the transfer of over 2,000 enterprises directly to private ownership, which amounted to about 25 percent of the 8,841 enterprises held by the government in July 1990; an additional 6 percent were transformed in to treasury-owned joint-stock companies. In 1994 an additional 321 enterprises were privatized and 244 were "commercialized," that is, converted into joint-stock companies with limited workers' council's influence; this raised the number of privatized enterprises to 29 percent of the total and the number of commercialized enterprises to 9 percent. In February 1995 Poland finally launched a voucher mass privatization program, with the selection of the management for 15 National Investment Funds; in July–October 1995, 413 enterprises were allocated to the Funds, with an additional 106 enterprises added by the end of 1995.[59] In July 1995 Poland passed a new Privatization Law, which emphasized commercialization, transferred authority away from the Ministry of Privatization to other ministries, and required parliamentary approval for sales firms in strategic sectors. Poland also liberalized its foreign trade by suspending or sharply reducing most tariffs and non-tariff barriers, and by ending the state monopoly on foreign trade. In January 1995 the average tariff on industrial goods went down to 9.3 percent and the import surcharge was reduced to 5 percent. In May 1995 Poland converted quantitative restrictions on agricultural imports into tariffs, as stipulated by the GATT Uruguay Round; in July 1995 it joined the WTO.[60]

The country's banking system was reformed by transforming the branches of nine regional departments of the Polish National Bank (NBP – Narodowy Bank Polski) into independent commercial banks. In 1993 two of the nine large state-owned commercial banks were privatized. All commercial banks have been licensed and supervised by the NBP.

As Poland entered 1996 some big economic issues remained to be addressed, especially in the area of a badly needed reform of the social security system and in the inefficient farming sector. Since 1989 the country has also needed substantial investment to improve its telecommunications and roads, including the planned construction of an expressway network. Unemployment has remained high, reaching 16 percent in 1994. Overall,

Table 3.9 *Indicators of economic trends in Poland since 1989*

	1989	1990	1991	1992	1993	1994	1995[a]
GDP	0.2	-11.6	-7.0	2.6	3.8	6.0	7.0
Industrial output	n.a.	n.a.	-8.0	2.8	6.4	11.9	9.4
Rate of inflation	251.1	585.8	70.3	43.0	35.3	33.2	27.8
% Labor force unemployed	0.1	6.1	11.8	13.6	15.7	16.0	14.9
GNP per capita	n.a.	n.a.	n.a.	n.a.	5,380	n.a.	n.a.
% Workforce in private activity	45.7	45.8	51.1	57.0	57.6	59.8	n.a.
% GDP from private sector	28.6	31.4	45.3	48.2	53.5	56.0	n.a.

Notes: GDP – % change over previous year; industrial output – % change over previous year; rate of inflation – % change in end-year retail/consumer prices; rate of unemployment as of end of year; GNP per capita – in US dollars at PPP exchange rates. [a]Estimate.

Sources: European Bank for Reconstruction and Development, *Transition Report 1995: Economic Transition in Eastern Europe and the Former Soviet Union* (London: EBRD, 1995); European Bank for Reconstruction and Development, *Transition Report Update, April 1996: Assessing Progress in Economies in Transition* (London: EBRD, 1996).

however, by 1996 Poland had made remarkable progress in the area of economic reform, especially when one remembers how deep was the economic crisis of the 1980s.

Democratic consolidation in progress

Successful democratization requires a mechanism that ensures the accountability and responsibility of those in power and political participation of the people. Democratization means in effect the establishment and consolidation of democratic and representative institutions that foster competition, participation, and civil and political liberties.[61] A democratic constitutional legal framework, competitive elections, and political parties are essential steps in establishing democracy. Political participation within the institutional framework is a necessary precondition for democratic consolidation, for it brings the state and the civil society into the process. It is encouraged by economic stability and a popular sense that the system favors the economic welfare of the citizenry.

Compared to the majority of postcommunist states, the Polish transition to democracy has been a success. The chaotic, even anarchic, nature of Polish politics notwithstanding, Poland has introduced democratic institutions and has continued economic reform despite social pressures generated by the Balcerowicz plan. The political parties have undergone a degree of consolidation at the level of parliamentary representation. Although "historically legitimate," democracy is still viewed by the Poles as something of an abstraction, but it is also a system preferred by the majority of the population. The long-term success of democratization in Poland will depend on the consolidation and maturation of the party system, and on the cumulative experience of the practice of democratic government. The process of consolidation will take time. However, inasmuch as the emergence of political parties is the function of the emergence of class and group interests, the extent to which Poland has succeeded in its transition to a market economy bodes well for that process.

The DLA's rise in particular raises an intriguing question about its future in relation to the UF, the largest post-Solidarity party in the parliament after the 1993 election. In 1995 and early 1996 both the DLA and the UF included a substantial centrist element, with the DLA also relying on the postcommunist left and the UF on post-Solidarity right for some of their support base. The recurrent discussion in Polish media on the possibility of a coalition between the DLA and the UF, albeit discounted publicly by both parties, suggests that Poland appears to have today two political parties that draw a substantial portion of their support from a Social-Democratic constituency.

The issue of the rise and consolidation of Polish civil society is a more complex question. One can appreciate the extent of change in Polish politics better when treating 1980–81 as the beginning of the breakdown of communist power. It is true that instead of working directly to bring down the communist state, the alliance of Solidarity served to marginalize it and in the process developed a nascent civil society. However, the experience of opposition may not in itself be sufficient to consolidate that civil society to the extent required by democracy.[62] Could it be that while it instilled in the population the values of civil society, the legacy of vigorous and determined dissident movement in Poland could itself be a contributing factor to the fragmentation and personalization of politics on the right of the spectrum? If that has been the case, the proliferation of nongovernmental organizations and grass-root activities may prove more important than ever to the consolidation of Polish civil society.

From the vantage point of the last six years of Polish reform it appears that the simultaneous implementation of economic and political reforms in postcommunist states can be sustained, but it involves trade-offs. Polish political reform suffered on occasion, as the energy of four Solidarity governments focused on the country's desperate economic conditions; the delay in addressing the constitutional question is a case in point as are the lingering questions about the communist legacy. In the early years of postcommunist transition, economic reform took precedence over the need to consolidate the new democratic institutions. Nevertheless, during six years since the collapse of communism a succession of Polish governments implemented an economic austerity program without undermining the overall popular support for democracy.

Institutional changes in Polish politics since 1989 have been impressive. In the six years since the anticommunist revolution Poland introduced an interim constitution and witnessed the rise of political parties. On four occasions the country went through an orderly transition of political power: after the 1991 and 1993 parliamentary elections and the 1990 and 1995 presidential elections. In 1995 the post-Solidarity parties on the right were weaker than the DLA and the PPP, but the divisions among the principal organizations appeared progressively less a matter of personalities and more a question of political programs, suggesting that a more unified Polish right-wing would eventually emerge as well.

The consolidation of Polish democracy will also be influenced by the degree of Western support for the country's long-term foreign and security policy objectives. Poland needs to become integrated in the Western economic and security system to foster stability and a sense of confidence about the future, the latter especially important in light of the residual fear of Russia and the remaining divisions over the country's communist past. Throughout the postcommunist transformation, the goal of becoming integrated with the West, including the European Union and NATO expansion, has been ever-present in Polish politics.

In 1996 the Polish political scene remained polarized. In the immediate aftermath of the election of DLA's Aleksander Kwaśniewski as the country's president one might have expected that the Poles would begin to come to terms with the legacy of communism; however, the 1996 resignation of Premier Józef Oleksy, who was being investigated on charges of espionage for Russia, revisited the old questions and deepened political cleavages in Polish society. The experience of the practice of democracy had caused some disappointment and lowered popular expectations. And yet, the Poles appeared to have remained committed to the principles of pluralism, freedom of expression, and accountability of elected officials while they criticized their government, their president, and their parliament.[63]

Acronyms of Polish political parties

CA	Center Alliance (Porozumienie Centrum)
CC	Conservative Coalition (Konserwatywna Koalicja)
CDP	Christian Democratic Party (Partia Chrześcijańskich Demokratów)
CEA	Catholic Election Action (Wyborcza Akcja Katolicka)
CfP	Concord for Poland (Przymierze dla Polski)
CIP	Confederation for an Independent Poland (Konfederacja Polski Niepodległej)
CNU	Christian National Union (Zjednoczenie Chrześcijańsko-Narodowe)
CP	Conservative Party (Partia Konserwatywna)
CPP	Christian Peasant Party (Stonnictwo Ludowo-Chrześcijańskie)
DLA	Democratic Left Alliance (Sojusz Lewicy Demokratycznej)
DU	Democratic Union (Unia Demokratyczna)
LDC	Liberal-Democratic Congress (Kongress Liberalno-Demokratyczny)
NATU	National Alliance of Trade Unions (Ogólnopolskie Porozumienie Związków Zawodowych)
NPBSU	Non-Party Bloc in Support of Reform (Bezpartyjny Blok Wspierania Reform)
PFBP	Polish Friends of Beer Party (Polska Partia Przyjaciół Piwa)
PPP	Polish Peasant Party (Polskie Stronnictwo Ludowe)
PPP-PA	Polish Peasant Party-Peasant Alliance (PSL-Porozumienie Ludowe)
SDRP	Social Democracy of the Republic of Poland (Socjaldemokracja Rzeczpospolitej Polskiej)
SDURP	Social Democratic Union of the Republic of Poland (Unia Socjaldemokratyczna Rzeczpospolitej Polskiej)
Solidarity	Solidarity Trade Union (NSZZ "Solidarność")
UF	Union of Freedom (Unia Wolności)
UL	Union of Labor (Unia Pracy)
URP	Union of Real Politics (Unia Polityki Realnej)

NOTES

1 Data for 1993 from *Transition Report 1995: Economic Transition in Eastern Europe and the Former Soviet Union* (London: EBRD, 1995) and *The Europa World Year Book 1995* (London: Europa Publications Ltd., 1995).

2 See Sarah Meiklejohn Terry, "Thinking about Post-communist Transitions: How Different are They?" *Slavic Review* 53, no. 2 (Summer 1993).

3 *Społeczna wizja ustroju demokratycznego* (Warsaw: Centrum Badania Opinii Społecznej, 1995), p. 18.

4 Torańska in her book *Them* gives a striking testimony to the endurance of the "us the people vs. them the state" paradigm in Polish politics through the communist era. It remains important in the present-day process through which the Polish political system is being consolidated. See Teresa Torańska, *Them: Stalin's Polish Puppets* (New York: Harper & Row, 1987).

5 It is interesting to note that among the greatest national heroes one finds Polonized ethnic Lithuanians, Ukrainians, or Ruthenians. The Polish national epic *Pan Tadeusz* by Adam Mickiewicz opens with the words "Lithuania, my country."

6 The other major ethnic groups in interwar Poland were West Ukrainian (14%), Jews (10%), Byelorussian (3.7%) and German (3.7%). See Roy E. H. Mellor, *Eastern Europe: A Geography of the Comecon Countries* (New York: Columbia University Press, 1975).

7 For a good discussion of culture and ethnicity as constitutive elements of the concept of nationalism in Eastern and Central Europe, see Juliana Geran Pilon, *The Bloody Flag: Post Communist Nationalism in Eastern Europe* (New Brunswick and London: Transaction Publishers, 1992).

8 Jacek Mojkowski, "Dwa buty na lewą nogę: Rząd kontra 'Solidarność,' bitwa o własność i budżet," *Polityka*, 10 June 1995.

9 Norman Davies, *God's Playground: A History of Poland* (New York: Columbia University Press, 1984), pp. 625-33.

10 See: Jacek Wasilewski i Włodzimierz Wesołowski, *Początki parlamentarnej elity: Posłowie kontraktowego sejmu* (Warszawa: Instytut Filozofii i Socjologii PAN, 1992).

11 *RFE/RL Daily Report*, 11 December 1990.

12 *Informator o partiach politycznych w Polsce* (Warsaw: Polska Agencja Informacyjna, October 1991). In addition to the more established groups, the parties included such bizarre organizations as the Party of the Owners of Video Cassette Recorders "V" (Partia "V" Posiadaczy Magnetowidów), the Polish Erotic Party (Polska Partia Erotyczna), or the Polish Friends of Beer Party (Polska Partia Przyjaciół Piwa).

13 "Wybory 91: Scena po pierwszym starciu," *Życie Warszawy*, 20-21 July 1991.

14 Ray Taras, "Voters, Parties, and Leaders," in *Transition to Democracy in Poland*, ed. Richard F. Staar (New York: St. Martin's Press, 1993), p. 26.

15 "Ustawa z dnia 28 czerwca 1991: Ordynacja wyborcza do Sejmu Rzeczypospolitej Polskiej," *Dziennik Ustaw Rzeczpospolitej Polskiej* no. 59 (Warsaw, 1991). The age eligibility requirements were retained unchanged in the 1993 revision of the law.

16 *RFE/RL Daily Report*, 28 October 1991.

17 *RFE/RL Daily Report*, 4 November 1991.

18 "Ze starego do nowego Sejmu," *Rzeczpospolita*, 6 November 1991.

19 "Polska geografia polityczna: Kto gdzie wygrał?" *Gazeta Wyborcza*, 7 November 1991.

20 *RFE/RL Daily Report*, 31 October 1991.

21 According to Bronisław Geremek, the floor leader of the Democratic Union, ideological polarization on issues such as abortion virtually precluded a majority vote on key civil rights issues. Conversation with author, Warsaw, 25 May 1992.

22 "Ustawa z dnia 28 maja 1993: Ordynacja wyborcza do Sejmu Rzeczpospolitej Polskiej," *Dziennik Ustaw Rzeczpospolitej Polskiej*, no. 45, 2 June 1993 (Warsaw). On electoral laws, see Stephen Holmes, "Designing Electoral Regimes," *East European Constitutional Review* 3, no. 2 (Spring 1994). Also see Louisa Vinton, "Poland's New Election Law: Fewer Parties, Same Impasse?" *RFE/RL Research Reports* 2, no. 28 (9 July 1993).

23 For a detailed discussion of the 1993 election results see: Louisa Vinton, "Poland Goes Left," *RFE/RL Research Report* 2, no. 40 (8 October 1993).
24 *The Europa World Year Book 1995*, p. 2,492.
25 *Aktualne problemy i wydarzenia: Czerwiec 1995* (Warsaw: CBOS, 1995).
26 "Polacy niezadowoleni z rozwoju demokracji," *Rzeczpospolita*, 19 December 1991.
27 On 19 December 1991, Wałęsa sent a letter to the Speaker of the Parliament Wiesław Chrzanowski withdrawing his draft proposal for the "Little Constitution." See: "Prezydent wycofuje projekt małej konstytucji," *Rzeczpospolita*, 20 December 1991.
28 Stanisław Podemski, "'Mała Konstytucja:' Koślawa szachownica," *Polityka*, 14 December 1991.
29 "Kariera szefa sztabu," *Gazeta Wyborcza*, 6 February 1995.
30 "Nowe kroki prezydenta," *Życie Warszawy*, 31 January 1995.
31 Piotr Zaremba, "Ile realnej władzy dla głowy państwa," *Życie Warszawy*, 13 June 1995.
32 See "Niemoralna konstytucja," *Gazeta Wyborcza*, 19 June 1995.
33 Already in 1993 Bronisław Geremek, a member of the Constitutional Commission, expressed doubt whether a new constitution would ever be passed in light of the intensity of ideological divisions on moral and ethical issues. Conversation with the author, June, 1993, Warsaw.
34 *OMRI Daily Digest*, 23 October 1995.
35 *OMRI Daily Digest*, 6 November 1995.
36 *OMRI Daily Digest*, 7 November 1995.
37 *OMRI Daily Digest*, 9 November 1995.
38 *OMRI Daily Digest*, 21 November 1995.
39 "Wybory prezydenckie przed Sądem Najwyższym: Ważne albo nieważne," *Gazeta Wyborcza*, 9-10 December 1995.
40 *Polskie Stronnictwo Ludowe: Program rozwoju wsi i rolnictwa* (Warsaw: Polish Peasant Party, 1992).
41 This section is based on "Political Parties in Poland," in *Political Parties in Eastern Europe* (RFE/RL, 10 February 1990), and Marek Burczyk, *The Polish Political Scene* (Warsaw: Ministerstwo Spraw Zagranicznych, 1995).
42 *Polskie Stronnictwo Ludowe: Dokumenty programowe* (Warsaw: Polish Peasant Party, 1993).
43 Arkadiusz Urban, "Perspektywy jedności prawicy," *Rzeczpospolita*, 13 June 1995.
44 For a good discussion of the Polish right on the eve of the 1993 election, see Anna Sabat-Swidlicka, "The Polish Elections: The Church, the Right, and the Left," *RFE/RL Research Reports* 2, no. 40 (8 October 1993).
45 "OBOP o partiach: Za i przeciw," *Gazeta Wyborcza*, 23 June 1993.
46 *Wybory parlamentarne: Potencjalne elektoraty w czerwcu '95* (Warsaw: Centrum Badania Opinii Społecznej, 1995).
47 Ibid.
48 *Społeczna wizja ustroju demokratycznego*, pp. 3–4.
49 Dariusz Fikus, "Demokracja jak trzcina," *Rzeczpospolita*, 22 May 1995.
50 "CBOS-pierwsze pokolenie III RP: Zagubieni w demokracji," *Gazeta Wyborcza*, 19 June 1995.

51 Ibid.
52 *Społeczna wizja ustroju demokratycznego*, pp. 9–10.
53 Ibid., p. 12.
54 Wiesław Władyka, "Nowi My i nowi Oni," *Polityka*, 13 May 1994.
55 The following is based on polls conducted between 5–10 May 1995. See *Społeczna wizja ustroju demokratycznego* (Warsaw: Centrum Badania Opinii Społecznej, 1995).
56 The following section is based on *Nations in Transition: Civil Society, Democracy and Markets in East Central Europe and the Newly Independent States* (New York: Freedom House, 1995), pp. 103–5, and Karol Jakubowicz, *The Media in Poland* (Warsaw: Ministerstwo Spraw Zagranicznych, 1995).
57 *Społeczna wizja ustroju demokratycznego*, pp. 9–10.
58 *Financial Times*, 3 May 1991.
59 *Transition Report 1995*, p. 52.
60 Ibid., p. 52.
61 Georg Sorensen, *Democracy and Democratization* (Boulder, CO: Westview Press, 1993), pp. 23–24.
62 Sally Terry views the continued weakness of civil society as the principal weakness of postcommunist transition. See Terry, "Thinking About Postcommunist Transitions."
63 The gains in the realm of political freedom, freedom of speech and freedom of religion were placed substantially ahead of the institutional changes within the structure of the state: 27 percent vs. 12 percent. See *Polacy o demokracji* (Warsaw: Ośrodek Badania Opinii Publicznej, 1991).

4 Party politics and political participation in postcommunist Hungary

Rudolf L. Tőkés

The fall of the old regimes in Eastern Europe in 1989–90 was a complex process which in some ways is still unexamined. With few exceptions, most Western postmortem accounts have tended to focus on small groups of visible political actors, founding elections, and the political institutions of the "new democracies." Data and interpretation of this kind, however valuable, have yet to explain the salience of personalities and events, such as the genesis of the new multiparty system, in a broader analytical framework of socioeconomic continuity and change in the affected countries. At issue are the "long-wave" processes of social mobility and restratification, value change, interest group politics, and macroeconomic transformation that helped define the social, ideological, and economic context of regime change in 1989–90.

It is axiomatic that the key components of postcommunist politics – actors, institutions, and processes – are products not of an areawide democratic parthenogenesis but of antecedent factors. Of these, precommunist traditions and the communist regimes' record of political mobilization, ideological indoctrination, social engineering, and institutional transformation were the most important. Therefore, assessments of postcommunist politics ought to be informed of the combined legacy of "communist universals" (one-party system, patterns of ideological legitimation, command structure, planned economy, and the like) and of indigenous national policy precedents.[1]

The universals denote systemic similarities among individual units of the Soviet-led international system of ruling party-states. By national policy precedents one understands (with the notable Czech exception) a combination of precommunist legacies of subject political culture, political decision making, particularly resource allocations, by small elites, and the paramount role of the state and its bureaucracy in public life. To a remarkable extent, these traditions were congruent with the East European communist regimes' goal of "building socialism" in countries under their immediate jurisdiction.

Over four decades of communist rule national hybrids of the general and the particular have yielded widely different political outcomes, and, in the end, regime capabilities to cope with and, as and when possible, to adapt to the threat of political collapse in 1989.

In any case, adaptation by East European leaderships to the regional hegemon's political expectations helped foster an external image of close institutional resemblance to the Soviet model. However, beneath the bland facade of institutional sameness among states of "existing socialism" there were significant national variations with respect to resource allocation priorities, leadership styles, patterns of internal political and social conflict management, and strategies of legitimacy building.

The task at hand is to examine the nature of party politics and analyze the dynamics of political participation in Hungary since the fall of the old regime in the spring of 1990. A full and adequately documented discussion of these matters is not possible within the confines of a brief essay. Therefore, I shall endeavor to develop a general framework and, within it, a selective summary of the key issues stemming from the origins and the record of the first ten years (1986–95) of the Hungarian party system. I date the onset of multiparty politics at the entry in 1985–86 of independent, that is, not regime-endorsed, MPs into the Parliament. My case for the explication of these matters is derived from my understanding of the generic and unique characteristics of regime change in Hungary. Much of what follows rests on the proposition that the structure of Hungarian postcommunist politics, including the party system and patterns of political participation, are products of a special kind of political transition from communism to parliamentary democracy in that Central European state.

The Hungarian transition scenario took its departure from the nation's "negotiated revolution."[2] By this I refer, as a critical explanatory variable, to a set of political agreements and understandings between the outgoing and incoming political elites that were concluded in 1989–90. The National Roundtable (NRT) negotiations of June-September 1989, the NRT Agreement of September 18, informal pacts between the new political forces and the incumbents, and the political agreement of May 1990 between the victor, the Hungarian Democratic Forum (HDF), and the runner-up Alliance of Free Democrats (AFD), of the March–April 1990 elections were the major road markers of this process.

The common objective of these agreements was to effect a qualitative change of political institutions and at the same time to preserve social peace and economic stability. The exclusion of the citizenry from the elites' negotiations, although conducive to the holding of confidential discussions between the "insurgents" and the "incumbents," made the outcome vulnerable to grassroots skepticism as to the legitimacy of the entire affair.

It is too early to tell whether these elite pacts should be seen as genetic flaws or eventually corrigible birth defects with adverse short-term effects on the nature of postcommunist politics.

Upon the surrender of its *nomenklatura* privileges in May 1989, the by-then only nominally ruling Hungarian Socialist Workers' Party (HSWP) ceased to be a source of coercive and state administrative power. Thanks to the combined efforts of the HSWP's reform wing under Imre Pozsgay, Miklós Németh, and Rezső Nyers, and of the incumbent state bureaucracy under Prime Minister Németh, the old regime's collapse was peaceful. In fact, it was so peaceful that the entire process of transition from one type of political regime to another may be likened to a "leveraged buyout" kind of business transaction. The participants were the "incumbent management," that is, the Németh government, and the insurgent hitherto nonvoting "minority shareholders," that is, the eight constituent parties and social interest groups of the Opposition Roundtable (ORT). The desired outcome was common survival and political relegitimation by way of free elections in March–April 1990 and the installation of a parliamentary government in May of that year.

My emphasis on *ex ante* political agreements and generally on the consensual essence of the old regime's replacement by a coalition of freely elected democratic parties seeks to call attention to one of the several regionally unique characteristics of Hungary's political evolution during the Kádár era of 1956–89. As I have discussed it elsewhere, Hungary's forty-year-long journey from Stalinist dictatorship to multiparty democracy was shaped by system-wide political-military-economic-ideological impera- tives and by the cumulative record of the Kádár regime's strategic policy decisions.[3]

The systemic imperatives were driven by the national interests of the USSR. In Hungary's case these called for the political incumbents' compli- ance with Moscow's general political-ideological line on the "nature of the present epoch." In a Cold War context this included all key issues of East–West relations; Hungary's partial integration into Soviet-dominated security and trade organizations; and the embedding of Soviet-style laws, institutions, and policymaking processes as integral parts of the political system.

Hungary's forty-year-long experience with communist rule was marked by several watershed events and unique policy precedents. The most important of these were the 1956 revolution and its bloody suppression; Kádár's leadership style; the launching and subsequent implementation of the New Economic Mechanism (NEM) of 1968; patterns of semi–public and non-confrontational interaction between the regime and its liberal democratic,

Populist, and socialist intelligentsia critics; and the negotiated transfer of power from Kádár's successors to the opposition in 1989–90.

The Hungarian regime's path between 1957 and 1990 was that of a strategic retreat – culminating in its negotiated surrender – from its politically, economically, and ideologically untenable original Stalinist positions. To survive as the national leader, Kádár chose to accommodate public aspirations for limited sovereignty, modest economic progress and, in the context of political-ideological demobilization, made provisions for the citizens' personal space under "existing socialism." Kádár also agreed to come to terms, by way of cooptation and selective marginalization, with the traditionally recalcitrant intellectuals. The remaining critical intellectuals – none of whom were jailed for political reasons after 1973 – were free (censorship and mild police harassment permitting) to have their say and thus became tolerated nay-sayers in the public arena. As will be shown below, these precedents had a decisive bearing on the form and substance of the party system and mass politics of postcommunist Hungary.

To make my case, I propose a three-part argument on the origins of the postcommunist party system, on party politics and political participation in 1990–94, and on the May–June 1994 elections and the consequent realignment of the Hungarian political spectrum.

Party system: origins, development, and social characteristics

The immediate origins of Hungary's postcommunist party system coincided with the commencement of the NRT negotiations between the HSWP, member parties and groups of the ORT, and the "third side" of public organizations on June 14, 1989.[4] This date was also the terminal point of an eight-year-long (1980–88) process of political succession in the HSWP. The *dramatis personae* of the succession process were the aging autarch János Kádár, his elderly associates in the HSWP's Politburo, leaders of the party's "successor generation," particularly Károly Grósz, Imre Pozsgay, and János Berecz, and the clients of both sides among Hungary's political elites. The object of the protracted intraparty struggle for power was the replacement of Kádár and the long overdue reconstruction of the political system.

Political succession and protopluralism

An unintended but, for purposes of eventual partification of public life, vitally important consequence of contestation within the ruling party was the creation of political space for new political actors in the early 1980s. The process of institutional devolution, including the separation of the party and the state and the growing administrative autonomy of the latter, had begun in the early 1970s. Much of this had been necessitated by the administrative imperatives of the regime's commitment to the consistent implementation of economic reforms. An important part of this process was the growing administrative autonomy of the regime's political auxiliaries, such as the Trade Union Federation (TUF), the Patriotic People's Front (PPF), and the Young Communist League (YCL). Other corporatist entities, such as those of Hungary's "red" and "green barons" of industry and agriculture and those of the technological-scientific establishment, particularly the Hungarian Academy of Sciences (HAS), were also parts of the political equation.

All "civil society"-type groups (much cherished by western political scientists as kernels of democracy in posttotalitarian states), such as "local heritage" clubs, amateur theater groups, and the like, functioned under the aegis of the PPF. With Cardinal József Mindszenty as an unwanted guest in the US Embassy until 1975, the Catholic Church, very much like the organizations of its Protestant brethren, were bureaucratic appendages of the state's Office for Religious Affairs. The state-approved hierarchy of both Christian churches saw to it that politically nonconformist clergymen, such as those promoting "basic communities" and lending moral support to conscientious objectors, were silenced and cut off from their flock. Neither the Vatican, nor the World Council of Churches objected. For both, the survival of the churches' organizational infrastructure took precedence over the parish priests' and ministers' spiritual autonomy and freedom of conscience.

By the early 1980s, the regime's policy lobbies began to function as protoparties within an increasingly pluralistic policy arena. Kádár's aspiring successors made use of the top nomenklatura elites' growing concerns about the HSWP's ability to keep the regime afloat and enlisted them to help unseat the incumbent leadership team of Kádár and his fellow gerontarchs in the Politburo and the Central Committee. At the May 1988 party conference this improbable alliance of younger party apparatchiki, policy lobbies, technocratic elites, and leaders of the provincial party organization prevailed and caused the removal of Kádár and several of his associates from the leadership.[5]

Kádár's successors – senior Politburo members Károly Grósz as secretary general, and János Berecz, Imre Pozsgay, Miklós Németh, and Rezső Nyers – tried to salvage what they could from the wreck of the old regime. In addition to the grave structural economic problems (the impact on living standards was marginal until the late 1980s) they inherited from Kádár, they also incurred several political IOUs to their political allies who had helped put them in power. Grósz and his colleagues finessed the issue by encouraging these groups to shed their bureaucratic image and become "social movements." As further incentive, these groups were offered enhanced consultative roles in political and economic decision making. However, these policy lobbies' political empowerment came too late to stem the tide of declining public confidence in the regime's social organizations.[6]

Evidence from the HSWP's archives and interviews with these party leaders indicate that from October 1988 on, Kádár's successors gave up on the idea of a one-party system and began preparations for the installation of a quasi-pluralistic political system in Hungary.[7] As the reform communists envisaged it, regime-supervised large-scale admission of "social organizations" and citizen groups – including noncommunist parties – in the political arena would still leave the incumbents with sufficient resources to remain in control over the commanding heights of power.

This optimistic scenario broke down in the winter months of 1988–89. Imre Pozsgay's bombshell announcement in late January 1989 calling the 1956 revolution a "popular uprising" (rather than a "counterrevolution") created a political *fait accompli*. Pozsgay's courageous move was designed to preempt yet another *Putsch*, that is, the inauguration of a martial law regime by Károly Grósz and a small group of fellow conservatives in the central apparat. Thanks to Pozsgay, the prudent internal security organs, and the military professionals, these preparations came to naught.[8] Thus, under the circumstances the Grósz-controlled Central Committee had no choice but to confront the central legitimacy dilemma of the Kádár era. The party elites had to decide whether to resist or to endorse the regime's orderly devolution into a multiparty system. With the adoption of the latter option, the HSWP was committed to recognize, tolerate, and accept the newly emerging "historic" and "new" political parties as legitimate representatives of the nonparty majority of the Hungarian people. As a result, by the end of March 1989, a *de facto* multiparty system came into being.

In early June 1989, following a complex process of public and behind-the-scenes dialogue between the divided HSWP and the united opposition, an agreement on the initiation of formal discussions was reached. The designated venue was the NRT. It was a political artifact created by the HSWP's reform leaders to broker an agreement on the modalities of the old regime's peaceful liquidation by the incoming and the outgoing elites. Participants of the NRT process included the HSWP, member parties and organizations of the ORT, and, as the "third side," representatives of the regime's transmission-belt agencies that were labeled as "social organizations."

Political parties: "historic" and "new"

The ORT was established in March 1989 as an *ad hoc* group of seven "historic" and "new" political parties and two civil-society-type organizations.[9] The historic parties were the Independent Smallholders' Party (ISP), the Hungarian Social Democratic Party (HSDP), the Hungarian People's

Party (HPP), and the Christian Democratic People's Party (CDPP). The new parties were the HDF, the AFD, and the League of Young Democrats (LYD, or Fidesz). The social organizations were an originally PPF-sponsored intelligentsia reform club, the Endre Bajcsy-Zsilinszky Society (EBZS), and the white-collar Democratic Union of Scientific Workers (DUSW). The Independent Lawyers' Forum (ILF), a group of proreform legal experts was ORT's convener and expert advisor. The "third side" consisted of official representatives from the PPF, the TUF, the YLC, and five additional regime-sponsored official interest groups.

The labels – historic, new, and regime-sponsored – are convenient but misleading terms (the first refers to parties that had been in existence prior to the communist takeover in 1947–48) that do not explain the origins and the political salience of these party and partylike groups in the summer of 1989. For this reason, a brief overview of the origins and post-1945 track record of each of these clusters seems to be in order.[10]

Hungarian Social Democratic Party (HSDP)

The HSDP, the oldest of the historic parties, was founded in 1889. Between 1922 and 1944, when it was driven underground by German occupation, the HSDP was a small opposition party in the Hungarian Parliament. In 1948 the HSDP was coerced into merging with the communist party and for the next forty years it ceased to exist as an independent political actor. The party's revival in late 1988 was materially supported by Károly Grósz, the HSWP's secretary general following János Kádár's exit from politics in May 1988. However, by 1989 the HSDP's traditional skilled blue-collar worker constituency had long disappeared: they either became part-time entrepreneurs in the "second economy" (and ended up voting for the AFD in 1990), or remained loyal to the old regime (and voted for the HSP in 1990). In either case, after forty years of communist rule the HSDP's elderly leaders were left with few followers. By the end of that year the party split into several feuding factions, and upon failing to receive four percent of the votes cast at the 1990 elections, it faded into oblivion.[11]

Independent Smallholders' Party (ISP)

The ISP, founded in the early 1920s and well represented in the Parliament prior to 1944, was another historic party. Unlike the HSDP, the ISP received 57 percent of votes cast at the first free postwar elections in November 1945 and was the largest political party. The ISP was also the principal victim of the communist party's "salami tactics." With its leaders driven to Western

Table 4.1 *Demographic trends in Hungary since the 1950s*

	1950s	1970s	1980s
Percentage of population	(1957)	(1970)	(1990)
Rural	59.7	54.8	38.1
Urban	40.3	45.2	61.9
Average annual rates of	(1953-59)	(1970-74)	(1980-90)
population growth (%)	0.6	0.3	0.3
Age distribution (%)	(1956)	(1977)	(1988)
15–24	14.7	15.4	13.9
25–49	34.9	34.2	35.0
50–59	11.8	11.9	11.6
Over 60	12.7	17.5	18.9
Levels of education[a] (%)	(1960)	(1970)	(1988)
Primary	90.1	84.1	59.2
Secondary	6.5	10.8	30.7
Post-secondary	3.4	5.1	10.1

Note: [a]Among persons over 25 years of age. Indicates attainment of completed or partial education at each level.

Sources: US Department of Commerce, *Statistical Abstracts of the United States*; Paul S. Shoup, *The East European and Soviet Data Handbook*; UNESCO, *Statistical Yearbooks*; United Nations, *Demographic Yearbooks*.

exile, or in jail, the party continued to exist through the persons of a few prominent fellow travelers. Although the ISP played an important role in Imre Nagy's coalition government in October–November 1956, its remaining leaders ended up in exile or in jail.

Unlike the HSDP, some of the ISP's natural constituency, that is, the small farmers and rural entrepreneurs of Hungary, survived, albeit mainly as members of forcibly collectivized farms throughout the Kádár era. However, rural Hungary had undergone radical social transformation between 1948 and 1989. From the late 1960s on, together with a new provincial proletariat, a new rural middle class of university- and college-trained experts, farm managers, and local professionals was born.[12] For the broader demographic context of this process, see table 4.1. Their interests had little in common with those of the ISP's traditional voters of the 1940s. Still, the ISP's "single-issue" platform, that is, the return of state-confiscated farming land to the former owners, had lost none of its salience in the preceding decades.

Christian Democratic People's Party (CDPP)

The CDPP's ideological forerunner was the Hungarian People's Party under the leadership of the prominent Catholic layman István Barankovics. Together with the rest of the democratic parties, this party too was swept away in 1948. The CDPP's likely mass support was an open question in 1989. On the one hand, the martyrdom of the Barankovics party's spiritual leader, Cardinal József Mindszenty, was a factor to reckon with. On the other hand, the open collaboration of Mindszenty's pliant successors with the Kádár regime helped tarnish the Catholic Church's image as a champion of political freedom and human rights.

Hungarian People's Party (HPP)

The Hungarian People's Party's origins lay in the left radical Hungarian Peasants' Party of the immediate postwar (1945–48) period. With the notable exception of Imre Kovács, who fled to the West in 1947, the rest of the HPP's leadership, particularly the writer Péter Veres and the sociologist Ferenc Erdei, chose to link up with the communist party and became the regime's steadfast supporters. The resurfacing of the HPP in 1988–89 as a "people's party" was the result of a political *deus ex machina* that had been engineered by the reform communist Imre Pozsgay through the vehicle of the PPF of which he had been the secretary general. In any case, the PPF, the EBZS, and at least initially the DUSW were the clever incumbents' (rather transparent) creatures with the mission to disrupt the political resolve of the opposition camp.

Real opposition parties

The regime's *real* opposition consisted of two radical liberal democratic parties, the Alliance of Free Democrats (AFD) and the League of Young Democrats (LYD, or Fidesz), and of a nationalist-Populist ideological hybrid, the Hungarian Democratic Forum (HDF). The intellectual and social origins of these parties could, with some effort, be traced back to the first part of the twentieth century. In this context the liberal democrats' forerunners had been the bourgeois radical parties of the Dual Monarchy (1867–1918); and the HDF's genesis may be linked to the rural left-wing radical and right-wing nationalist traditions of Hungarian politics in the interwar (1920–39) period.[13] These precedents, though helpful for establishing these parties' historic credentials and ideological legitimacy, were largely irrelevant to the issues of 1989. What did matter was that unlike the other parties, the AFD,

LYD, and the HDF called themselves political heirs to Hungary's native revolutionary traditions, particularly those of 1956.

The "newness" of these parties consisted of their political agenda and the leaders' social background. Both were rooted in the social and political dynamics of the post-1968 "mature Kádárist" era of economic reforms, social transformation, and institutional change. The three parties' political agendas displayed striking similarities in several policy areas:

– all were committed to free elections, political pluralism, rule of law, and the reestablishment of parliamentary democracy;

– all were in favor of recapturing Hungary's national independence and of the peaceful severance of the nation's multiple military, economic, and political ties to the Soviet Union;

– all were in (tacit) agreement on preserving, and subsequently gradually modifying, the basic institutions of the Kádárist welfare state and on assigning to the state the principal responsibility for the protection of the people's political rights, economic well-being, and cultural opportunities; moreover,

– as beneficiaries of an elite-brokered process of political transformation, all three – particularly the two liberal – parties assigned to the intelligentsia a leading role in the political and cultural guidance of postcommunist Hungary.

However, beneath the consensual elements of the opposition's political platform there were significant ideological cleavages that became manifest in the course of the electoral campaign of February–March 1990. The HDF's emphasis on Hungary's historic identity as a Christian and European nation, the AFD's harsh rejection of the communist era and its advocacy of Western models of liberal democratic institutions, and the LYD's brand of "new politics" of the young generation were the first harbingers of the coming clashes of ideas, policies, and personalities in postcommunist Hungary.

From latent pluralism toward a multi-party system

The new party elites and the early joiners were, almost without exception, members of the new Hungarian middle class that came into being in the 1970s. By "middle class" I refer to middle-aged and, to a substantial extent non-HSWP member, university graduates at the outer fringes of the official nomenklatura system. As educated, socially well-situated, and respected professionals – physicians, lawyers, engineers, educators, writers, and artists – this social cluster made its first appearance as independent or spontaneously nominated candidates at the contested, albeit regime-manipulated, national and municipal elections of 1985. The latter was the regime's last-ditch attempt to endow the Parliament and the municipal assemblies with a semblance of legitimacy. The elections had been preceded by a process of staged debates between regime-approved, and in one-third of the cases, among the "official" and spontaneously nominated candidates. At the end, for the first time since 1947, the Hungarian voters had a *choice* to make at the ballot box. Although regime-sponsored candidates prevailed in most cases, the *issues* – bureaucracy, corruption, resource misallocation, and neglect of community needs – that motivated the 1985 voters to support officially non-endorsed independent candidates and local reformers acquired even greater salience by the end of the 1980s.

It was neither intolerable oppression nor large-scale economic deprivation but a nonrevolutionary yet deeply felt sense of malaise that prompted the more courageous local notables to enter the public arena. They stood for reforms through incremental change within the existing political system. With the exception of a few scores of Budapest intellectuals of the democratic opposition, no one questioned the regime's right to rule or advocated an independent stance in international affairs.

The Hungarian reformers' terms, "soft dictatorship" and "paternalistic rule" of the late Kádár era, adequately characterize the HSWP's style of governance. The HSWP was a catch-all mass party that, thanks to Kádár, was equally concerned with the promotion of the regime's developmental objectives and with the people's material well-being. The party, to which 13 percent of the adult population belonged, was a bureaucratic and, at the end, ideologically permissive host to a representative cross-section of the society. According to reliable survey evidence from the early 1980s, the membership's views, policy preferences, and social values were essentially the same as those of the nonparty majority.[14]

With the HSWP's gradual retreat from its traditional high-profile management of public affairs toward a rearguard posture of an "all-people's party," new political space was created in and out of the ruling party for the advocacy of radical reforms of all kinds. This new space was the spawning ground for assorted clubs and other – ostensibly nonpolitical – organizations, as well as for unstructured intelligentsia-led social movements for the airing of the unofficial "second" society's growing concerns about a wide range of social and economic issues.[15]

Kádár's exit from the political scene in May 1988 removed the principal obstacle, that is, the living symbol of the crushing of the nation's bid for freedom in October–November 1956, to a new political contract between the regime and the society. Kádár's successors were anxious to distance themselves from the regime's bloody origins. They sought, but eventually failed, to relegitimate the political system by a large-scale cooptation of nonparty groups – the regime's own corporatist policy lobbies, civic groups, and reformist political opponents alike. Thus, it was in this ideologically fluid and politically ambiguous context that the regime's Populist-nationalist critics were given a chance to establish the HDF in September 1987; the democratic opposition to create first the Network of Free Initiatives, and subsequently the ADF as a political party in November 1988; and, after initial police harassment, the radical university students to establish Fidesz in March 1988.

The rebirth and the official recognition of political pluralism in Hungary in the summer of 1989 marked the end of a complex two-decades-long process of economic reforms, social restratification, institutional transformation and cognitive change. Still, however ripe the internal conditions were for substantive political change, these were insufficient to bring the regime to the negotiating table. Rather, it was a combination of a new international correlation of forces, particularly Gorbachev's hands off posture with respect to Hungarian internal developments and the US-led diplomatic offensive in Eastern Europe, and the ascendance of the HSWP's reform wing, that was responsible for the political outcomes of 1989.

Political pacts and elite realignment

By agreeing to negotiate, as political equals, with the self-selected political representatives of the reform intelligentsia and by exiling the regime's own social auxiliaries to the "third side" of the bargaining table, Kádár's heirs defined the essential boundaries of postcommunist politics in Hungary. As shown in table 4.2, in March–April 1990 all but two (the HSDP and the HPP) parties of the ORT and none of those excluded from the NRT managed to gain seats in the Parliament. The four percent electoral threshold served as an invisible political hand that separated the eventual winners from the losers of the Hungarian transition process. The voters' exclusion of the "third side's" quickly improvised Trojan horse types of electoral parties, and of the HSWP's left-wing successor party (subsequently renamed as Workers' Party), from the postcommunist legislature put the seal of legitimacy on the restricted scope of the party spectrum in the postcommunist Parliament. The electoral outcome made for a governable polity – that is, one controlled by the NRT parties rather than by the economic and social marginals of Hungary that the "third side" spoke for in summer 1989.

Unlike the Polish national roundtable discussions between the regime and Solidarność that yielded an agreement of sorts on economic and social issues, and provided for semi-free elections, parties of the Hungarian NRT confined the agenda to legal and procedural matters and rolled over the burden of making hard, and inevitably unpopular, economic decisions to the post-communist regime. In any case, the critical political difference between the Polish and the Hungarian negotiations lay in the agreement on the restricted and unrestricted scope of elections in June 1989 and March–April 1990, respectively.[16]

The incoming and the outgoing Hungarian elites all wanted change, but chose not to leave footprints on the snowy path of transition to a postcommunist Hungary. In doing so, the pact-makers gravely compromised the chances of prompt implementation of overdue macroeconomic reforms. The task of promptly addressing matters such as the downsizing the state's social welfare expenditures and that of the bloated state bureaucracy; the restructuring of industry and agriculture; and confronting the country's crushing foreign indebtedness called for a shared vision and the courage of the elites' political convictions. For understandable reasons, such quixotic virtues were conspicuously absent from the Hungarian political power brokers' pragmatic agenda. Whereas the Polish pact-makers had no choice but to confront the consequences of Poland's economic free fall since 1979, Kádár's "goulash communism," albeit in a more modest fashion, still worked in Hungary.

In the summer of 1989 public opinion polls on voting preferences at hypothetical elections still gave a decisive majority to the HSWP. The ruling party's leading personalities, such as Imre Pozsgay, Miklós Németh and Rezső Nyers, still enjoyed what seemed an unassailable lead in popularity rating and name recognition.[17] Yet, three months later the HSWP was on the brink of collapse and the HSWP new leadership was in total disarray. What had happened?

The regime's unilateral empowerment of the ORT parties as bona fide participants in the political process and the HDF's stunning victories at four parliamentary by-elections in July and August helped level the political playing field in the insurgents' favor. At this point the incumbents were faced with the choice between revitalizing and thus salvaging at least a part of the HSWP's membership of 700,000 (as of September 1989) and reinventing the party as a new reform-oriented democratic socialist party. Instead of a difficult salvage operation, they chose the latter. However, by the time the new Hungarian Socialist Party (HSP) – itself a conglomerate of a half dozen miniparties – was launched in early October, the political document of the NRT Agreement of September 18, 1989 was already in place. Although the party's reform leaders Nyers, Pozsgay and Németh managed to oust Grósz and the apparat deadwood, they ended up dismissing the party's membership as well.[18] Moreover, Németh's government saw to it that the disoriented Parliament promptly enacted into laws the letter (and some of the spirit) of the NRT Agreement. All of this left the HSP high and dry and compelled it to function not as a "leading force," but as *one* of the several "old-new" parties in the political arena.

Pacta sunt servanda: *the NRT precedent*

The NRT Agreement was a multipurpose political instrument that defined the rules of the political game for the transition period and in many respects well beyond the first free elections.[19] The agreement provided for a substantially revised Constitution and the renaming of the state from a People's Republic to a Republic. The creation of a constitutional court and the revival of the office of president of the Republic were also parts of the institutional package that subsequently became important elements of a postcommunist system of new checks and balances.[20] The Constitutional Court was made up of "new democrat" and reform socialist law professors. The Court has exceptionally broad jurisdiction that ranges from being the court of first instance with respect to citizen grievances concerning the constitutionality of ongoing litigation to being an agency of legislative oversight with respect to pending bills and enacted laws. Though the Court is to be "above politics," the record of its decisions has made it the principal guardian of the old regime's social safety net and a sharp critic of government attempts to curtail the same. The incumbent president of the Republic Árpád Göncz who was reelected for another term in 1994, has had a choice of being a figurehead, or becoming a political activist. By siding with his own party (the AFD) and even more with the HSP, Göncz chose to become the champion of Hungary's *homo Kádáricus* and thus the hands-down winner of popularity contests with the incumbent prime minister – Christian Democrat and socialist alike. Other items on the agenda included guidelines for a complex campaign and electoral procedure, as well as the unconditional lifting of press censorship for the time that remained for the old regime.

These businesslike arrangements were supplemented by a series of political confidence-building measures. In return for the new parties' legal immunity from police interference in the preelection period, the ORT negotiators extended similar guarantees to all officeholders of the outgoing regime. A comparable tradeoff between short-term government subsidies for the new parties and the opposition's long-term commitment of extending state subsidies for the electoral runnerups that received at least one percent of the national vote was another pragmatic component of the transition arrangements. Come what may at the first free elections, all but the truly fringe political forces were financially provided for in the postcommunist period.

In sum, the rebirth of multiparty politics in the waning years of the old regime in Hungary was the result of latent longitudinal trends in political devolution, institutional pluralism, elite politicization, and the incumbents' declining performance with respect to legitimacy building, resource allocation, and political management. By the mid-1980s the issues, policy options, and escape strategies, as well as the postcommunist political leaders

Table 4.2 *Votes for party ballot and distribution of seats in parliamentary elections in Hungary, 1990*

Party or coalition	Votes		Seats in parliament	
	N	%	N	%
Hungarian Democratic Forum	1,214,359	24.73	164	42.49
Alliance of Free Democrats	1,050,799	21.39	92	23.81
Independent Smallholders' Party	576,315	11.73	44	11.40
Hungarian Socialist Party	535,064	10.89	33	8.55
League of Young Democrats	439,649	8.95	21	5.44
Christian Democratic People's Party	317,278	6.46	21	5.44
Hungarian Socialist Workers' Party	180,964	3.68	–	
Hungarian Social Democratic Party	174,434	3.55	–	
Agrarian Alliance	154,004	3.13	1	0.26
Entrepreneurs' Party	92,689	1.89	–	
Patriotic Electoral Coalition	91,922	1.87	–	
Hungarian People's Party	37,047	0.75	–	
Hungarian Green Party	17,951	0.36	–	
National Smallholders' Party	9,944	0.20	–	
Somogy County Christian Coalition	5,966	0.12	–	
Hungarian Cooperative and Agrarian Party	4,945	0.10	–	
Independent Hungarian Democratic Party	2,954	0.06	–	
Freedom Party	2,814	0.06	–	
Hungarian Independence Party	2,143	0.04	–	
Nonparty independent	–	–	6	1.55
Jointly endorsed by two or more parties	4	1.04		
Total	4,911,241	100.00	386	100.00

Source: *Parlamenti Választások, 1990*, ed. György Szoboszlai [Parliamentary Elections, 1990] (Budapest: MTA Társadalomtudományi Intézet, 1990), pp. 455–76.

and institutional vehicles were present, albeit only partly visible, in the public arena. The survivalist old and the emerging new elites were all in place and well prepared to act on new opportunities to escape from the Kádárist quagmire.

Public apathy and widespread disinclination to engage in demonstrative behavior, such as strikes and protest marches, were an important characteristic of the pretransition period. Indeed, prior to the electoral campaign of February–March 1990 there had been no more than a half dozen instances when the people took to the streets to protest (on national holidays), to celebrate (as on October 23, 1989), or to vote at by-elections and plebiscites, such as those held in July and on November 26, 1989, respectively. The flood of uncensored information, though helpful for the airing of issues, contributed to information overload and to the blurring of partisan distinctions among eighty-odd parties, associations, electoral alliances, and whimsical groups that entered the electoral process. On the other hand, after a sluggish start in the fall of 1989, the hitherto disinterested public had no difficulty in making early decisions as to party preference and choice of electoral platforms.

On the eve of Hungary's founding elections both the parties and the public were "flying blind" with respect to the correspondence between party programs and the social groups and the spatial distribution of voting blocs whose interests the parties claimed to represent. Although the electoral turnouts – 65 percent on March 25 and 45 percent on April 8 – do not quite show it, there was no doubt that the overwhelming majority were anxious to be rid of the old regime. On the other hand, it was equally clear that the public's voting preferences were motivated by the parties' campaign slogans rather than by the substantive message of their programs.[21]

The NRT Agreement was a well-crafted political contract and its crown jewel was a technically complex electoral system that was designed to yield a stable "winners take all" (or most) type of parliamentary representation of political parties. As the Hungarian constitutional lawyer György Szoboszlai explained,

The number of elected MPs was defined as 386 of which 176 were to be elected in individual districts, 152 from within the competition of regional party lists (20 regions were determined, in 19 counties and in Budapest, the capital), and 58 on the basis of competing national lists. The electoral law was liberal with respect to preconditions of candidacy. Each registered party or other electoral organization could present a candidate by collecting 750 recommending signatures in the individual district. The same rule was valid for the independent candidates, but they had difficulties in collecting the signatures. Only registered parties could create regional lists provided they were able to run in one-fourth of the constituencies, at least in two. Those parties could compose national lists who were able to stand at least 7 regional lists. These thresholds resulted in certain selections. In the individual districts there were 10–12 candidates in average; 18 parties and other organizations could enter the competition on regional level, but only 12 could present a national list from among the 65 registered parties.

The voters voted for an individual candidate and for a regional party list in each constituency. In the first round the regional competition was over, but the distribution of the regional seats was not possible until the completion of the second round because of the compensating system. According to this procedure those votes not counted to get a regional seat (on the basis of the well-known d'Hondt system) on the one hand and the votes given for a non-elected party-backed candidate were to be collected on the national level. Seats assigned to the national list were distributed on the basis of this compensating system, counting the so-called lost votes. The minimum number of national seats was fixed in the law as 58, but because of the disproportion-ality of the regional distribution the actual number turned out to be 90 . . . The combination of the principles of proportionality and disproportionality made the system selective and proportionate for those remaining in competition. This seems to be a rational and just system and justified by the electoral results, except the independent candidates.[22]

In sum, the 1990 electoral outcomes could be seen both as the result of the Hungarian people's collective one-time ideological temper tantrum – as bounded by a complex electoral system – and that of the citizens voting their immediate political aspirations and long-term socioeconomic interests. In the end, the voters eliminated all but six parties. The finalists may be positioned at the left of, and at the right of the ideological center. In the final analysis what mattered was that the people endorsed and democratically legitimated the NRT pactmakers' right to represent the public interest in postcommunist Hungary.

Party politics in a new democracy: toward a bipolar system?

Hungary's founding elections gave birth to what proved to be postcommunist Eastern Europe's most stable government and party system. The Christian democratic three-party (HDF-ISP-CDPP) coalition government under József Antall and, after his untimely death in December 1993, Péter Boross was (with the arguable Czechoslovak exception wherein the split of the country into two sovereign states in 1992 may been seen either as evidence of continuity, or that of change) the first postcommunist regime that completed its designated term of service. Moreover, it seems certain that the present HSP-AFD coalition government under the reform communist Gyula Horn will remain in power until the next elections in 1998. It is equally likely that the six parties that passed the 4 percent threshold in 1990 (and the 5 percent threshold in 1994) that are still in the Parliament today will again be electoral frontrunners in 1998.

The postcommunist polity's institutional structure, including the party system, owes its remarkable stability to several factors. Of these the most important are Hungary's in some ways still semi-Kádárist, preparticipant political culture; patterns of social cohesion of, and ideological cleavages among, the party elites; well-crafted and continuously reinterpreted political pacts; and the political, institutional, and economic checks and balances that define the power relationships among institutional actors. Each of these points requires a brief commentary.

Public expectations and political participation

Political stability in the late Kádár era rested on an unwritten social contract between the people and the regime. Both were traumatized survivors – victims and ostensible victors – of postwar East Europe's only *real* revolution. Driven by the people's sense of abandonment by the west as well as by the regime's fears of total Soviet domination, both sides were ready to come to terms with one another. Thus, it was not – as uninformed western skeptics would have it – the public's latent procommunist sympathies, but a shared desire for national survival in a, to Hungary's fate indifferent, Cold War international environment, that facilitated this process.

The terms of the "contract" called for the regime's satisfaction of the public's consumerist expectations and trade-offs between the citizens' political passivity and the regime's "self-limiting" exercise of its coercive powers. The outcome made for a depoliticized and inward-looking society that, from the early 1970s on, became wedded to the "good king" János Kádár's brand of predictable, non-coercive, and stable political authority. It was not the resurgence of deeply embedded revolutionary aspirations – these had been crushed in 1956 and never again contemplated thereafter – but the regime's defaulting on its economic commitments and the crisis of political leadership after Kádár's exit that prompted the Hungarian public to give a chance to the new and the historic parties of 1989–90.

After the 1990 elections the public quickly put aside its partisan preferences and demanded – as respondents to public opinion polls, rather than through spokesmen for nonpolitical "civil society"-type organizations which remained silent on the subject – an all-party coalition government.[23] Instead, the public got what many called a "parliamentary circus" in the form of – for the Western publics, perfectly normal – divisive partisan disputes in the legislative chamber. And that has been one, perhaps the main, reason that only a small minority of the citizens – perhaps 100,000, or less than 2 percent of the eligible voters – became declared and dues-paying party members in postcommunist Hungary. Although political patronage is alive and well, the traditional advantages (higher pay, access to scarce goods, and the like) of membership in the ruling party (or party coalition after 1990) ceased to be available to the rank-and-file party faithful. Thus, by default, nonelectoral partisan involvement in politics has become the domain solely of professional politicians; economic, cultural, and other single-issue interest groups; and those directly linked up with the parties' patronage network.

The Hungarian electronic and printed media played an important, and still not fully examined, role in thwarting and to a lesser extent aiding, public participation in political events. It is a complex story, but the "media wars" of 1991–93 notwithstanding, it would be fair to say that prior to the implementation of the new media law in late 1995, the TV and the radio tended to serve the government of the day. In any case, neither gavel-to-gavel TV coverage of the parliamentary proceedings (hence the image of "political circus"), nor cleverly edited visual excerpts depicting unconventional events, such as strikes and occasional public protests, have inspired much confidence in the possible efficacy of citizen involvement in politics. On the other hand, during the Antall-Boross era the printed media was (and still is) under overwhelming AFD and HSP control. As the result, nonelite issues have received selective and often muted coverage in the press. With the exception of the ex-nomenklatura-led HSP-supporter trade unions, news generated by the rest of the social, cultural and generational interest groups tend to see daylight either with a "man-bites-dog" kind of editorial slant, or in small circulation journals and occasionally in the "letters to the editor" and the Op Ed pages of the national press. Consequently, mass political participation and demonstrations of the kind that one could witness at one time or another elsewhere in Eastern Europe rarely happened in Hungary prior to 1992.[24] The absence of the "street" from political deliberations has thus helped firm up the elites' grip on mass politics.

Intellectuals as party elites

With the exception of the HSP, the rest of the political parties had begun as small intelligentsia circles that found themselves together in the same proreform cultural and political trenches in the mid-1980s. Each of these groups consisted of organizers, activists, resident ideologues, and designated spokesmen (only the Free Democrats had a few women in the inner circles) with similar educational and professional backgrounds. Hungarian analysts described these preparty clusters as "tribal" and "clan-like" and the leading members as being totally preoccupied with their personal intellectual agenda.[25] At any rate, while these groups' evolution from friendship circles to "social movements" and, from there, to political parties tended to weed out many political amateurs, behind the party facade most of them remained debating clubs of querulous intellectuals.

The "hard core" of the new parties' "founding fathers" were prudent enough to coopt a few *real* experts (lawyers, successful entrepreneurs, and experienced administrators) into the leadership.[26] They were also pragmatic enough to put themselves in the top twenty to thirty slots of their parties' national lists that virtually guaranteed a seat in the Parliament. However, with the socialists' exception, (all seasoned veterans of apparat politics), once elected, they were not disciplined enough to stick together as members of the same party caucus. As Bill Lomax explained, the root causes of disunity lay in the new parties' sense of identity and political style:

The self-identities of the parties are . . . rooted in emotive commitments rather than on rational choice. The political identities and cleavages they represent are based neither on social interests, nor social programs, nor structured belief systems, but on cultural, emotional or even spiritual identifications through which their members come to belong to socio-cultural camps with common life styles and behavior patterns. Such political styles are very good at identifying enemies and scapegoats, but they are highly detrimental to the processes of bargaining and the pursuit of compromises that are the essence of pluralist democracy.[27]

Parties-in-Parliament: the government coalition

The 1991–94 Parliament began with six parties and a small group of independents. Four years later there were about twenty parties (some of them with one or two MPs) as well as countless "platforms," "factions," and policy caucuses within each of the six main parties.[28] What had happened? As Bill Lomax explains in an other essay, each of the six parties were, or became, Western European-style catch-all "people's parties" that reflected, sometimes in an extremely distorted fashion, the left-center-right ideological spectrum of the society at large.[29]

In its original configuration the HDF was a party of left- and right-wing Populist intellectuals. When the conservative József Antall took the helm as party chairman and especially after he became prime minister, the socialist sympathizers were driven out of the party. In the next two years the István Csurka-led radical rightists broke with the HDF, launched a party of their own, and they left "Forum" divided among Christian democratic, national liberal, and moderate Populist factions.[30] From 1992 on, along with the HDF's waning fortunes in the polls, more than two score backbenchers joined other parties or the caucus of nonparty independents.

The authoritarian schoolmaster-style leadership of prime minister and party chairman József Antall, though important in keeping the backbenchers in line, was also responsible for the stifling of intraparty disputes on policy alternatives.[31] Antall's conservative ideological agenda tolerated no internal dissent and drove his party into politically damaging confrontations with the predominantly liberal and socialist-sympathizer intelligentsia, particularly with the media elites. This strategy, though helping to keep party divisions alive, as shown in table 4.3, undermined his party's standing in the polls and, in 1994, at voting booths as well.

The HDF's coalition partners, the ISP and the CDPP, underwent similar experiences. The major difference between the two was the remarkable ability of the Smallholder József Torgyán-led faction of nine MPs to wrest the party's leadership from the ISP's thirty-three coalition loyalists. The case in point, as demonstrated from time to time in similar intraparty feuds, may be called the "in the kingdom of the blind the one-eyed man is king" syndrome. In other words, true to classical democratic and nondemocratic political traditions, it was always the "born politicians" and shrewd parliamentary tacticians who typically prevailed in confrontations with the political innocents of the backbenches. The outcome may have seemed

Table 4.3   *Quarterly trends in party preferences in Hungary, January 1990–March 1994 (in % of respondents; n = National representative samples)*

Year by quarters	1991				1992				1993				1994
	I	II	III	IV	I	II	III	IV	I	II	III	IV	I
Parties:													
HDF	11	12	11	9	11	8	8	8	8	7	7	6	7
AFD	15	11	10	11	8	7	7	9	7	8	7	8	9
ISP	7	8	6	6	6	6	4	5	5	5	5	5	4
HSP	6	4	4	6	6	7	7	6	10	11	14	17	18
Fidesz	20	20	20	21	29	27	29	30	25	26	23	18	11
Other party	3	4	3	3	2	7	6	5	8	7	8	7	7
Don't know (or would not vote)	34	40	41	39	29	27	29	30	34	31	32	35	38

Question: "If elections were held next Sunday, which party would you vote for?"
Percentages are rounded and add up to more or less than 100 in some columns.

Source: Tibor Zavecz, "A pártok megitélése a két választás között" [Public Opinion on the Political Parties between Two Elections] in *Társadalmi Riport, 1994* [Social Report, 1994], ed. Rudolf Andorka (Budapest: Tarki, 1994), pp. 448–9.

chaotic but, at least in Hungary, it was only a facade for the pragmatic politicking – based on compromises and the swapping of favors – among the handfuls of professionals of both the government and the opposition parties.[32] The result was manifest instability and latent stability in Hungarian party politics.

Parties-in-Parliament: the opposition

In ideological terms, the parliamentary opposition was divided between liberal (AFD and LYD) and socialist (HSP) camps. As the second largest parliamentary party, the AFD was an odd conglomerate of a small, tightly knit, all-intellectual party executive, originally headed by the philosopher János Kis; middle-class professionals; small entrepreneurs; and an assortment of single-issue constituencies. The party's subsequent splintering, realignment, and reunification are a complex story that need not be discussed here.[33] What stands out is the pattern of battles between oversize egos, clashes among proponents of nonnegotiable philosophical postures, and periodic showdowns between pragmatists and ideologues. Withal, it is a small wonder that in the midst of internecine feuds, the party became an effective advocate of solid policy alternatives on issues such as privatization, budget reform, and social welfare policies that managed, despite some defections to other parties, to hold its own as a united political force both in and out of the Parliament.

Unlike the rest (save the socialists), the League of Young Democrats, with twenty-two MPs, was a party of highly skilled lawyers and economists who became hardworking young political professionals. For the first three years the party's parliamentary caucus remained a close-knit team that advocated sensible legislative priorities and was widely admired as effective critics of the internally divided government coalition. The turning point came in 1993 when, as shown above, the party's popularity rating eclipsed, by a significant margin, that of its parliamentary rivals at either side of the aisle. To stay at the top, party chairman Viktor Orbán decided to remold the party's image from that of the representative of "young people and their grandmothers" to that of a mainline right-of-center liberal party. This, in turn, prompted a leadership split between the left-wing minority and the centrist majority. To Fidesz' misfortune, its internal divisions were fully exploited by the liberal and socialist printed media. To say that the party was "lynched" by the partisan media would be an overstatement. Yet, no political organization could have survived the barrage of AFD- and HSP-inspired vicious publicity to which Fidesz was subjected in 1993–94. In any case, in 1994 Fidesz did survive the socialists' electoral landslide and managed to remain in the Parliament. However, the defection of the popular deputy leader Gábor Fodor to the AFD and the maladroit politicking of the party's founder and incumbent leader left the party as a still visible, but for the foreseeable future, a marginal player in Hungarian politics.

The HSP was a "quarantined" political outcast in the first three years of Hungary's postcommunist politics. At the beginning, neither the well-entrenched government coalition nor the then viscerally anticommunist liberal parties had any use for survivors of the old regime. The party's electoral defeat, however painful for the socialist faithful, was far from complete in April 1990. In September–October 1990, the nominally "independent" holdover village and small-town apparatchiki of the former ruling party (of whom 84 per cent were reelected) made a clean sweep at the village government elections. The "new democrat" HDF-ISP-CDPP coalition and AFD, Fidesz, and HDF, as individual parties, may have controlled the national government and the large cities, respectively, but much of the countryside remained in socialist hands.

After the departure of Imre Pozsgay from the HSP and the forced resignation of Rezső Nyers, former foreign minister Gyula Horn became the party's leader. The principal advantage of the party's parliamentary isolation lay in the leaders' ability to distance the party's parliamentary caucus from the other parties' record of trying, but inevitably failing, to satisfy unrealistic public demands for stable living standards, full employment, and growing social-welfare benefits. Given the resource constraints on the government's ability to satisfy these expectations, all the socialists had to do was to keep a low profile, behave correctly, and await the, to them inevitable, downturn of their rivals' public support.

Unlike the rest of the party elites, the HSP leadership was a disciplined team of seasoned political veterans with a great deal of previous administrative experience as top party and government policy managers. To their credit, they redefined the party's identity as "social democratic" and willingly embraced the rules of the democratic political game.[34] Instead of engaging in self-destructive ideological disputes, Horn and his colleagues diligently rebuilt the party's grassroots organizations and maintained close political ties with the growing and increasingly affluent community of "party apparatchiki and red/green-barons-turned-entrepreneurs" of Hungary. Though initially shunned by the other parties, the HSP, as discussed above, retained its influence over key social and communications resources in the postcommunist era.

The HSP's political prospects were further strengthened by the party's substantial real estate holdings, business assets, and well-invested cash that the leaders managed to salvage from the shipwrecked, but immensely wealthy HSWP.[35] Again, unlike its competitors with their hand-to-mouth existence on state subsidies and meager income from membership dues, the HSP's campaign chest was never short of money to finance local and national elections. The solid string of the HSP-sponsored candidates' by-election victories in 1991–94 was important evidence of the party's continued viability as a cohesive and well-financed political machine.

Partisanship: old issues and new cleavages

From the parliamentary interaction of the six parties and the growing cluster of independents and one-man to two-men miniparties there developed new patterns of party politics. Together with the growing professionalization of legislative politics, there has been a growing distance between the parties-in-Parliament and their grassroots organizations.[36] The latter, with the socialists' signal exception – their trade union auxiliaries gained new strength in the Antall era – have become scattered remnants of the (short-lived) political movements whence the new and historic parties originated in the late 1980s. As part of this process, new power centers of party politics have come about in Budapest, in the counties, and various regions of Hungary.

The political configurations of these local centers were not mirror images of national politics but issue-oriented multi- and occasionally all-party *ad hoc* coalitions on behalf of local, regional, and other sectorial interests. Here again, the socialists' administrative experience and efficient "old comrades' networks" were important assets for the overcoming of their political rivals' well-meaning but inexperienced local activists. The point is that due to the top party politicians' inevitable preoccupation with the technical minutiae of the workings of the legislature or, at the local level, with the administrative details of contentious issues – privatization, public housing, water supply, waste disposal, and school budgets – party labels lost their immediate salience.[37]

Between 1989 and 1992 the number of registered "civil associations" increased from 8,574 to 19,950.[38] The potential efficacy of these groups for the promotion of sectorial interests was attenuated by the party system, by the existence of corporatist bodies of "interest reconciliation," and by the parliamentary party caucuses' modus operandi. Let us consider each of these built-in impediments:

(1) The party system, particularly the method of selection for the parties' national lists, was designed to preempt potentially powerful sectoral interests by the cooptation of token representatives of religious, ethnic, cultural-scientific, business, labor, female, and so forth, constituencies. In doing so, artificial "rainbow coalitions" were created – under the watchful eyes of the political professionals.

(2) "Civil groups," such as assorted professional and business "chambers," have their origins in the late Kádár era when these nomenklatura peer groups served as the regime's lightning rods within their respective constituencies. The largest is the National Council for Interest Reconciliation. It is made up of representatives of business, labor and other social organizations to deal with the *government* to craft "social pacts" – mainly to set national wage scales indexed to next year's inflation.

(3) Because individual MPs are bound by strict party discipline, they are by and large immune to constituency pressures and, by posing as guardians of public (versus particular, such as pressure group) interests, they tend to be impervious to most kinds of extra-party civil pressures.[39]

Because of the parties' relative immunity to grassroots pressures, the inevitable consequence was the blurring of party identification and the public's reemerging "them-and-us," kinds of zero sum adversarial attitudes toward that powers that be. Dichotomous perceptions of "parties and party leaders in power" versus "parties and party leaders in opposition," and the "local (all parties) versus national" (the ruling coalition) were evidence of growing public distrust of Hungary's postcommunist political institutions.[40] The main line of division was between those who saw themselves as victims (the overwhelming majority) and those who were beneficiaries (few cared to admit to have done well since 1990) of the parties' legislative record in postcommunist Hungary. In any case, whereas at least initially, most key

Table 4.4 *Indicators of economic trends in Hungary since 1989*

	1989	1990	1991	1992	1993	1994	1995[a]
GDP	0.7	-3.5	-11.9	-3.0	-0.8	2.9	2.0
Industrial output	-1.0	-9.6	-18.2	-9.8	4.0	9.6	4.8
Rate of inflation	17.0	28.9	35.0	23.0	22.5	18.8	28.2
% of labor force unemployed	0.3	2.5	8.0	12.7	12.6	10.9	10.4
GNP per capita	n.a.	n.a.	n.a.	n.a.	6,310	n.a.	n.a.
% Workforce in private activity[b]	n.a.	n.a.	n.a.	n.a.	59.4	n.a.	n.a.
% GDP from private sector[b]	29.0	n.a.	41.0	48.1	55.6	n.a.	n.a.

Notes: GDP – % change over previous year; Industrial output – % change over previous year; Rate of inflation – % change in end-year retail/consumer prices; Rate of unemployment as of end of year; GNP per capita – in US dollars at PPP exchange rates. [a]Estimate. [b]Including cooperatives.

Sources: European Bank for Reconstruction and Development, *Transition Report 1995: Economic Transition in Eastern Europe and the Former Soviet Union* (London, 1995); European Bank for Reconstruction and Development, *Transition Report Update, April 1996: Assessing Progress in Economies in Transition* (London, 1996).

legislative items – legal reforms, institutional transformation and foreign policy – enjoyed all-party support,[41] all shortfalls – unemployment, inflation, and budget deficits – were laid at the Antall-Boross government's door by the disenchanted public.[42] Data on economic trends since 1989 tend to support these propositions. (On this, see table 4.4.)

There is a great deal of survey evidence on public attitudes toward political parties, party leaders, and political institutions.[43] The general trend has been that of the public's negative/suspicious/hostile attitudes toward the national government and the top incumbents of the state bureaucracy. Whereas the ADF-affiliated president of the Republic Árpád Göncz was always at the top of the monthly popularity charts, by 1992–93 the prime minister's popularity (on a scale of 1 to 100) had sunk from the mid-60s to the mid-30s. The opposition leaders Viktor Orbán, Gábor Fodor, Iván Pető, and Gyula Horn were perennial favorites – more or less in an inverse ratio to their parties' capacity to effect desired outcomes in the national legislature.

Paradoxically, the public's low esteem for the government, that is, the agency held responsible for inflation, taxes, and unemployment, was also shared by the Parliament and the political parties. According to three 1992 and 1993 surveys on public trust in political institutions, on a scale of 1 to 100, the president of the Republic, the army, and the police enjoyed 50-plus percent support, whereas the Parliament and the political parties were trusted by less than one-third and about one-fourth of the postcommunist public, respectively.[44] The net winners, as recipients at the level of 45 to 55 percent of public support, were the Constitutional Court, the judicial system, and the local governments. The trade unions, particularly the unreformed Trade Union Federation, though initially trusted only by 28 percent, gradually rose in public esteem and by May 1993 was the winner of nationwide elections for bargaining representative of the still largely unionized blue-and white-collar employees of Hungary.

The consistent gap between the opposition politicians' high personal popularity rating and the much lower level of their parties' public support represents an important analytical dilemma for the study of Hungary's new party system.[45] On the one hand, precommunist Hungary's traditions of identification of the names of prominent political leaders with that of their party – such as the "Bethlen party" in the 1920s – served as a convenient label for the general public. From this it seems to follow that a leader's personal popularity is readily convertible into his party's electoral support. However, such has not been the case.

The larger than life-size role of party standard-bearers as top political spokesmen on all matters helped obliterate their parties' ideological identity in the public eye. Whenever possible, chairmen of each of the six parliamentary parties' sought to appear as a *national* leader – often with little or no reference to his partisan affiliation. Because it was these party leaders' individual standings in the Hungarian media's monthly "beauty contests" that legitimated, albeit only in the opposition parties, their position in the party hierarchy, the question of the political salience of personal versus party popularity could be fully resolved only at the quadrennial national elections. At such occasions – much to the credit of the Hungarian voting public – the party standard bearers' national popularity ratings proved to be *not* automatically convertible into personal parliamentary mandates in individual electoral districts.

To a somewhat lesser extent, the same was true of the relationship between the party leaders' personal popularity and votes cast for candidates in individual voting districts. With the exception of few scores of "safe" seats – usually for "native sons" – the top party leaders entered the Parliament via national and regional party lists rather than through the inherently chancy individual districts. From this one might advance a tentative hypothesis on the declining salience of "great men" and charismatic political leaders in Hungarian party politics. In my view, the only "great man" (of sorts) who still matters is the "good king" János Kádár of 1968–80 – not the man, but his still cherished legacy as provider and guardian of the nonelites' interests. (Since József Antall's death, some of his heirs in the HDF have been seeking to capitalize on their late leader's "intellectual patrimony" – with no visible results to date.) In any case, the Kádárist model of party politics tended to overshadow personalities, thwart divisive disputes, and cater to public yearnings for manifest stability and predictable political outcomes. Much of this is compatible with the institutional dynamics of Hungary's postcommunist politics.

Institutional safeguards: holdover elites at the helm

The NRT Agreement, as modified by party pacts and all-party constitutional amendments since the summer of 1990, still serves as the basic framework of institutional checks and balances in Hungarian politics. Central to the arrangements are the built-in obstacles to removing the incumbent government by parliamentary vote of no confidence. This is augmented by the powers vested in the "semistrong" president of the Republic and those of the Constitutional Court.[46] Prior to the local government elections of 1994, the opposition-dominated municipal and local governments served as important counterweights to the political center. These new political artifacts, however important to the formal functioning of a pluralistic polity, were kept afloat by the unwritten parts of *ex ante* and *ex post facto* agreements between the outgoing and incoming political elites of 1989–90.

At issue is the overwhelming – and inherently undocumentable – influence of the holdover state bureaucracy and that of the old/new entrepreneurial and media elites over public policy. The state bureaucrats' jobs are de facto entitlements that are protected by ironclad guarantees of the Labor Code and by the 1991 Law on Public Employees. Yesterday's "red barons" are today's managers and key stockholders in partly state-owned enterprises and business firms. These creatures of the old party state have retained and converted their administrative-managerial control of state resources into public-private "recombinant property."

The term was coined by David Stark in his excellent case study on industrial privatization in Hungary.[47] As he explains, official data on the size of the private sector and the reported share of national income derived from this sector are wholly misleading. The actual size of the private industrial sector is 12 to 15 percent, rather than 60-plus percent. The difference lies in the *partly* state-owned, that is, with state ownership of less than 50 percent of shares, mixed-ownership firms wherein the incumbent management is free to divert company assets to insider-owned satellite firms, and bill the state for costs of depreciation and operating deficits. Thus, "recombinant property" is

a form of organizational hedging, or portfolio management, in which actors are responding to extraordinary uncertainty in the organizational environment in diversifying their assets, redefining and recombining resources. It is an attempt to have resources in more than one organizational form – or similarly – to produce hybrid organizational forms that can be justified or assessed by more than one standard of measure. . . . [P]arallel to the decentralized reorganization of assets is a centralization of liabilities, and these twinned moments blur the boundaries of public and private: On the one hand, privatization produces criss-crossing lines of recombinant property; on the other, debt consolidation transforms private debt into public liabilities.[48]

This legal hybrid shelters key economic actors from the exigencies of party politics, as well as from political responsibility for the government's unpopular measures in aid of marketization, balanced budgets, and the like. Thus, the parties may pass laws and enact budgets, but their implementation is still the discretionary domain of the nonparty and still predominantly prosocialist holdover state bureaucracy. The same, as discussed above, is true for the country's still largely state-owned, but only indirectly controlled, productive assets in the hands of yesterday's captains of industry and commerce. All this makes for manifest "stability" – if Hungary's glacial regression toward ever-higher foreign indebtedness may be called such – and even "social peace" of sorts, but begs the question of the parties' role in the process.

Political parties: cui bono?

The leading Hungarian political scientist, Mihály Bihari, characterized the party system as a *libegő* (hovering, or floating in midair) phenomenon that is detached from the mainstream of politics and public affairs.[49] The term is apt because it denotes the thus far only superficial integration of the parties into a broader matrix of what the Hungarian public have traditionally understood by "politics." Until now both precommunist and communist party politics have been elite affairs that admitted few outsiders into the profession-al politicians' *boszorkánykonyha* (witches' kitchen). Precommunist popular perceptions of party politics were heavily laden with suspicion of "chicanery of the gentlefolk," and with skepticism as to what, if any, good might come from party politics. The Hungarian people have yet to accept the political parties as indispensable to democracy and good government.

The public's traditionally low sense of political efficacy is still a major factor that affects political participation and electoral turnout. The by now habitual absence of one-third to one-half of voters from the polls at national

Table 4.5 *Votes for party ballot and distribution of seats in parliamentary elections in Hungary,*
1994

Political party or electoral coalition	Votes		Seats in parliament	
	N	%	N	%
Hungarian Socialist Party	1,781,504	32.99	209	54.14
Alliance of Free Democrats	1,065,889	19.74	70	17.88
Hungarian Democratic Forum	633,770	11.74	38	9.84
Independent Smallholders' Party	476,272	8.82	26	6.74
Christian Democratic People's Party	379,523	7.03	22	5.70
League of Young Democrats (Fidesz)	379,344	7.03	20	5.18
Workers' Party	172,109	3.19	–	
Party of the Republic	137,561	2.55	–	
Agrarian Alliance	113,384	2.10	1	0.26
Party of Hungarian Justice and Life	85,737	1.59	–	
Hungarian Social Democratic Party	51,110	0.95	–	
United Smallholders' Party	44,292	0.82	–	
Entrepeneurs' Party	33,367	0.62	1	0.26
National Democratic Alliance	28,075	0.52	–	
Hungarian Green Party	8,809	0.16	–	
Consolidated Smallholders' Party	5,918	0.11	–	
Conservative Party	2,046	0.04	–	
Green Alternative	849	0.02	–	
Hungarian Market Party	635	0.01	–	
Total	5,400,194	100.00	386	100.00

Source: István Stumpf, "A politikai erőtér átrendeződése a választások után" [The Realignment
of Political Power after the Elections] in *Parliamentary Elections*, 1994, ed. Luca Gábor et al.,
pp. 574–75.

and local government elections, though essential to keeping the six- (now
seven) party system afloat, raises new questions about the long-term stability
of the postcommunist party system in Hungary. A partial answer (and a
tentative prognosis) may be inferred from the citizens' habit of bypassing
established political structures in the pursuit of their private interest.

The Kádárist tradition of individual *érdekérvényesítés* (interest realization)
by means of one-on-one bargaining with members of the state bureaucracy
is alive and well in Hungary today. The survival of such informal channels
has kept the doors wide open to corruption and fostered contempt for official
venues, such as the hopelessly overloaded civil courts, of interest adjudication
between the citizens and the state. Hungary's *homo Kádáricus* sees no moral
contradiction between expressing high regard for the judicial system – as an

abstract proposition from the local to the Constitutional Court – and going about his business and routinely violating a dozen laws and regulations a day.

The well-heeled party leaders – in late December 1995 the government coalition announced a 30 percent pay hike for top public servants, including MPs – make for poor role models for the average citizen. He will be lucky if his next pay raise will be only one-third less than the inflation rate of 30 per cent forecast for 1996. The parties, yet again, proved to be irrelevant to the satisfaction of citizen interests at the constituency level.

The 1994 elections: political sea change, or back to the future?

The ex-communists' return to power in May 1994 marked the end of the Christian democrat-dominated $3+3$ party system in Hungary.[50] The HSP's spectacular electoral victory was all the more convincing: its candidates in individual electoral districts captured 150 of the total of 176 available individual mandates. In 1990 the top vote-getter, HDF, had managed to win in only 111 of the 176 districts. Moreover, as shown below, the HSP landslide victory was sealed with the help of 32.99 percent (versus 24.73 percent that the HDF received in 1990) of votes cast for the party ballot. Thanks to the built-in multiplier effects of Hungary's majority cum PR electoral system, the HSP ended up with 209, or 54.1 percent of the seats, and thus an absolute majority in the 1994–98 Parliament.

Political democratization: an interim balance sheet

The task at hand is not that of an electoral postmortem – a subject fully and perceptively discussed by Hungarian political scientists – but an analysis of the likely impact of this remarkable outcome on the party system and the future of democracy in Hungary.[51] The discussion should begin with some general observations about the record of Hungary's "first-round" government. The positive aspects of the record were:

– the instauration and the firm embedding of basic laws, institutions, and procedural guarantees for the rule of law in Hungary;

– the enactment of legislation to facilitate the transformation of the national economy from a centrally planned command economy to a market economy, with special reference to measures to promote privatization and, in a trickle-down fashion, the citizens' access to private property;

– the development of modern continental European parliamentary procedures, the growing professionalization of lawmaking, and the routinization of the rules of political interaction among the parliamentary parties, particularly between the government and opposition;

– the beginning of the development, by way of *ad hoc* interaction, of dialogue between independent-minded members of parliamentary parties and extraparliamentary interest groups, policy lobbies, and civic associations; and

– the universal acceptance by all political actors of democratic, court- and state bureaucracy-supervised and enforced rules of the political game at all levels of the political system from the Parliament down to local governments.

The legitimacy of elected officials, of new and reformed institutions, and of the political processes of Hungary's parliamentary democracy was firmly established by 1994. Much of this may be summarized by calling the outcome institutional stability with built-in capacity for incremental change.[52] Though "full democratic consolidation" – whatever it means – will not be achieved until the enactment of a new constitution, the institutional and political achievements of the transition period are firmly embedded in Hungary.

Items on the negative side of the ledger must be attributed to the still unresolved legacies of the past, particularly to the country's still semitraditional political culture that the party elites of the first-round postcommunist polity could not, and have not been particularly anxious to, overcome. These include intractable issues of

– social justice that could not be made available to all members of the society. The Hungarian people – at least 60 to 70 percent of the voting public – had become accustomed to cradle-to-grave economic security that the government of the deeply indebted state can no longer provide;

– political justice, by way of full compensation for all victims of the old regime, and vigorous screening and prosecution of those guilty of crimes against the society, cannot be delivered in a political system that owes its immediate origin to an elite-pacted, "forgive and forget" negotiated revolution. The postcommunist regime has neither the resources nor the political will to satisfy such public expectations;

– intelligentsia politics that entailed the gratuitous "ideologization" of intra- and interparty disputes among the new party elites, as well as between them and the HSP and its political auxiliaries, such the TUF and the media elites.

Prime Minister Antall's confrontation-seeking "symbolic politics" of pursuing political legitimacy through the government-assisted revival of Hungary's precommunist ruling elites' values and ideologies was responsible for the awakening of Hungarian public opinion to the threat of backsliding into the authoritarian past. The liberal and the socialist opposition made good use of Antall's ideological posturing and rallied the post-Kádárist middle class for the defense of the postcommunist status quo.[53]

The HSP and the AFD were subsequently joined by the intelligentsia and, at the end, by the majority of the voting public. The HSP and AFD-sponsored "Democratic Charter" movement of 1992 – itself a reaction to István Csurka's ravings and rantings – though began as a political cabal, was legitimate democratic political strategy that helped mobilize the public and cleared the way for the realignment of party loyalties.

Party politics of the "second round"

With their absolute majority of seats in the Parliament the victorious socialists could, if they so chose, have governed alone. On the other hand, the socialists' parliamentary majority fell short of the two-thirds necessary to pass "fundamental" laws or to amend the Constitution. Moreover, to retake the helm only four years after the spectacular collapse of the HSWP and assume sole responsibility for the combined economic debt of not one but two previous regimes entailed unacceptable political risks. In any case, as beneficiaries of another, possibly one-time, protest vote, it was uncertain whether the HSP had a solid enough electoral mandate to go it alone.

The AFD was the socialists' "natural" coalition partner as well as a relatively low-risk choice with which to share some of the governing power and, in case something went wrong, all the political responsibility for keeping the economy afloat. The two parties' political mating dance took the form of protracted negotiations held behind closed doors. The entire affair bore an uncanny resemblance to the HFD-AFD negotiations of April–May 1990 – with the critical difference that the two-party pact of June 1994 was not a zero-sum but a "win-win" game for the participants.[54] For the HSP, coalition with the liberals responded to the ex-communists' need for a democratic fig leaf, as well as to the HSP technocrats' demands for continued marketization and privatization.

As the liberals saw it, the HSP's offer of, inevitably junior, partnership in a coalition government entailed risks and opportunities. The outcome had a vital bearing on the very survival of the AFD as self-declared standard-bearer of a liberal democratic Hungarian society that has yet to be born, let alone provide a 30 percent-plus share of the electoral support necessary to form a liberal-led government coalition. In September–November 1989 the AFD-led ad hoc coalition had to resort to the desperate measure of forcing a plebiscite against the HDF- and HSP-sponsored candidacy of the still very popular reform politician Imre Pozsgay for the presidency of the Republic. The gamble paid off: the outcome eliminated Pozsgay, secured the AFD's second place at the 1990 elections, and subsequently the presidency for the AFD backbencher Árpád Göncz.

The AFD's repeat performance as electoral runner-up, albeit with a huge gap of 13 percent (and 139 parliamentary seats) behind the winner, four years later posed a set of difficult political alternatives for the party's real leader (party chairman Iván Pető of the original "hard core") and its electoral standard-bearer (the ethnic German Gábor Kuncze, the AFD's candidate for prime minister). On the one hand, the AFD could have become the leading force of a deeply divided cluster of five opposition parties – only to see its legislative priorities savaged by the HSP, by the parties of the defeated Christian democratic coalition, and, for good measure, by the vengeful Fidesz. On the other hand, by joining the HSP government and shackling Prime Minister Horn with the terms of the coalition pact, the AFD could gain valuable administrative experience yet preserve the option of bailing out as and when it seemed expedient.[55] In the meantime, the AFD leadership is in a position to reward its party faithful by political patronage and access to lucrative opportunities in the state-controlled economic sector.

The Horn government's political record has been adequately covered in a recent collection of studies on that subject and need not be discussed here.[56] However, the transformation of the party system from a 3+3 to a 2+4 model and its likely consequences merit a brief assessment cum prognosis on the future of party politics in Hungary.

Government and opposition: a preliminary assessment

According to a July 1994 survey of HSP voters, they had, in declining order, supported the Horn team in expectation of quick remedies for inflation, rising prices, unemployment, poverty, environmental degradation, and the Parliament's legislative performance.[57] In any case, 69 per cent of the socialist voters were convinced that with the HSP in power, the "advantages of the pre-1990 regime would be restored."[58] If these views are indeed widely shared among the nearly 1.8 million HSP voters, prospects of the socialists' medium- and long-term political hegemony are open to doubt. At issue is the political cohesion of the HSP's parliamentary caucus of 209 MPs, of whom more than 170 are new to the Parliament. The point is that 150 of them had come in as winners in individual electoral districts – most often on the strength of unmet local economic demands.

Unlike the party-machine-appointed candidates who gained their seats via party lists, MPs from individual voting districts have been an unpredictable lot. In the previous Parliament 30 of the 164 HDF MPs – most of them originally from individual districts – defected to other parties or joined the independents' caucus. In any case, though segmented (with the party chiefs' blessing) into several "factions" and "interest groups," the HSP's parliamentary contingent should be seen not as one but at least three to four nascent parties with policy priorities of their own. Should push come to shove, one or more of these ad hoc clusters might, as they have several times in 1995, defy the leadership on key policy issues. The record to date has been one of simmering disputes, the isolation of radical economic reformers, and the appeasement of the trade union caucus by the neo-Kádárist HSP executive.

(1) By hitching its wagon to the HSP, the AFD has lost some of its earlier public image as a vigorous promoter of sound legislative alternatives and a source of policy innovation. The party's toehold in the government, by way of two substantive ministries (Internal Affairs, and Education and Culture) headed by Kuncze and, until the end of 1995, by the Fidesz defector Gábor Fodor, respectively, and some other subcabinet appointments, have yet to stem the liberals' eroding popularity in the polls. On the other hand, the AFD's "me-too" parliamentary role is more than balanced by the liberals' function as political counterweight to the HSP's antimarket, antiprivatization redistributionists as equal partners in the standing HSP-AFD interparty consultative committee. Other than the government's financial experts and Hungary's Western creditors, this body is about the only impediment to the government succumbing to Horn's periodic relapses into demagoguery and his caving in to demands of his party's welfare lobby.

The AFD's role as the government's "internal opposition" has tended to preempt the agenda of the four opposition parties in the Parliament. The shouting match between the government – "the last four years of the Antall government brought Hungary to the brink of ruin" – and the opposition – "lets talk about the preceding forty years" – has yet to subside into routine parliamentary interaction. Instead, what seems to be emerging is a new kind of political interplay between the "1+1" government and a "4+1" opposition.

(2) The HDF is the largest opposition party and, next to the upstart LYD, the greatest loser in the 1994 elections. In several ways, the party is captive to its political record and to "Antall's orphans," that is, to the tired politicians who served their late political master rather than the voters who brought them to power in 1990. Long simmering disputes between the party's Populist and liberal wings came to a head in March 1996. Under the leadership of Iván Szabó who had been minister of finance in the Antall government, a group of sixteen HDF MPs left the party to form the Hungarian Democratic People's Party (HDDP). The remaining twenty-two HDF MPs (one of them chose to join the independents' caucus) rallied around Sándor Lezsák – a village school teacher and a self-taught Populist ideologue. Since neither faction has much of a political identity, let alone wide popular following of its own, the Lezsák group is likely to end up joining forces with some extra-parliamentary right-wing parties, while the HDDP might want to team up with the CP-Fidesz (if the young liberals will have them) prior to the 1998 elections.

(3) The CDPP is the only party of the Antall coalition that lost no votes in 1994. Though much courted by the HSP – the Catholic vote was dispersed

among all parties both in 1990 and 1994 – the party's new leadership is staying the course. Whichever party ends up at the top in 1998 would do well to take on the CDPP as a respected, but politically lightweight, coalition partner.

(4) By the end of 1994, the LYD – having changed the party's name to Citizens' Party-Fidesz – has more or less recovered from the devastating impact of its precipitous slide from the top of the polls in mid-1993 to barely passing the 5 percent parliamentary threshold a year later. Viktor Orbán is still at the helm, albeit his powers are now shared with his extremely able deputies. If tenacity, political savvy, and professionalism will matter to the Hungarian voters in the years to come, CP-Fidesz could be a key player in the next elections. In the meantime, the party is trying to keep the opposition together and its leaders on speaking terms with one another.

(5) The ISP under József Torgyán is the "1" in the "4 + 1" equation of the parliamentary opposition. At this time it is unclear whether the ISP is a "Torgyán party" and the personal political vehicle of a shrewd provincial lawyer cum populist demagogue, or the kernel of an emerging rural nationalist protest movement with an excellent chance to double is electoral support in the next three years. (In August 1995 and again a year later, ISP caught up with and overtook HSP in the popularity polls, and the end is not yet in sight).[59]

Party politics: short-term perspectives

Unlike the rest of Hungary's postcommunist political institutions that will at best be fine-tuned but not drastically modified by a new constitution, the party system is still in the process of transformation from a unipolar toward a bi- or possibly tripolar configuration. In early 1995 the leaders of HDF, CP-Fidesz, and CDPP came to a tentative agreement on the forming of Citizens' Federation (CF) to coordinate parliamentary strategy. CF was also meant to be the kernel of a multi-party right-of-center electoral alliance for 1998. The would-be partners have yet to act in unison: the CDPP, having learned its lesson of playing second fiddle to HDF under Antall, wants to see thorough house cleaning there as a condition of cooperation – the HDPP might fit the bill; the veteran oppositionist CP-Fidesz, especially Orbán, are not about to defer to the former helmsmen of the Antal-Boross "Titanic" – though probably not averse to take on Iván Szabó, former foreign minister Géza Jeszenszky and the rest as "third fiddlers"; and, more to the point, none of them can get along with the ISP's feisty leader, József Torgyán.

As befitting a pluralistic democracy, Hungary's party system will be shaped by the interplay of newly surfacing social forces, the "invisible hand" of a slowly emerging market economy, and the powerful remnants of the country's Kádárist political legacy.[60]

It is axiomatic that the "long-wave" restratification of Hungarian society will continue to yield unexpected electoral results in the years to come. Given the share of nonvoters and that of ballots cast for electoral runner-ups that are redistributed among the finalists, the present party system will have to find a way to respond to currently unmet social interests. Foremost of these is the challenge of fiscally prudent political representation of the needs of the economic victims of the state's inevitable retreat as provider of last resort.

The Horn government's decision to trim the social safety net in March 1995 – followed by backtracking and further watering down of austerity measures by the Constitutional Court – is the first of many attempts yet to come to implement needed but unpopular measures to keep Hungary afloat. Similar efforts to downsize the state bureaucracy that have come to naught under every postwar regime from the Stalinist Mátyás Rákosi to the Christian democrat József Antall must be actually implemented by the quintessential apparatchik-bureaucrat Gyula Horn himself.

The jury of public opinion is still out with its verdict on the Horn regime. However, the steadily declining living standards and the snowballing, since mid-1995, of widely publicized scandals involving the misappropriation and brazen embezzlement of extremely large sums of money (bank bailouts, kickbacks from secret privatization transactions, and astronomical profits from government contracts) by Horn's cronies from the old HSWP apparat suggest that the countdown for the next elections may have begun in the fall of 1996.

The political parties' staying power and eventual constituency support will depend on some foreseeable and many unpredictable contingencies. What seems certain is that due to the loss of substantial amounts of state subsidies (apportioned according to respective shares of seats in the Parliament) the opposition parties' financial resources will be inadequate to match the incumbents' campaign chests.[61] However, as shown by the socialists' modest campaign expenditures yet stunning success in May 1994, this need not be a fatal handicap. Money helps, but it is the issues, more precisely the state of the economy, rather than campaign advertising that will, as it did in 1990 and 1994, determine electoral outcomes in Hungary in 1998 and beyond.

NOTES

1 The term is Ezra Vogel's and its specifics are discussed in *Change in Communist Systems*, ed. Chalmers Johnson (Stanford: Stanford University Press, 1970), pp. 27-8.

2 The term is mine, and it is one of the central themes of Rudolf L. Tőkés, *Hungary's Negotiated Revolution: Economic Reforms, Social Change, and Political Succession, 1957-1990* (Cambridge: Cambridge University Press, 1996).

3 Ibid., ch. 9.

4 See András Bozóki, "Út a rendszerváltáshoz: az Ellenzéki Kerekasztal" [Road to the Change of the System: The Opposition Roundtable] *Mozgó Világ*, no. 8 (1990), 23-37.

5 George Schöpflin, Rudolf L. Tőkés, and Iván Völgyes, "Leadership Change and Crisis in Hungary," *Problems of Communism* 37, no. 5 (September-October 1988), especially pp. 27-39.

6 László Bruszt and János Simon, "Politikai orientációk Magyarországon a rendszerváltás évében" in *A lecsendesitett többség* [The Silenced Majority] ed. László Bruszt and János Simon (Budapest: Társadalomtudományi Intézet, 1990), pp. 33-74.

7 On this, see Imre Pozsgay, *1989 - Politikuspálya a pártállamban és a rendszerváltásban* [1989 - A Political Career in the Party State and in the Change of the System] (Budapest: Puski, 1993) and my interviews with Károly Grósz and János Berecz cited in Tőkés, *Hungary's Negotiated Revolution*, ch. 8.

8 Tőkés, *Hungary's Negotiated Revolution*, ch. 7.

9 On the new and historic parties, see *Magyarország Politikai Évkönyve, 1988*, ed. Sándor Kurtán, Péter Sándor and László Vass (1988, hereafter *Hungarian Yearbook*) (Budapest: R-Forma Kiadó, 1989), pp. 699-709; *Az Ellenzéki Kerekasztal. Portrévázlatok*, ed. Anna Richter [The Opposition Roundtable, Portraits] (Budapest: Ötlet, 1990).

10 Cf. Tamás Fricz, "A magyarországi pártrendszer kialakulásáról és jellemzőiről: 1987-1992" [The Development and Characteristics of the Hungarian Party System: 1987-1992], unpublished dissertation, Budapest: Institute for Political Studies, 1993. See also András Körösényi, "Stable or Fragile Democracy? Political Changes and Party System in Hungary," in *Flying Blind. Emerging Democracies in East-Central Europe*, ed. György Szoboszlai (Budapest: Hungarian Political Science Association, 1992), pp. 344-56.

11 György G. Márkus, "Parties, Cleavages in Post-Communist Hungary: Is the Weakness of Social Democratic Forces Systemic?" in *Flying Blind*, pp. 331–42.

12 Cf. Iván Szelényi, *Socialist Entrepreneurs* (Madison, WI: University of Wisconsin Press, 1988).

13 Tőkés, *Hungary's Negotiated Revolution*, ch. 4.

14 Lajos Géza Nagy, "Történelem képek és jövő-képek" [Images of History and Ideology. The Stratification of Ideological Beliefs in the Early 1980s], unpublished dissertation, Budapest, 1989.

15 Cf. Elemér Hankiss, *East European Alternatives* (Oxford: Clarendon Press, 1990), chs. 6–8.

16 Text of the Polish Roundtable Agreement is in *Trybuna Ludu*, 7 April 1989 and in *FBIS-EEU* Daily Report, 5 May 1989, pp. 19–35. For the full text and appendices, see *Poruzumenia Okralego Stolu* [The Roundtable Agreement] (Warsaw, 1989). Photocopy of the typewritten original of the Hungarian NRT agreement is in Richter, *The Opposition Roundtable*, pp. 310–15.

17 On trends in public opinion in 1989, see Ágnes Bokor, "Public Opinion Concerning the Process of the Regime's Change," in *Social Report, 1990*, ed. Rudolf Andorka, Tamás Kolosi and György Vukovich (Budapest: TARKI, 1992) pp. 418–45; Bruszt and Simon, *The Silenced*, passim; and György Csepeli and Antal Örkény, *Alkonyat. A magyar értelmiség ideológiai-politikai optikája a 80-as évek végén* [Sunset – Hungarian Intelligentsia Perceptions of Ideology and Politics in the late 1980s] (Budapest: Institute of Sociology, ELTE, 1991).

18 In a politically self-destructive leadership decision, the disbanded HSWP's membership was given three weeks to decide whether or not to join the HSP. Only 20,000 to 25,000 did so by the end of 1989.

19 Tőkés, *Hungary's Negotiated Revolution*, chs. 7 and 8.

20 On the structure and functions of Hungary's postcommunist political institutions, see *Alkotmánytan* [Constitutionalism], ed. István Kukorelli (Budapest: Osiris-Századvég, 1994). See also György Szoboszlai, "Political Transition and Constitutional Changes," in *Democracy and Political Transformation*, ed. György Szoboszlai (Budapest: Hungarian Political Science Association, 1991) pp. 195–212.

21 For a full discussion of voluminous survey evidence on the voters' political motivations in early 1990, see Rudolf L. Tőkés, *From Post-Communism to Democracy: Party Politics and Free Elections in Hungary* (Sankt Augustin bei Bonn: Konrad Adenauer Stiftung-Forschungsinstitut, 1990). See also, Bokor, "Public Opinion."

22 Szoboszlai, "Political Transition," pp. 207–8.

23 László Bruszt and János Simon, "A 'választások éve' a közvéleménykutatás tükrében" [The "Year of Elections" in the Mirror of Public Opinion] in *Hungarian Yearbook, 1990*, especially pp. 633–46.

24 Máte Szabó, "The Taxi Driver Demonstration in Hungary – Social Protest and Policy Change," and András Bozóki, "Democrats Against Democracy? Civil Protest in Hungary since 1990," in *Flying Blind*, pp. 357–81 and 382–97.

25 See Miklós Gáspár Tamás, *Másvilág* [Otherworld – Political Essays] (Budapest: Uj Mandátum Kiadó, 1994).

26 For a biographical directory of MPs elected in 1990, *Az 1990-ben Megválasztott Országgyűles Almanachja I.*, [Parliamentary Almanac, 1990], vol. I., ed. József Kiss et al. (Budapest: Magyar Országgyűlés, 1990).

27 Bill Lomax, "Hungary: The Development of Democratic Politics," unpublished manuscript, 1994.

28 See "Pártpreferenciák és Tagoltságok" [Party Preferences and Cleavages] in *Parlamenti Választások 1994* [Parliamentary Elections, 1994], ed. Luca Gábor, Ádám Levendel and István Stumpf (Budapest: Osiris-Századvég, 1994), pp. 70–149.

29 Bill Lomax, "Obstacles to the Development of Democratic Politics," *The Journal of Communist Studies and Transition Politics* 10, no 3 (September 1994), 81–100.

30 The split in the HDF was precipitated by the publication of a bitter right-wing nationalistic and anti-Semitic pamphlet by the playwright HDF vice-president István Csurka. It was an alarming episode that prompted the US media and Hungary's postcommunist neighbors to reach premature conclusions about the extent to which such beliefs are held in Hungary. Csurka's Party of Hungarian Life and Justice received 1.59 percent of the votes in the 1994 elections, or about

one-half of the votes (3.19 percent) cast for the communist Workers' Party. These numbers are fair indicators of public support for right-wing nationalist and left-wing Leninist extremist groups in Hungary in the 1990s.

31 On Antall, see Tőkés, *Hungary's Negotiated Revolution*, ch. 10 and Sándor Révész, *Antall József Távolról, 1932–1993* [József Antall in perspective, 1932–1993] (Budapest: Sik Kiadó, 1995).

32 Party politics has been the subject of countless, mainly unsystematic and frequently partisan studies in the Hungarian press and literary-political journals. The most useful accounts on political parties can be found in the Hungarian Political Science Association's *Politikatudományi Szemle* and the Hungarian Yearbooks for 1990–95. Three works, *A többpártrendszer kialakulása Magyarországon, 1985–1991* [The Development of Multi-party System in Hungary, 1985–1991], ed. Mihály Bihari (Budapest: Kossuth, 1992), István Schlett, *Színjáték vagy háború? A magyar politika négy évéről* [Theater or War? Four Years of Hungarian Politics] (Budapest: Cserépfalvi, 1995), and Tamás Fricz's monograph cited above are still the best sources on this subject.

33 The most authoritative account is by the party's former chairman, AFD MP Péter Tőlgyessy, "A kerekasztaltól a koalicióig" [From the NRT to the (HSP-AFD) Coalition], *Népszabadság*, 18 November 1995. See also, Zoltán Ripp, *Szabad Demokraták* [Free Democrats] (Budapest: Napvilág Kiadó, 1995).

34 Attila Ágh, "Organisational Change in the Hungarian Socialist Party," *Budapest Papers on Democratic Transition* 1994. [Also on Internet:gopher://gopher.mek.iif. hu:7070/00/porta/szint/tarsad/politika/agh76.hun]

35 On the basis of the HSWP's (incomplete) financial report to the Parliament in the fall of 1989, I estimated the fair market value of the party's assets at HUF 150Bn, or $3Bn at the October 1989 rates of exchange. Tőkés, *Hungary's Negotiated Revolution*, ch. 8. The party's current (1995) assets consist of (a) over 300 office buildings; (b) several party-owned business firms; (c) several party-controlled "nonprofit" foundations; (d) partly party-financed privatized enterprises controlled by former HSWP officials; (e) state budgetary subsidies; and (f) dues and gifts from members and sympathizers. See Gábor Juhász, "Pártpénzek Magyarországon" [Party Finances in Hungary], *Mozgó Világ*, no. 8. (August 1993); Gábor Juhász, "1993-as pártmérlegek" [Party Balance Sheets for 1993], *Heti Világgazdaság* (6 May 1994), pp. 95–100; Gábor Juhász, "Pártképviselők az állami cégekben" [Party MPs in State Enterprises], *Heti Világgazdaság* (24 June 1995), pp. 83–9; and János Dobszay, "Törvénysértő alapítványok" [Illegal Foundations], *Heti Világgazdaság* (14 October 1995), pp. 109–11.

36 Cf. Attila Ágh, "Bumpy Road to Europeanization: Policy Effectiveness and Agenda Concentration in the Hungarian Legislation, 1990–1993," in *The Emergence of East Central European Parliaments: The First Steps*, ed. Attila Ágh (Budapest: Hungarian Centre for Democracy Studies, 1994) pp. 69–85.

37 On this, see the essays by György Csepeli, László Lengyel, István Stumpf, Ágnes Bokor and László Kéri in part I, "Pártok és kötődések" [Parties and Attachments] in *Parliamentary Elections, 1994*, ed. Luca Gábor et al., pp. 18–69.

38 Cf. László Vass, "Europeanization of Interest Groups in the New Hungarian Political System," *Budapest Papers on Democratic Transition*, 1990. As of December 1994, 110 of these were national organizations with the mission of

148   *Rudolf L. Tőkés*

érdekvédelem [protection of interest]. For a full list, see *Hungarian Yearbook, 1994*, pp. 755–60.
39 Kathleen Montgomery, "Interest Group Representation in the Hungarian Parliament," *Budapest Papers on Democratic Transition*, 1994. Because two-thirds of the MPs polled refused to respond to Montgomery's survey, her findings, however sensible, require further corroboration.
40 According to a March 1993 survey, the least trusted political institutions, on a "distrust-trust" scale of 1 to 100, were the political parties, the trade unions, and the Parliament with 27, 28, and 31 percent, respectively. *Hungarian Yearbook, 1993*, p. 732.
41 About one-half of the 107 bills enacted into laws between May 1990 and late 1991 were passed unanimously. Sándor Kurtán, "Pártok és Törvények," *Budapest Papers on Democratic Transition*, 1991.
42 Cf. Máté Szabó, "Adaptation and Resistance: the Institutionalization of Protest Movements, 1990–1994," in *Democratic Legitimacy in Post-Communist Societies*, ed. András Bozóki (Budapest: T-Twins Publishing House, 1994), pp. 137–54.
43 "A politikai közvélemény a Medián kutatásainak tükrében, 1991–1994" [Public Opinion on Politics, 1991–1994 in the Mirror of Surveys by Median, Inc.], ed. Béla Marian, in *Hungarian Yearbook, 1994*, pp. 718–56.
44 Ibid., pp. 731–4.
45 Ágnes Bokor, "A pártok és a politikusok népszerűségének összefüggéséről" [On the Relationship between Party Preference and Personal Popularity] in *Parliamentary Elections, 1994*, ed. Luca Gábor et al., pp. 88–97.
46 For an excellent description of the workings and interaction of the key branches of the government and those of the media with the powers that be, see Béla Pokol, *Magyar Parlamentarizmus* [Hungarian Parliamentarism] (Budapest: Cserépfalvi, 1994).
47 David Stark, "Recombinant Property in East European Capitalism," *Public Lectures*, no. 8 (Budapest: Institute for Advanced Study, Collegium Budapest, 1994).
48 Ibid., p. 7.
49 *A többpártrendszer kialakulása Magyarországon*, ed. Bihari, *passim*.
50 Mihály Bihari, "Parliamentary Elections and Governmental Change in Hungary in 1994," in *Hungarian Yearbook, 1995*, pp. 31–45.
51 See András Körösényi, "The Reasons for the Defeat of the Right," *Occasional Paper* no. 1 (Budapest: Windsor Klub, July 1994); Luca Gábor, "Értékelések" [Assessments], in ibid., pp. 491–585; and György Szoboszlai, "Változások a választási térképen: parlamenti és önkormányzati választások" [Changes in the Electoral Map: National and Local Elections], *Hungarian Yearbook, 1995*, pp. 82–98.
52 See *Balance. The Hungarian Government, 1990–1994*, ed. Csaba Gombár et al. (Budapest: Korridor Center for Political Research, 1994).
53 István Schlett, "A politika nyelvezetének alakulása a rendszerváltás után" [The New Language of Politics after the Change of the Regime], *Társadalmi Szemle* 49, nos. 8–9 (1994), 28–34.
54 The text of the two parties' voluminous "political prenuptial contract" is in *Hungarian Yearbook, 1995*, pp. 648–729.

55 On the AFD's political options in June 1994, see Iván Pető, "Az MSZP-SZDSZ kormánykoalició" [On the HSP-AFD Government Coalition], in *Hungarian Yearbook, 1995*, pp. 168-86.

56 See *Question Marks: The Hungarian Government, 1994-1995*, ed. Csaba Gombár et al. (Budapest: Korridor Center for Political Research, 1995).

57 Ágnes Bokor, "Az MSZMP szavazótáborának három rétege" [Three Clusters of HSP Voters], *Hungarian Yearbook, 1995*, p. 542.

58 Ibid., p. 546.

59 Endre Hann, "Pártok és politikusok népszerűsége" [The Popularity of Parties and Politicians], *Heti Világgazdaság*, 9 September 1995, pp. 90-92, and *Népszava*, 11 December 1995.

60 The Horn government's most comprehensive attempt to come to terms with these issues has been a major planning document, "Magyarország az új Európában. A Kormány modernizációs programjának politikai koncepciója" [Hungary in the New Europe. Political Theses of the Government's Modernization Program], Special supplement to *Magyar Hirlap*, 18 November 1995.

61 Cf. Béla Pokol, *Pénz és politika* [Money and Politics] (Budapest: Aula Kiadó, 1993).

5 Democratization and political participation: the experience of the Czech Republic

David M. Olson

The Czech Republic is an example of a postcommunist country well on its way toward a consolidated democratic political system. Building upon its democratic past in the interwar period, its postcommunist political and economic system closely follows a western democratic model. Not only does the Republic wish to "join Europe" in foreign policy and economic relations, it also seeks to become fully democratic in its internal life.

The sudden and unexpected dissolution of the Czech and Slovak Federation in 1993 did not disrupt the development of democracy, economic reform, or the new party system within the Czech Republic. Though the Czech Republic as an independent sovereign nation dates only from 1993, political developments within that Republic are a continuation of the "velvet revolution" and democratization process initiated within the Czechoslovakian Federation in 1989–90.

The Czech Republic would appear as one of the more stabilized and successful of the postcommunist states in both politics and economics. The major democratization developments within the Czech Republic include the rapid growth of a multiparty system, the slower growth of an interest group system, and the abrupt increase in parliamentary activity. In economics, rapid privatization in all retail and profitable industry sectors has been accompanied by continued state ownership of either unprofitable or critical sectors. The public, as measured through opinion polling, seems to have an accepting, if reserved, attitude toward these postcommunist changes.

This chapter examines these elements of postcommunist reform, both economic and political, beginning with a review of past events with consequences for current developments.

Influences of the past

Current developments in the Czech Republic did not, unlike the Republic itself, emerge suddenly, seemingly without connection to the past. The present is closely related to selected elements of both the communist and interwar experiences, and to the hectic moments of the transitions, both democratic and national.

The First Republic

The memory of the Czechoslovakian Republic between the wars is a strong one in the contemporary Czech Republic. Newly created at the end of World War I on the northern rim of the Austro-Hungarian Empire, the Czechoslovakian Republic was the only Eastern European nation to experience a continuous democracy until the beginning of World War II. Parliamentary elections were held regularly, and governments were selected as a consequence of those elections. The multiparty system and the proportional election system continued through the entire, if brief, period. The dominant governing mode within parliament was a five-party coalition, the "Petka," within which the coalition partners negotiated their differences by agreements among the party leaders prior to the formulation of official cabinet level policy.[1] This model is echoed in the postcommunist 1992–96 four-party government coalition.

Likewise, the current proportional representation electoral law is a revival of the First Republic election system. The similarity of today's election system with that of the First Republic was based on the expectation in 1989–90, that the new democracy would continue the multi-party system of the First Republic.[2]

While most parties of today do not directly trace their antecedents to the parties of this earlier period, both the Communist Party and one of the Christian parties are "historical" parties. Both their organizations and sources of voter support are continuations from the interwar Republic. The currently named Christian Democratic Union-Czech Peoples' Party, especially, retains its earlier strong regional support in Moravia.[3]

Another source of continuity from the pre-war Republic is in economic structure. Prewar Czechoslovakia was more industrial and commercial than were other countries in the region, and that status was, in turn, an inheritance from the Austro–Hungarian Empire.

An important related characteristic, however, was that industry and commerce were found more in the Czech than in the Slovakian portions of the new republic. As one indicator, literacy was much higher in the Czech than Slovak sections.[4] Their differential status, also, was an inheritance of the old Empire. That difference has had a major impact upon contemporary events.

Related to both democratic politics and the industrial economy were the large numbers of voluntary and civic associations, at least in the Czech portion of the Empire.[5]

In retrospect, one other development in the First Republic assumed major significance: within Slovakia, voting support for nationalist parties slowly increased. While the major parties in the Republic had leadership, organization and voter support in all regions, voter support for pan-Czechoslovakian parties slowly decreased during this period.[6] This trend was accentuated in the 1946 election.[7] The potential for separatist appeals was increased when the Slovak People's Party split from the Czechoslovak People's Party, both based upon Catholic support and policies.[8]

At the end of the First Republic, Hitler not only assumed control over Czechoslovakia, but treated the Czech and Slovak portions differently. A source of current controversy is the question of the interpretation of the separate Slovakian state created during the Nazi occupation.[9]

The communist experience

That communist rule might be transitory both in time and in effect was indicated, though briefly, by the "Prague Spring" of 1968, when attention turned to the possibilities of both economic reform and less rigidity within the Communist Party. The clearest expression of the possibility of a return to the democratic past was the increased visibility and importance of the parliament, and public opinion in support of a freer election system.[10]

The two most immediate and major inheritances from communist rule include federalism and depressed interest group formation. The one lasting structural remnant of communism was the legal change of the unitary structure of the state to a federation. While continued central rule by the Communist Party vitiated the practice of federalism, certain formal structures were created which persisted, without legal change, until the collapse. This change reflected the ability of the Slovakian section of the Communist Party to act independently from the Prague center.[11] Two new formal mechanisms to express the federal structure, the formation of two republic-level National Councils and the federalization of the National Assembly, assumed major importance two decades later with democratization.

First at the provincial republic level, National Councils were created for both republics. Serving as elected assemblies, both bodies were institutional revivals of earlier "national councils" from World War II and World War I independence experiences. These bodies have, with independence for both Republics, become the new sovereign parliaments of their respective

Republics. Their personnel fear that those bodies were doubly handicapped in facing today's realities: they were neither structured nor equipped for the rigors of competitive democratic debate and decision-making; and they were inexperienced in facing the substantive responsibilities of the internationally sovereign state. As an external indication of their revised status, the initial US congressional direct aid program for legislatures was directed to the Federal Assembly, not to the Republic Councils. The new parliaments of the new Republics have made a double transition.[12]

The second critical federal decision under communism was to alter the composition and balance of political forces within the National Assembly. The unicameral body became the bicameral Federal Assembly. Furthermore, within one of the two houses, the two Republics had equal representation, and even more crucially, constitutional decisions required separate majorities among each of the two Republic delegations.[13] The significance of these formal provisions could not have been foreseen until the democratic transition; they were designed, but could never have been tested, under communism. The formal powers allocated to the Republic delegations were of no use under single party control.

While federalism is the first lasting inheritance of the communist experience, depressed interest group formation is the second. Not only political parties, but any form of voluntary group organization, is now distrusted. This anti-organization inheritance may be common to all postcommunist democracies.[14] Just as political parties in Central Europe now exist with voters rather than members,[15] so interest groups may appear more with self declared leaders acting in the name of potential groups than with real members.

The common anti-organization inheritance of postcommunist societies has, however, had different expressions in different countries. The rigid repression of "normalization" following the 1968 Prague Spring, brought two decades of suppression of independent thought and action either by individuals or through groups. Though it was not possible to form a Solidarity type organization, the group Charter 77 did emerge. Disavowing an interest in control of either government or the economy, it concentrated on petitions to official leaders to observe strict legality in the treatment of individuals.

Charter 77 was more a network of communication and artistic expression than a formal association for action.[16] It also came to provide the basis for the expression of an alternative view of life, the "second polis," suggesting the formation of modes of action separate from, but parallel to, those of the state.[17] As specialists in communication, their written and symbolic expression had an influence far beyond its membership of 2,000 or so. This network formed the small and highly personal nucleus of the pro-democracy reform groups at the moment of the transition.[18]

Nevertheless, the National Front with two parties in the Czech Republic, and a different two in Slovakia, in addition to the communists, provided the structure for those two Czech parties to continue to exist at the beginning of the democratic transition. Their organizational shell and their property and newspapers became valuable resources. They quickly shed their old leadership, and played a vital role in mediating between the Communist Party and the new reform groups in the early stages of the transition.[19]

There are two main economic consequences of communism for the postcommunist era, for agriculture and industry. First, in agriculture, the large collective and cooperative farms under communism will apparently remain in place; though now privatized and not directly linked to the state, they are not being replaced by small private holdings. Through this means, the social structure of the rural areas will remain very different from the prewar rural society, and it is possible that the old rural voting patterns will become very different as well. It is striking that neither peasant nor agricultural parties of any size have appeared in the new Czech Republic. To the extent there is a distinctive rural electorate, it now votes for both Christian and Communist Parties in local as well as national elections.

Second, industry was developed differently in the two republics during the communist period, with heavy industry and armaments concentrated in the Slovak Republic. Furthermore, this period marked Slovakia's initial industrialization, while the Czech Republic had industrialized and urbanized earlier, beginning in the Austrian period. This pattern created different economic circumstances between the two republics at the time of communist collapse. Slovakian towns, for example, were more dependent upon single industries than were Czech towns.[20]

The democratic transition

The democratic transition in Czechoslovakia was abrupt; the system imploded. The immediate observable consequence was that the democratic reformers were neither numerous nor prepared. The other but more important consequence was that the reform groupings in Prague and Bratislava were not able either to merge their organizations or to coordinate their activities. The same observations could apparently be made about reform groupings in Košiče as well.

When the sudden absence of repression made independent group formation possible, many small parties quickly appeared, some of which were survivals of prewar democracy. They were submerged, however, in the formation of the Civic Forum in Prague, and the Public Against Violence in Bratislava. Both were amorphous reform groupings, united for the single purpose of removing communists from power. Having quickly achieved their goal, they as quickly lost the source of their cohesion. They remained as single organizations in their respective Republics only until after the initial democratic election in June 1990.

The period November 1989 to June 1990 is one of confusion, and as many participants have observed, euphoria. The enthusiasm of hundreds of thousands of persons in Wenceslas Square was translated into improvised organization at the Magic Lantern theater, and into negotiations with the communist leadership who, by that time, wished to exit.[21]

Three consequences for democratic life developed from the non-violent implosion of communism, celebrated by the sobriquet, "Velvet Revolution": parliamentary activism, the Republic centric party system, and the parliamentary basis for party formation.

Firstly, the moribund Czechoslovakian Federal Assembly and the two National Councils were galvanized into action. They were "reconstructed," meaning that more than half of the communist members resigned, to be replaced by new appointees of the reformer groups. Both the non-communist parties already in the Assembly, and the communists, also replaced some of their own members. The reconstructed legislatures promptly enacted the legal measures to transform the political system, as agreed by the negotiations between the communist leaders (who were also replaced) and the reform groups. Václav Havel was elected by the Federal Assembly as president, replacing communist Gustav Husak. The constitution was immediately amended, removing the most obnoxious symbols of the past, especially the "leading role" of the Communist Party. Furthermore, as part of the negotiated package of regime and personnel changes, the chairman of the Assembly (Alexander Dubček) and the prime minister (Marian Čalfa) were newly selected.[22]

These early actions established the parliaments as the center of political reform and of legality. Their subsequent policy activism was built upon these early weeks of the transition. It was the reconstructed parliaments which adopted the new election law for the 1990 elections.[23]

The second consequence of the rapid transition was the clear difference in political party systems between the Czech and Slovak Republics. The two separately created anti-communist reform movements, one in each Republic (Civic Forum in Prague; Public Against Violence in Bratislava) were predictive of the party systems which subsequently emerged through splits of those reform movements.

The "common state" did not have a common party system, but two. Each Republic had its own party system. The new political parties of democracy did not split from a common organization, but from two, one for each Republic. The party system was, at the moment of the democratic beginning, Republic-centric.[24] The 1990 election law itself reflected the separate

Republic political identities, in that the vote counting procedures and seat allocation rules to the Federal Assembly were calculated and applied separately to the two Republics within the common federation. The 1990 law in this respect followed the 1946 law.[25]

As the third consequence of the rapid transition, the party systems developed through splits within parliamentary based parties. Parliaments became the only institutional location which gathered the aspirants to the new political elite and became, by default, the only forum within which new political actors could interact. The longer process of political group discovery and formation outside of parliament in Hungary and Poland was completely lacking in Czechoslovakia; parliaments became the negotiation locale. If the interaction between elites and voters, and among elites, can be conceptualized as a "market," parliament became the market place for Czechoslovakia.

But in retrospect, not all parliaments were equal within the federation: The main dynamics occurred in the Slovakian National Council for the parties in that Republic, while the Federal Assembly was the source of the main dynamics among political elites in the Czech Republic.

The national transition

The split of Czechoslovakia into two sovereign states has occasioned much discussion and argument; somewhat less examined is the peaceful means of that split. What factors contributed to the "velvet divorce," and especially to the "velvet" character of the split?

One consideration is that the whole country consisted of only two political entities, thereby simplifying many related geosocial characteristics. Their borders were clear and long established, and there was a low mixture of population. Neither the volatile admixture of the Yugoslavian population, nor the dispersal of the Russian population into neighboring regions, had occurred. Second, violence was not a factor. Neither the military nor police were actors in the independence issue. They did not participate in the decision, but were fully engaged in the ensuing negotiations about how to split military assets. In addition, crowd or anomic violence was not present, either. Third, the international objective of Slovakian autonomists was acceptance by the European Union as a future member state. The Union insisted upon a democratic polity. As a corollary, means of national separation other than through negotiation and peaceful means were discouraged. Fourth, the prior existence of the Slovakian Republic parliament, government and ministries permitted not only the formation of an electorally based political leadership, but one predisposed to a negotiation oriented independence strategy. Fifth and finally, the arena which became decisive in the split of the state was the election system, especially the elections in 1992, held simultaneously to all three parliaments. The electoral sequence hypothesis suggests that if the initial democratic elections are held initially at subordinate levels, the tendency to separation is increased (for example, Yugoslavia), whereas if the initial democratic elections are held initially at the country-wide level (for example, Spain), the tendency to unity is increased.[26] Czechoslovakia held initial democratic elections simultaneously at both levels. If one consequence has been to increase separatist pressures, another has been to direct those pressures into negotiated paths.

The evolution of political society

Political parties dominate electoral politics, government formation, and the internal organization of parliament. Proto-interest groups, or perhaps, proto-lobbies, are becoming active in decision making, especially in association with ministries. These observations are much more applicable to national level politics than to local. Research on group formation and activity is only in the beginning stage.

Interest groups

Interest groups are most visible as the state encourages, or even requires, their formation, of which the clearest example is in the corporate model tripartite labor market negotiation bodies. Both workers and employers are required to join their respective regional and national bodies.[27] Parliament has no similarly structured means of encouraging interest group participation, and thus group formation and action centered upon parliament is found much less than, or at least is not as visible as, in administrative settings.

The broad and neutral category of "interest group" in American political science does not exist in Czech thinking. There seem to be two broad categories: the economic based groups and a more general category of citizen (or "civic") groups.

Economic sector organizations

Economic reforms appear to have affected labor and business much more than agriculture (table 5.1 shows some economic trends since 1989). Interest groups in all three economic segments have been created, often as continuations of communist front groups, and function in relation to the government and ministries.

Table 5.1 *Indicators of economic trends in the Czech Republic since 1989*

	1989	1990	1991	1992	1993	1994	1995[a]
GDP	1.4[b]	-0.4[b]	-14.2	-6.4	-0.9	2.6	5.2
Industrial output	0.8	-3.5	-22.3	-7.9	-5.3	2.1	9.1
Rate of inflation	2.3[b]	10.8[b]	56.7	11.1	20.8	10.0	9.1
Rate of unemployment	0[b]	0.8[b]	4.1	2.6	3.5	3.2	2.9
GNP per capita	n.a.	n.a.	n.a.	n.a.	7,910	n.a.	n.a.
% Workforce in private activity[c]	1.3	6.9	18.8	31.1	47.1	n.a.	n.a.
% GDP from private sector	11.2	12.3	17.3	27.7	45.1	56.3	n.a.

Notes: GDP – % change over previous year; industrial output – % change over previous year; rate of inflation – % change in end-year retail/consumer prices; rate of unemployment – end of period; GNP per capita – in US dollars at PPP exchange rates. [a]Estimate. [b]Years 1989, 1990 are for Czechoslovakian Federation; beginning with 1991, data are Czech Republic only. [c]Excludes cooperatives.

Sources: European Bank for Reconstruction and Development, *Transition Report 1995: Economic Transition in Eastern Europe and the Former Soviet Union* (London: EBRD, 1995); European Bank for Reconstruction and Development, *Transition Report Update, April 1996: Assessing Progress in Economies in Transition* (London: EBRD, 1996).

Organized labor unions have continued in the Czech Republic in the same organizations and buildings, and industrial sectors, as during the communist era. Economic reform has affected the large and heavy industries the least, so that the major sources of union membership have been least affected by privatization.[28] Privatization has proceeded much more quickly in the retail and distribution sectors than in large industry.[29] Union membership, in addition, does not include the workers in the new and rapidly growing smaller businesses and industry, much of which is either small scale retail or in "high tech" sectors. The growth sectors of the economy are thus nonunion.[30]

In imitation of the continental democracies, labor unions culminate in a "peak" association, the Bohemian-Moravian Chamber of Trade Unions (CMKOS), a direct lineal descendant of the official communist union structure (Revolutionary Trade Union Movement, ROH). It has inherited the former unions' building, members and financial and physical assets. There are, in addition, a Christian Trade Union Coalition, the Association of Independent Trade Unions, and a variety of independent unions.[31] The new

Chamber of Trade Unions was admitted to the European Union's trade union consultative group in late 1995, thus achieving in labor the broader goal of "joining Europe."[32]

Business associations are much more variable and also flexible than are labor associations. Managers of just a few enterprises can form their own sectoral or regional group. They are often the managers of the previous state-owned enterprises, and simply reconstitute themselves as a private association. The state owned system grouped enterprises together in a common monopoly organization; that existing structure has become the basis for private organization of the same managers and the same enterprises as under the communist system.

The largest economic sectors are the most easily organized, and the most visible: steel, textiles, chemicals, banks, forestry, glass. In addition, Chambers of Commerce serve as "peak" associations at both national and regional levels.[33]

Agriculture was largely collectivized through cooperatives.[34] Privatization in agriculture proceeds on the basis that land had remained in private ownership; productive activity was required to be organized through the cooperatives. Apparently many private owners continue their joint production through the existing agricultural cooperative which then becomes a private economic unit. According to the minister of agriculture (Josef Lux, Christian Democratic Union), 40 percent of the state farms remain under government control; restitution claims appear the greatest obstacle to privatization.[35]

To be represented in the tripartite Council for Dialogue of Social Partners, as it has been called since June 1995, the organizations of business, labor and agriculture must be nation-wide, include organizations from several sectors, and have a specified minimum membership.[36]

While avoidance of partisan affiliation is one of the requirements for official registration of a private association, the tripartite negotiation structure has placed the peak economic associations in direct contact with not only the ministries, but the government. Proposed Government legislation affecting the economic organizations must be discussed beforehand within the tripartite Council, and their views must be communicated to Parliament.

While the formal organizational structure resembles the old communist system, the jurisdiction and government linkages of the tripartite Council follow the pattern of western European democracies. The Council negotiates not only wage settlements, but on a wide range of government proposed legislation affecting business prosperity, social benefits, and labor-management relations. The resulting "social compact" has a wide policy and constituency reach.[37]

Contacts with parliament can be expected to increase and to become more visible and organized. The committee structure of parliament, in parallel with the ministries, is the most easily available and structured, means of access to parliament. Lobbying as an activity may also become organized. On the British model, a private profit business consulting firm has opened offices in Prague to "monitor . . . parliamentary discussions and register . . . how local deputies vote on bills in addition to using Western lobbying techniques." The group's president admitted, "'We will even be inviting parliament members to lunches.'"[38]

The economic based interest groups have not affiliated with political parties. They proclaim their lack of partisanship and seem reluctant to create even the impression of partisan preferences or actions. This reluctance is part of the rejection of political participation in the communist period. Political parties can, as has the Czech Social Democratic Party, create affiliated interest groups for both businessmen and women; such groups, however, do not constitute a formal affiliation between parties and interest groups. The pattern of party-group relations is more similar to the German than the British.

Party and campaign finance provide occasional surface indications of both political preferences and actions by people in their economic capacity. Not much is known about political finance, but occasional fund raising events are held, and parties have taken bank loans to pay for campaigns.

One particularly difficult topic in campaign finance concerns those economic enterprises which are partially privatized. Some companies have a considerable share of state ownership, even though they are managed as private for-profit enterprises, and the share structure permits their eventual complete privatization. The managers and directors of such mixed ownership enterprises experience difficult and conflicting norms, both legal and unofficial, about their proper involvement in partisan activity. For example, three state owned firms paid 250,000 Koruna for their managers to attend a fund raising dinner for the leading government party, a practice since made illegal.[39]

Direct public action in economic matters, such as protests, demonstrations and strikes, have been few. They have been directed by labor unions at specific economic issues. Those issues, however, have affected the public sector. Railway unions threatened to strike in summer 1995, as did some physicians in the fall, over wages and management issues, and since both the railroads and the health care system are state owned and managed, the relevant ministries were the target of those public actions. While the few actions had no direct consequences for state policy earlier, those in 1995 have resulted in ministerial shifts, wage increases, and administrative reorganizations.[40]

Political parties and interest groups as vehicles for the accumulation of personal wealth by the participants is a topic which surfaces mainly in allegations of conflict of interest directed at members of parliament. There are similar accusations directed at members of the government and their family members. The entire privatization process, in addition, creates many opportunities for allegations, at least, of improper personal gain.[41]

Civic associations

The civic category of interest groups is similar to the "non governmental organization" or NGO type, and to the "public interest groups" in American thought. One term, used mainly by the groups themselves, *neziskovem sektoru*, indicates nonprofit sector.

The formation of these types of interest groups is encouraged by international sources including the United Nations and the European Union, American and British government assistance projects, and private sources such as the New York-based group, Charter 77. These types of foreign sponsorship have created lobbying organizations within the Czech Republic which seek legal recognition and financial support for non-profit organizations. Such groups as "the Information Center for Foundations" and special features in the Prague Post, sponsored by the Prague Post Foundation, are illustrations. Even the few studies on civic groups are sponsored by international sources.[42] Their legal status was formalized in Fall 1995 under the heading of "common beneficial corporations."[43]

Several researchers report, separately, that many of the civic and non-profit groups which have been created, seem to disappear rapidly, suggesting that many are formed in response to encouragement (including financial) from foreign sponsors. The director of the Civil Society Development Foundation, supported by the European Union's PHARE program for Central Europe, estimated that more than half of the funds for nonprofit organizations had come from foreign sources.[44]

It is difficult to obtain a clear view of the extent of membership in civic and political organizations. No analyst credits the self-reported membership figures released by either political parties or interest groups about themselves. Public opinion researchers apparently find it difficult to phrase questions which are meaningful to the public.

One public opinion survey indicated that 27 percent of the public report themselves as members of groups and associations, while 34 percent are members of labor unions, and 12 percent report themselves as members of political parties.[45] Another survey found a much higher rate of group participation, at the local level: 53 percent reported themselves as active in groups, of which sports (31 percent) were by far the most common.[46] The proportion (16 percent) reporting themselves active in a political party is much closer to the national level survey reported immediately above than is the group participation rate.

Over 20,000 groups had registered with the Ministry of Interior by mid-1994. The largest topical and membership categories are sports, hunting, and school groups. Many receive state funding through a variety of ministries, including Education, Health, and Culture.[47] By 1995, the estimated number of nonprofit groups was 30,000.[48]

Civic associations for population groups do exist for women, for Romanies (or Gypsies), and of course for religions. Postcommunist women's organizations appear small in membership, largely discredited by the communist experience.[49] Romany organizations find it difficult to organize their scattered eligible population.[50]

Churches and religious organizations have a long-standing existence. They register with the Ministry of Culture (21 denominations in 1995), and all but six accept financial support from the state. The larger and historic groups are mainly in the news as involved in the property restitution process.[51] Some religious groups, especially those with foreign (that is, American) origins, have been named in a report of the Interior Ministry on extremist organizations.[52]

The typical public-private distinction in American thought is not completely applicable to current conditions in the Czech Republic. Some share of ownership of economic enterprises and agriculture remains in state hands. The associations of firms with at least partial state ownership may more resemble, in American examples, associations of housing authorities than of trade associations. Likewise, the civic associations are largely dependent upon, or seek to obtain, state financial support.

Ethnicities and regionalisms

There were markedly different attitudes toward the Czechoslovakian Federation between Slovaks and Czechs, though they substantially agreed on both political and economic reform. The major differences in their attitudes and preferences were directed toward their mutual relations within the federation.[53]

Since the split of the federation, the ethnic composition of the Czech Republic has become more simple, but less tangible and clear. The single largest ethnic group is the Slovakians, who tend to be clustered in the western border area, as new settlers following the expulsion of the Germans after World War II.

Another sizeable grouping is the Moravians: those persons (about one-third of the total) who live in the Moravian region and who identify their ethnicity as Moravian rather than as Czech.[54] While they tended to vote for the

Moravian-Silesian based party, the policy demands of that party have more concerned local decentralization than economic or social policy questions. That party has disappeared since the 1992 election. This region also provides disproportionate voter support for the Christian Democratic Union–Czech Peoples Party, reflecting and continuing interwar patterns.

The most distinctive ethnic group is the Romanies, or Gypsies, numbering approximately 300,000, and concentrated in economically depressed regions and city neighborhoods. Their relatively small numbers, and lack of education and steady employment, reduce their presence in public opinion data. The districts of their concentration tend to provide disproportionate electoral support to the one avowedly nationalist party in the Czech Republic, the Republican Association.[55]

While all social policy questions affect the Romany, it is the citizenship law which has a particular impact upon this group. Romanies frequently have moved to and from the Slovak and Czech portions of the Federation, and thus have difficulty in meeting the two-year permanent residence requirement for Czech citizenship.[56] The strict citizenship law has been strongly criticized by international human rights groups.[57]

Media

The only media subject to government control are television, while radio and newspapers are now regarded as private economic investments. The number of radio stations has been increasing. There seem to be few controversies over attempted government control.

Television is a more potential source of difficulty. That the Czech Republic has had only two parliamentary elections (1990, 1992) has reduced the opportunities for complaint. In 1992, political commercials were restricted to certain time slots, and news programs were prohibited from showing partisan political activity. While TV programming during that campaign was dull, it was at least not a source of controversy. The opportunity for allegations of partisanship were reduced by this policy. Television seems to not have been a factor in the 1995 local elections.

The public policy question of government financial support for, and governance of, the two TV channels is a continuing controversy. There is now, in addition, a new private TV channel, while cable provides increasing access to international channels. The behavior and control of private media is becoming a new source of controversy. The private TV channel offered weekly free air time to the prime minister, to which all other political parties objected. A second controversy, affecting all media, concerns foreign ownership and control over Czech media. More than 50 percent of the Czech press are reported to have foreign owners.[58]

Some newspapers have clear political party preferences. *Telegraph* was founded as an organ of the current plurality party, the Civic Democratic Party. It even carries a weekly article by the prime minister, Václav Klaus. The several papers sponsored by political parties clearly do not earn a profit.

The officially permitted paper of the communist government, *Rude Pravo* (Red Truth) has survived as an independent and widely respected newspaper. While its editorials are vaguely "left" and skeptical toward the current government coalition, journalists and political figures of all persuasions respect the accuracy and professionalism of its news reports. It has retained the building and equipment of its predecessor, and has had the advantage of a large and experienced professional staff.[59] It has recently changed names to the plain and simple *Pravo*.

Many newspapers are loosing their political identity, for they are purchased by foreign newspaper companies as investments. The change in ownership leads to personnel dissatisfaction and resignations, with the new managers and commentators having more an economic success than policy orientation toward their work. Some newspapers do commission public opinion polls, but mainly report as neutral news the relative standings of political parties and their changes over time. As the 1996 election approached, public figures commented on their own standings in the polls, which were then reported as news.[60]

One public policy controversy concerns the Czech Press Service. Maintained on public funds, there is now a strong push to convert it to a self-supporting financial base. There are also occasional criticisms that the Service does not provide as complete coverage of an event or press release as the originators, even the prime minister, would prefer.[61]

Crime, corruption, and improprieties

Crime is seen by the public as a problem of individual behavior and threat more than as a collective event. Organized crime, usually referred to loosely as the mafia, is seen more as a source of drugs and personal violence than as a participant in broader economic activity. There are no allegations of linkages between criminal activity and/or criminals, and political parties. There are no reports of murders by crime syndicates.

Misbehavior, whether legal or ethical, is sometimes attributed to public officials. In the clearest case, the official in charge of privatization (Jaroslav Lizner) was convicted of taking a $300,000 bribe in Czech currency in the sale of a dairy enterprise.[62] Public officials are also seen as accepting personal favors from both governmental and private sources. The prime minister finally decided, after publicity, to not accept an apartment from a local government authority. Other officials were accused of accepting the use of foreign autos from foreign firms. Also within the category of unseemly official behavior, several members of parliament were shielded from prosecution for personal criminal behavior by the parliament's refusal to rescind their parliamentary immunity.

Allegations of either illegal or unethical behavior have also affected political party and campaign finance. In a celebrated case, which was finally not prosecuted, one of the coalition parties, Civic Democratic Alliance (ODA), did not repay a bank loan for the 1992 election campaign, amounting to about $2 million. The loan disappeared in a series of transactions among the bank, the party, and a transient private company. The major penalty, so far, has been the resignation of several party leaders and a disastrous decline in the party's public opinion ratings.[63] In 1995 the parliament adopted a conflict of interest law covering all public officials and members of their immediate families. Though financial penalties were debated, the only sanction adopted was publicity.[64]

Public awareness and attitudes

The Czech public supported the change from communism in 1989, and continues to support the new democratic political system. While there are many attitudes of cynicism tinged with fatalism toward the behavior of individual politicians and political parties, the public is cautiously supportive of the democratic political system. This complex mixture of particularistic cynicism and system support varies both by political attitudes and by demographics.

Public attitudes toward the new democracy in the new state are expressed in cautious and moderate terms. Responses to public opinion survey questions tend to avoid both the "strong yes" and "strong no" options.[65]

The new democratic political system

The public is, on the whole, optimistic toward changes in the country since the events of 1989. Those most strongly approving have declined slightly, while the most strongly disapproving have remained constant over a two year period. Most were and remain in the cautious middle (table 5.2). Age of respondents provides a strong gradient of approval/disapproval of the post communist changes. Below age 45, those approving the changes greatly outnumber the disapprovals, while those disapproving the changes are predominant in the ages 45 and above (table 5.2b). By education the differences in approval rates are equally large (table 5.2c). Only the vocationally educated category disapproves the changes. Those with higher

Table 5.2 *Evaluation of changes in the Czech Republic since November 1989*

A. Evaluation of changes since November 1989 in two time periods

Evaluation	1991 %	1994 %
Positive	20	24
Positive with reservations	61	56
Negative	19	20
Total	100	100

B. Evaluation of changes by age, 1994

Age	Positive %	Negative %	Index of difference
15-19	38	11	27
20-29	33	11	22
30-44	25	17	8
45-59	19	22	-3
60 +	15	32	-17

C. Evaluation of changes by education, 1994

Education	Positive %	Negative %	Index of difference
Primary school	22	21	1
Secondary school incomplete	18	23	-5
Secondary school complete	32	15	17
Higher education	41	11	30

Question: "How do you think about the evolution of our society since November 1989?" (N=969)

Source: *IVVM Bulletin 94–12*, questions 32, 33.

education more approve the changes than disapprove by a margin of 30 percentage points.

In evaluations of the economy separately from politics, Czechs tend to be more approving of their "economic situation" than the "political situation." The evaluations in table 5.3 have been relatively stable over the 1993–95 period, with the disapproving rate declining slightly. The demographic correlates of both political and economic evaluations are similar: the young and well educated approve of both economic and political developments,

Table 5.3 *Evaluation of economic and political situation in the Czech Republic*

A. Evaluation of economic and political situation in two time periods (%)

	Economy		Politics	
Evaluation	1993	1995	1993	1995
Positive	26	30	38	39
Half and half	42	44	n.a.	n.a.
Negative	26	16	58	55
Index of difference	0	14	-20	-16

B. Evaluation of economic and political situation by party, 1995 (%)

	Economy				Politics		
Party	Positive	Half	Negative	Index	Positive	Negative	Index
CDP (ODS)	65	30	2	63	75	23	52
CDA (ODA)	40	54	6	34	45	52	-7
CSDP (CSSD)	20	50	23	-3	25	72	-47
Communist	34	34	9	-46	9	90	-81
Undecided	20	51	14	6	25	65	-40

Questions: "How do you think about our political situation?" Answer: "satisfied."
"How do you think about the Czech economic transition?" Answer: "successful." (N=959)
Source: *IVVM Bulletin 95-04*, questions 48, 49.

while the older and less educated persons are less approving. By occupation, businessmen are positive toward the economy (52 percent) and political situation (54 percent), while a smaller proportion of both workers and the retired approve the economic transformation (22 and 21 percent), and the political situation (31 percent and 29 percent). These evaluations are strongly related to party preferences (table 5.3b). Supporters of the government coalition parties tend to approve of both the economic and political situations of their country, while voters for the non-government parties tend to disapprove. The Civic Democratic Party, the largest government party, and the Communist Party (and related parties), are at opposite extremes of evaluation of both the economy and political situation, while the supporters of Civic Democratic Alliance, a government party, the Social Democrats, and the undecideds occupy intermediate positions. The distribution of the public by party preferences is indicated in table 5.13.

Table 5.4 *Evaluation of the party system in the Czech Republic*

A. Evaluation of system of political parties as guarantors of democracy, 1993–95

Evaluation	% July 93	% Jan. 94	% Oct. 94	% April 95
Definitely yes	7.3	5.8	8.6	7.4
Rather yes	44.1	48.8	46.9	49.1
Rather no	37.0	34.2	34.7	36.5
Definitely no	10.6	11.3	9.8	6.9

B. Evaluation of party system by left-right identity, 1995

Evaluation	% Left	% Center	% Right
Definitely yes	2.1	4.5	13.6
Rather yes	29.5	47.6	63.2
Rather no	53.4	42.9	19.2
Definitely no	15.0	4.9	4.0

Question: "Do political parties of the Czech Republic act as guarantors of democratic politics?" (N=1,505)

Source: STEM (Center for Empirical Research), July 1995.

Political entities

Separate questions have been asked about political parties, interest groups, and the institutions of government.

Parties

One question, repeated over time, has asked people to evaluate the political party system as a guarantor of democracy (table 5.4). During the 1993–95 period, the "definitely yes" and "definitely not" categories each have fluctuated between 7 and 11 percent. The "rather yes" category has gradually grown from 44 percent to 49 percent, while the "rather not" category has remained constant at 34 to 37 percent. The "yes" responses together have slowly grown from 51 percent in 1993 to 56 percent in 1995. The distribution of the public's attitudes on this question has been stable. Evaluations of the party system are related to respondents' self-placement on a political left-right scale, but all categories remain within the cautious range. The highest negative evaluation ("definitely no") is provided by "left" voters, at 15 percent, while 14 percent of their opposites, the "right" voters, give a "definitely yes" response (table 5.4b). By party preference, the strongest negative evaluation is provided by supporters of the Left Block at 27 percent. The largest strongly affirmative response of 17 percent comes from supporters of the Civic Democratic Party (data not shown). Popular assessments of their political and economic circumstances in the new postcommunist democracy vary by both age and education. On all questions, the better educated and the younger persons are more optimistic about the changed situation than their opposites. For example, in assessments of political parties as guarantors of the new democracy, the university educated respondents were the most strongly positive (but only 13 percent), while the least educated were most strongly negative (but only 9 percent).

By age, there is more variation in the strong "no" responses than in the other responses on this question. The oldest age category is more than twice as negative (10 percent) than is the youngest (4 percent).

Interest groups

Interest groups, as a type of participant in political life, have not been the object of public opinion testing, for their formation and activity are much less visible to the public than are political parties. Terms such as "interest group," "NGO," "voluntary association," or "lobby" apparently have little currency in postcommunist Czech society.

Trade unions are the single exception; their visibility during the communist period, and their prominence in public attention in the new democracy, make them known to the general public. The public has been asked about their degree of trust in trade unions. The "definitely not" responses are larger than in the previous party system question, but also cluster in the cautious middle. By self-placement on a left-right scale, even 9 percent of the "left" voters strongly negatively evaluate trade unions (table 5.5). By party preference, the strongest support is provided by 24 percent of the Communist Parties' supporters, while only 13 percent of the Social Democrats are strongly positive toward labor unions. Supporters of the government coalition parties vary in their assessment of organized labor: the "strong no" evaluation of unions is at 23 percent for the Civic Democratic Party and Civic Democratic Alliance voters, but only 12 percent for the Christian Democratic Union–Czech Peoples Party supporters (data not shown).

Governmental institutions

Public attitudes toward the institutions of the governmental system reflect the typical pattern of more established democracies. Greatest trust or confidence is placed in the president, and least in parliament, with attitudes toward the government more moderately stated. In the past year, public trust in the

Table 5.5 *Trust in trade unions in the Czech Republic (by left–right identification)*

| Degree of trust | % All | Political identity | | |
		% Left	% Center	% Right
Definitely yes	9.6	17.8	9.6	4.9
Rather yes	39.1	51.9	43.9	26.8
Rather no	35.0	21.4	34.6	43.5
Definitely no	16.3	8.9	11.8	24.9

Note: N = 1,513

Source: STEM (Center for Empirical Research), July 1995

president rose from 69 percent to 77 percent, while it also rose slightly from 25 percent to 29 percent for parliament (table 5.6).

Evaluations of government institutions vary strongly by political party and also by satisfaction with one's living standards. Among the supporters of all parties, the president is more positively evaluated than the other institutions, with parliament the least. Why Civic Democratic Party supporters should more strongly trust the president, whom they do not control, than either the government or parliament, which they do control, is not clear. Why Civic Democratic Alliance trust in Parliament and government should be lower than that expressed by the former party supporters – both parties share in the control of parliament – is not clear. Why Social Democratic and Communist supporters should trust president and government, neither of which they control, more than parliament in which they have a significant presence, is not clear, either.

By degrees of satisfaction with living standards, trust toward government institutions varies as much as by party preferences. But both the satisfied and the dissatisfied rank the three institutions in the same descending order, from president to parliament. Whether by party or living standard evaluations, the president ranks highly, and parliament ranks low; it is government trust which varies the most, and predictably, by party and by living standards evaluations.

The range of government institution trust by these factors is sufficiently large that one must wonder what the general question – trust – actually measures.

Beyond general assessments of parliament, the public has been asked for the reasons for which they give a low evaluation of parliament. The largest proportion of persons (31 percent) speak of parliamentary activity and

Table 5.6 *Trust in government institutions in the Czech Republic*

A. Trust in government institutions, 1994–95

Institution	% July 94	% Jan. 95	% June 95
President	69	77	78
Government	54	58	54
Parliament	25	30	29

B. Trust in government institutions by party, 1995

Institution	% CDP	% CDA	% CSDP	% Comm. parties	% Independent
President	94	79	74	46	82
Government	87	78	34	21	53
Parliament	52	38	13	11	26

C. Trust in government institutions by living standard satisfaction, 1995

Institution	% Satisfied	% Dissatisfied
President	84	69
Government	67	37
Parliament	37	19

Source: *IVVM Bulletin 95–06*, question 1. (N=998)

functions, referring to poor preparation of the members and of enactment of "bad laws." The second largest proportion (21 percent) refer to personal misuse of office, such as pursuit of money or property, and abuse of parliamentary immunity (data not shown). These references are topical; they are stated after news of scandal and allegations of undesirable activity by members or parties in parliament.

If the question shifts from the whole parliament as a single institution to the activity of one's representatives in the institution, however, a different and more positive pattern emerges. On the question "Do your party deputies act in support of your ideas," the "definitely yes" responses varied from 12 percent to 24 percent on the left-right scale, with the "center" voters at the low end of that range. A majority of all three sets of voters responded "rather yes" to the question (table 5.7). By party, the Left Block and Communist Party supporters were the most split between the strongly positive and the most negative. The distributions of responses, both for the whole public and by party, vary markedly from the other questions discussed in this section.

Table 5.7 *Beliefs about representation by party deputies in the Czech Republic (by party identification)*

Beliefs	% All	Government parties			Opposition parties	
		% CDP	% CDA	% CDU-CPP	% CSDP	% Communist
Definitely yes	19.1	22.1	11.3	23.5	17.1	29.7
Rather yes	52.5	60.3	61.3	58.8	62.0	43.9
Rather no	18.6	14.7	21.8	12.6	16.1	15.5
Definitely no	6.6	2.5	4.8	4.2	4.1	10.8

Question: "Do your party deputies act in support of your views?"

Source: STEM (Center for Empirical Research), July 1995.

Public problems and government performance

Public opinion is much more differentiated on specific social problems than in general evaluations. Over 90 percent named three major social problems: crime, corruption in the state, and organized crime. At the other end, 50 percent or fewer rated Romany, refugees, Slovakian relations, and definition of territorial subunits as serious problems. Economic reform, however, was rated as a problem by 85 percent.

These social condition evaluations do have direct consequences for public evaluations of government performance. Over 50 percent evaluated government performance as "good" in two categories": economic reform and relations with Slovakia, while 12 percent or fewer evaluated government peformance as "good" on the three top problems of crime, state corruption, and organized criminality (data not shown). Analysts speculate that the popular worry about crime and corruption has not directly translated into cynicism about either the state or democracy.

Who understands what?

As a final view of the Czech public in relationship to their many systemic changes, they have been asked, "Do you understand what's happening in politics?" Only 5 percent said "definitely yes," while 14 percent responded, "definitely no." By self-placement on a left–right scale, the highest "definitely yes" responses came from the right, at 7 percent. The centrists were the most "definitely no," at 19 percent. By party, two government parties and the communists expressed the greatest confidence in their understanding (the highest at 8 percent), while the independents, along with the Christian Democratic Union–Czech Peoples Party as a government party, gave the highest "definitely no" responses. In only the plurality government party, did the combined "yes" responses outnumber the combined "no" responses (data not shown). In conjunction with the previous question about party deputies, the supporters of most parties seem to like, but not understand, what they see in contemporary politics.

The Czech public seems to have an approximate understanding of their new political and economic circumstances, and gives cautious, more pragmatic than cynical, approval.

Political parties and the party system

The party system predates the formation of the new Republic. The political parties of the Czech Republic individually, and their collective relationship in a party system, were formed in the first years of the democratic transformation within the Czechoslovakian Federation. With the dissolution of the Federation, the whole party system and its leaders within the Czech Republic simply shifted their actions from the Federation to the Republic, from one side of the Vltava to the other.

Nothing more symbolized the dissolution of the Federation than the decision, immediately following the 1992 elections, of Václav Klaus, leader of the plurality Civic Democratic Party, that he would become prime minister of the Czech Republic rather than of the Czechoslovakian Federation. When the Federation collapsed, the Republic became the one existing sovereign state available to the existing parties and their leaders.

Three elections

In the half decade of postcommunist democracy, the Czech Republic has held only three elections. The parliament elected in 1992, and the government coalition formed from that election, served a full four year term. In the whole region, only Hungary has had a similar record of cabinet longevity in its early postcommunist electoral term.

The three elections have been very different. The initial one, in 1990, was part of the regime change process. It, like most of the other initial elections of the region, was a referendum on the fall of communism (table 5.8). It was not a choice of parties and programs; neither was it a "founding" election as in the Latin transitions. Rather, it was a plebiscite on the end of communism. The democratic system remained to be "founded."

One of the early actions of the reconstructed Federal Assembly was adoption of a new law to not only permit, but to encourage the formation of political parties.[66] By March 1990, thirty-eight groups had registered at the Interior Ministry; by June, seventy-nine groups were registered, while

Table 5.8 *Party votes and seats in elections to the Federal Assembly and National Councils in Czechoslovakia, 1990*

| | Chamber of People | | | Chamber of Nations | | | | National Councils | | | |
| | Votes | | Seats | Votes | | Seats | | Votes | | Seats | |
Republic and party	N	%	N	N	%	N	%	N	%	N	%
Czech Republic											
Civic Forum	3,851,172	53.15	68	3,613,513	49.96	50	66.67	3,569,201	49.50	127	63.50
Communist Party	976,996	13.48	15	997,919	13.80	12	16.00	954,690	13.24	32	16.00
Christian & Democratic Union	629,359	8.69	9	633,053	8.75	6	8.00	607,134	8.42	19	9.50
Moravian Silesian Movement (MSDMS)	572,015	7.89	9	658,477	9.10	7	9.33	723,609	10.03	22	11.00
Subtotal	6,029,542	83.21	101	5,902,962	81.61	75	100.00	5,854,634	81.19	200	100.00
All others	1,215,908	16.79	–	1,329,163	18.39	–	–	1,356,413	18.81	–	–
Republic total	7,245,450	100.00	101	7,232,125	100.00	75	100.00	7,211,047	100.00	200	100.00
Slovakia											
Public Against Violence (PAV)	1,104,125	32.54	19	1,262,278	37.28	33	44.00	991,285	29.35	48	32.00
Christian Democratic Movement	644,008	18.98	11	564,172	16.66	14	18.67	648,782	19.21	31	20.67
Communist Party	468,411	13.81	8	451,740	13.43	12	16.00	450,855	13.35	22	14.67
Slovak National Party	372,025	10.96	6	387,387	11.44	9	12.00	470,984	13.94	22	14.67
Coexistence	291,287	8.58	5	287,426	8.49	7	9.33	292,636	8.66	14	9.33
Democratic Party	149,310	4.40	7	124,561	4.67	–	–	148,567	4.40	7	4.67
Green Party	108,542	3.49	6	87,366	4.00	–	–	117,871	3.49	6	4.00
Subtotal	2,879,856	84.87	49	2,953,003	87.30	75	100.00	2,854,542	92.40	150	100.00
All others	513,190	15.13	–	433,152	12.70	–	–	256,746	7.60	–	–
Republic total	3,393,046	100.00	49	3,386,155	100.00	75	100.00	3,111,288	100.00	150	100.00
Federation total			150			150					

Notes: Includes parties over 3% or 5% in one Republic per Republic. The entries "all others" include all parties under threshold for each chamber per Republic. Parties listed by size for Chamber of People by Republic. Slovakia total votes tabulated by author.

Source: Statisticka ročenka, Ceske a Slovenske Federativne Republiky (1991), pp. 629–30.

Table 5.9 *Party formation in the Czechoslovakian Chamber of People, by republic, April 1, 1991*

Republic/Party	No. of seats	% of seats
Czech Republic		
Civic Forum (CF)		
Civic Democratic Party (CDP)	30	20.00
Civic Democratic Alliance (CDA)	5	3.33
Civic Movement (CM)	21	14.00
Social Democrat Orientation	7	4.67
Independent	3	2.00
subtotal	66	44.00
Moravian Silesian Movement (MSDMS)		
MSDMS I	4	2.67
MSDMS II	5	3.33
Christian Democratic Union (CDU)		
Christian Democratic Union (CDU-CPP)	7	4.67
Christian Democratic Party (ChDP)	3	2.00
Subtotal	85	56.67
Slovakia		
Public Against Violence (PAV)		
Civic Democratic Union-Public Against Violence	8	5.33
Movement Democratic Slovakia (MDS)	8	5.33
Subtotal	16	10.67
Christian Democratic Movement	8	5.33
Slovakian Christian Democratic Movement	4	2.67
Slovakian National Party	4	2.67
Hungarian Minority-Coexistence	5	3.33
Subtotal	37	24.67
Both regions		
Communist		
CPBM Czech Communist	13	8.67
SDL Democratic Left-Slovakia	8	5.33
subtotal	21	14.00
Other/Independents	7	4.67
Subtotal	28	18.67
Total	150	100.00

Sources: Czechoslovakian Federal Assembly Directory and roll call documents.

another twenty-seven were denied registration for failure to meet the formal criteria such as a full list of officers.[67] As of January 1, 1996, eighty-six parties and movements had been registered, of which thirteen had ceased activity, leaving a pool of seventy-three electoral organizations to begin the 1996 election year.[68]

In the June 1990 initial election, thirteen electoral lists were offered to the Czech National Council, of which four won seats. The Civic Forum won

Table 5.10 *Party votes and seats in elections to the Federal Assembly and National Councils in Czechoslovakia, 1992*

	Chamber of People			Chamber of Nations				National Councils			
	Votes		Seats	Votes		Seats		Votes		Seats	
Republic and Party	N	%	N	N	%	N	%	N	%	N	%
Czech Republic											
Civic Democratic Party (CDP-ChDP)	2,200,937	33.90	48	2,168,421	33.43	37	49.33	1,924,483	29.73	76	38.00
Left Bloc (LB)	926,228	14.27	19	939,197	14.48	15	20.00	909,490	14.05	35	17.50
Czech Social Democrats (CSDP)	489,030	7.67	10	440,806	6.80	6	8.00	422,736	6.53	16	8.00
Republican Association (RA-RPC)	420,848	6.48	8	413,459	6.37	6	8.00	387,026	5.98	14	7.00
Christian Dem. Union (CDU-CPP)	388,122	5.98	7	394,296	6.08	6	8.00	406,341	6.28	15	7.50
Liberal Social Union (LSU)	378,962	5.84	7	383,182	6.06	5	6.67	421,988	6.52	16	8.00
Civic Democratic Alliance (CDA)								383,705	5.93	14	7.00
Moravia/Silesia Movement (MSDMS)								380,088	5.87	14	7.00
Subtotal	4,804,127	74.14	99	4,749,361	73.22	75	80.89	5,235,857	80.89	200	100.00
All others	1,679,335	25.86	–	1,736,378	26.78	–	19.11	1,237,393	19.11	–	–
Republic total	6,483,462	100.00	99	6,485,739	100.00	75	100.00	6,473,250	100.00	200	100.00
Slovakia											
Movement Dem. Slovakia (MDS)	1,036,459	33.53	24	1,045,395	33.85	33	44.00	1,148,625	37.26	74	49.33
Democratic Left (PDL)	446,230	14.44	10	433,750	14.04	13	17.33	453,203	14.70	29	19.33
Slovak National Party	290,249	9.39	6	288,864	9.35	9	12.00	244,527	7.93	15	10.00
Christian Democratic Movement	277,061	8.96	6	272,100	8.81	8	10.67	273,945	8.88	18	12.00
Coexistence	227,925	7.37	5	228,219	7.39	7	9.33	228,885	7.42	14	9.33
Slovak Social Democrats				188,223	6.09	5	6.67				
Subtotal	2,277,924	73.69	51	2,456,551	79.53	75	76.19	2,349,185	76.19	150	100.00
All others	813,050	26.31	–	631,875	20.47	–	23.81	733,511	23.81	–	–
Republic total	3,090,974	100.00	51	3,088,426	100.00	75	100.00	3,072,696	100.00	150	100.00
Federation total	9,574,436		150			150				150	

Note: Includes parties over 5% in one Republic per chamber. The entries "all others" include all parties under 5% for each chamber per Republic. Parties are listed by size for Chamber of People by Republic.

Sources: ČSTK, "Volby 92," June 7, 1992; Federal Election Commission, "1992 Report Disk"; and *Rude Pravo*, June 11, 1992.

49.5 percent of the vote and 63.5 percent of the seats. It was not a political party in a Western sense, and indeed, aspired to be something very different and better: a broad social movement uniting diverse and even opposed groups, leaders and policies. It was "above" politics.

The electoral groupings participating in the initial elections were regime-change movements and proto-parties. The formation of political parties occurred after the initial election, and largely occurred within the three parliaments of the Federation.

Much of the dynamic of the subsequent formation of political parties originated by splits, which were anticipated, within the Civic Forum following the initial regime change election (table 5.9). The Civic Forum knowingly included a variety of party groups which, knowingly, joined the Civic Forum electoral umbrella in the hopes of gaining at least some parliamentary seats.[69]

In the 1992 election, by contrast, political parties were the main contenders (table 5.10). The surviving organization of the original Civic Forum, the Civic Movement, did not win any seats in the new parliaments. It was the one group which insisted on maintaining the "movement" name and diversity, as opposed to becoming a mere "political party."

The 1992 election had the unexpected (and perhaps unintended) consequence of splitting the Federation into two separate Republics. The plurality winners in the two Republics could agree on only two items: first, they agreed they could not agree on how to govern together, and thus second, they agreed to split the state.[70]

The 1992 election was, in effect, two separate elections, one in each of the two Republics. The issues were different, as were the participants. While the broad regime change movement had disappeared in a series of successor parties in the Czech Republic, in Slovakia, one regime change movement (Public Against Violence) was succeeded by another (Movement for a Democratic Slovakia).

In the Czech Republic, the plurality winner succeeded in forming a four party coalition, with 105 of the 200 seats, which remained in office for the entirety of the stipulated four year term. Only two parties (Republican Association and Liberal Social Union) entered parliament in the 1992 election which previously had no parliamentary members, illustrating the broader trend that party formation in the new democracies of Central Europe tends to be parliamentary-centered.[71]

The 1996 parliamentary election was doubly complicated by the new Senate: not only was a new legislative chamber added to the Chamber of Deputies, but it had an entirely different election system, with elections occurring in November following the June elections to the Chamber of Deputies.

The June election produced a near-stalemate, with the incumbent government coalition of three parties obtaining ninety-nine seats, two seats short of an absolute majority (table 5.12). Among the non-government parties, the orthodox Communist Party completely eclipsed the more moderate Left Bloc, and two small centrist parties were eliminated from the Chamber. The nationalist Republican Association, which had been losing seats during the term, gained seats and votes over 1992. The Czech Social Democrats became the second largest party in the Chamber of Deputies.

Though there was no clear single winner in this election, by either party or ideology, nevertheless the party system was simplified in that fewer parties entered the Chamber of Deputies than previously, and further, only 9 percent of the votes were cast for small below-threshold parties, contrasting with 19 percent in the 1992 election.

The inconclusive results in June greatly escalated the importance of the Senate elections in November. The government parties won fifty-two (64 percent) of the total of eighty-one senate seats, thus somewhat strengthening the position of the government. The beginning year of a new parliamentary term, 1996, ended with an unstable balance between government and non-government parties.

In voter participation, the series of three elections began at an astoundingly high rate of 96 percent in 1990, the initial regime change election. In the second, 1992, voter turnout was 85 percent, while it declined further to 76 percent in the June 1996 elections for the Chamber of Deputies, and even further to 35 percent and 30 percent in the two rounds of senate elections.

Party changes, 1992–96

Within the relatively long time span of a four-year term, and below the surface appearance of political stability, there were many changes among the parliamentary political parties. Changes occurred more among the opposition than government parties.

The Communist Party split, the nationalistic Republican Association lost members, and the loose and heterogeneous electoral coalition, LSU, also split. The Moravian-based party (MSDMS) changed names and membership several times.[72] Among the opposition parties, only the Czech Social Democrats gained parliamentary members and also gained in the public opinion polls (tables 5.11 and 5.12). In fall 1995, the Liberal National Socialist Party, the remnant of the LSU electoral coalition of 1992, merged with the Free Democrats. The latter is the renamed remnant of the Civic Forum and then the Civic Movement, led by Jiři Dienstbier. By this merger, the Civic Movement group once again gained a parliamentary foothold, in the hopes of building a centrist party for the 1996 elections.[73] The merged party

Table 5.11 *Changes in number and percentage of party seats in the Czech Parliament, 1992–95 (by government alignment of parties)*

Party and Government Status	1992 Election N	1992 Election %	Aug. 1994 N	Aug. 1994 %	May 1995 N	May 1995 %	Oct. 1995 N	Oct. 1995 %
Government								
CDP	66	33.00	65	32.50	66	33.00	66	33.00
CDU-CPP	15	7.50	15	7.50	18	9.00	24	12.00
CDA	14	7.00	15	7.50	16	8.00	16	8.00
ChDP	10	5.00	10	5.00	5	2.50	6	3.00
ChDP-I					5	2.50	0	0.00
Subtotal	105		105		110		112	
Opposition								
Left Bloc	35	17.50	24	12.00	24	12.00	23	11.50
CPBM	10	5.00	10	5.00	10	5.00		
CSDP	16	8.00	18	9.00	20	10.00	24	12.00
LSU	16	8.00	9	4.50	0	0.00		0.00
LNSP	5	2.50	5	2.50	6	3.00		
MSDMS	14	7.00	7	3.50		0.00		0.00
CMCP	9	4.50		0.00		0.00		
CMCU	16	8.00	15	7.50				
RA-RPC	14	7.00	8	4.00	6	3.00	5	2.50
Independents			5	2.50	9	4.50	5	2.50
Subtotal	95		95		90		88	
Republic total	200	100.00	200	100.00	200	100.00	200	100.00

Notes: Acronyms: CDA – Civic Democratic Alliance; CDP – Civic Democratic Party; CDP-ChDP – Civic Democratic Party-Christian Democratic Party; CDU-CPP – Christian and Democratic Union-Czechoslovakian People's Party; CMCP – Czech-Moravia Center Party; CMCU – Czech-Moravian Center Union; CPBM – Communist Party of Bohemia and Moravia; CSDP – Czech Social Democratic Party; CSDP – Czech Social Democratic Party; LNSP - Liberal National Socialist Party; LSU – Liberal Social Union; MSDMS – Movement for Self-Governing Democracy-Society for Moravia and Silesia; RA-RPC – Association for the Republic-Republican Party of Czechoslovakia.

Sources: 1992 Election: Federal Election Commission, "1992 Report Disk"; August 1994: Reschova and Syllova, "The Legislature of the Czech Republic," in *The New Parliaments of Central and Eastern Europe*, ed. Olson and Norton (1996), Table 7; May 1995: *Parliamentni Zpravodaj* 5/1995, p. 200; October 1995: *Parliamentni Zpravodaj* 2/1995-96, p. 67.

began life with a combined name, Free Democrats–Liberal National Socialists (FD-LNSP).

The four government parties also experienced internal changes. The Christian Democratic Party (ChDP) decided to merge with the plurality Civic Democratic Party, leading to a split among its parliamentary delegation into two separate clubs. The parliamentary dissidents, grouped in the club

Table 5.12 *Chamber of Deputies votes and seats in the Czech Republic: winning parties by alliances, 1992 and 1996*

1992 Party grouping	Votes %	Seats N	Seats %	1996 Party grouping	Votes %	Seats N	Seats %
Government				**Pro-CDP**			
CDP-ChDP	29.73	76	38.00	CDP	29.62	68	34.00
CDU-CPP	6.28	15	7.50	CDU-CPP	8.08	18	9.00
CDA	5.93	14	7.00	CDA	6.36	13	6.50
Subtotal		105		Subtotal		99	
Opposition				**Anti-CDP**			
Left Bloc	14.05	35	17.50	CPBM	10.33	22	11.00
CSDP	6.53	16	8.00	CSDP	28.44	61	30.50
RA-RPC	5.98	14	7.00	RA-RPC	8.01	18	9.00
LSU	6.52	16	8.00	CNM		0	.00
MSDMS	5.87	14	7.00	CMCU		0	.00
Subtotal		95		Subtotal		101	
Combined subtotal	80.89			Combined subtotal	90.84		
All others	19.11			All others	9.16		
Republic total	100.00	200	100.00	Republic total	100.00	200	100.00

Notes: 1996 votes/seats are preliminary/unofficial; acronyms: CDA – Civic Democratic Alliance; CDP – Civic Democratic Party; CDP-ChDP – Civic Democratic Party-Christian Democratic Party; CDU-CPP – Christian and Democratic Union-Czechoslovakian People's Party; CMCU – Czech-Moravian Center Union; CNM – Civic National Movement; CPBM – Communist Party of Bohemia and Moravia; CSDP – Czech Social Democratic Party; LSU – Liberal Social Union; MSDMS – Movement for Self-Governing Democracy-Society for Moravia and Silesia; RA-RPC – Association for the Republic-Republican Party of Czechoslovakia.

Sources: for 1992, ČSTK, "Volby 92," June 7, 1992; Federal Election Commission, "1992 Report Disk"; and *Rude Pravo*, June 11, 1992; for 1996: CTK News Summary, June 3, 1996 (e-mail).

Christian Democrats–Independent, soon merged with the Christian Democratic Union–Czech Peoples' Party club (CDU-CPP).

The net result in the distribution of parliamentary power was a slight increase in the strength of the government coalition, the emergence of independent members, and a series of splits among the opposition parties.

These party changes paralleled shifts in public opinion, with the Social Democrats becoming more popular, rivaling the Civic Democratic Party, and the others in danger of falling below the 5 percent threshold. The parties, including the Christian Democratic Party, are attempting to find an organizational vehicle to both define their program and to attract voter support.

A pattern of three coalitions could have developed within the first term: a Civic Democratic Party group on the political right, a Social Democratic Party group on the left, with a Centrist coalition among the newly created Free Democrats-Liberal group joined by the Christian Democratic Union-Czech Peoples Party. If the results of the 1996 election had duplicated those of 1992, the latter party could have occupied the swing position.

This potential pattern of three coalitions, however, also depended upon the electoral fate of the other parties, including the two communist groups, the nationalist Republican Association, and the Czech-Moravian Center Union. In the 1996 election to the Chamber of Deputies, the government coalition of three parties lost their majority, but no other viable coalition was possible to form a new government. Though the Social Democrats were by far the largest single gainer in seats, the relative gain by the Communists and Republican Association, and the loss of centrist parties, deprived them of potential cooperative partners.

It was the Social Democrats who came to occupy the critical swing position after the 1996 election. They were awarded seats in the new parliament's management structure, of Speaker and also of several committee chair positions, and they, in turn, supported the continuation of the old government as a minority government. Unlike Poland and Hungary, in which the elections have produced a change in governments, in the Czech Republic, the new election continued the existing government coalition (see table 5.12).

The Czech party system includes several parties with an historical continuity back through the communist era to the prewar Republic, while others are more clearly "post-Forum" and post-transition new parties. The paths of party formation are indicated in table 5.13. The dynamics of party changes, and their consequences for governmental stability, have been very different between the Czech and Slovak Republics since their independence from each other. In the latter, the government parties lost enough members to force a change in governments, while in the former, party changes have concentrated among the opposition parties. Indeed, the Czech Republic is the only postcommunist democracy in the whole region in which the government has gained strength in parliament rather than losing seats within a single term of office.

Issue dimensionality

The effort by researchers, both West and East, to interpret the emerging kaleidoscope of political parties in the new democracies of Central Europe in left–right terms is much easier in the Czech Republic than elsewhere. There

Table 5.13 *Paths of party formation in the Czech Republic, 1946–95, and by government alignment, 1992–95*

1946 vote %	Communist era	Seats in Parliament	1990 Czech National Council	Vote %	1990 Local vote %	Party & alignment 1992–95	1992 vote %	1994 local vote %	1995 public opinion
						Government			
			Civic Forum	49.5	35	CDP	29.7	29.5	29
						CDA	5.9	7	7
					3	ChDP	0	1	1
20	Cz.-Slov. Peoples	5	CDU	8.4	11	CDU-CPP	6.3	8.6	8
						Opposition			
40	CP	75	CP	13.2	17	Left Bloc	14.1	.3	2
						CPBM	14.7	9	
16	CSDP		CSDP	4.1	5	CSDP	6.5	8.7	24
			Agric. Party	4.1	3	LSU	6.5	.1	
24	Czech Nat'l Soc.	5	Social. Party	2.7	3	LNSP		1.2	
			Green Party	4.1	3	Green Party		.2	
			MSDMS	10	4	MSDMS	5.9	0	
						CMCU		.8	1
						RA-RPC	5.9	2.6	3
			Independents		10	Independents		11.5	
	Other	15	Other	3.9	9	Other	19	13.8	16
100		100		100	100	Total	99.8	100	100

Note: For acronyms, see table 5.12.

Sources: 1946, 1990 and 1990 Local: Gordon Wightman, "Czechoslovakia," in *New Political Parties of Eastern Europe and the Soviet Union*, ed. B. Szajkowski (1991); Communist: Marek Bankowicz and J. Dellenbrant, "The Party System of Czechoslovakia," in *East European Multi-Party Systems*, ed. Sten Berglund et al. (1988); 1992 Parliamentary Election: Federal Election Commission, "1992 Report Disk"; 1994 Local: Czech Statistical Office, "Vysledky voleb '94"; 1995 Public Opinion: STEM (July).

is not, however, complete agreement on where the parties fit on such a continuum.

Two major issue dimensions seem present in contemporary Czech politics: economic issues and liberty-authority issues. Most post-Forum parties are on the right on economic issues (pro-market with low state involvement), and are on the liberty end of the authority scale. The two Christian parties, however, while they tend toward the market end of the economic scale, defend Church prerogatives in general and on property restitution questions in particular.

On the left, the two communist parties, and the Social Democrats, are market reform parties with a relatively greater emphasis on state involvement, and, like the secular postforum parties, are on the liberty end of the other dimension.

By one schema, the parties could be expected to align on a two-dimensional scale in a clear ordering: Communist and Socialist parties on the left, postforum parties on the right, with Christian parties on the economic right but on the authoritarian end of the liberty scale.[74]

Within parliament, in 1995 at least, the political parties have tended to vote somewhat differently, in two clusters. The postforum parties, both Christian parties, and the Liberal Social Union groupings, have voted together, forming a right coalition. On the left, the two communist parties and the Social Democrats tend to vote together, with the Social Democrats and Left Bloc sometimes together, leaving the Communist Party to define the left end of a voting continuum.

Two parties, however, do not fit this clustering pattern. The nationalist Republican Association tends to vote differently from all the others; more closely, however, to the Communist Party on the left, than to any other party. The Czech–Moravian Center Union has been the most variable party in its positioning relative to the others. At times, it has voted with the right, at times with the left, and at other times, has formed a centrist coalition with the Social Democrats.[75]

The electoral system

The apparent stability of the Czech party system is sustained by several features of the electoral system: bicameralism, timing and frequency of elections, and the vote threshold.

Bicameralism is important because of the new Czech Constitution: The Senate's consent would be required to dissolve parliament prior to a regularly scheduled election. Since, however, the Senate was not created until 1996, there was no legal means by which earlier elections could have been called.

Elections are action-forcing events. Had elections been held two or even three years following the formation of the Republic, the party system could have experienced more change. Either new parties could have attempted to win election, or their relative strength could have changed. In new democracies in this region with more frequent elections, the party results have shifted dramatically from one election to the next; this possibility has not existed in the Czech Republic.

The sure knowledge in 1995 that a parliamentary election would be held in 1996 stimulated election-oriented activity. Among the governmental coalition parties, the Christian Democratic Party (ChDP) formally decided to merge with the plurality party, Civic Democratic Party (CDP) with which they were affiliated in an electoral coalition in 1992. That party had never faced the electorate as a free-standing party (only in coalition) in parliamentary elections, and did not do very well in the 1994 local elections.

The impending election also spurred efforts to create the constitutionally-mandated Senate. The chief obstacle to its formation had been disagreements within the government coalition over the election system. The four government coalition parties agreed on a single member majority election system,[76] but only one year in advance of the election. The 1996 elections were held for both chambers, but with very different election systems, presenting a similar contrast as in Poland between the two chambers.

The Czech Republic also suggests that electoral thresholds are important in proportional representation election systems. The 5 percent threshold in 1992 had the effect of completely removing from parliaments (both Federal and Republic) the leaders of the democratic reform movement of 1990 who were both federalist in state questions and centrist on economic policy. The 5 percent threshold figure was directly copied from the German example, without thought about possible results of different levels of the threshold. It is possible that five percent is too strict a barrier in the beginning stages of new democratic political systems. A three percent threshold in 1992, for example, would have permitted the entry of three additional parties in the Federal Assembly, three in the Slovak National Council, and one in the Czech National Council.[77] While in stable democracies, the threshold is thought to restrain the growth of small extremist parties, in the Czech and Federation experience, the threshold has removed from all three parliaments the moderate parties, those which were centrist in economic policy and federalist in state policy.

There is a fourth characteristic of the Czech election system which has an effect on the party system. The entire country is divided into only eight election districts, with 13–41 seats per district. The large number of seats per districts has the effect of increasing proportionality in seat distribution. In combination with the high electoral threshold, however, the result is to reduce the number of parties in parliament. Proportionality is increased only among the winning parties. In 1992, 19 percent of the vote went to parties not winning any seats because of the threshold, while that number decreased to 9 percent in 1996.

It is in this respect that the proposed single member district system for the Senate may have its greatest differential impact on the party system. The eighty-one single-member districts, may produce a very different constellation of parties than does the large multi-member district Chamber of Deputies. The majority requirement, forcing two rounds of elections as in the French system, may lead to a variety of unanticipated coalitions. On the other hand, Poland has the same contrast in electoral systems between the two chambers; yet, similar party configurations have been found in the two chambers at each election period. The Czechs, however, have added a new variation: the election to the two chambers occurs several months apart.

Campaign finance

Campaign finance has an important impact on political parties. Quite apart from the sheer amount of funds required for an active party to wage an active campaign, campaign finance has been important in the Czech Republic in at least five respects.

First, there have been allegations of favoritism, or attempts to gain favor, between fund providers and receivers. Some of the allegations raise accusations of legal violations. Second, campaign finance has an important consequence for the internal distribution of power within parties. For example, local units of parties are permitted to design and publish their own election materials, but the funding for those materials comes from national headquarters.[78] There is a third consequence for parties from campaign finance. Some parties are still carrying a heavy debt burden incurred from bank loans for the 1992 campaign. Their ability to campaign effectively in the next election is correspondingly reduced. Fourth, parties in parliament receive public funding for parliamentary offices. Space, phones, equipment, a car, supplies and staff are provided each parliamentary party. While needed for their work in parliament, those facilities also have an election campaign utility. Fifth, campaign finance carries its own threshold. While 5 percent is the minimum vote required to gain parliamentary seats, 3 percent is the minimum to receive public funding for campaign expenses, raised from 2 percent minimum in the 1992 election. As parliamentary parties have split and reformed, the connection between them and their electoral parties weakened.

Public funding for the 1992 election, for those parties winning seats, ranged from 15 ml korun to 94 ml korun. The 1994 law on political parties provided an annual public payment to parties based upon both their votes in the last election and upon the number of seats won in parliament. The largest sums (from 9 to 37 ml korun annually) were paid to the Republican Association (lowest) to the Civic Democratic Party (highest) in the 1995–96 period. Several parties without representation in parliament also receive funding by this formula; the largest sum, 3.3 ml korun, went to the Free Democrats.[79] Some parties survive on campaign funding but lack current parliamentary seats, while some parliamentary clubs lack the support of an external party.

Governmental structure

The broader structure of the governmental system also impacts the stability of the party system. The characteristics of the presidential office and the absence of federalism both have had the effect of increasing the importance of parliament and of the parties within parliament.

The presidential office is filled by parliamentary selection. The current incumbent, Václav Havel, was the obvious choice for president of the Federation in 1989; he was then selected by parliament as the first president of the new Czech Republic. The president has been restrained in his conduct of the office; he has raised no demands or even suggestions which would interfere with parliament and its functioning. His several legislative vetoes have been overridden. It was the president, however, who resolved the disputed question among the government parties, of the timing of Senate elections to be held separately from the lower chamber elections in 1996.[80]

In the new and unitary Czech Republic, a constant and unresolved policy question concerns the definition, functioning, and authority of lower regional units of government. In the absence of either formal constitutional autonomy or independent finance, the many local municipalities do not act as a restraint upon the organization and conduct of national policy or politics. Though the 1994 local elections produced many results in electoral coalitions which contradict national level relationships, the general vote pattern was consistent with the levels and sources of votes for parties in the 1992 parliamentary elections. The suggestion of a federal structure, advocated by Moravian groups, has largely been ignored, perhaps as a reaction to the release from the tensions produced by that same question in relationship to Slovakia.

Ministries have, as a practical matter, wide powers of discretion. Questions have not been raised about the independence of a state bureaucracy, or of quasi-governmental entities, from the government. There are questions of parliamentary knowledge and control over such bodies, but these questions occur more within the context of policy disputes than of partisan or government–opposition relations. Parliament introduced in 1995 the new practice of interpellation, as a means of increasing its knowledge of government and ministry activity.

Communist, nationalist and regional parties

The Communist Party has split in parliament into an orthodox Communist Party of Bohemia and Moravia (CPBM) and a more reformist Left Bloc (LB). Earlier, the Federation-wide Communist Party split into two regional groups, with very different political attitudes; the Slovakian Party was clearly reformist, while the Czech party remained orthodox.[81]

In parliament, the communist parties act as normal parties within democratic deliberative and voting assemblies. Their deputies work within existing parliamentary procedures, debate freely, and accept the outcome of legislative voting, both in committee and on the floor. In the three elections held within the Czech Republic, the Communist Party and its candidates have acted as have all other parties. They identified their likely sources of electoral strength, held campaign meetings, and accepted the results of the vote on election night. The geography of their current vote is strikingly similar to the 1946 elections.[82]

One party is less conventional in its participation in the political process. The Republican Association (RA-RPC) is a nationalist party, with rhetoric, parades and street meetings in defense of Czech people and in attacks against foreigners and Gypsies. In the 1992 election, they demanded that Ruthenia, the eastern portion of the Federation taken by the Soviets at the end of World War II, be returned to the Federation. The Party was, however, silent at the time of the split of the Federation.

This group has engaged in highly visible actions. Its first moment of parliamentary notoriety was a verbal attack upon Václav Havel as presidential candidate during the live TV broadcast of the presidential selection.[83] Its second moment of undivided attention in both parliament and mass media occurred in July 1995, when the question was raised of removing parliamentary immunity from one of its deputies.

One example of high publicity action has been to take physical control of the area surrounding the statue of King Wenceslas at the annual observance of Czech independence. Another has been publication and distribution of a false document, attributed to Chancellor Kohl, in which Kohl allegedly assured the Sudeten Germans that the Czech government would honor their claims to expropriated property. This pamphlet was traced directly to the leader of the Republican parliamentary group, raising questions of the applicability of parliamentary immunity to prosecution for criminal acts.[84]

Its parliamentary contingent steadily lost members in the 1992–96 term. It demands membership on important committees, but its members are reported to not participate in committee work. It lost additional members following the immunity debate and vote.

Parties do tend to have different regional and local sources of electoral support. One, the Moravian-Silesian Movement, has appealed only to the two electoral districts in Moravia, while the Christian Democratic Union–Czech Peoples Party mainly appeals to Catholic inclined voters, who tend to be more found in the Moravian districts than elsewhere in the country. Both the Communists and the Christian parties appeal to the rural electorate. Only the communists and Civic Democratic Party have support throughout the whole country.

Violence has not been part of the activity of leaders and groups active in electoral politics or active through political parties. The provocative actions of the Republican Association have not included acts of physical violence. So far, there is little evidence to directly associate skinhead attacks upon Romany youth with either tactics or policies of political parties,[85] even though Republican Association voter support concentrates in districts with high Romany population.[86]

Government coalition

The ability of a coalition of four parties to gain a majority of votes and parliamentary seats, and their ability to not split from the coalition, both created and sustained a single government since the 1992 elections. The government's policies have been clearest on the two issues of the split of the Federation, and on economic reform. The combination of economic success has validated both policies.

Other issues have found ample divisions within the coalition. The questions of regional boundaries and their legal competence have split the several parties within the coalition, while the issue of church property restitution has split the two Catholic oriented parties (ChDP and CDU-CPP) from the other and more dominant parties (CDP and CDA) in the coalition. Social services and health policies have also divided the coalition parties. Though one of the coalition parties (ChDP) split over the question of affiliation with the larger coalition party (CDP), neither faction from that party withdrew support from the government. A long standing dispute within the coalition over the electoral law to the Senate was resolved only under the time pressure of an election.

Conclusion

The Czech Republic has experienced a double transition; first, from communism to democracy, and second, from one part of a larger country to sovereignty as its own complete country. It gives every appearance of having made both transitions thoroughly and smoothly.

Both transitions, while rooted in the past, reflect current developments. The collapse of the Soviet Union permitted, and the collapse of communist rule in the countries of East Central Europe led, as was expected, to the democratic transition. Less anticipated, however, was the eruption of the question of the legal structure binding Czechs and Slovaks in a common state.

The state question could be traced back to the origins of Czechoslovakia, as a newly independent state created at the end of World War I. The Slovaks and Czechs, each in a different part of the Austro-Hungarian Empire, had never previously shared a common state. A sense of Slovakian nationalism slowly grew during the First Republic, and was given added impetus during both Nazi occupation and the communist reform period of 1968–69. If, with the collapse of communism, freedom meant economic reform in the Czech Republic, it meant increased autonomy in the Slovak Republic.

Both democratic and economic reform could also be traced back to the First Republic. The commercial and industrial base of the new country, especially the Czech portion, provided both the experience and facilities for economic reform in 1989. Likewise, the governmental institutions of cabinet and parliament, and the institutions of political parties and elections, provided the pattern for the reconstruction of, interpreted as a return to, a democratic political system.

The simultaneity and interaction of state and political reform in the Czechoslovakian Federation, led to the split of the state. Perhaps the history of Slovak-Czech relations increased the possibility of the split of the Federation; it was the democratic political system which directed the "velvet divorce" into peaceful channels.

The first government and parliament of the newly independent Czech Republic has had the luxury of serving a full four-year term of office. Based upon a four-party majority (beginning with 105 seats of 200), government and parliament have had the opportunity both to define a consistent set of policies and to build themselves as stable institutions. The multiparty system with proportional representation and a government coalition all reflect the legacy of the First Republic. It did take a full three years, however, for the government parties to agree among themselves on the formation of the new Senate.

Within the context of institutional and policy stability, both political parties and interest groups have had an opportunity to develop their own organizations. Political parties, especially in opposition, have formed and dissolved new groupings, and members of parliament have joined and departed from parliamentary parties. This process of party definition and discovery accelerated in the year preceding the Spring 1996 election.

Interest group formation is more problematic. Economic groups, both sectoral and general, have developed more rapidly than nonprofit and civic organizations. The former have been required by the government in its development of a tripartite negotiation body for both economic and social policy questions. It is only in 1995 that the legal and financial status of the latter have been defined in law. Many groups, including church denominations, receive financial support from the state through relevant ministries.

The Czech public seems to welcome political democracy and economic reform in general, but to also have a restrained or cautious sense of approval of specific policies, and of governmental institutions and practices. The mass media have undergone dramatic change. The few communist era newspapers have been replaced by many privately owned papers, radio stations are numerous and private, and the two government TV channels have been complemented by one new private channel. Cable TV also provides numerous channels from other countries. Questions of both foreign control and of ethics have arisen in the new media environment.

Many questions of both ethics and law are faced in a period of rapid transition. Potential conflicts of interest among public officials, especially in the mix of public authority and private financial gain, are newly created in a newly privatizing economy. Furthermore, in a democratic system, these issues are publicly reported and argued. The news reports of potential conflicts of interest, as well as of legal prosecutions, create a public skeptical of the integrity of their own officials and institutions.

Both the forty years of communism and the rapidity of the communist collapse have conditioned the pace and content of the postcommunist transition. Communism provided little preparation for the open expression and orderly resolution of the many conflicts inherent in a complex society. The rapidity and unexpected collapse of communist rule provided little opportunity for replacement democratic elites to be either identified or prepared for the responsibilities of governance. The transition occurred through improvisation. The words of dissident playwright Václav Havel during the most severe period of communist repression, have proved prophetic: "I am worried about the price we as a people will have to pay once we come into our own."[87]

Compared to other postcommunist countries of Central Europe, however, the Czech Republic has been relatively stable, and successful in both political and economic reform. Communism has created a severe and rushed agenda of difficult and complex issues – definition of the political system, rebuilding of an economic system, and definition of state boundaries – which Western democracies have resolved over centuries.

Communism has provided the agenda of difficult issues to be faced all at once, but provided postcommunist elites and public with little preparation for the magnitude of their tasks. The Czech Republic has called upon its resources from the First Republic in the first half of this century to overcome the communist legacy of the second half.

Acronyms of Czech parties and organizations

ChDP	Christian Democratic Party – Křestanskodemokraticka strana (KDS)
CDU-CPP	Christian and Democratic Union-Czechoslovakian People's Party – Křestanska a demokraticka unie – Československa strana lidova (KDU-ČSL)
CDA	Civic Democratic Alliance – Občanska demokraticka aliance (ODA)
CDP	Civic Democratic Party – Občanska demokraticka strana (ODS)
CF	Civic Forum – Občanske forum (OF)
CM	Civic Movement – Občanske hnuti (OH)
CDUP	Committee for the Defense of the Unjustly Persecuted – Vybor na Obranu Nespravedlivě Stihanych (VONS)
CPBM	Communist Party of Bohemia and Moravia – Kommunisticka strana Čech a Moravy (KSČM)
CPCS	Communist Party of Czechoslovakia – Kommunisticka strana Československa (KSČS)
CMCU	Czech-Moravian Center Union – Českomoravska unie středu (CMUS)
CMTUC	Czech and Moravian Trade Union Confederation – Českomoravska komora odborovych svazů (CMKOS)
CSDP	Czech Social Democratic Party – Česka strana socialně demokraticka (ČSSD)
FD	Free Democrats – Svobodni demokrate (SD)
FD-LNSP	Free Democrats – Liberal National Socialist Party – Svobodni demokrate – Liberalni strana narodně socialni (SD-LSNS)
LB	Left Bloc – Levy blok (LB)
LNSP	Liberal National Socialist Party – Liberalni strana narodně socialni (LSNS)
LSU	Liberal Social Union – Liberalně socialni unie (LSU)
MDS	Movement for Democratic Slovakia – Hnutie za demokoraticke Slovensko (HZDS)
MSDMS	Movement for Self-Governing Democracy – Society for Moravia and Silesia – Hnuti za samospravnou demokracii – Společnost pro Moravu a Slezsko (HSD-SMS)
PAV	Public Against Violence (Slovakia) – Veřejnost Proti Nasili (VPN)
RA-RPC	Association for the Republic-Republican Party of Czechoslovakia – Struženi pro republiku – Republikanska strana Československa (SR-RSC)

NOTES

1   Milan E. Hapala, "Political Parties in Czechoslovakia," in *Czechoslovakia Past and Present*, ed. Miloslav Rechcigl, Jr. (The Hague: Mouton, 1968), I, p. 134; Victor S. Mametey, "The Development of Czechoslovak Democracy, 1920–1938," in *A History of the Czechoslovak Republic, 1919–1948*, ed. Victor S. Mamatey and Radomir Luza (Princeton: Princeton University Press, 1973), p. 108; Milso Trapl, *Political Catholicism and the Czechoslovak People's Party in Czechoslovakia, 1918–1938* (Boulder, CO: Social Science Monographs, 1995), p. 55.

2   Oskar Krejci, *History of Elections in Bohemia and Moravia* (Boulder, CO: East European Monographs, 1995); Jindriska Syllova, "The Transition to Democracy in Czechoslovakia in the Field of Electoral Law," in *The Transnational Future of Europe*, ed. Ziemowit J. Pietras and Marek Peitras (Lublin: Maria Curie-Sklodowska University Press, 1992).

3   Petr Jehlicka, Thomas Kostelecky and Ludek Sykora, "Czechoslovak Parliamentary Elections 1990: Old Patterns, New Trends and Lots of Surprises," in *The New Political Geography of Eastern Europe*, ed. John O'Loughlin and Herman van der Wusten (London: Belhaven Press, 1993); Tomas Kostelecky, "Changing Party Allegiances in a Changing Party System: the 1990 and 1992 Parliamentary Elections in the Czech Republic," in *Party Formation in East-Central Europe*, ed. Gordon Wightman (Hants, UK: Edward Elgar, 1995), p. 86.

4   Václav Benes, "The Development of Czech Democracy," in *A History of the Czechoslovak Republic, 1919–1948*, p. 49; Mamatey, "The Development of Czechoslovak Democracy, 1920–1938," p. 117; Sharon L. Wolchik, "Czechoslovakia," in *Columbia History of Eastern Europe in the Twentieth Century*, ed. Joseph Held (New York: Columbia, 1992), pp. 119–63.

5   Wolchik, "Czechoslovakia," p. 124; "Zakladni informace o neziskovem sektoru v CR" (Prague: Nadace Rokzvoje Obcanske Spolecnosti, 1994), p. 14.

6   Carol S. Leff, *National Conflict in Czechoslovakia* (Princeton, NJ: Princeton University Press, 1988).

7   Marek Bankowicz and Jan Ake Dellenbrandt, "The Party System of Czechoslovakia," in *East European Multi-Party Systems*, ed. Sten Berglund, M. Grzybowski, J. Dellenbrandt, and M. Bankowicz (Helsinki: Finnish Society of Sciences and Letters, 1988), p. 95.

8   Trapl, *Political Catholicism and the Czechoslovak People's Party in Czechoslovakia, 1918–1938*, pp. 57–58.

9   Lubomir Brokl and Zedenka Mansfeldova, "Zerfall der Tschechoslowakei – strukturelle Ursachen und Parteihandeln," in *Parteien in Osteuropa: Kontext and Akteure*, ed. Dieter Segert and Csilla Machos (Westdeutscher Verlag, 1995), pp. 133–47.

10 Bankowicz and Dellenbrandt, "The Party System of Czechoslovakia," pp. 102–3; Jaroslaw A. Piekalkiewicz, *Public Opinion Polling in Czechoslovakia, 1968–69: Results and Analysis of Surveys Conducted During the Dubček Era* (New York: Praeger, 1972); Gordon H. Skilling, *Czechoslovakia's Interrupted Revolution* (Princeton: Princeton University Press, 1976); Otto Ulc, "Political Participation in Czechoslovakia," *Journal of Politics*, no. 33 (May 1971), 422–47.

11 Joseph Rothschild, *Return to Diversity* (New York: Oxford University Press, 1993), pp. 168–70.

12 David M. Olson, "Party Formation and Party System Consolidation: Parties in the New Democracies of Central Europe in the First Half-Decade," paper read at Fifth World Congress for Central and East European Studies, Warsaw, 1995.

13 *Kronika Demokratickeho Parlamentu, 1989–1992,* ed. Frantisek Ciganek (Prague: Cesty, 1992); Karen Henderson, "Czechoslovakia: The Failure of Consensus Politics," Discussion Papers in Politics, University of Leicester, 1993; David M. Olson, "Dissolution of the State: Political Parties and the 1992 Election in Czechoslovakia," *Communist and Post-Communist Studies* 26, no. 3 (September 1993), 301–14; David M. Olson, "The Sundered State: Federalism and Parliament in Czechoslovakia," in *Parliaments in Transition,* ed. Thomas F. Remington (Boulder, CO: Westview, 1994), pp. 97–124; David M. Olson, Jindriska Syllova, and Jana Reschova, "Prvni volebni obdobi demokratickeho parlamentu v CSFR: Federalni shromazdeni 1990–92: komparacni pohled," *Pravnik* 132, no. 2 (1993), 125–41. [The First Term of the Democratic Parliament of the Czech and Slovak Federal Republic: A Comparative Perspective]; Sharon L. Wolchik, *Czechoslovakia in Transition* (London: Pinter, 1991).

14 David M. Olson, "Political Parties and Party Systems in Regime Transformation: Inner Transition in the New Democracies of Central Europe," *The American Review of Politics, Special Issue: Political Parties in a Changing Age,* ed. William Crotty, no. 14 (Winter 1993), 619–58; Jirina Siklova, "Are Women in Eastern Europe Conservative?" in *Gender Politics and Post Communism,* ed. Nanette Funk and Magda Mueller (New York: Routledge, 1993), pp. 74–83; Josef Skala and Christoph Kunkel, "Auf dem Weg zu einem konsolidierten Parteiensystem?" *Geschichte und Gesellschaft* 18, no. 3 (1992), 292–308.

15 Olson, "Political Parties and Party Systems in Regime Transformation," pp. 619–58.

16 Mary Hrabik Samal, "Dissent's Challenge to East European Political Systems: The Case of Charter 77 in Czechoslovakia," *East European Quarterly* 21, no. 4 (Winter 1987), 469–90; Gordon H. Skilling, "Independent Currents in Czechoslovakia," *Problems of Communism,* no. 34 (January–February 1985), 32–49.

17 Gordon H. Skilling, *Charter 77 and Human Rights in Czechoslovakia* (London: George Allen & Unwin, 1991).

18 Jindriska Syllova, "Czechoslovakia 1990: Transition to Democracy," *Journal of East West Studies* 21, no. 1 (April 1992), 75–93; Wolchik, "Czechoslovakia," pp. 140–41.

19 Bankowicz and Dellenbrandt, "The Party System of Czechoslovakia," pp. 89–108; Syllova, "Czechoslovakia 1990: Transition to Democracy," pp. 75–93.

20 Brokl and Mansfeldova, "Zerfall der Tschechoslowakei – strukturelle Ursachen und Parteihandeln," p. 139.

21 Timothy Garton-Ash, *The Magic Lantern* (New York: Random House, 1990); Gordon Wightman, "Czechoslovakia," in *New Political Parties of Eastern Europe and the Soviet Union,* ed. Bogdan Szajkowski (Essex, UK: Longman Current Affairs Group, 1991); Wolchik, *Czechoslovakia in Transition.*

22 Syllova, "Czechoslovakia 1990: Transition to Democracy," pp. 75–93; Wightman, "Czechoslovakia," pp. 319–26.

23 Syllova, "The Transition to Democracy in Czechoslovakia in the Field of Electoral Law."

24 Olson, "The Sundered State: Federalism and Parliament in Czechoslovakia," pp. 97–124.

25 Wightman, "Czechoslovakia," pp. 53–54.

26 Juan Linz and Alfred Stepan, "Political Identities and Electoral Sequences: Spain, the Soviet Union, and Yugoslavia," *Daedalus* 121, no. 2 (Spring 1992), 123–39.

27 Martin Myant, "Czech and Slovak Trade Unions," *Journal of Communist Studies* 9, no. 4 (December 1993), 59–84; Zdenka Mansfeldova, "Tripartism in the Czech Republic," paper read at conference on "Tripartism in Central and Eastern Europe," Budapest, 1994; Zdenka Mansfeldova, "Social Partnership in the Czech Republic," paper read at Fifth World Congress for Central and East European Studies, Warsaw, 1995.

28 Myant, "Czech and Slovak Trade Unions," pp. 59–84.

29 Steve Kettle, "Foreign Investment and the SPT Telecom Deal," *Transition*, 22 September 1995, 52–55; Jeff Freeman, "A Long Wait for Oil-Refinery Privatization," *Transition*, 22 September 1995, pp. 56–59.

30 Myant, "Czech and Slovak Trade Unions," pp. 59–84.

31 Mansfeldova, "Social Partnership in the Czech Republic"; "Vznik organizaci od roku 1989" [Growth of Organizations from 1989], manuscript, Institute of Sociology, Czech Academy of Science, 1995.

32 CTK News Highlights, 14 December 1995 (internet).

33 *Prague Post*, 25 January 1995; "Vznik organizaci od roku 1989," pp. 11–12.

34 Otto Ulc, *The Judge in a Communist State* (Athens, OH: Ohio University, 1972), pp. 196–97.

35 Lubomir Sedlak, "Agriculture Minister Stands His Ground," *Prague Post*, 19 April 1995, p. 5.

36 Mansfeldova, "Social partnership in the Czech Republic."

37 Ibid.

38 Lubomir Sedlak, "Eye on Business," *Prague Post*, 22 March 1995, p. 5.

39 *Economist*, 11 February 1995, p. 45.

40 Myant, "Czech and Slovak Trade Unions," 59–84; *Prague Post*, 18 June and 22 November 1995; Byron Sebastian, "Debts and Disgruntled Doctors," *Transition*, 29 December 1995, pp. 46–50.

41 Zdenek Zboril, "Impediments to the Development of Democratic Politics: A Czech Perspective," in *Party Formation in East-Central Europe*; Zdenek Zboril, "Korupce, zneuzivani moci a zmena rezimu," *Politologicka Revue* (June 1995), 29–38.

42 "Zakladni informace o neziskovem sektoru v CR."

43 *Parlamentni Zpravodaj* 1 (1995–96), 34–35.

44 *Prague Post*, 22 November 1995.

45 Focus 1994.

46 Institute for Public Opinion Research 94–21.

47 "Zakladni informace o neziskovem sektoru v CR."

48 *Prague Post*, 22 November 1995.

49 Barbara Einhorn, *Cinderella Goes to Market* (London: Verso, 1993); Jirina Siklova, "Are Women in Eastern Europe Conservative?" pp. 74–83; Jaroslava Stastna, "New Opportunities in the Czech Republic," *Transition*, 8 September 1995, pp. 24–26ff.
50 Zoltan Barany, "Roma: Grim Realities in Eastern Europe," *Transition*, 29 March 1995, pp. 3–8.
51 Steve Kettle, "Rise of the Social Democrats," *Transition*, 28 July 1995, pp. 70–74.
52 *Prague Post*, 21 June and 29 November 1995.
53 Richard Rose, *Czechs and Slovaks Compared*, Studies in Public Policy, no. 198 (Glasgow: University of Strathclyde, Centre for the Study of Public Policy, 1992).
54 Tomas Kostelecky, "Changing Party Allegiances."
55 Barany, "Roma: Grim Realities in Eastern Europe," pp. 3–8.
56 Ibid., p. 5.
57 Janusz Bugajski, *Ethnic Politics in Eastern Europe* (Armonk, NY: M. E. Sharpe, 1994), p. 304.
58 Steve Kettle, "Czech Republic Struggles to Define an Independent Press," *Transition*, 6 October 1995, pp. 4–6.
59 Michal Klima, "The Glut of Dailies Threatens Market," *Prague Post*, 9 August 1995, p. 9.
60 *Telegraph*, 28 July 1995, p. 3.
61 *Prague Post*, 8 February 1995.
62 *Economist*, 11 February 1995; *OMRI Daily Digest*, 19 October 1995 (e-mail); *Prague Post*, 25 October 1995.
63 *Prague Post*, 20 September 1995.
64 Daniel Kummermann, "New Law: What's Crucial? The Conflict or the Interest," *Prague Post*, 15 November 1995, p. 11.
65 The public opinion data reported here are from a time series of public opinion surveys, "Trends," conducted by STEM (Center for Empirical Research), and a battery of questions conducted over the past three years by the Institute for Public Opinion Research (IVVM). The directors of each, Dr. J. Hartl of STEM and Dr. E. Rendlova of IVVM, have been most helpful in providing these data.
66 Jindriska Syllova, "Ceska narodni rada v roce 1990: Analyza slozeni a cinnosti," *Sociologicky Casopis* 28, no. 2 (April 1992), 237–46; Syllova, "The Transition to Democracy in Czechoslovakia in the Field of Electoral Law"; Wightman, "Czechoslovakia."
67 Jaroslav Hudacek and Zdenka Mansfeldova, "Erste Schritte der tschechoslowakischen Gesellschaft im Transformationsprozess," in *Abbruch and Aufbruch*, ed. Michael Thomas (Berlin: Akademie Verlag, 1992), pp. 226–38.
68 Private communication, Institute of Sociology, Czech Academy of Science.
69 Olson, "Political Parties and Party Systems in Regime Transformation," pp. 619–58; Olson, "Dissolution of the State," pp. 301–14; Skala and Kunkel, "Auf dem Weg zu einem konsolidierten Parteinsystem?" pp. 292–308; Gordon Wightman, "The 1992 Parliamentary Elections in Czechoslovakia," *Journal of Communist Studies*, no. 8 (December 1992), 293–301; Sharon L. Wolchik, "Repluralization of Politics in Czechoslovakia," *Communist and Post-Communist Studies* 26, no. 4 (December 1993), 412–31.

70   Brokl and Mansfeldova, "Zerfall der Tschechoslowakei – strukturelle Ursachen und Parteihandeln," pp. 133–47; Zora Buterova and Martin Butora, "Political Parties, Value Orientations, and Slovakia's Road to Independence," in *Party Formation in East-Central Europe*; Ales Gerloch, "Teorie federalismu a rozdeleni Ceskoslovenska," *Politologicka Revue* 1 (June 1995), 13–28; Henderson, "Czechoslovakia: The Failure of Consensus Politics"; Olson, "The Sundered State: Federalism and Parliament in Czechoslovakia," pp. 97–124; Gordon Wightman, "The Czech and Slovak Republics," in *Developments in East European Politics*, ed. Stephen White, Judy Batt and Paul Lewis (Durham: Duke University Press, 1993).

71   Olson, "Party Formation and Party System Consolidation."

72   Steve Kettle, "Straining at the Seams," *Transition*, 9 June 1995, pp. 8–12.

73   *OMRI Daily Digest*, 4 December 1995.

74   Brokl and Mansfeldova, "Zerfall der Tschechoslowakei – strukturelle Ursachen und Parteihandeln," pp. 133–47; Herbert Kitschelt, "The Formation of Party Systems in East Central Europe," *Politics and Society* 20, no. 1 (March 1992), 7–50; Herbert Kitschelt, "The Formation of Party Cleavages in Post-Communist Democracies: Theoretical Propositions," paper read at conference on Party Formation and Public Opinion in Eastern Europe, Duke University, 1995.

75   These broad statements are based on diagrams of roll calls in successive issues of *Parlamentni Zaprovodaj* for 1995.

76   *OMRI Daily Digest*, 15 September 1995.

77   Olson, "Dissolution of the State," p. 311.

78   Ibid.

79   Krejci, *History of Elections in Bohemia and Moravia*, pp. 296, 311.

80   *OMRI Daily Digest*, 19 and 27 December 1995.

81   Jiri Pehe, "Divisions in the Communist Party of Czechoslovakia," *Report on Eastern Europe*, 26 July 1991, pp. 10–13.

82   Tomas Kostelecky, "Economic, Social, and Historical Determinants of Voting Patterns," *Czech Sociological Review* 2, no. 2 (1994), 209–28.

83   Lubomir Brokl and Zedenka Mansfeldova, "Bilanz der tschechisen Innenpolitik im Jahre 1993," *Berichte des Bundesinstituts fuer ostwissenschaftliche und internationale Studien*, no. 8 (1995), 26.

84   *Lidove noviny*, 26 July 1995.

85   Bugajski, *Ethnic Politics in Eastern Europe*, p. 305.

86   Kostelecky, "Economic, Social, and Historical Determinants of Voting Patterns," pp. 209–28.

87   Václav Havel, "Václav Havel to Gustav Husak: Letter, 1979," in *Since the Prague Spring*, ed. Hans-Peter Riese (New York: Vintage Books, 1979), p. 38.

6 Democratization and political participation in Slovakia

Sharon L. Wolchik

In November 1989, citizens of Slovakia joined those in the Czech Lands in mass demonstrations that brought about the rapid end of one of Central and Eastern Europe's most oppressive communist regimes. With the end of the Communist Party's monopoly of political power, political life in Slovakia changed radically. The proliferation of groups and voluntary associations that followed was paralleled by the rapid repluralization of the party system in Slovakia as in the Czech Lands.

By the June 1992 elections, it was clear to most observers that the Czechoslovak federation would not last. In January 1993, the federation was replaced by independent Slovak and Czech states. In the Czech Lands, developments in both the political and economic realms continued to progress smoothly. Under the leadership of Prime Minister Václav Klaus, Czech political leaders continued their rapid reintroduction of a market economy. Czech political institutions also appeared to be more stable than those in most other postcommunist states.

In Slovakia, where political life differed in many important respects from trends in the Czech Republic prior to the break-up of the federation and where the shift to the market caused far greater economic hardship, political life after independence was more tumultuous. In contrast to the situation in the Czech Lands, where public support for Václav Klaus and the move to the market remained high, Slovak politics continued to be characterized by high levels of conflict among political leaders. Evident in the acrimonious relationship between Prime Minister Vladimír Mečiar and President Michal Kováč, as well as between the members of the ruling coalition and within Mečiar's political movement itself, these conflicts resulted in the ousting of the prime minister as the result of a parliamentary vote of no confidence in March 1994. The grand coalition government formed at that time included political forces that spanned the left-right spectrum, but nonetheless demonstrated a good deal of consensus in dealing with pressing public issues such as privitization and minority relations. However, this coalition proved unable to cooperate in the September–October 1994 elections, and Vladimír Mečiar once again became prime minister in December 1994 in coalition with the Slovak National Party and the newly formed Association of Slovak Workers. Despite the high level of elite conflict, alternation of governments has take place peacefully to date. There are also encouraging signs in terms of the development of other elements of civil society, including non-governmental organizations.

As this brief recital illustrates, the effort to create stable democratic political institutions has faced a number of challenges in Slovakia since the end of communist rule. The pages to follow examine an important aspect of this process, the development of the party system and other mechanisms for citizen participation in politics. As the experiences of other countries in transition from authoritarian rule in other contexts indicate, the development of such mechanisms, which both link citizens to the political system and provide feedback to political leaders, is an essential part of creating and maintaining democratic institutions. The development of what has often been called "civic society," that is, non-governmental, voluntary associations, as well as of attitudes that support democracy, are also critical aspects of this process.[1]

The chapter to follow examines the extent to which democracy has been consolidated in Slovakia. After examining the factors that have influenced the formation of political groups and parties, it turns to the development of voluntary associations and interest groups, political parties and the party system, and popular perceptions of political leaders, institutions, and the political system. It concludes with an evaluation of the impact of the party system and other mechanisms for citizen participation on the way in which policies are made, citizen support for the political system, and the con-solidation of democracy in Slovakia.

Factors influencing the formation of political groups and parties

The formation of political parties and groups in Slovakia has been influenced by many of the same factors that have influenced the formation of such groups in other postcommunist states.[2] These include the impact of the communist era on the political attitudes and values of citizens and leaders, and the impact of rapid and large-scale economic change on citizens' perceptions of politics and political entities. The formation of such groups as well as broader trends in political life have also been influenced by a number of factors that are specific to Slovakia. These include its precommunist history and political traditions; the interrelationship between Slovak and Hungarian as well as Czech culture; the delayed industrialization of the region; and the country's multiethnic composition. They also include the impact of the break-up of the joint state with the Czechs and the tasks Slovak leaders have faced in state-building in the postcommunist era. To a larger extent than in many other countries, Slovak politics and the development of the party system have also been influenced in important ways by the characteristics, personality, and beliefs of a single dominant political leader, Vladimír Mečiar.[3]

The precommunist legacy

In Slovakia as in other postcommunist countries, the development of political groups and parties has been shaped in important ways by the pre-communist legacy of its people. Slovaks' sense of national identity developed in reaction to Hungarian and Czech culture. Living in a multi-ethnic region that was part of Hungary for nearly 1,000 years, Slovaks had very little opportunity for the development of a national movement until the interwar period. In contrast to the situation in the Czech Lands, where Austrian rule allowed the formation of citizens' groups that developed into a mass based national movement, Slovaks experienced strong pressures from their Magyar rulers to assimilate and to give up their national identity. These pressures became particularly strong in the second half of the nineteenth century. Very few Slovaks (6 percent) were able to vote, and Slovak representation in the Hungarian parliament's lower house (7 of 413 in 1906 and 3 of 413 in 1911) was very low.[4] Levels of illiteracy were high into the early twentieth century, and educational levels among Slovaks were low. Slovaks also had few opportunities to be educated in their own language. Again in contrast to the situation in the Czech Lands, which were among the more industrialized areas of the Austro–Hungarian Empire, Slovakia remained predominantly agrarian.[5]

These factors had an important impact on political life in Slovakia after the formation of the Czechoslovak Republic in 1918. Brought together with the Czechs, as well as sizeable Hungarian and German minorities, for the first time in a common state, Slovaks entered the new state with political experiences, levels of economic development and urbanization, educational levels, and cultural orientations that were very different from those of the Czechs.[6] These differences soon led to resentment and fed the growth of Slovak nationalism, as many Slovaks felt that Hungarian rule had merely been exchanged for rule from Prague. Although Slovaks were able to and did participate in multiparty elections, many Slovaks became increasingly alienated from the political system.

The growth in national identity and the politicization of ethnicity in interwar Slovakia reflected a variety of factors that influenced the ability of ethnic Slovak leaders to mobilize the population around ethnic issues. Efforts to promote the industrialization of Slovakia largely failed during this period, in part as the result of the Great Depression. Economic hardship, which fueled large-scale emigration from Slovakia, coupled with the perception that economic and political decisions made in Prague did not really take Slovakia's interests into account, led to widespread disaffection with the government and to growing support for political actors, such as the leaders of the People's Party, who would articulate national grievances. At the same time, although Slovakia's economy virtually stagnated,[7] the marked increases in educational levels that occurred during the interwar period provided new resources for Slovak leaders to use to mobilize the population. Voluntary associations developed, and Slovaks also organized a variety of political parties.[8]

Given the low levels of urbanization and education of Slovak society, Catholic priests emerged as important political as well as spiritual leaders. As the interwar period progressed, Slovak resentment grew and fueled support for extreme nationalist movements. Thus, Slovaks as well as Czechs lived in a political system that was democratic for much of the interwar period. However, because most Slovaks saw the interwar government as an instrument of Czech hegemony, this experience did not provide the same grounding for the effort to recreate democratic political life in Slovakia as it did in the Czech Lands.[9]

The extent to which Czechs and Slovaks viewed the interwar government differently was evident in the results of public opinion polls conducted in Czechoslovakia in the 1960s. Czechs surveyed in October 1968, for example, were most likely to identify the interwar republic as the most glorious period of their history (39 percent), followed by the age of Jan Hus (36 percent) and the reign of King Charles IV (31 percent). Slovaks, on the other hand, were most likely to identify the time of L'udovit Štur, the 1840s (36 percent), the period after January 1968 (36 percent), and the Slovak National Uprising, which occurred in 1944 (26 percent). Among Slovaks, the interwar republic was perceived as the most glorious period by only 17 percent of respondents;[10] 13 percent of Slovaks ranked the Slovak state as the most glorious period.[11] As Brown notes in a discussion of these results, far more Slovaks regarded the Slovak state as the least glorious or most unfortunate period for their nation (44 percent).[12] A 1992 survey found that most Slovaks also identified figures important to the development of Slovak national identity, such as Štur, M.R. Štefanik, or Alexander Dubček as the most important personalities in Slovak history. However, 11 percent identified Father Andrej Hlinka (founder of the People's Party that came to dominate Slovak politics in the interwar period) and 5 percent Jozef Tiso (president of the Slovak state established in 1939 under Hitler's aegis) as the most important figures. As in 1968, 11 percent of respondents identified the period of the Slovak state as the most famous period in Slovaks' history.[13]

Although their numbers are not large, then, for certain Slovaks, the Slovak state created in 1939 was a more relevant symbol than the interwar republic. Given the nature of this state and the actions of its leaders, efforts to link the postcommunist government of Slovakia to it have been extremely controversial. Nominally independent, the Slovak state created on March 14, 1939 followed Nazi Germany's lead in almost all areas and in fact was largely a puppet of Hitler. During its reign, anti-Jewish legislation increasingly restricted the rights of the country's Jewish inhabitants. Beginning in the early 1940s, 70,000 Slovakian Jews were deported to death camps, where they perished.[14] Although the country retained the form of a democratic government, Slovakia's political life was dominated by the People's Party which ruled in an increasingly authoritarian way. Some political groups, such as the Communist, Social Democrat and Jewish parties, were banned in 1938. Others, with the exception of the National Party, which disbanded voluntarily, were forced to merge with the People's Party, which became a means for mobilizing the population to carry out the leadership's orders. As in other states under Nazi influence, freedom of the press and other democratic liberties were suspended. Leaders of the Slovak state also adopted laws that abridged the rights of the Hungarians and other minorities.[15]

Discussions of the place of Jozef Tiso and Andrej Hlinka, as well as of the Slovak state itself, in Slovak history have been heated. Apologists and critics alike note that the creation of the Slovak state fulfilled the aspirations of many Slovaks for their own state, despite the way in which it was created and its nature.[16] The experience of having a state of their own, however limited its actual powers, also influenced Slovak views of the government after World War II when a joint state with the Czechs was recreated.

It has been primarily the nationalist Slovak National Party's leaders who have tried to resurrect Tiso and the Slovak state as honorable parts of Slovakia's history. Certain other nationalist groups active in the interwar period have also been resurrected. These include Matica Slovenská, a patriotic association founded in 1863 that existed for much of the Communist period, but operated under many of the same restrictions as other organizations. After 1989, this organization once again came to be active in pressing Slovak national claims, including the demand for Slovak sovereignty.

The legacy of the interwar nationalist movement has also been evident in patterns of support for political parties in the postcommunist period. Support for the Slovak National Party and the Movement for a Democratic Slovakia, the most nationalist parties in Slovakia for example, has not varied consistently by level of economic hardship. Rather it has been highest in those districts in which support for the Slovak People's Party was highest in the interwar period.[17]

The legacy of the interwar period has also led to problems in creating what has been termed a "usable past," that is, a past compatible with democratic values and forms of politics.[18] Since most Slovaks do not see the leaders and experiences connected with the interwar republic as positive, it has been difficult for Slovaks who support democracy to find figures to use to help create a democratic identity. The fact that most of the historical figures seen most positively by Slovaks are associated with the Slovak national movement at various points in history also creates problems for the effort to foster a sense of identity that is inclusive of members of other ethnic groups. This problem is compounded by the fact that Hungarians in Slovakia also identify individuals associated with the development of Hungarian history as the most important figures in their history.[19]

The pattern of relations between Slovaks and Hungarians during the interwar period was also an important element of the pre-communist legacy. The Hungarians who found themselves in Czechoslovakia after 1918 suffered from an abrupt loss of status; the citizenship status of many was also unclear for some time. The constitution guaranteed those who could claim citizenship the right to use their own language in schools and in court under certain conditions.[20] However, many Hungarians felt themselves to be disadvantaged and welcomed the reincorporation of the southern part of Slovakia into Hungary brought about by the first Vienna Award of 1938, which also allowed Hungary to annex southern Ruthenia, also previously part of Czechoslovakia. Those Hungarians who remained in Slovakia, along with other minorities, were subjugated to heavy pressure to become Slovak.[21] These events and the exchange of Hungarian and Slovak populations after World War II complicated ethnic relations during the communist period and continue to be reflected in the attitudes of Hungarians and Slovaks toward each other in the postcommunist period.[22]

The communist legacy

The communist period left several important legacies in Slovakia. Many of these, including the impact of a command economy on economic performance and the structure of the economy, the widespread alienation of the population from the political system, distrust of political leaders, lack of interest in joining political organizations, and the erosion of morality in the public and private spheres that Václav Havel has described so eloquently, were similar in Slovakia and the Czech Lands. Others, however, were peculiar to Slovakia and reflected the many ways in which the two regions differed from each other at the outset of the communist period.

Several of these were particularly important. These include the impact of a unitary political system on Slovak national aspirations and identity; the pattern of industrialization that occurred in Slovakia during the communist era; the impact of the Communist Party's monopoly of power and control of the media on ethnic relations within Slovakia; and the different patterns the political reforms of 1968 took in Slovakia and the Czech Lands and the resulting differences in the political climate after their suppression.

The Košice Government program which formed the basis of the Czecho-slovak state re-created in 1945 included guarantees of Slovak autonomy. However, these provisions were largely ignored after the communists came to power in February 1948. As the Stalinist system was consolidated in Czechoslovakia, Slovak national bodies such as the Slovak National Council lost much of their authority and Slovak leaders, including Vladimír Clementis and Gustáv Husák, were accused of being bourgeois nationalists and executed or forced to leave political life during the purges. Promises of autonomy were forgotten, and decision-making once again was centered in Prague. Due to the party's monopoly of power and control of the media, Slovak leaders lost the ability to raise ethnic issues. Several of the parties that had championed Slovak national causes during the interwar period, including the People's Party, were banned after World War II. Others, such as the Democratic Party which had been active in the period between 1945 and 1948, were abolished after 1948.

It was only in the context of the process of theoretical renewal that preceded the reform period of 1968 that Slovak leaders and intellectuals were once again able to voice Slovak national claims openly. As the process of rethinking the nature of socialist society that took place at the elite level spread, Slovaks began to question the unitary organization of the state and call for greater attention to Slovak issues and needs. It was during this period that Slovak national organizations, such as Matica Slovenska, were once again allowed to act as advocates of Slovak national interests. In the context of the reform, Slovak leaders were also able to bring about the federation of the country.[23]

Many of the powers granted to the republic governments as the result of federalization, which was one of the few elements of the reform agenda to survive the August 1968 Soviet-led Warsaw Pact invasion of Czechoslovakia and subsequent "normalization" and which entered into effect in January 1969, were subsequently rescinded. The reduction in the powers of the republic governments, especially in the economic area, in turn was reflected in the growing dissatisfaction among Slovaks with the federation that became evident after November 1989. The change in the structure of the state had an important impact on political developments in the late communist and early postcommunist period. The lack of power of the republic governments was one of the factors that fueled Slovak dissatisfaction with the notion of a federation and provided a rallying point for Slovak leaders who wanted to see either a radical change in the state's structure or independence for Slovakia.

As numerous analysts have noted, most Slovaks as well as most Czechs opposed the break-up of the Czechoslovak federation, and the dissolution of the state was ultimately accomplished at the elite level.[24] But while political leaders, particularly Václav Klaus and Vladimír Mečiar, negotiated the break-up without consulting the broader populations directly, large numbers of citizens in Slovakia wanted to see some change in the structure of the state. It is telling, for example, that only 8 percent of respondents in Slovakia surveyed in 1991 by the Institute for Public Opinion Research were satisfied with the federation.[25] Most Slovaks wanted to see a "confederation;" however, few were clear about what such an arrangement would involve. Many of those who wanted to see a confederation also supported Vladimír Mečiar's Movement for a Democratic Slovakia in the June 1992 elections.[26]

The concentration of decision-making power in Prague during the late communist period allowed Slovak leaders to blame the Czechs for the ills the system created. The continuation of the existing federal structure after the November 1989 revolution also allowed them to blame the Czechs for the negative results of the introduction of the market in Slovakia. At the same time, the fact that political life had been organized in a federal system for some time made it easier for political leaders to agree to divide the country and to do so peacefully.

The timing of Slovakia's industrialization also had an important influence on political developments in the postcommunist period. Because most of Slovakia's industrialization took place during the communist era, its economy was particularly vulnerable to the disruptions caused by the transition to the market. The closing or downsizing of many of the large, inefficient enterprises in the arms and other heavy industries contributed to rates of unemployment that were much higher in Slovakia than in the Czech Lands prior to the break-up of the state. The proportion of families living in poverty was also much greater in Slovakia than in Bohemia and Moravia. This situation fed resentment against the federal government and the Czechs and increased support for parties that called for a change in the strategy of economic change to better suit Slovakia's economic conditions.

The impact of the leadership's approach to Slovakia's sizeable Hungarian minority during the communist era was another important part of the communist legacy in Slovakia. Citizenship and other restrictions on Hungarians after the end of World War II were lifted during the communist era. Hungarians living in Slovakia also had an officially established cultural organization. However, like other mass organizations under communist rule, this organization existed to mobilize the population to do the bidding of the

Communist Party rather than to articulate or promote the interests of the Hungarian minority. There were also a number of schools, particularly at the elementary level, that taught in Hungarian. Control of public debate by the Communist Party and the inability of citizens to form independent groups meant that only a few activists gave voice to the grievances of the Hungarian minority during the communist period. However, Hungarian resentment over what many considered to be their second class status in Slovakia and lack of opportunity for education in Hungarian, particularly at the secondary and higher levels, continued to grow. When the communist system fell, then, the ground was prepared for Hungarian activists to mobilize Hungarians living in Slovakia around Hungarian ethnic claims.

Finally, the formation of interest groups and parties in the postcommunist period was influenced by the impact of the reform period of 1968 and its aftermath in Slovakia. The 1968 reforms and their suppression had a profound impact on political and economic life in Czechoslovakia. Due to the Husák leadership's fear that any discussion of economic or other significant reform would have political repercussions, it was virtually impossible to speak of reform in any area for much of the rest of the communist period. The replacement of Husák by Miloš Jakeš in 1987 and the impact of Gorbachev's policies in the Soviet Union in Czechoslovakia led to some change in this respect. The Communist Party adopted a new approach to economic issues in January 1987 that highlighted the need for significant economic reforms, for example. Change in the composition of top party bodies was accompanied by an increased willingness on the part of the population to challenge the regime by participation in activities organized by dissidents, particularly in the Czech Lands. Dissent also spread to groups previously not involved, such as young people and people in the official world.[27]

In Slovakia, the end of the reforms of the Prague Spring reflected the nature of the reform process itself. Although certain Slovaks supported the effort to create a more democratic system, many were more concerned with national issues in 1968. The purge of supporters of democratization, therefore, was not as deep in Slovakia as in the Czech Lands.[28] Intellectual life also was not as tightly controlled after 1968 as in the Czech lands. As a result, many Slovaks who had they lived in the Czech Lands would have been classified as dissidents by the regime were able to keep their jobs in the official world while at the same time engaging in what Martin Bútora, one of the founders of Public Against Violence, has called "constructive deviance." In the late 1980s, activist intellectuals were able to use officially approved organizations, such as the Guardians of Nature, to organize and engage in activities to support the environment and other non-conformist actions.

Table 6.1 *Demographic trends in Slovakia since the 1950s*

	1950s	1970s	1980s
Percentage of labor force in:	(1950)[a]	(1969–73)[a]	(1980)[a]
Agriculture	53.5	21.6	15.5
Industry & construction	25.2	42.0	45.1
Average annual rates of		(1970–74)[b]	(1980–90)
population growth	n.a.	0.6†	0.6[c]
Age Distribution (%)	(1961)[d]	(1970)[e]	(1990)[f]
15–24	15	19	15
25–49	32	32	35
50–59	11	9	9
Over 60	11	14	15
Levels of education‡ (%)	(1950)[g]	(1970)[g]	(1991)
Primary	77.6	55.9	38.6
Secondary	4.3	13.4	50.9
Post-secondary	0.7	3.3	9.5
Apprentice programs	8.7	20.2	
Trade school	6.6	5.9	

Notes: †Population growth rates for 1970–74 are for Czechoslovakia. ‡Among persons 15 and over. Indicates attainment of completed or partial education at each level.

Sources: [a]Sharon L. Wolchik, "Regional Inequalities in Czechoslovakia"; [b]*United Nations Statistical Yearbook 1975* (New York: United Nations, 1976), p. 71; [c]US Department of Commerce, *Statistical Abstracts of the United States*; [d]*Statistická Ročenka Československé Socialistické Republiky 1963* (Praha: Ústřední Komise Lidové Kontroly A Statistiky, 1963), p. 109; [e]Ibid., 1971, p. 86; [f]Ibid., 1992, p. 104; [g]Sharon L. Wolchik, *Czechoslovakia in Transition: Politics, Economics and Society* (London: Pinter Publishers, 1991), p. 164.

The numbers of people who participated in these activities was not large; like their counterparts in the Czech Lands they were for the most part intellectuals and developed few links to broader groups within the population. Several of the leaders of this group became leaders in Public Against Violence in 1989, and the informal networks created at this time continued to have an influence on politics after 1989. At the same time, because they operated within the framework of official organizations, leaders of these groups did not gain the experience that Polish and Hungarian dissidents did in mobilizing large groups of people or openly engaging in politics, or the support of large groups of citizens. Nor did their actions earn them the same moral authority as that of many of the Czech dissidents. The primary exception to this pattern occurred in the case of a few writers and philosophers, such as Milan Šimecka and Miroslav Kusý, and the growing numbers of religious activists, such as Ján Čarnogurský who became more active in the late 1980s in challenging restrictions on the freedom of religion. The actions of the latter included pilgrimages to shrines, which grew from approximately 100,000 people in the early 1980s to an estimated 800,000 people in 1988.[29] A 1988 candlelight demonstration in Bratislava was a particularly important step in the development of religious activism.

The impact of the communist period on levels of development in the Czech Lands and Slovakia also affected ethnic relations and the development of the political system after 1989. Investment in Slovakia succeeded in reducing many of the disparities between the Czech Lands and Slovakia during the communist period. As I have demonstrated more fully elsewhere, these results were evident on almost all indicators of development, including occupational structure; educational levels; urbanization patterns; and living standards.[30] In 1948, for example, 59.8 percent of the labor force was employed in agriculture in Slovakia, compared to 33.1 percent in the Czech Lands. The difference between the two regions had decreased substantially by 1970 (23.6 percent in Slovakia, 14.6 percent in the Czech Lands), and continued to decrease throughout the rest of the communist period. By 1989, 12.6 percent of the population was engaged in agriculture in Slovakia, compared to 8.4 percent in the Czech Lands.[31] Access to education in the two regions also became more equal. In 1949, the ratio of students in higher education per 1,000 population between 20 and 29 years of age was 0.70. This ratio was 0.93 in 1955 and, in the 1960s and 1970s, 1.13 to 1.41. The ratio decreased somewhat to 0.91 by 1985 and 0.87 by 1987, but educational access in Slovakia was still closer to that in the Czech Lands by the end of the communist period than at its inception.[32]

A similar picture emerges if one considers average monthly wages in the socialized sector of the economy (excluding agricultural cooperatives), which were slightly lower in Slovakia at the outset of the communist period, but had reached 0.98 percent of those in the Czech Lands by the mid-1960s.[33] Because a somewhat larger proportion of the population was employed in agricultural cooperatives in Slovakia than in the Czech Lands, and average wages of cooperative members were somewhat lower than those in the rest of the socialized economy, average incomes were still slightly lower in Slovakia than in the Czech Lands in the 1980s. However, these differences did not lead to great differences in standards of living in the two regions. Information about the equipment of homes with consumer goods and automobile ownership, for example, indicates that differences in the two regions had all but disappeared by 1980.[34] However, the near-equalization of conditions in the two regions did not lead to a decrease in ethnic identity among Slovaks or ethnic tensions in Czechoslovakia. After 1989, political conditions allowed Slovak leaders to use the resources modernization created to mobilize the population around ethnic issues.

The impact of the transition: the repluralization of politics

The sudden end of communist rule in Czechoslovakia, coupled with the tight political control exercised by the regime until the end of the system, meant that Slovaks as well as Czechs were faced with the need to respond rapidly to the unexpected after November 1989. As in the Czech Lands, Slovaks could not rely on existing institutions or groups, such as Solidarity in Poland, to take the lead in bringing about the end of the communist system and reorganizing of the polity and economy. Rather, they faced had to create a new organization to deal with the rapidly changing demands of the situation. In the Czech Lands, Václav Havel and other dissidents centered around Charter 77 moved quickly to create Civic Forum and were the obvious choice to negotiate with the government and coordinate the mass demonstrations that spread after the November 17 beating of peaceful student demonstrators. In Slovakia, it was a loose coalition of the non-conformist intellectuals discussed above, cultural figures, and people who had been involved in the old regime but quickly came to support the call for its end who established Public Against Violence. As in the case of Civic Forum in the Czech Lands, this umbrella organization included individuals with what would prove to be very different ideas about how to deal with the tasks of the immediate postcommunist period.

The involvement of large numbers of ordinary citizens in the mass demonstrations that brought about the end of communism was a positive resource for the new leaders in the Czech Lands and Slovakia. However, this public support soon faded, to be replaced by skepticism about political movements and parties and, in many cases, about political institutions and leaders. Because the old regime fell so quickly, citizens in Slovakia had a limited opportunity to participate openly in politics prior to the effort to recreate democratic political life. The transition therefore did little to contribute to the legitimacy of the new government or create new symbols or myths that democratic leaders in Slovakia could use to develop a political culture supportive of democracy. Because the "Velvet Revolution" began in Prague and there was initially a high level of cooperation between Czech and Slovak leaders, many of the Slovak intellectuals who led the movement to end communist rule were vulnerable to being depicted as insufficiently dedicated to pursuing Slovak national interests. The short period of the transition meant that citizens had little opportunity to become familiar with those who would emerge as leaders in 1989. It also meant that there were few leaders in Slovakia apart from those associated with the Communist system who had any experience in negotiating with the Communist leadership, or in leading a mass based political party or movement.[35]

The end of communist rule in Slovakia, as in the Czech Lands, was followed by a rapid effort to re-create democratic political life. Most of this effort focused in the immediate postcommunist period on removing those leaders compromised by their roles in the old system and reorienting the style of work of existing institutions. Changes were made in the composition of the Federal Assembly in December 1989 and early 1990 by coopting new people to replace those communist deputies who resigned. Competitive elections, held in June 1990 and 1992 for Federal and Republic legislatures and in September/October 1994 for the Slovak National Council as well as in November 1990, November 1992 and November 1994 for local offices were the primary means of selecting new leaders.[36] The rapid repluralization of politics that occurred after the end of Communist rule provided citizens with the opportunity to articulate their views and join or form voluntary organizations to defend their interests, advocate policies and pressure political leaders.[37]

Electoral legislation and the timing of elections in Slovakia were influenced by the desire of Czechoslovakia's new leaders to move quickly to legitimate the ad hoc personnel changes and changes in government that occurred immediately after the end of the communist system; the need to take the multiethnic nature of the country and its tradition of proportional representation into account; and the desire to prevent an extreme degree of fragmentation of political forces in parliament. Thus, a system of proportional representation with thresholds of 5 percent for the Federal Assembly and the Czech National Council, and 3 percent for the Slovak National Council, was adopted. In 1992, the threshold for the Slovak National Council was increased to 5 percent. Political considerations including the situation of the Hungarian minority have influenced recent discussions of electoral districts.

In the June 1990 elections, Civic Forum and Public Against Violence emerged as the clear winners in their regions. Public Against Violence gained 32.5 percent of the vote and 19 of the 51 Slovak seats in the House of the People and 37.3 percent of the vote, or 33 of the 75 Slovak seats in the House of Nations in the Federal Assembly. The movement also won 29.3 percent of the vote to the Slovak National Council, which gave it 48 of the 150 seats in that body. The Christian Democratic Movement was the second most popular party, with approximately 19 percent of the vote to the House of the People and 16.7 percent to the House of Nations of the Federal Assembly and 19 percent of the vote to the Slovak National Council. The Communist Party of Slovakia won 13.8 percent of the vote for the House of the People and 13.4 to the House of Nations of the Federal Assembly; the

Table 6.2 *Parliamentary elections in Slovakia, 1990*

Political Parties	House of the People				House of Nations				National Council			
	No. votes	% vote	No. seats	% seats	No. votes	% vote	No. seats	% seats	No. votes	% vote	No. seats	% seats
PAV	1,104,125	32.54	19	39	1,262,278	37.28	33	44	991,285	29.34	48	32
KDH	644,008	18.98	11	22	564,172	16.66	14	19	648,782	19.20	31	21
SNS	372,025	10.96	6	12	387,387	11.44	9	12	470,984	13.94	22	15
KSS	468,411	13.81	8	16	454,740	13.43	12	16	450,855	13.34	22	15
ESWMK	291,287	8.58	5	10	287,426	8.49	7	9	292,636	8.66	14	9
DS	149,310	4.4	–	–	124,561	3.68	–	–	148,567	4.39	7	5
SZ	108,542	3.20	–	–	87,366	2.58	–	–	117,871	3.48	6	5
SD	64,175	1.89	–	–	51,233	1.51	–	–	61,401	1.81	–	–
SSL	49,012	1.44	–	–	42,111	1.24	–	–	60,041	1.77	–	–
SZV	87,604	2.58	–	–	71,204	2.10	–	–	85,060	2.51	–	–
ČSS	2,086	.06	–	–	2,073	.06	–	–	1,166	.03	–	–
SB	6,145	.18	–	–	5,643	.17	–	–	3,326	.09	–	–
VDS									6,755	.20	–	–
ČSDF	562	.20	–	–	499	.01	–	–	338	.01	–	–
HČSP	13,947	.41	–	–	16,943	.50	–	–	13,417	.39	–	–
DURS	22,670	.67	–	–	20,445	.60	–	–	24,797	.73	–	–
VDSPR	8,577	.25	–	–	7,169	.21	–	–	7,023	.21	–	–
HOS	580	.02	–	–	914	.03	–	–				

Notes: Voter turnout: 95.39% of eligible voters; Acronyms: ČSDF – Czechoslovak Democratic Forum; ČSS – Czechoslovak Socialist Party; DS – Democratic Party; DURS – Romanies; ESWMK – Coexistence-Hungarian Christian Democratic Party; HČSP – Movement of Czechoslovak Understanding; HOS – Movement for Civic Liberty; KDH – Christian Democratic Movement; KSS – Communist Party of Slovakia; PAV – Public Against Violence; SB – Free Bloc; SD – Social Democratic Party; SNS – Slovak National Party; SSL – Freedom Party; SZ – Green Party; SZV – The Alliance of Farmers & the Countryside; VDS – All-People's Democratic Party; VDSPR – People's Democratic Party-Rally for the Republic

Sources: Sharon L. Wolchik, *Czechoslovakia: Politics, Economics, and Society* (London: Pinter Publishers Ltd., 1991), pp. 72, 75; Oskar Krejčí, *History of Elections in Bohemia and Moravia* (New York: Columbia University Press, 1995), pp. 341–52; *FBIS-EEU*, Slovakia, June 11, 1990, pp. 31–34 and June 15, 1990, p. 18.

party won 13.3 percent of votes for the Slovak National Council. The Slovak National Party won approximately 11 percent of the vote to the two houses of the Federal Assembly and 14 percent to the Slovak National Council. A coalition of two Hungarian parties, Coexistence and the Hungarian Christian Democratic Party, gained about 8.5 percent of votes to all three bodies. In addition to these parties, which passed the 5 percent threshold required to seat deputies in the Federal Assembly, the Democratic Party, with 4.4 percent of the vote and Green Party with 3.5 percent passed the three percent threshold required to seat deputies in the Slovak National Council (see table 6.2).

As in 1990, no party won a majority of the vote in the 1992 elections in Slovakia. Vladimír Mečiar's Movement for a Democratic Slovakia gained the largest share of the vote (33.5 percent to the House of the People and 33.9 percent to the House of Nations of the National Assembly and 37.3 percent to the Slovak National Council). The Party of the Democratic Left, the successor to the Communist Party of Slovakia, came in second with approximately 14 percent of the vote for all three bodies, followed by the Christian Democratic Movement with approximately 9 percent. The Slovak National Party won 9.4 percent of the vote for both houses of the Federal Assembly and 7.9 percent for the Slovak National Council. In addition, coalitions of Hungarian parties gained approximately 7 percent of the vote and seated deputies in both the federal and Slovak bodies. The Social Democratic Party, with 6 percent of the vote, also passed the threshold to seat deputies in the House of Nations of the Federal Assembly. The Civic Democratic Union, however, the center right successor of Public Against Violence, with 4.0 percent of the vote for all three bodies, did not pass the threshold required to seat deputies at either the federal or republic level (see table 6.3).

Since independence, Slovakia has experienced early parliamentary elections brought about by the parliamentary ouster of Vladimír Mečiar as prime minister in March 1994. In these elections, which were held in September–October 1994, the Movement for a Democratic Slovakia won the largest share of the vote (34.96 percent). Common Choice, a coalition of the Party of the Democratic Left, the Social Democratic Party of Slovakia, the Green Party of Slovakia and the Farmers Movement of the Slovak Republic, was second with 10.41 percent; and the Hungarian Coalition was third with 10.18 percent. Unable to convince leaders of the Party of the Democratic Left to enter into a coalition with him, Mečiar formed a coalition with the Slovak National Party which won 5.40 percent of the vote, and the Association of Slovak Workers which won 7.43 percent. Together, the coalition holds 83 of the 150 seats, eight more than a majority in parliament (see table 6.4).

Table 6.3 *Parliamentary elections in Slovakia, 1992*

Political Parties	House of the People				House of Nations				National Council			
	No. votes	% vote	No. seats	% seats	No. votes	% vote	No. seats	% seats	No. votes	% vote	No. seats	% seats
HZDS	1,036,459	33.5	24	47.0	1,045,395	33.9	33	44.0	1,148,625	37.3	74	49.3
SDL	446,230	14.4	10	19.6	433,750	14	13	17.3	453,203	14.7	39	26.0
SNS	290,249	9.4	6	11.7	288,864	9.4	9	12.0	244,527	7.9	15	10.0
KDH	27,061	9.0	6	11.7	272,100	8.8	8	10.7	273,945	8.9	18	12.0
MKDH	–	–	–	–	–	–	–	–	–	–	–	–
MKDH/MSL	227,925	7.4	5	9.8	228,219	7.4	7	9.3	228,885	7.42	14	9.3
SDSS	–	–	–	–	188,223	6.1	5	6.6	123,426	4	–	–
ODU	122,359	4	–	–	124,649	4	–	–	123,426	4	–	–
MOS	72,877	2.3	–	–	71,122	2.4	–	–	70,689	2.3	–	–
DS/ODS	122,266	3.7	–	–	113,176	3.4	–	–	102,058	2.3	–	–

Notes: Voter turnout: 83% of eligible voters;   Acronyms: DS/ODS – Democratic Party/Civic Democratic Party; HZDS – Movement for a Democratic Slovakia; KDH – Christian Democratic Movement; MKDH – Coexistence-Hungarian Christian Democratic Movement; MKDH/MSL – MKDH/Hungarian People's Party; MOS – Hungarian Civic Party; ODU – Civic Democratic Union; SDL – Party of the Democratic Left; SDSS – Social Democratic Party; SNS – Slovak National Party

Sources: Jiri Pehe, "Czechoslovakia's Political Balance Sheet, 1990–1992," *RFE/RL Research Reports*, June 19, 1992; "Volby 1992," *Respekt*, June 8–14, 1992); Sharon L. Wolchik, "The Repluralization of Politics in Post-Communist Czechoslovakia," *Journal of Post-Communist Studies*, no. 1 (1994), 419; Oskar Krejčí, *History of Elections in Bohemia and Moravia* (New York: Columbia University Press, 1995), pp. 341–52; and *FBIS-EEU*, Slovakia, June 8, 1992, pp. 15–17 and June 11, 1992, p. 9.

Table 6.4 *Parliamentary elections in Slovakia, 1994*

Political Parties	No. votes	% vote	No. seats	% seats
Movement for Democratic Slovakia (HZDS)/Peasant Party of Slovakia (RSS)	1,005,488	34.96	61	40.7
Common Choice[a] (SU)	299,496	10.41	18	12.0
Hungarian Coalition[b] (MK)	292,936	10.18	17	11.3
Christian Democratic Movement (KDH)	289,987	10.08	17	11.3
Democratic Union (DU)	246,444	8.57	15	10.0
Workers' Assoc. of Slovakia (ZRS)	211,321	7.34	13	8.7
Slovak National Party (SNS)	155,359	5.40	9	6.0
Democratic Party[c] (DS)	98,555	3.42	–	–
Communist Party of Slovakia (KSS)	78,419	2.72	–	–
Christian-Social Union (KSU)	59,217	2.05	–	–
New Slovakia (NS)	38,369	1.33	–	–
Party against Corruption (SPK)	37,929	1.31	–	–
Movement for a Prosperous Czechia and Slovakia (HZPC+S)	30,292	1.05	–	–
Romany Civic Initiative (ROI)	19,542	.67	–	–
Social Democracy (SD)	7,121	.24	–	–
Realistic Social-Democratic Party (RSDSS)	3,573	.12	–	–
Assoc. for the Republic-Republicans (ZPR)	1,410	.04	–	–

Notes: Voter turnout: 75.65% of registered voters [a]Coalition of Party of the Democratic Left (SDL), Social-Democratic Party of Slovakia (SDSS), Movement of Farmers of the Slovak Republic, and the Green Party of Slovakia (SZS). [b]Coalition of Coexistence, Hungarian Christian Democratic Movement (MKDH), and Hungarian Civic Party (MOS). [c]Including Party of Businessmen and Self-Employed.

Sources: FBIS-EEU, Slovakia, October 5, 1994, p. 11; "1994 Elections," by EUnet (Internet source), October 2, 1994; *Slovakia: Parliamentary Elections 1994*, ed. Soňa Szomolányi and Gregorij Mesežnikov (Bratislava, Slovakia: Slovak Political Science Foundation, 1995); *1994 Parliamentary Elections in the Slovak Republic*, TA SR, Slovakia News Agency, September 27, 1994.

The break-up of the Czechoslovak Federation

The development of the party system and other forms of citizen participation in politics in Slovakia was also influenced by the break-up of the Czechoslovak Federation in 1993. As I have argued in greater detail in an earlier discussion of this issue, the end of the Czechoslovak state was the reflection of a variety of historical, cultural, economic, and political/institutional factors.[38] Cooperation between Czech and Slovak leaders after November 1989 soon gave way to conflict over the division of labor between the federal and republic governments as well as to the increasingly open expression of different views on the speed and extent of economic reform.

The inability of leaders to come to an agreement on the power-sharing issue and the much harsher impact of the shift to the market in Slovakia, given the differences in the timing and nature of industrialization discussed earlier, resulted in growing dissatisfaction with the federation in Slovakia. As the results of the 1992 elections illustrate, this dissatisfaction, coupled with psychological and historical factors, as well as with the differences in opinion among Czechs and Slovaks concerning many of the most important issues of the day, led to the victory of a center–right coalition led by Václav Klaus in the Czech Lands and a coalition of the Movement for a Democratic Slovakia and the Slovak National Party led by Vladimír Mečiar in Slovakia.

The actual process by which the common state ended was initiated by political elites and confined to the elite level. The public, which continued to oppose the break-up in both the Czech Lands and Slovakia even as their leaders negotiated it, was not consulted by means of a referendum. The Federal Parliament eventually approved a plan for dividing the state, but it is clear that neither the federal nor the republic legislatures played a significant role in the process.[39] At the same time, the different perspectives of Czechs and Slovaks on issues such as the nature of the state and the pace and extent of economic reform provided the background for these actions. Thus, among those Slovaks who wanted to see a common state continue, most favored a "confederation"; however, the nature of this arrangement was not clearly understood or specified.[40] Similarly, Vladimír Mečiar's promise to find a road to the market that would take Slovakia's specific features into account resonated with the desire of many Slovaks to see the state continue to play a larger role than most Czechs wanted as well as with the lower levels of support among Slovaks for privatization of large state enterprises. Differences in the perspectives of Czechs and Slovaks, then, allowed political leaders, particularly in Slovakia, to mobilize citizens around these issues.

In contrast to the situation in the former Yugoslav federation, the break-up of Czechoslovakia occurred peacefully. The peaceful nature of the end of the Czechoslovak state reflected the fact that the Czech leadership was willing to agree to Slovakia's independence after the June 1992 elections. It also reflected the fact that Czechs and Slovaks had never slaughtered each other in mass numbers and the absence of a history of violence between the two peoples. The concentration of settlement in the two regions was also an important factor. In contrast to the situation in former Yugoslavia, the numbers of Czechs living in Slovakia and Slovaks living in the Czech Lands was not large.[41]

From the perspective of the development of the party system and other avenues of citizen participation in politics in Slovakia, the break-up of the federation was significant in a number of ways. Questions about the nature and future of the state played a dominant role in public life in the first two and a half years of the postcommunist era. Particularly as economic hardship due to the shift to the market increased in Slovakia, those political leaders and political parties who supported both reform and the continuation of the federation were doubly disadvantaged in their efforts to gain electoral support. After the elections of June 1992 they were marginalized from politics.

The fact that the split occurred peacefully was also important for the further development of the party system as well as of other political organizations and institutions in Slovakia. In contrast to the situation in former Yugoslavia, the leaders and citizens of Slovakia were able to continue to engage in political life without the threat or presence of war after independence.

Social and ethnic cleavages in postcommunist society

Ethnicity, which was one of the most important cleavages in Czechoslovakia during the interwar and communist periods, continues to be the most politically salient cleavage in independent Slovakia. Slovaks comprise 85.7 percent of the population. There are approximately 567,000 Hungarians concentrated in the southern part of Slovakia; 17,200 Ruthenians; and 13,300 Ukrainians.[42] There are also smaller Polish and Czech communities and a sizeable Romany, or gypsy community, unofficially estimated to be between 100,000 to 250,000.[43] During the communist era, members of the Hungarian minority as well the Ukrainians/Ruthenians concentrated in Eastern Slovakia were more likely than Slovaks to work in agriculture.[44] However, most members of both groups were workers or employees. The educational levels of Ukrainians/Ruthenians were substantially lower than those of other citizens of Slovakia.[45]

Political life after independence, just as it was before, is organized along ethnic lines. Hungarian voters in particular vote for Hungarian parties. As a later section of the paper will discuss, there are also important differences in the political perspectives of young and old voters. Political values and attitudes also differ by educational levels, as well as by gender.

As I have argued in greater detail elsewhere,[46] there are important differences in the status of men and women in Slovak society. As the result of policies adopted during the communist era, women's educational levels have increased and now equal or exceed those of men, particularly in the younger age groups. Most women are also employed outside the home. However, substantial inequalities still remain in the workplace. Women are less likely to hold leading positions and also have lower incomes. In the postcommunist period, women's share of the unemployed has generally been larger than their representation in the labor force. Women have also faced increasingly open discrimination in the workplace and in society at large. The exclusion of women from positions of political power has continued in the postcommunist period.[47] Slovak society is also becoming more stratified along economic lines as a result of the reintroduction of the market.

The shift to the market

At the end of the communist period, Slovakia's development level was nearly on a par with that of the Czech Lands. However, because it took place largely during the communist era, the nature of Slovakia's industrialization differed. Much of Czechoslovakia's arms industry was concentrated in Slovakia, and more of Slovakia's industries were of the very large, inefficient type typical of centrally planned economies. There were also large numbers of towns that were in effect one-industry towns and thus extremely vulnerable once market conditions were introduced.[48]

Slovak leaders agreed to the plan for the rapid reintroduction of the market adopted by the federal and republic governments in September 1990. However, given the timing and nature of industrialization, the Slovak economy was more susceptible to disruptions caused by the shift to the market. Unemployment rates soon reached 12 to 13 percent, rates several times higher than those in the Czech Lands. Part of the source of Vladimír Mečiar's electoral victory in the 1992 elections was his promise to adjust economic strategy to better reflect the specific needs and conditions in Slovakia.

As in other postcommunist societies, the impact of the economic transition has been differentiated. Those who are young, better educated, and live in urban areas have benefited most from the opportunity to establish or work for private businesses, increase their skills through contact with foreign experts and travel abroad, or work for international corporations. They and a larger group have also benefited from the ability to practice their professions or work in their occupations without political or ideological interference.

Table 6.5 *Indicators of economic trends in Slovakia since 1989*

	1989	1990	1991	1992	1993	1994	1995[a]
GDP	1.4[b]	-0.4[b]	-14.5	-6.4	-4.1	4.5	6.6
Industrial output	-0.7	-3.6	-17.5	-14.4	-10.2	6.4	8.4
Rate of inflation	2.3[b]	10.8[b]	61.2	10.1	23.2	13.5	9.9
% Labor force unemployed	0	1.5	11.8	10.3	14.4	14.8	13.1
GNP per capita	n.a.	n.a.	n.a.	n.a.	6,660	n.a.	n.a.
% Workforce in private activity	1.0	5.0	12.8	18.4	22.2	31.9	n.a.
% GDP from private sector	n.a.	n.a.	n.a.	22.0	24.6	43.8	n.a.

Notes: GDP – % change over previous year; industrial output – % change over previous year; rate of inflation – % change in end-year retail/consumer prices; rate of unemployment as of end of year; GNP per capita – in US dollars at PPP exchange rates. [a]Estimate. [b]Years 1989, 1990 are for the Czechoslovak Federation; beginning with 1991 data are for Slovakia only.

Sources: European Bank for Reconstruction and Development, *Transition Report 1995: Economic Transition in Eastern Europe and the Former Soviet Union* (London: EBRD, 1995); European Bank for Reconstruction and Development, *Transition Report Update, April 1996: Assessing Progress in Economies in Transition* (London: EBRD, 1996).

For many Slovaks, however, the shift to the market has created a good deal of hardship. Unskilled workers, older workers, and women have borne the brunt of the transition. Vulnerable groups in the population, such as the elderly and single mothers,[49] have been particularly hard hit. Workers in the many one-industry towns and cities in Slovakia in which the main enterprises are not competitive in the new conditions have also suffered high levels of unemployment and economic hardship.[50] Different groups in society have had different experiences with privatization. Many Slovaks benefited from their participation in the first wave of coupon privatization, which took place before the break-up of the federation. Since that time, critics of the Mečiar regime have charged that privatization has benefited largely those who support Mečiar and members of the old apparatus.[51] Hungarian activists in particular have claimed that members of the Hungarian minority are being systematically excluded from participation in privatization.[52] Economic performance began to improve in 1995, when the Slovak economy grew at the rate of 6.6 percent. However, as in a number of other postcommunist countries, progress at the macroeconomic level has yet to be reflected in the living standard of many sectors of the population (see table 6.5).

Large-scale privatization virtually stopped after Vladimír Mečiar became prime minister in 1992. The coalition government of Jozef Moravčik adopted plans to reinstitute coupon privatization in 1994, and the first sales were made prior to the September–October 1994 elections. The Mečiar government formed in December 1994 as the result of the September–October 1994 elections invalidated these sales, including several that had involved foreign investors. Under pressure from the IMF, the government announced a new plan in June of 1995 to privatize large scale economic enterprises later that year. However, this plan would provide citizens with bonds redeemable only in five years. In addition, many enterprises were sold by means of direct sales.[53] In July 1995, the parliament ended coupon privatization.[54] A December 1995 poll by FOCUS found that 40 percent of respondents in a nationwide survey were critical of the government's privatization strategy. Over 66 percent felt that privatization was not proceeding in the proper direction in Slovakia.[55]

Despite the reluctance of the government to continue the privatization of state enterprises, the private sector has continued to grow in Slovakia. By 1992, private enterprises accounted for 32.4 percent of GDP. This figure had increased to 58.2 percent by 1994 and 62 percent in the first half of 1995.[56] Approximately 40.5 percent of the labor force was estimated to be engaged in the private sector by 1994.[57]

The political evolution of society

Political parties and movements are the dominant political actors in Slovakia. As the section to follow on political parties and the party system details, many new political parties were formed after the end of communist rule. The Communist Party and other small parties permitted to exist during the communist period also continued to exist and took steps to reform themselves in order to compete electorally.

Other associations and organizations, including business groups, professional and voluntary associations, and trade unions, also took advantage of the new political conditions to organize and attract members. The NGO sector grew particularly quickly after the end of restrictions on forming new organizations. There were an estimated 9,800 NGO's in Slovakia in late 1995. This represents a sizeable increase since 1993 when there were approximately 6,000 NGOs registered with the government.[58] These figures compare to the approximately 16,000 associations that Mannová notes existed in Slovakia in the interwar period.[59]

Information on all of the NGOs registered with the government is not available. However, analysis of data gathered by SAIA-SCTS (Slovak Academic Information Agency-Service Center for the Third Sector) on 1,571

NGOs provides some insight into their fields of activity and focus. In 1995, the largest category of NGOs registered with SAIA-SCTS worked in the area of education and training (59 percent); 58 percent worked with youth, 46 percent with children; 35 percent with charity and social welfare; and 33 percent with disabled people. In addition, 25 percent focused on issues related to the environment and 20 percent on issues related to business development. These organizations encompassed approximately 380,400 volunteers in 1995.[60] Originally concentrated in Bratislava, NGOs have increasingly spread to other parts of the country.[61]

In March 1994, a Council, or Gremium, of the Third Sector was formed by sixteen people who represented different areas of the NGO sector. In 1995, this group was expanded to include seventeen individuals representing five areas of NGO activity. This body meets monthly and attempts to influence legislation that affects the NGO sector.[62]

A study of volunteerism conducted in Slovakia in April 1994 as part of an international study of volunteering provides some information about the number and kinds of citizens who take part in the work of voluntary organizations. In 1994, 11 percent of the 1,015 individuals surveyed indicated that they had participated in some kind of unpaid work for a voluntary organization in the previous year, and 12 indicated that they had done specific types of such work.[63] Of these over half (56 percent) did so at least once a month; 41 percent of those who regularly volunteer spent 10 hours a month doing so. Fialová notes that these proportions, as those in other formerly communist European countries, were considerably lower than those in countries such as Belgium (where 30 percent of respondents volunteered), Denmark (28 Percent), the Netherlands (34 percent) and Sweden (32 percent). Volunteers in Central and Eastern Europe are more likely than those in the rest of Europe to become volunteers through their work; they are also more likely to volunteer to provide services. Levels of satisfaction with volunteering are also lower.[64]

Equal proportions of men and women were regular volunteers; individuals with university education, as well as those who are older than 35, were most likely to volunteer.[65] These figures correspond to the results Zora Bútorová, Jan Hartl, and I found in our December 1994 survey which found that women were more likely to be active in non-partisan organizations than in political parties.[66] Men are more likely to volunteer for sports and recreation related organizations; women are more frequently found as volunteers in groups that deal with health and social service issues.[67]

In addition to groups that focus on providing services and recreational groups, a wide variety of other nongovernmental organizations developed that focus on issues ranging from the environment to feminism. Religious denominations also expanded the groups they organized for youth, women, and other groups of the population, as did political parties.

The introduction of the market and privatization have been accompanied by the formation of numerous groups and associations by business people and managers. To a large extent, these groups focus primarily on professional development and business related issues. However, a small party, the Party of Businessmen and Tradesmen, was formed in 1990. This party, which favors the rapid reintroduction of the market and creation of a positive environment for small and medium-sized businesses, ran as part of the Democratic Union's electoral slate in the 1994 elections. The Party also cooperates with business organizations abroad, including those in the Czech Republic and Hungary. On August 1, 1994, the party began a regular column in the daily *Sme* to provide advice for business people and information on issues that affect them.[68] Disagreement among the leaders of the party led to a split in February 1995; a new party, the Union of Tradesmen, Businessmen, and Farmers of the Slovak Republic, was formed.[69] In October 1995, the Party of Businessmen and Entrepreneurs agreed to cooperate with Mečiar's Movement for a Democratic Slovakia.[70]

In addition to these groups, there are also numerous business groups and associations that are affiliated with international bodies. The Slovak Association of Employers Unions and Associations represents employers groups in the Tripartite Commission, a body that brings together the trade unions, employers and the government to negotiate wage and other agreements.[71]

Privatization and the introduction of the market have also sparked efforts to organize on the part of agricultural workers. As in the case of business groups, most groups have focused on issues related to their members' occupations, such as agricultural production techniques. Agricultural workers and farmers have divided their votes among a variety of different political parties. These include the small Peasant Party that ran in the 1994 elections in coalition with the Movement for a Democratic Slovakia; the Christian Democratic Movement; and the Party of the Democratic Left.[72] The farmers movement, which formed part of the Common Choice coalition in 1994, also represents agricultural interests.

The end of communism has allowed trade unions to be more active protecting the interests of their members. However, the action of the trade unions has been limited by their participation in the deliberations of the tripartite commission. First established under the federation, the tripartite commision that brings unions, employers and the government together was continued after Slovakia became independent. Union representatives signed a General Agreement for 1994 designed to promote social peace in August 1994.[73] There have been few strikes in Slovakia since independence.

However, individual trade unions such as KOVO, the union of workers in mining, geology, and the oil industry, staged protests against the government's social policies in 1995.[74] Dissatisfaction with the government's effort to revamp social policies led representatives of the confederation to walk out of the tripartite agreement discussions in September 1995.[75] There have also been demonstrations such as that of 20,000 people in Bratislava organized by the Confederation of Trade Unions to protest government policies.[76] Leaders of the Confederation have also accused the Mečiar government of trying to break up the unions.[77]

The military, which was rapidly downsized, has played virtually no role in the selection of government leaders in Slovakia during the period between 1989 and 1993 or since Slovakia's independence.[78] During the communist era, the army was unpopular as the result of its politicization and subordination to the Soviet Union.[79] However, as in the former Soviet Union, the military was subordinated to Czechoslovakia's political authorities and did not play an independent role in politics. In the course of the reforms of 1968, steps were taken to reduce political influence in the military as well as to increase the number of Slovak officers and reduce discrimination against Slovaks in advancement.[80] The purge of reformist officers who supported the political reforms of 1968, which involved almost all of the junior officers, resulted in the dominance of officers who supported the repressive policies of the Húsak regime, particularly after Soviet support for Húsak became clear. For the remainder of the communist period, the army suffered from funding problems and demoralization.[81] The low educational levels of officers and evident subordination of the military to the Soviet command were additional factors that led to low public trust in the military and to the low prestige associated with military careers.[82]

The army's role in the events that brought about the end of communism in Czechoslovakia is disputed. As Barany notes, there is evidence that elements within the military as well as in the political leadership contemplated the use of force against the growing number of demonstrators in November 1989, but the resignation of the Communist Party's leadership prevented a decision about this issue from being reached.[83] In October 1990, then Defense Minister Miroslav Vaček was replaced when an investigation revealed that he had been a central figure in a November 1989 plan to control radio and television broadcasting.[84]

As in other postcommunist states, the military underwent important changes in its size, staffing, doctrine, and international links after the end of communist rule. Steps were taken to increase the military's professionalism. A significant number (23.6 percent) of officers and other professional soldiers left the military either because they did not pass competence testing or at their own request.[85] Slightly over one-half of all generals and 23.6 percent of all professional soldiers did not sign the new loyalty oath. Most of those who worked as political officers also left military service.[86] The Czechoslovak government also established greater civilian control over the military and took steps to eliminate the influence of foreign intelligence in the military.[87]

The Slovak army which came under the control of the new Slovak Republic in 1993 is uninvolved in political life. When the Czechoslovak federation brokeup, Czech and Slovak leaders agreed to split the army's assets and equipment on a two to one ratio. The division of the army was facilitated by the redeployment of army troops from the Czech Republic's western borders, where they had been concentrated during the communist period, to a more uniform distribution throughout the county. Czech officers serving in Slovakia and Slovak officers serving in the Czech Republic were given the option of remaining or returning to their own country when the federal state broke up. Most of the Slovaks who returned to Slovakia were younger and less experienced than those who remained in the Czech Lands. This factor complicated the task of creating a national Slovak army. As was the case for numerous other institutions such as the foreign service, for example, Slovaks had to build new institutions while Czechs could use federal institutions as a framework for the creation of Czech institutions. The weakness of the military as an institution and the fact that it has been largely preoccupied with its own internal affairs in Slovakia since independence, are additional factors, then, that have limited the military's political influence.

The direct political role of the political or secret police also appears to have been minimal. However, in Slovakia certain political leaders have allegedly influenced the decisions of their opponents as to whether or not to seek office or to continue in office by using information provided by the intelligence service or from police files. In these cases, the intelligence services provided information used by political leaders rather than initiating action or playing a role as independent political actors.

To date, violence has played a similarly limited role in the selection of political leaders in Slovakia. There have been several changes of government that have occurred peacefully in Slovakia. However, there are indicators that violence or the threat of violence may play an increasing role. The beating of František Mikloško, Deputy Chair of the Christian Democratic Movement, in September of 1995, is widely thought to have been politically motivated. The August 1995 kidnapping of President Kovač's son, who was forced to drink large quantities of alcohol and taken across the border into Austria, is another example of a politically motivated violent act.[88] President Kovač has accused Ivan Lexa, the head of the Slovak Information Service, Slovakia's secret service, of directing the kidnapping of his son.[89] Other opposition leaders, including Ján Čarnogurský, head of the Christian Democratic Party, have also charged that the SIS was involved in the abduction.[90] Two police investigators on the case who had alleged that the secret service was involved were removed from the case. The Director of the SIS filed criminal charges against the investigators as well as a lawsuit against President Kovač.[91]

At present, the process of selecting political leaders by democratic means is threatened more by political factors than by the use of violence. Hungarian activists charge that the government coalition's plans for redrawing the borders of Slovakia's districts threaten the ability of Slovakia's Hungarians to elect Hungarian leaders, for example. Originally approved by the government on March 22, 1996 and reapproved on July 3 after President Kovač's veto, the administrative reform recreated eight regions in Slovakia. It reduced the numbers of districts from 83 to 79.[92] The Deputy Chair of Coexistence, one of the members of the Hungarian Coalition, notes that the government plan incorporates the districts of two of the main centers of Hungarian settlement, Komarno and Dunajska Streda, into three different regions. Other districts and sub-districts with large Hungarian populations have also been separated and have become parts of different regions.[93]

The efforts of the Slovak National Party and the Movement for a Democratic Slovakia to revoke the mandates of Democratic Union deputies in March 1995 and the effort of the Mečiar government to force President Kovač to resign are examples of the attempted use of non-electoral, but legal means to influence the composition of the country's leadership. In January 1996, the Chair of the Mandate and Immunity Commission of the National Council announced that the conclusions reached by the earlier temporary mandate committee that the mandates of the Democratic Union deputies elected in 1994 were invalid was legally irrelevant because of procedural abnormalities in the temporary committee's handling of the issue. This judgement relied on the Constitutional Court's ruling to that effect in March 1995.[94] As the failure of both of those attempts illustrates, the ability of leaders to use such measures has been limited to date by the powers of other institutions, such as the Constitutional Court, despite the fact that the current government coalition holds a majority of legislative seats. International pressure also appears to have served as a restraint.

As in other postcommunist countries, rumor abounds concerning the influence of organized crime in Slovakia. International criminal organizations, including "mafias" from Ukraine and Russia, have moved into Slovakia in addition to Slovak criminal groups and networks. For obvious reasons, there is little systematic data about such groups and their activities.[95] Public opinion surveys indicate that Slovaks rank crime of all types second in importance after health concerns as a public problem.[96] Public officials have enacted new laws designed to deal with organized crime.[97] They have also begun to cooperate with agencies of other governments, including the FBI, to combat organized crime. However, in contrast to the situation in several postcommunist countries, where such groups appear to have infiltrated governmental bodies as well as economic institutions and many new private businesses, the direct political influence of such groups on politics appears to be small.

The greater threat to the persistence of democracy appears to come from antidemocratic actions on the part of certain elements of the legitimate political elite, including remnants of the old apparatus.[98] It is this influence rather than the influence of organized crime *per se* that appears to have most impact on citizens' perceptions of political life and institutions. As the section to follow illustrates, many citizens in Slovakia continue to be suspicious of the motives and actions of people in positions of political leadership. They are also reluctant to get involved in politics themselves, in part because of their belief that most people in politics are active in political life primarily to enrich themselves rather than to promote the common good.[99]

Since the end of communist rule, the media have developed into an independent source of information and opinion in Slovakia. Several political parties have newspapers that are either affiliated with them or favorable to their point of view. Efforts by the government to control newspapers have occurred frequently and led in some cases to the formation of new, more independent, dailies. After their 1994 electoral victory, Mečiar and his coalition partners attempted to change what they perceived to be the hostile press and other media by a number of means, including the replacement of the members of the board of governors of Slovak television and pressure on editors and journalists. These changes were followed by more extensive personnel changes in the media. A Council for Mass Media was also established in February 1995 to make sure that the media respect the constitution.[100] Political influence has been particularly noticeable in the broadcast media. Although there are several regional television stations and private radio stations, these stations cannot compete effectively with state owned channels, which remain more popular with viewers and listeners. A survey conducted by the State Television Board in May 1995 found that coalition parties and figures received markedly more coverage than the opposition or the president.[101]

The print media have not been as susceptible to measures to control them as the broadcast media. However, the government has taken a number of steps to attempt to correct what its members see as an anti-governmental bias in the journalism world. In February 1995, a law was discussed in a parliamentary committee that would have imposed a very high VAT on all dailies that were partly owned by outside investors. This measure provoked a common protest by thirteen dailies against what they described as undue economic pressure designed to muzzle a free press, and the government measure was shelved.[102] Opposition activists also see the removal of the license of the majority shareholder of the publisher of *Sme* and the purchase of another independent journal, *Pravda*, by the Harvard Investment Fund, which is closely connected to Ivan Lexa, head of the SIS, as efforts to limit the independence of the press.[103] The law on the protection of the republic which Parliament passed in December 1996 after President Kováč vetoed an earlier version of the law, calls for sanctions against those who spread false news that endangers the security of Slovaks or damages its interests, including those that are potential threats, and gives the government an additional tool to silence its critics in the media and other areas.[104]

Public support for democratization

Survey research conducted since the end of communist rule demonstrates that most Slovak citizens support democratization in general terms.[105] However, there have been important changes over time in the levels of this support, and there are significant differences in the degree of such support among different social groups. In general, younger, better educated, urban males tend to be more supportive of both the move to the market and the effort to recreate a democratic political system.[106]

As the survey results discussed below illustrate, a sizeable number of citizens in Slovakia continue to be unconvinced that it was necessary to change the pre-1989 system. Prior to the break-up of the Czechoslovak federation in 1993, Slovaks tended to be less favorable than Czechs toward a rapid move to the market. They also were less willing to accept greater unemployment and more fearful of a decline in the standard of living. Respondents in Slovakia were also less favorable toward the privatization of large enterprises and more likely than those in the Czech Lands to want the state to continue to play a major role in providing social welfare and security for citizens.[107] In a November–December 1994 survey on which I collaborated with colleagues in Bratislava and Prague, 41 percent of respondents in Slovakia (compared to 68 percent of those in the Czech Lands) believed that extensive changes were necessary in the economy.[108] The less positive attitudes of Slovaks toward economic reform and the introduction of the market can be traced in part to the high levels of unemployment in Slovakia since the end of communist rule and in part to the persisting legacy of certain values and expectations dating from the communist era.

Respondents in Slovakia also were less favorable toward the political changes that occurred after 1989. The proportion of those who felt that the current system had more disadvantages than advantages increased from approximately 20 percent in May 1991 to 55 in October 1993. In December 1994, approximately 42 percent of respondents in Slovakia, compared to 20 percent in the Czech Republic, felt that the present political regime had more disadvantages than the pre-1989 system. Most citizens in Slovakia as well as in the Czech Lands, however, felt that the current system gave their children advantages the previous system could not offer.[109]

Citizen evaluations of political leaders and institutions have generally not been as favorable in Slovakia as those toward the overall idea of democratization. A majority of respondents surveyed in the Slovak Republic in November–December 1994, for example, disagreed with the statement that most politicians act in an unselfish and moral way (approximately 76 percent). Approximately 91 percent of respondents agreed with the statement that the powers that be do not care about the opinion of common people.[110]

Trust in political institutions fluctuated in Slovakia after independence.[111] In early 1991, for example, 57 percent of the population trusted the president of the federation; 48 percent the Federal Assembly; 67 percent the Slovak National Council; and 77 percent the Slovak government.[112] In October 1993, 73 percent of those surveyed trusted the president of Slovakia; 43 percent the Slovak National Council; and 41 percent the government of Slovakia. Levels of trust in the National Council increased slightly during the period of the coalition government in Slovakia (May 1994), while those in the government increased substantially (to 55 percent).[113] In late 1994, trust in the president had increased to 80 percent; and in the government to 61 percent. Trust in parliament remained substantially lower at just under 40 percent.[114] As is the case for general attitudes toward the transition, trust in political institutions, as well as in individual leaders, varies considerably by the political orientations of respondents. In 1994 and 1995, those affiliated with the opposition parties put more trust in the president, who has often opposed the policies of Prime Minister Mečiar; those who voted for the ruling coalition were more likely to trust the government and National Council.[115]

Attitudes concerning political parties have tended to be negative in Slovakia as well as in the Czech Republic. Thus, many citizens think that a strong leader is more important for democracy than strong political parties.[116] Slovak respondents were also less likely than those in the Czech Lands (15 percent compared to 27 percent) to be members of interest groups and civil associations, but nearly equally likely (32 percent and 34 percent) to be members of trade unions.[117] Respondents in Slovakia and the Czech Lands were equally unlikely to view at least two strong political parties which compete in elections as the most essential feature of a democracy.[118]

Many citizens in Slovakia feel that they do not understand politics. The majority of those surveyed in 1994 also felt that they had little ability to influence government decisions that adversely affect their interests at either the national (74 percent) or local level (50 percent). A majority (55 percent) did not feel that parliamentary elections allow citizens to influence decision-making; only a slightly higher proportion (58 percent) saw local elections as a way of influencing local decisions.[119]

As in the case of general evaluations of the process of democratization and the move to the market, opinions on these issues vary considerably by social category and, particularly, partisan political affiliation or sympathy. Supporters of parties that are in the government that was formed in late 1994 tend to be less supportive of a liberal conception of democracy and less favorable toward the market. However, partisan affiliation does not differentiate among citizens with different potentials for participation. Younger and better educated people, as well as students, entrepreneurs, and professionals are more likely to indicate that they are willing to participate in political activities than workers or retired people. Men were more likely to participate than women.[120]

Differences in attitudes and inclinations to take part in political action are particularly noticeable between men and women. Women are less likely than men to feel that they understand politics and far less likely to feel that they can influence political decisions at either the national or local level. They are less often members of political parties and less often indicate that they are likely to take part in the activities of political parties.[121]

As the discussion above indicates, the economic transition has had a major impact on citizens' attitudes toward the transition and their roles in it. In general, those who have benefited from the shift to the market or have the ability to benefit from it in the future are more likely to have a liberal concept of democracy. They are also more likely to indicate that they are active or are likely to be active in a variety of forms of political action in addition to voting.

Political parties and the party system

Slovakia's party system shares certain features with those of other postcommunist European countries. Chief among these is the fact that there is still a good deal of fluctuation in both political parties and popular affiliation with particular parties. These features are evident in the changing roster of parties that have competed in each of the parliamentary elections held since 1989 and the number of new parties that continue to be formed; they are also evident in survey research that indicates that a significant number of citizens are not firmly anchored to a single political party but rather float among different parties in their electoral support and choices.[122] Two of the seven parties that won enough votes to seat deputies in the 1994 parliamentary elections, for example, had been created after the last elections.[123] Another, Common Choice, was a newly formed coalition of left of center parties including the Party of the Democratic Left, the Social Democratic Party, the Christian

Social Union, and the Farmers' Movement among others. Vladimír Mečiar's Movement for a Democratic Slovakia also entered into coalition with the small Peasant Party. (See tables 6.2–6.4 for the results of the postcommunist parliamentary elections.) There have also been a number of changes in political parties since the 1994 elections, including a split in the Social Democratic Party.

Most parties continue to have small memberships. This tendency, which parallels the decline in party membership in certain West European democracies, is compounded by low levels of party identification among voters. As noted above, many citizens in Slovakia have rather low opinions of political parties and are not convinced that they are essential to democracy. In reaction to the communist period when party membership was required to advance in one's career or influence politics, most citizens do not want to join any political party. Most of the respondents in our 1994 November–December survey did not participate in the work of party organizations. Thus, 8 percent of those surveyed in Slovakia, compared to 12 percent in the Czech Lands, were members of political parties in late 1994. Men were more likely than women to be party members in both countries. Both men and women were more likely to be involved in the work of nonpartisan voluntary organizations.

As in other postcommunist systems, many of the umbrella organizations and groups that united people with a wide variety of political perspectives have fragmented in Slovakia. The split in Public Against Violence in April 1991 that was followed by the formation of Vladimír Mečiar's Movement for a Democratic Slovakia and the eventual formation and electoral demise of the Civic Democratic Union was paralleled by the splits that occurred within the Christian Democratic Movement, the Slovak National Party, and other political groupings.

However, the fragmentation of non-traditional movements has not been followed, as it has in the Czech Republic, by the domination of political life by political parties that can be easily placed on the left-right spectrum similar to those that exist in more established political democracies. Vladimír Mečiar's Movement for a Democratic Slovakia, for example, has supported economic and social policies often associated with leftist parties; however, its symbols and appeal to national sentiments are more typical of radical right-wing parties.[124]

There are some indications that party divisions are beginning to crystalize in Slovakia. This tendency has been particularly evident among the Hungarian political parties, which saw the least shift in their supporters in the 1994 elections. The Christian Democratic Movement has been the most stable of the right of center parties.[125] However, there has been considerable fluctuation in both the levels of support and individuals supporting most other political parties and movements.

The electoral laws adopted after the fall of the communist system have influenced the structure and durability of political parties in Slovakia in important ways. Based largely on the electoral law used for the 1946 elections, the electoral law adopted to govern the June 1990 elections, which relied on a system of proportional representation with a threshold, was instrumental in both ensuring that the various cleavages in Slovak society would be reflected in parliament and in limiting the number of political parties that would be represented in parliament. Coupled with the retention of the federated system of government, the electoral system, which required a party to achieve a threshold in only one republic in order for deputies to be seated in one of the houses of the Federal Assembly, also reinforced the division of political life and party formation by republic.

The threshold requirement succeeded in limiting the number of competing political parties that would be active in parliament to a manageable number. However, it also meant that there were a large number of "lost" votes for parties that did not gain the percentage of the vote required to seat deputies in the legislature. The increase in the threshold from 3 percent to 5 percent for single parties in the Slovak National Council and the introduction of a 7 percent threshold for a coalition of two or three parties and a 10 percent threshold for coalitions with more than three parties further increased the number of parties that did not pass the required threshold.[126] However, it did succeed in reducing the number of lost votes from 23.8 percent in the June 1992 elections to 13.02 percent in the 1994 elections.[127]

As Zemko notes, despite the impetus toward consolidation that threshholds might be expected to create, most small parties did not unite with others but rather joined or formed electoral coalitions of larger parties to ensure that some of their candidates would be elected to parliament in the 1994 elections. As a result, of the approximately sixty political parties that existed in Slovakia in the spring of 1994, eighteen parties and coalitions participated in the elections. However, these included a total of thirty-one parties, organized into coalitions of one sort or another.[128]

As noted earlier, the structure of the state, as well as ethnic cleavages, had a major impact on the organization of parties during the period in which Slovakia remained part of the Czechoslovak federation after 1989. However, the existence of a unitary system within Slovakia after independence has not decreased the salience of the ethnic division as a focus for political organizing. This fact suggests that the form of the state has been less important in Slovakia than underlying ethnic cleavages in influencing party formation.

Analysts of other societies in transition differ concerning the impact of parliamentary and presidential systems on political stability.[129] The president in Slovakia is elected by parliament and has relatively limited formal powers. However, as the role President Kováč's speech to parliament played in bringing about the ouster of the Mečiar government in March 1994 illustrates, the occupant of the office can play an important political role in certain circumstances. The close relations between the president and the parties that participated in the broad coalition government in 1994 that became the opposition after the September–October 1994 elections, however, did little to bolster the drawing power of those parties in the 1994 elections.

The latter point illustrates a further factor that has been very important in influencing the development of the party system in Slovakia as in other postcommunist states: the role of personalities and personal rivalries. The pivotal role of Vladimír Mečiar in Slovak politics since 1989 is the clearest example of this factor. Several new parties have formed directly as the result of their leaders' conflict with Mečiar. Personal rivalry has been at least as if not more important than policy or programmatic differences in the splits that have occurred and led to the formation of other new parties in other political groupings. As noted earlier, Mečiar's dominant role and the conflicts that have occurred between him and his former supporters, as well as between him and the opposition have contributed to the polarization of political life in Slovakia.[130]

Research conducted in Slovakia indicates that supporters of parties in the government and in the opposition differ from each other in their commitment to pluralistic values, as well as in their levels of belief in egalitarianism and nationalism. Differences in value orientations and attitudes toward the institutions and principles of parliamentary democracy in turn are among the factors that make compromise between the two groups unlikely.[131] Thus, supporters of the Democratic Union, the Christian Democratic Movement, the Party of the Democratic Left, the Social Democratic Party of Slovakia, the National Democratic Party, the Green Party of Slovakia, the Hungarian Christian Democratic Movement and the Hungarian Civic Party have followers who tend to be supportive of democratic procedures and the development of a more differentiated civil society. The commitment of leaders and supporters of the three parties in the government coalition to democratic principles is not as clear. None of these parties openly espouses the use of violence, although the leader of the Slovak National Party has argued that all Hungarian political organizations in Slovakia are working against the state and should therefore be banned. None is linked with paramilitary forces or with forces outside the state that openly advocate the overthrow of democratic institutions.

Leaders of the Movement for a Democratic Slovakia and the Slovak National Party left office peacefully in March 1994 when their government received a vote of no-confidence in parliament. However, many of the supporters of these parties and the Association of Workers of Slovakia, do not support many of the principles of democratic political life, such as tolerance, compromise, negotiation, and the need to respect the rights of opponents and minorities.[132] The Slovak National Party draws on many of the traditions of the Slovak interwar clerical movement. Survey research indicates that its supporters, as well as those of the other members of the ruling coalition, include sizeable numbers of individuals who do not have a strong faith in democratic principles. SNS supporters also score very low on measures of ethnic tolerance. They differ from supporters of their coalition partners in their strong pro-market orientation.[133]

Leaders of these parties have engaged in efforts to limit the rights of expression of their political opponents and tried to use legal means including their majority in parliament to change the rules of the political game in a way that would ensure their continuation in power. As discussed earlier, in October 1994, Mečiar and his coalition partners attempted to remove fifteen deputies of the Democratic Union, a party formed in March 1994 by Josef Moravčik and several other deputies who were originally elected to parliament as members of the Movement for a Democratic Slovakia, from Parliment. The coalition's supporters also have tried repeatedly to force President Kováč from office. In addition to investigations into Kováč's role in Mečiar's ouster by parliament in March of 1994, the parliament passed a nonbinding vote of no-confidence in the president in May of 1995. The budget of the president's office has been severely cut, necessitating drastic staff reductions and limiting the activities in which he can engage.[134] As noted earlier, in addition to these actions which violate the spirit of democratic political life but are not strictly illegal, political institutions and actors controlled by or affiliated to the government have been associated with politically motivated violence in a number of cases since the 1994 elections.

The need to compete in competitive elections has clearly had an influence on the successor to the Communist Party of Slovakia, the Party of the Democratic Left. Leaders of the party, which has consistently earned more of the votes than its social democratic competition, have worked hard to reorient the image and policies of their party. The party defines itself as a social-democratic party, and its leaders participated in the broad coalition in power between March and December 1994 which included the Christian Democrats and other center–right parties. Public opinion data gathered in late 1994 indicate that supporters of the coalition Common Choice which the party joined in the last elections see the parties affiliated with the coalition as the most leftist of the parliamentary parties. However, in their opinions on economic issues, most supporters fall closer to the center of the political spectrum. Coalition supporters tended in November and December 1994 to have views on economic and foreign policy issues closer to those of Vladimír

Mečiar and the other parties that joined his governing coalition in December 1994. However, their views on democracy and other political principles, as well as on the Hungarian minority, were more similar to those members of the political parties that were in opposition to Mečiar.[135] Most supporters of Common Choice have higher educations and support social-democratic positions.[136]

The formation of the left-wing Association of Slovak Workers by a former deputy of the Party of the Democratic Left who broke away from the Party is another indication of how far the Party of the Democratic Left has moved from hard-line leftist positions. In addition to the Association of Slovak Workers, there is also a very small hard-line Communist Party of Slovakia which is not represented in parliament. This party opposes privatization and most of the changes that have been made since 1989. It is not a threat to democratic political life in Slovakia because it is so small.

There is a strong ethnic dimension to Slovakia's party system. Two of the three Hungarian political parties, the Hungarian Civic Party and the Hungarian Christian Democratic Movement, are differentiated primarily by their lay or religious character. Both are center–right parties whose leaders and followers support the move to the market and democratic principles. Coexistence, the third Hungarian party, which also includes Ruthenian/Ukrainian as well as Roma supporters, is less well-defined. It is the primary example of a political movement that crosses ethnic lines, although it is part of the Hungarian Coalition in Parliament and is generally viewed as a Hungarian movement. Most Hungarians support Hungarian parties. In May 1994, for example, Coexistance was the most popular party among Hungarian respondents surveyed (31 percent) followed by the Hungarian Christan Democratic Movement (28 percent). The Party of the Democratic Left and the Hungarian Civic Party had approximately equal degrees of support (9 and 8 percent respectively.[137] There is also a Romany Civic Initiative which draws support from the Roma.

In addition to the Hungarian Christian Democratic Movement, the Christian Democratic Movement and Christian–Social Union are religiously based parties. The strongest of these is the Christian Democratic Movement. Supporters of the CDM, which defines itself as a center–right party, support liberal economic principles and adhere to democratic political values. Almost all are religious.[138]

Conclusion: the impact of the party system on governmental efficiency and the consolidation of democracy in Slovakia

The party system in Slovakia has not facilitated the formation of a government able to carry out coherent public policies to date. In the period between 1990 and 1992, Slovak politics, as well as that of the federation as a whole, was dominated by the issue of constitutional reform and the future of the joint state. These issues complicated the process of economic reform and increased citizen dissatisfaction with political institutions and leaders. In Slovakia, the June 1992 elections saw the marginalization of the liberal leaders of the former Public Against Violence and the victory of the Movement for a Democratic Slovakia, which endorsed economic policies at odds with those adopted by the previous coalition and also attracted supporters dissatisfied with Slovakia's position in the federation.

After Slovakia became independent, the divisions within the country that had been evident regarding the issue of independence continued to color political life. Vladimír Mečiar's informal coalition with the Slovak National Party was unstable; defections from his own party eventually made his government a minority government. Coupled with Mečiar's conflict with the president, these problems led to his ouster by parliament in March 1994.

The broad coalition government formed at that time made a good deal of progress in dealing with Slovakia's problems and restarting economic reform. However, its leaders proved unable to form an electoral coalition and Mečiar, as leader of the party with the largest share of the votes, was once again able to form a coalition, despite the fact that his party did not gain a majority of the vote in the September–October, 1994 parliamentary elections.

Political life also continues to be highly polarized in Slovakia. In late 1995–early 1996, representatives of the Party of the Democratic Left flirted with cooperating with the Movement for a Democratic Slovakia. However, party representatives indicated that one of the conditions of such cooperation would be the removal of the Slovak National Party from the coalition. The prime minister's coalition, which brings together the right of center National Party and the left of center Association of Slovak Workers, has only a slim majority of votes. Disagreements within the coalition or defections from the coalition parties could easily upset the balance that prevailed through 1995 and early 1996. Significantly, the primary example of cooperation between the opposition parties and the government in 1995 occurred in the passage of the language law, a measure which threatens the interests of the Hungarian minority.

These factors call into question the extent to which democracy has been consolidated in Slovakia. In formal terms, Slovakia has a democratic government. The Mečiar government formed in December 1994 reflected the results of free, open, and contested elections. To date, the actions of the leaders of the coalition have remained within the framework of the law. However, as noted earlier, leaders of the coalition have attempted to use their parliamentary majority to remove vocal opponents of their policies from their positions and restrict the influence of the opposition. The government has also used legal means to consolidate its power in the bureaucracy at the district and local as well as central level and in the police forces. It has attempted to use legal means to control the media and has taken actions to make the future of non-governmental organizations more difficult. The sporadic violent attacks on and harassment of prominent members of the opposition as well as of the president's son are widely attributed to the government. The law on the protection of the republic which the government approved in December 1996, in effect subjects anyone who makes a critical remark about the country or publishes information that is critical to possible prosecution.

On the side of the opposition, the unity of the period of the coalition government in 1994 appears to have been short lived, as the parties that participated chose not to form an electoral coalition. There also appears to be little willingness among the lay center–right parties to put aside personal and other differences to form a strong center–right party. Nor have these parties been able to recruit or develop a leader who could match Vladimír Mečiar's ability to appeal to the populace or challenge his position as the dominant personality in Slovak politics. The inability of the governing coalition and the opposition to compromise or establish a system to institutionalize and mediate the conflicts that separate them are further signs democracy has yet to be consolidated in Slovakia.

The situation of the Hungarian minority in Slovakia is also problematic from the perspective of the consolidation of democracy, if consolidation is also understood to include the requirement that all significant groups in society have a chance of having their interests heard. Efforts by the Mečiar government in 1995 to assert greater central control over the selection of principals in local schools and introduce so-called "alternative education," that is, education in Slovak in Hungarian language schools, if parents request it further increased the distrust members of this group felt toward the government. Parliament's failure to ratify the state treaty with Hungary signed in March 1995 in a timely way due to opposition from the Slovak National Party, and the passage of a law making Slovak the official language and requiring its use in a wide variety of official, cultural, and other contexts also increased tensions between the two groups.[139] In early 1995, Hungarian activists gathered 45,000 signatures to protest the introduction of "alternative education," that is, classes in Slovak in Hungarian schools.[140] Hungarian representatives have expressed the fear that the law will lead to the restriction of the use of Hungarian in official contacts, a right which is guaranteed to members of national minorities by the constitution.[141] The difficulty of resolving this situation is illustrated by the fact that most opposition deputies (apart from those of the Christian Democratic Movement) supported the language law.

To date, most Hungarians appear to accept the boundaries of the state, as well as the need to work within the framework of democratic institutions.[142] However, the policies discussed above may in time lead to the perception among Slovakia's Hungarians that they are being systematically marginalized and that there is little hope that they can achieve their aims or defend their interests by using established institutions. Evidence of this possibility is found in the fact that Coexistence, whose leaders have occasionally advocated more direct forms of protest and whose supporters have demonstrated less support for democratic norms and values than those of leaders of other Hungarian parties, has consistently gained the largest share of the Hungarian vote.

The progress of democratic consolidation in Slovakia will be influenced by many factors in addition to the development of the party system. Despite efforts to restrict their influence, opposition activists and intellectuals continue to have the possibility to publish, travel abroad, and organize with others to criticize or question government actions. Citizens also are able to engage in active protests, as occurred in the November 1994 and March 1995 demonstrations for democracy and free speech.[143]

The growth of the non-governmental sector in Slovakia is also positive. Many of these organizations are dependent on foreign funding; most are small; and many consist largely of those who staff them in Bratislava or other large cities. However, such organizations provide a ground for the development and fostering of attitudes supportive of democracy among citizens. They also allow citizens to organize independently of the existing political parties to protest government policies and attempt to mobilize public opinion to bring new issues to the political agenda. The fact that young people tend to be more supportive of democratic values than older people is also an encouraging sign for the future.[144]

The fate of Slovak democracy and the likelihood that democracy will be consolidated will also be influenced by economic factors. The economic hardship many Slovaks experienced as a result of the shift to the market in the early postcommunist period was one of the factors, together with national grievances, that fueled support for the Movement for a Democratic Slovakia. The growth in the Slovak economy in 1994 and 1995 surprised many analysts. Despite the effective end of large-scale privatization of state enterprises after the Mečiar government returned to power, the private sector continues to grow in Slovakia. The improvement in economic performance has yet to be reflected in a decline in the rate of unemployment or a widespread increase in the standard of living. However, should it continue, it may increase the number of individuals who feel they have a stake in a market economy and a democratic political system. The political impact of a decline in economic performance is perhaps easier to anticipate. As in the early 1990s, increased economic hardship would in all likelihood increase support for parties, such as those in the ruling coalition, that promise to buffer the population from the hardships of the market.

International factors will also have an important impact on the outcome of political developments in Slovakia. The desire of Slovakia's leaders to be a part of the European club, to join the EU and become a member of NATO, is one of the factors that puts certain limits on the extent to which the government will infringe upon the rights of the opposition and of minorities. Demarches by the United States and several EU ambassadors in October 1995 expressed concern about unsettling political developments in Slovakia including the campaign to remove President Kovač from office and called for greater attention to toleration of different views and for full respect for constitutional rights.[145] The passage of the slaw on language and the protection of the republic, despite the protests of the Hungarian government and the concern expressed by European institutions as well as by representatives of individual governments indicates the limits of such influence. However, as the signing of the treaty with Hungary in 1994 and the dropping of overt attempts to force President Kovač from office illustrate, the actions of outside groups and the desire to be a respected member of Central Europe can have a positive influence.[146]

Outside support is also crucial for the development of the non-governmental sector. Although such support makes NGOs vulnerable, there are few alternative sources of support for such organizations at present. Those groups that support activities to foster the development of civic values and values supportive of democracy are particularly dependent on outside support. Until the private sector develops in such a way as to generate more philanthropists within Slovakia, such support will be a critical factor in determining the outcome of the transition from communist rule in Slovakia.

As the pages above illustrate, the party system has contributed to the polarization of political opinion that has occurred in Slovakia, as well to the bitter conflict among political elites in the coalition and opposition that prevents compromise. But the instability of political coalitions and volatility of political life in Slovakia since 1989 cannot be traced to the party system alone. Rather, both the functioning of political parties and the conflictual nature of politics reflect deeper social and attitudinal cleavages as well as the impact of the transition within the electorate, and the lack of consensus on political values and the rules of the game among the members of the political elite.

NOTES

I would like to thank the International Research and Exchanges Board (IREX), which funded part of the research on which this chapter is based. I would also like to acknowledge the research assistance of Nancy L. Meyers, Spencer Smith, and Jay Honigstock.

1 Robert D. Putnam, *Making Democracy Work: Civic Traditions in Modern Italy* (Princeton: Princeton University Press, 1992).
2 See Herbert Kitchelt, "The Formation of Party Systems in East Central Europe," *Politics and Society* 20, no. 1 (1992), 7–50, for a general treatment of the development of party systems in the region. See Sharon L. Wolchik, "The Repluralization of Politics in Post-Communist Czechoslovakia," *Journal of Post-Communist Studies*, no. 1 (1994), 412–31 for an early analysis of the development of the party system in the Czech Lands and Slovakia. See also Zora Bútorová and Martin Bútarova, "Political Parties, Value Orientations and Slovakia's Road to Independence," in *Party Formation in East-Central Europe: Post-Communist Politics in Czechoslovakia, Hungary, Poland and Bulgaria*, ed. Gordon Wightman (London: Edward Elgar, 1994); Darina Malová, "The Relationship Between the State, Political Parties and Civil Society in Postcommunist Czecho-Slovakia," in *The Slovak Path of Transition to Democracy?*, ed. Soňa Szomolanyi and Grigorij Mesežnikov (Bratislava: Slovak Political Science Association, 1994), pp. 111–58; David M. Olson, "Dissolution of the State: Political Parties and the 1992 Election in Czechoslovakia," *Communist and Post-Communist Studies* 26, no. 3 (September 1993), 301–14; and Carol Skalnik Leff and Susan Mikula, "Institutionalizing Party Systems in Multiethnic States: Integration and Ethnic Segmentation in Czechoslovakia, 1918–1992," paper prepared for presentation at the convention of the American Political Science Association, Chicago, September 1995.
3 Sharon L. Wolchik, "Slovak Politics Since Independence," paper presented at the conference Fünf Jahre nach der Wende – Bilanz in Mittel- und Südosteuropa, Magdeburg, Germany, 11 June 1994.
4 Victor Mamatey, "The Establishment of the Republic," in *A History of the Czechoslovak Republic*, ed. Radomir Luza and Victor Mamatey (Princeton: Princeton University Press, 1973), pp. 7–8.
5 Peter Brock, *The Slovak National Awakening* (Toronto: University of Toronto Press, 1976).
6 Sharon L. Wolchik, *Czechoslovakia in Transition: Politics, Economics and Society* (New York: Pinter Publishers, 1991), pp. 1–59. See also Owen Johnson, *Slovakia in 1918–1938: Education and the Making of a Nation* (Boulder, CO: East European Monographs, 1985).
7 Zora Pryor, "Czechoslovak Economic Development in the Interwar Period, 1918–1948," in *A History of the Czechoslovak Republic*, pp. 188–215.
8 Martin Bútora, "Volunteerism as a Multidimensional Phenomenon," in *Non-profit Sector and Volunteering in Slovakia*, ed. Zora Bútorová and David P. Daniels (Bratislava: SAIA-SCTS and FOCUS, 1995), p. 15. See also Eva Broklová, *Československá Democracie, Politický Systém ČSR 1918–1938* (Prague: SLON, 1992).

9   Wolchik, *Czechoslovakia in Transition.* In addition, see H. Gordon Skilling, *Czechoslovakia's Interrupted Revolution* (Princeton: Princeton University Press, 1976), pp. 49–56.
10 From data in tables 6.1 and 6.3, pp. 164 and 168 in *Political Culture and Political Change in Communist States*, ed. Archie Brown and Jack Grey (New York: Holmes & Meier Publishers, 1979).
11 Ibid., p. 118.
12 Ibid., p. 169.
13 FOCUS, *Current Problems in Slovakia* (Bratislava: FOCUS, 1992), pp. 25–26.
14 Ivan Kamenec, *Po stopach tragedie* (Bratislava: Vydavateľstvo Archa, 1991), p. 171.
15 See Yeshayahu Jelinek, *The Parish Republic: Hlinka's Slovak People's Party, 1939–1945* (New York: East European Quarterly, 1976), p. 20. For more information on the history of the Slovak state, see Kamenec, *Po stopach tragedie*, and Ladislav Lipscher, *Židia v Slovenskom štáte, 1939–1945* (Munich: R. Oldenbourg, 1990).
16 Edita Bosak, "Slovaks and Czechs: An Uneasy Coexistence," in *Czechoslovakia, 1918–88: Seventy Years from Independence*, ed. H. Gordon Skilling (London: Macmillan, 1991), pp. 65–81.
17 Vladimir Krivý, "The Parliamentary Elections 1994: The Profiles of Supporters of the Political Parties, the Profile of Regions," in *Slovakia and the 1994 Elections*, ed. Soňa Szomolányi and Grigorij Mesežnikov (Bratislava: Slovak Political Science Association, 1995), pp. 114–35.
18 See Andrew Michta's chapter in this volume for a discussion of comparable issues in the Polish case.
19 Sándor Bordás et al., *Counter-Proof* (Bratislava: Kiadó Vydavateľstvo Verlag, 1995), pp. 33–57.
20 C. A. Macartney, *Hungary and Her Successors: The Treaty of Trianon and Its Consequences, 1919–1937* (Oxford: Oxford University Press, 1937), pp. 158 and 164, as cited in Paul Robert Magocsi, "Magyars and Carpatho–Rusyns," in *Czechoslovakia, 1918–1988*, pp. 106, 107, 127.
21 See Jelinek, *The Parish Republic*.
22 FOCUS, *Current Problems of Slovakia*, May 1993, December 1993, May 1994, and December 1994. See also Bordás et al., *Counter-Proof*.
23 See Skilling, *Czechoslovakia's Interrupted Revolution*.
24 See, for example, Zora Bútorová, "Premyslené 'áno' zániku ČSFR? Image strán a rozpad Česko-Slovenska očami občanov Slovenska," *Sociologický časopis* 29, no. 1 (March 1993), 88–104.
25 Sharon L. Wolchik, "The Politics of Ethnicity in Post-Communist Czecho-slovakia," *East European Politics and Societies* 8, no. 1 (Winter 1994), 179.
26 Ibid., p. 157. See also the analyses in *The End of Czechoslovakia*, ed. Jiří Musil (Budapest: Central European University Press, 1995) and Fedor Gál et al., *Dnešní krize česko-slovenských vztahů* (Prague, 1992).
27 Wolchik, *Czechoslovakia in Transition*, ch. 1.
28 See Skilling, *Czechoslovakia's Interrupted Revolution* and Carol Skalnik Leff, *National Conflict in Czechoslovakia: The Making and Remaking of a State, 1918–1987* (Princeton: Princeton University Press, 1988) for discussions of the reform era and its aftermath.

29 Wolchik, *Czechoslovakia in Transition*, p. 215.
30 Sharon L. Wolchik, "Regional Inequality in Czechoslovakia," in *The Politics of Inequality*, ed. Daniel Nelson (Lexington, MA: Lexington Books, 1983). See also Leff, *National Conflict*.
31 Wolchik, *Czechoslovakia in Transition*, pp. 188–89.
32 Ibid., pp. 189–90.
33 Ibid., p. 190.
34 Ibid., p. 191; see also Wolchik, "Regional Inequality in Czechoslovakia."
35 See Wolchik, "The Politics of Ethnicity," pp. 153–88 and *The End of Czechoslovakia*.
36 See Siváková, "The New Slovak Parliament," and David M. Olson, "The New Parliaments of New Democracies: The Experience of the Federal Assembly of the Czech and Slovak Federal Republic," in *The Emergence of East Central European Parliaments: The First Steps*, ed. Attila Ágh (Budapest: Hungarian Center of Democracy Studies Foundation, 1994), pp. 48–54 and 35–47.
37 Wolchik, "The Repluralization of Politics in Post-Communist Czechoslovakia."
38 See Wolchik, "The Politics of Ethnicity."
39 See Siváková, "The New Slovak Parliament," pp. 48–54 and Jana Reschová, "Parliaments and Constitutional Change: the Czechoslovak Experience," in *The Emergence of East Central European Parliaments*, pp. 55–68.
40 Wolchik, "The Politics of Transition," in *The End of Czechoslovakia*, ed. Musil, p. 225–44.
41 Sharon L. Wolchik, "The Politics of Ethnicity and the Breakup of Czechoslovakia," paper presented at the Conference on the Breakup of Communist States and Nation/Statebuilding in Post-Communist States, Cornell University, April 21–22, 1995.
42 Štatistický úrad Slovenskej republiky, *Štatistická ročenka Slovenskej republiky 1992* (Bratislava: Štatistický úrad Slovenskej republiky, 1993), p. 47.
43 Janusz Bugajski, *Ethnic Politics in Eastern Europe: A Guide to Nationality Policies, Organization, and Parties* (New York: M. E. Sharpe, 1994), p. 322. Official sources state that there were 75,800 Roma in Slovakia in 1991, a figure equal to 1.5 percent of the population. *Štatistický úrad*, p. 47.
44 Ivan Čorný, "Úspežné riešenie sociálno-ekonomických problémov a životnej úrovne obyvateľstva ukrajinskej narodnosti v ČSSR," in *Socialistickou cestou k národnostnej rovnoprávnosti* (Bratislava: Pravda, 1975).
45 Paul Robert Magocsi, *The Rusyn-Ukrainians of Czechoslovakia* (Vienna: Wilhelm Braumuller, 1985).
46 See Sharon L. Wolchik, "Gender Issues During Transition," *East-Central European Economies in Transition: Study Papers Submitted to the Joint Economic Committee, Congress of the United States, November 1994* (Washington, DC: US Government Printing Office, 1994), pp. 147–70; Sharon L. Wolchik, "Women's Issues in Czechoslovakia in the Communist and Post-Communist Periods," in *Women and Politics Worldwide*, ed. Barbara Nelson and Najma Chowdhury (New Haven: Yale University Press, 1994), pp. 208–25; and Sharon L. Wolchik, "Women and the Politics of Transition in Central and Eastern Europe," in *Democratic Reform and the Position of Women in Transitional Economies*, ed. Valentine M. Moghadam (New York: Clarendon Press, 1993).

47   Sharon L. Wolchik, "Gendered Democracy: Women in the Transition in the Czech and Slovak Republics," in *Trying Democracy: Women in the Transition in Latin America and Central/Eastern Europe*, ed. Jane S. Jaquette and Sharon L. Wolchik (Baltimore: Johns Hopkins University Press, forthcoming); and Liba Paukert, "The Changing Economic Status of Women in the Period of Transition to a Market Economy System: The Case of the Czech and Slovak Republics After 1989," in *Democratic Reform*.

48   See Josef C. Brada, "The Slovak Economy After One Year of Independence," in *East-Central European Economies in Transition: Study Papers Submitted to the Joint Economic Committee, Congress of the United States, November 1994*, p. 523.

49   Branko Milanovic, "Poverty and Inequality in Transition Economies: What Has Actually Happened," in *Economic Transition in Russia and the New States of Eurasia*, ed. Bartlomiej Kaminski (Armonk, NY: M. E. Sharpe, 1996).

50   Ján Bunčak and Valentina Harmadyová, "Transformacia sociálnej struktury," *Sociólogia* 25, nos. 4–5 (1993), 389–402.

51   Sharon Fisher, "Privatization Stumbles Forward," *Transition* 1, no. 8 (26 May 1995), 44–49.

52   Interviews in Bratislava, April and June 1995; interview with leaders of the Hungarian coalition, Washington, DC, June 1995.

53   See Vladimír Tvaroska, "Priame predaje za 29 miliárd," *Pravda*, 14 September 1995, pp. 1–2; see also "Government Announces Privatization Principles," *Hospodarske noviny*, 7 June 1995, p. 7, *FBIS-EEU*, 1 November 1995, pp. 13–17.

54   "Vo včerajšom hlasovani NR SR rozhodlo 76 poslancov o ukončení kupónky na Slovensku," *Sme*, 13 July 1995, pp. 1–2.

55   "Občania hodnotia privatizáciu kriticky," *Sme*, 1 January 1996, p. 2.

56   "WTO: Tempo privatzácie je nízke," *Sme*, 7 December 1995, p. 7.

57   European Bank for Reconstruction and Development, *Transition Report 1995: Economic Transition in Eastern Europe and the Former Soviet Union, 1995* (London: EBRD, 1995) p. 4.

58   Martin Bútora, "Volunteerism as a Multidimensional Phoenomenon," in *Non-profit Sector*, p. 27.

59   E. Mannová, "Spolky v období sociálno-politických zmien na Slovensku 1938–1951. Analýza spolkových stanov," in *Občianska spoločnost' na prahu znovuzrodenia* (Bratislava: Sociologický ústav SAV, 1992), pp. 21–30, as cited in Bútora, "Volunteerism as a Multidimensional Phenomenon," p. 15.

60   Zuzana Fialová, "Third Sector in Figures," in *Non-profit Sector*, p. 67.

61   Ibid.

62   *Non-profit Sector*, p. 83.

63   Fialová, "Third Sector in Figures," p. 65.

64   Ibid.

65   Ibid.

66   Sharon Wolchik, Zora Bútorová, and Jan Hartl, "Citizen Political Values and Attitudes Toward Democracy in the Czech and Slovak Republics," data files from November–December 1994 survey.

67   Fialová, "Third Sector in Figures," p. 67.

68   *Sme*, 1 August 1995, p. 13.

69   "Nový politický subjekt," *Pravda* (Bratislava), 11 February 1995, p. 2.
70   "Slovak Ruling Party Signs Agreement with Businessmen," *OMRI Daily Digest*, 13 October 1995.
71   Iveta Radičová, "Sociálny potenciál podnikavosti a prijímanie ekonomickej reformy," *Sociologia* 25, nos. 4-5 (1993) pp. 410–11.
72   Dušan Leška and Viera Kogánová, "The Elections 1994 and the Crystallization of the Political Parties and Movements in Slovakia," in *Slovakia: Parliamentary Elections 1994*, ed. Soňa Szomolányi and Gregorij Mesežnikov (Bratislava, Slovakia: Slovak Political Science Foundation, 1995), pp. 86–102.
73   *Slovenský dennik*, 12 August 1994, p. 2.
74   "Odborári vystupujú tvrdšie proti vláde," *Sme*, 20 July 1995, pp. 1–2.
75   "Odborári dvere nezabuchli," *Pravda* (Bratislava), 31 August 1995, p. 2.
76   "Odborári demonštrovali proti zlej sociálnej situácii, ale nie proti vláde," *Sme*, 25 September 1995, p. 1.
77   "A. Engliš viní vládu, že chce rozbiť odbory," *Sme*, 16 May 1995, pp. 1, 2. See also Malová, "The Relationship Between the State, Political Parties and Civil Society," pp. 145–46.
78   Wolchik, "The Repluralization of Politics in Post-Communist Czechoslovakia."
79   See Condoleezza Rice, *The Soviet Union and the Czechoslovak Army, 1948–1983: Uncertain Allegiance* (Princeton: Princeton University Press, 1984) and Jiří Valenta and Condoleeza Rice, "The Czechoslovak Army," in *Communist Armies in Politics*, ed. Jonathan R. Adelman (Boulder, CO: Westview Press, 1982).
80   Rice, *Soviet Union and the Czechoslovak Army*, pp. 127–28.
81   Zoltan D. Barany, "East European Armed Forces in Transitions and Beyond," *East European Quarterly* 26, no. 1 (March 1992) pp. 3–4.
82   Miroslav Purkrabek, "Politická, sociální a vojenská transformace ČSA," *Sociológia* 24, no. 3 (1992), 137–43.
83   Barany, "East European Armed Forces in Transitions and Beyond," p. 13.
84   Ibid., p. 21; and Martin Komárek, "Odvolán s plnou důvěrou," *Mlada frontá dnes*, 19 October 1990, p. 2.
85   Rotislav Valašek, "Atestace v plném proudu," *Rudé právo*, 28 August 1990, pp. 1, 5.
86   Marie Königová, "Doktrína večí nejen generální," *Rudé právo*, 4 October 1990, p. 5.
87   Wolchik, *Czechoslovakia in Transition*, pp. 102–04 and Barany, "East European Armed Forces in Transitions and Beyond," pp. 15–22; see also Purkrabek, "Politická, sociální a vojenská transformace ČSA."
88   See "Prezident SR píše Ivanovi Lexovi," *Národná obroda*, 15 December 1995, p. 2 and "Prezident Kováč píše riaditeľovi SIS," *Sme*, 15 December 1995, p. 2. See also "J. Čarnogurský sa strtol s Oskarom F. zahraničí," *Národná obroda*, 8 December 1995 p. 2.
89   See "Prezident SR píše Ivanovi Lexovi," *Národná obroda*, 15 December 1995, p. 2.
90   "Carnogursky Meets Oskar F., 'Convinced' His Claims Are True," *CTK National News Wire*, 7 December 1995.
91   Timea Spitková, "Kovac Case Investigator Files Charges," *Prague Post*, 18 October 1995.

92 "Bude 8 krajov a 80–90 okresov," *Pravda* (Bratislava), 17 January 1996, p. 1; Ivan Samel and Helena Budinska, "NR SR. S. Kozlik informovol o plnení štátného zaverečného učtu," *Narodná obroda*, 6 July 1996.

93 Jozef Kvarda, "Counties as a Solution," *Pravda* (Bratislava), 26 January 1996, p. 4, *FBIS-EEU*, 31 January 1996, p. 13.

94 "Kauza hárky DU: Správa A. Poliaka konštatuje protizákonnosť záverov Macuškovej komisie," *Sme*, 1 February 1996, p. 1.

95 "Horor takmer na pravé poludnie," *Pravda* (Bratislava), 7 July 1995, p. 3 for a report on the links between the car explosion in Bratislava and Mafia groups in Slovakia.

96 See FOCUS, "Aktualné problemy Slovenska, Maj 1994," p. 2 for an overview of change in the importance attached to crime in surveys conducted since 1990.

97 "Poradíme si s mafiami?" *Pravda* (Bratislava), 17 March 1994, p. 5.

98 See Soňa Szomolányi, "Does Slovakia Deviate from the Central European Variant of Transition?" in *The Slovak Path of Transition to Democracy*, pp. 8–39.

99 Wolchik, Bútorová, and Hartl, "Citizen Attitudes and Political Values in the Czech and Slovak Republics," 1994 survey.

100 See Sharon Fisher, "Slovak Media Under Pressure," *Transition* 1, no. 18 (6 October 1995), p. 7.

101 Fisher, "Slovak Media Under Pressure," p. 8.

102 See "Znepokojeni," *Sme*, 6 March 1995, p. 1.

103 Fisher, "Slovak Media Under Pressure," p. 9.

104 See Fischer, "Slovak Justice Ministry Prepares Draft Law on Protection of Republic," *OMRI Daily Digest*, 5 March 1996 and Martin Krno, "Rozhodli Puptákovci," *Pravda* (Bratislava), 16 December 1996, p. 1.

105 See FOCUS surveys, 1990 to 1995.

106 Ibid.

107 Wolchik, *Czechoslovakia in Transition*, ch. 2; FOCUS, "Current Problems of Slovakia After the Split of the CSFR," March 1993 (Bratislava: FOCUS, 1994); FOCUS, "Aktualné problemy Slovenska," May 1994 (Bratislava: FOCUS, September 1994); Wolchik, Bútorová, and Hartl, 1994 survey results.

108 FOCUS, "Aktualné problemy Slovensky," May 1994, p. 27.

109 Results of Wolchik, Bútorová, and Hartl survey, as discussed in FOCUS, "Current Problems of Slovakia, December 1994" (Bratislava: FOCUS, 1994), pp. 1–2.

110 Ibid., pp. 35–37.

111 See Wolchik, *Czechoslovakia in Transition*, ch. 2 and the results of public opinion surveys reported in FOCUS, "Current Problems of Slovakia, December 1994."

112 Ivan Tomek and Václav Forst, "Postoje čs. veřejnosti k zakladním politickým institucim," *IVVM*, February 1991.

113 "Aktualné problemy Slovenska," May 1994, p. 77.

114 FOCUS, "Current Problems of Slovakia, December 1994," pp. 68–69.

115 Ibid., p. 68.

116 See Wolchik, *Czechoslovakia in Transition*, ch. 2 for references to studies illustrating these tendencies.

117 FOCUS, "Current Problems of Slovakia, December 1994," p. 38.

118 Ibid., p. 54; see this source as well for a brief overview of other differences in conceptions of democracy and kinds of political participation in the two countries.

119 Ibid., p. 35.

120 Ibid., p. 41.

121 See Wolchik, "Gendered Democracy."

122 FOCUS, 1993 surveys.

123 The Association of Slovak Workers and the Democratic Union.

124 Slovak analysts have noted that the party system in Slovakia differs from those which exist in many other postcommunist states in the importance that parties and movements that have no connection to broader political movements and similar parties in other countries still have in Slovakia. See Leška and Koganová, "The Elections in 1994 and the Crystallization of the Political Parties and Movements in Slovakia," p. 90.

125 Ibid., pp. 93-6.

126 Milan Zemko, "Political Parties and the Election System in Slovakia: Retrospective on the Last Three Elections to the Slovak National Council and the National Council of the Slovak Republic," in *The Slovak Path of Transition to Democracy*, pp. 44-46.

127 Zemko, "Political Parties," pp. 46-49.

128 Ibid., p. 48.

129 See Juan Linz, "Presidential or Parliamentary Democracy: Does It Make a Difference," and Alfred Stepan, "Presidentialism and Parliamentarism in Comparative Perspective," in *The Failure of Presidential Democracy*, ed. Juan J. Linz and Arturo Valenzuela (Baltimore: Johns Hopkins University Press, 1994), pp. 3-87, 119-136; see also Sharon L. Wolchik, "The Presidency in the Czechoslovak Federation and the Czech Republic," in *The Post-Communist Presidencies*, ed. Ray Taras (Cambridge: Cambridge University Press, forthcoming).

130 Wolchik, "Slovak Politics Since Independence."

131 Ibid., p. 109.

132 FOCUS, "Current Problems in Slovakia, December 1994," pp. 59-60.

133 Ibid.

134 Sharon Fisher, "Prime Minister and President Grapple for Power," *Transition* 1, no. 11 (30 June 1995), 38, 42, 70.

135 FOCUS, "Current Problems in Slovakia, December 1994," pp. 63-64.

136 Leška and Koganová, "The Elections 1994 and the Crystallization of the Political Parties and Movements in Slovakia," p. 91.

137 FOCUS, "Current Problems of Slovakia, May 1994" (Bratislava: FOCUS, 1994) p. 60.

138 Ibid., p. 63.

139 See *The Hungarian Minority*, ed. Pavel Frič, Fedor Gál, Péter Hunčik, and Christopher Lord (Prague: The Institute of Social and Political Science, 1993), p. 43. See also Ondrej Dostál, "Od konfrontácie k rezervovanosti," *Quo Vadis, Slovensko?* (Bratislava: Open Society Fund, January 1995), pp. 101-26.

140 See Bordás et al., *Counter-Proof*.

141 See František Buda, "The Language Law Has Many Pitfalls," *Pravda* (Bratislava), 29 January 1996, pp. 1 and 4, *FBIS-EEU*, 7 March 1996, p. 12.

142 See FOCUS, "Current Problems of Slovakia," May 1994, p. 54.
143 "Vyhlásenie študentov k 17. novembru," *Národná obroda*, 18 November 1994, p. 2. See also "Milan Markovič: moc sa naľakala smiechu," *Sme*, 10 March 1996, p. 2 and "Podľa výskumu pre Európsku úniu 79% Slovákov nesúhlasí s vývojom demokracie," *Sme*, 10 March 1996, p. 3.
144 Marek Boguszak and Vladimír Rak, *Czechoslovakia – May 1990 Survey Report* (Prague: Association for Independent Social Analysis, 1990).
145 "Juraj Schenk: Keby som mohol konzultovať s prezidentom, možno by sa predišlo komplikáciám," *Národná obroda*, 31 October 1995, p. 1. See also Mim, "Podla ministra Schenka obavy zo strany EÚ v prípade Slovenska nie sú opodstastnené," *Sme*, 31 October 1995, p. 2. See the following articles in *FBIS-EEU*, 31 October 1995: "Daily: EU Demarche Warns Mečiar to Respect Kovač," p. 16; "Daily: Demarches 'Constructive,' 'Not Hostile,'" p. 17; "Commentary on Demarches Urges Parliamentary Debate," p. 18; "Schenk Questions EU, US Attitudes Toward SR," p. 13; and "US-EU Demarche 'Serious Diplomatic Step,'" p. 13.
146 Representatives of the European Commission noted in Brussels in early February that Slovakia must allow greater freedom of the press and respect the rights of minorities if it wants to participate in preparations for joining the EU. "EÚ: Slovensko musí pripustiť väčšiu slobodu tlače a rešpektovať práva menšin," *Sme*, 8 February 1996, p. 1.

7   Democratization and political participation in postcommunist societies: the case of Latvia

Andrejs Plakans

On September 30–October 1, 1995, Latvia conducted its second parliamentary (Saeima) election since the August 1991 resumption of national independence. A new government (cabinet) was not formed until shortly before Christmas of that year, however. In the intervening eleven weeks, the "right," "center," and "left" parties, under the watchful eye of the country's President Guntis Ulmanis, negotiated intensely for the right to form a cabinet that would reflect the voters' preferences. But these preferences, reflected in the comparative strength of parties, were not clear. The first cabinet – proposed by the "right bloc" – failed to receive a majority in the parliament (49 for, 51 against), as did the second – proposed by the "left bloc" (50 for, 45 against, 5 abstaining). Ulmanis, as was his constitutional right, finally reached outside the competing "blocs" for a prime minister – Andris Šķēle, formerly a deputy minister of agriculture and now a successful entrepreneur. Šķēle's cabinet, merging persons from parties in both "blocs," received on December 22 a 70-vote majority (24 against, 6 not voting or absent) in the Saeima – an impressive mandate. The interregnum permitted the Latvian media ample time to ponder whether the post-election wheeling and dealing was appropriate in a "democracy," how an ostensibly democratic election could have brought so close to power as "irresponsible" a party as the right-wing National Movement for Latvia and its adventurer-leader Joachim Siegerist (who did not even speak Latvian), and whether Šķēle's cabinet – composed of ministers with diametrically opposed views on many basic questions – would be capable of governing. There were also reflections on how, in a system in which the legislature was supposed to be dominant, the national president had suddenly moved to center stage.

To outside observers, the "bloc"-building and negotiating that resulted in a viable cabinet could easily have been read as a sign that the democratization of Latvia's politics was continuing. The old Saeima and cabinet, after all, stood peacefully by to turn over power. The new cabinet was the product of

245

political leaders (and parties) pulling back from extreme positions in order to obtain ministerial posts, and assenting, at least until the next election, to be part of a "team" that would have to enter into many compromises in designing new legislation. Until recently to many in Latvia, "compromise" had still sounded like "surrender of principle," and the absence of quick solutions to identifiable national problems had been a sign of a malfunctioning system.

Thus four years into renewed independence there were lingering doubts in Latvia about the extent of democratization. The political machinery for resolving national problems was clearly present. Thus Egīls Levits, a former Latvian minister of justice (and in 1995 the Ambassador to Austria), argued just before the 1995 elections that "since the 1993 parliamentary elections there has come into being in Latvia a political party system with relatively clear contours . . . We no longer automatically view each other as enemies but accept each other as partners who think differently but have the welfare of Latvia at heart." Yet in August 1995, in its coverage of election preparations, the principal Latvian newspaper *Diena* [The Day] was less certain about how deeply the democratic impulse had taken hold: "in the transitional postsocialist society in which we are living, *the preparations for and the conduct of precisely this [the 1995] election will demonstrate how deeply democracy has taken root here* and whether the majority of the residents of Latvia support a course of reform meant to consolidate an independent and democratic state" (emphasis added). And immediately after the election, *Diena* found little to be cheerful about: "Are we going to continue on the path of reform and well-being and security as a modern European nation, or, are we, after this second free and democratic election, going to step off that path, having permitted a relatively developed party system to be destabilized by charlatans? One hopes that the election results will have served as a cold shower to the politically active segment of Latvian society and to the forces of progress."[1] Thus to *Diena*, the 1995 elections were indeed free and democratic and the system of political parties well-developed, but the process was still not producing encouraging results.

In order to place these 1995 political events and attitudes in some perspective, we shall try to delineate, first, the mood of uncertainty in Latvia that the 1995 elections did not succeed in dissipating; and, second, the role played by the various historical legacies in shaping that mood. We shall then survey the post-1991 elections (1993, 1994) and the system of political parties that emerged in these years; and, finally, we will return to the 1995 parliamentary election and investigate its significance for the post-1991 political history of the Latvian state. A concluding section will analyze the question of whether, and to what extent, the current political situation signals the presence in the Latvian body politic of a democratization process.

The mood of uncertainty

The question of whether the Latvian political world has experienced "democratization" has a formal answer. The Latvian Constitution (officially renewed in 1993) declared Latvia to be a democratic republic and the term "democracy" appears repeatedly in Latvians' descriptions of their political system. In plain fact, the country now has a functioning electoral system in which the leaders of government are regularly chosen by competitive elections from many candidates by secret balloting; and, since 1991, the working of that system, as will be described later, has been amply demonstrated in the first Saeima elections of 1993, the municipal elections of 1994, and the second Saeima elections in 1995. But more outreaching versions of the question – is there a democratic political culture? have democratic political values been internalized? is there a shared view that a democratic political system can handle the country's problems? – are less easily answered. The post-1991 elections were all conducted in an atmosphere more suffused with uncertainty than with confidence. The hardships that were earlier thought to be temporary – natural aspects of a "transition" from a communist to a post-communist society – seem now to have become a permanent state of affairs. Confidence in the new political institutions was very uneven in mid-1993[2] and remained so over the next year. At the end of 1994 only 21 percent of Latvians in Latvia gave a positive valuation to the current partially reformed economic system, and only 43 percent evaluated the current political system positively. Among the so-called "Russian-speakers" in Latvia (that is, ethnic Russians and other Slavs) the evaluations were even less positive, 24 percent and 9 percent in these two categories, respectively.[3] Though public opinion in Latvia, as elsewhere, is continually shifting, socio-political changes since 1991 clearly have not produced the strong popular satisfaction with the new independence that could have been forecast from the enthusiastic pre-1991 oratory of the Latvian Popular Front, which led the country to independence. There are, in fact, few domains of Latvian life that can be described as sources of satisfaction, as examples of things turning out well.

By 1995, demographically speaking, the total population of the Latvian state had diminished by 5.1 percent from a total of 2,666,567 in 1989 to 2,529,543 in 1995.[4] Life expectancy at birth had declined by 1994 to 72.9 years for women and a dramatically low 60.7 years for men.[5] Infant mortality (perinatal mortality) had risen steadily from 1988 to 1992, when it reached a high of 19.6 deaths per 1000 births; and, while in 1993 and 1994 this figure has been 18.6 for both years, that rate (though a decline from 1992) was still substantially higher than in the last decade of Soviet rule (when it ranged from 10.0 to 12.1).[6]

Table 7.1 *Demographic trends in Latvia since the 1950s*

	1950s	1970s	1990s
Percentage of population	(1959)	(1979)	(1994)
Rural	43.9	32.2	30.8
Urban	56.1	67.8	69.2
Average annual rates of population growth (%)	.9	1.0	-.9
Age distribution (%)		(1979)	(1989)
15–24		15.5	13.4
25–49		35.8	34.1
50–59		11.6	12.7
Over 60		16.8	18.8
Levels of education[a] (%)			
Primary			34.1
Secondary			49.9
Post-secondary			16.0

Note: [a]Indicates attainment of completed or partial education at each level.

Sources: Paul S. Shoup, *The East European and Soviet Data Handbook*; UNESCO, *Statistical Yearbooks*; *United Nations, Demographic Yearbooks*; *Demographic Yearbook of Latvia* (Riga: Central Statistical Bureau of Latvia, 1995), pp. 25, 41, 57, 58; *Statistical Yearbook of Latvia* (Riga: Central Statistical Bureau of Latvia, 1995), p. 135.

The proportion of infants born with congenital defects has also increased. All these disturbing demographic trends and patterns were communicated to the general population quickly, due to the extraordinary number of academic specialists who published in the daily press the results of research that in other countries remain known only to specialists.

The fact that the country's ethnic balance had continued to change relatively slowly after 1991 disappointed many Latvians (see table 7.2).[7] In fact, ethnic cleavages of various kinds persisted as an important aspect of everyday life. The population of the capital city Riga, as of five of the other six largest cities in Latvia, continued to have non-Latvian majorities (see table 7.2), which in 1995 stood in sharp contrast with the results of the political transformation. The ethnic composition of the new political elite (president, Saeima, cabinet ministers) was almost exclusively Latvian, and the official state language – required in the functioning of all governmental bodies – was Latvian. But in some sections of the country (for example, in areas of Latgale, the easternmost segment of the country) and in areas of the main cities (for example, in Riga in such suburban "micro-raions" as Imanta and Purvciems) the Latvian language was scarcely heard at all.

Table 7.2   *Ethnic composition of the population of Latvia and proportion of Latvians in cities (in percent)*

Ethnic group	1935	1989	1993	1994
Latvians	77.0	52.0	53.5	54.1
Russians	8.8	34.0	32.5	33.1
Belorussians	1.4	4.5	4.2	4.1
Ukrainians	.1	3.5	3.2	3.1
Poles	2.5	2.3	2.2	2.1
Lithuanians	1.2	1.3	1.3	1.3
Jews	4.9	.9	.6	.5
Gypsies	.2	.3	.3	.5
Estonians	.4	.1	.1	.1
Germans	3.3	.1	.1	.1
Others	.2	1.0	1.0	1.0

Proportion of Latvians in the cities of Latvia (beginning of 1995)

Riga	38.0
Daugavpils	13.9
Jelgava	51.2
Jūrmala	45.5
Liepāja	43.5
Rēzekne	38.7
Ventspils	45.9

Sources: National statistics – *Statistical Yearbook of Latvia* (Riga: Central Statistical Bureau of Latvia, 1995), p. 54; city statistics – *Demographic Yearbook of Latvia* (Riga: Central Statistical Bureau of Latvia, 1995), p. 36.

These residential patterns continued to roil emotions: on the Latvian side among those who had hoped that after 1991 the "Russians" would somehow "disappear" quickly, and on the non-Latvian side among those who had lost the security of belonging to a superpower – the USSR – in which the Russian language and culture were dominant. Though the proportion of Latvians within the population of Latvia was creeping slowly upward, it was at a much lower pace than many expected.

The political significance of these ethno-demographic facts was not patently clear. Some 35 percent of the non-Latvians in Latvia were already citizens (and therefore voters), and the citizenship/naturalization law of 1994 ensured that by 2002 all residents of Latvia meeting citizenship requirements would be able to become citizens (and voters). To some, the law introduced unjustifiable obstacles to immediate citizenship (and political participation) and the citizenship requirements (especially the language requirement) were seen as unduly harsh; to others, the law accepted as a *fait accompli* the results of the Soviet-era industrialization policy that brought to Latvia hundreds of thousands of non-Latvians as the labor force in large state enterprises. It was hardly clear, however, that such large-issue resentments were all-consuming: the proportion of ethnically Latvian men and women with spouses of a different nationality has remained stable since independence (men – 18.2 percent in 1990, 18.3 percent in 1994; women – 18.6 percent in 1990; 18.2 percent in 1994).[8]

By 1995, economic indicators – in decline from 1990 to 1992 – had not shown improvements dramatic enough to allay fears about the near future. The reversal of GNP decline in 1994 and 1995[9] was not large enough to overshadow the dramatic long-term collapse of wages and salaries for many segments of the population, particularly for those with so-called "budget" incomes (that is, incomes from positions funded from the national budget). The fact that the majority of erstwhile "cultural workers" (academics, writers, artists, and so forth) – the articulate intelligentsia – had been cut adrift from the national budget added to complaints the charge that the government did not care about "culture." State pensions (also a "budget" expenditure) continued to be very low. By comparison with incomes, the cost of living had risen steadily: foodstuffs and housing expenses in 1994 comprised 51.6 percent and 13.9 percent of household budgets, respectively (in comparison with 42.5 percent and 4.0 percent in 1990).[10] The 1995 collapse of sixteen "private" banks affected the savings accounts of tens of thousands of persons and contributed to the atmosphere of uncertainty.[11]

The growth in the number of private commercial and retail establishments (especially in Riga, the capital) – while impressive to visitors – serve to local residents as a grating reminder of their own relative impoverishment, because high prices placed most goods out of their reach. Income polarization – symbolized, on the one hand, by overcrowded busses and streetcars, and, on the other, by expensive western automobiles – was not only a matter of abstract economic statistics but also a visible source of socio-economic resentment. In a study of socio-economic self-identification (using nine socio-economic strata) from 1991 to 1995, a substantially larger proportion of the inhabitants of Latvia (that is, both ethnic Latvians and minority nationalities) placed themselves in the three lowest strata in 1995 than they did in 1991 (Latvians – 1991, 43.1 percent; 1995, 56.0 percent; non-Latvians – 1991, 45.0 percent; 1995, 63.3 percent).[12]

Crime and official corruption were frequently portrayed by the Latvian press as an overwhelming problem, but accurate statistics on both counts remained scarce. Economic success was frequently linked by public opinion to corruption, even in the absence of any direct evidence. Those of the post-1991 political elite who practiced conspicuous consumption were

Table 7.3 *Indicators of economic trends in Latvia since 1989*

	1989	1990	1991	1992	1993	1994	1995[a]
GDP	6.8[b]	2.9	-10.4	-34.9	-14.9	0.6	0.9[b]
Industrial output	n.a.	0	0.6	-35.0	-32.1	-9.9	n.a.
Rate of inflation	4.7[b]	10.5[b]	124.4[b]	951.2[b]	109.1[b]	36.2[b]	25[b]
Rate of unemployment	0	0.5	0.6	1.6	5.7	7.3	6.3
GNP per capita	n.a.	n.a.	n.a.	n.a.	5,170	n.a.	n.a.
% Workforce in private activity	13.9[b]	19.2	22.5	43.7	55.2	66.7	68.8

Notes: GDP – % change over previous year; Industrial output – % change over previous year; Rate of inflation – % change in end-year retail/consumer prices; Rate of unemployment as of end of year; GNP per capita - in US dollars at PPP exchange rates. [a]Estimate [b]EBRD; other statistics from Latvian sources cited.

Sources: *Monthly Bulletin of Latvian Statistics* (Riga: Central Statistical Bureau of Latvia, 1995), no. 11; *Statistical Yearbook of Latvia 1995* (Riga: Central Statistical Bureau of Latvia, 1995); European Bank for Reconstruction and Development, *Transition Report 1995: Economic Transition in Eastern Europe and the Former Soviet Union* (London: EBRD, 1995); European Bank for Reconstruction and Development, *Transition Report Update, April 1996: Assessing Progress in Economies in Transition* (London: EBRD, 1996).

assumed to have obtained their wealth illegally; by contrast, the number of officials charged, tried, and punished for corruption was relatively small (which can be attributed as well to imprecise laws and a badly functioning legal system).

Uncertainty about the honesty of political leaders went hand in hand with fears about individual safety. By definition, there were as few reliable statistics about criminality as there were about corruption. A widely shared general assumption was that most criminal activity in Latvia is a matter of active "mafias." The number of registered crimes per 10,000 population increased after 1990, though the trend reversed in 1993 (1990 - 129; 1991 - 157; 1992 - 236; 1993 - 204; 1994 - 161).[13] Yet official statistics about crime may not have been reliable, because further analyses also reported that probably fewer than 40 percent of all punishable crimes were officially registered.[14] In the realm of everyday safety, however, statistics were less important than perceptions, and the perception among the country's residents was that life (especially in urban areas) was much less safe than it used to be.[15] In spite of the decreasing population, the absolute number of murders in Latvia increased from 111 cases in 1988 to 429 in 1993 (by 286 percent); serious bodily injury cases from 199 cases in 1988 to 725 in 1993 (by 264 percent); and theft from 205 cases in 1988 to 1179 in 1993 (by 475 percent).[16]

Economic reform – initiated by the Soviet-era Supreme Council in 1990 and continued by a succession of post-independence governments since that time – on balance had not produced sufficient forward momentum to persuade many that they were in a "transition" to something better. Privatization of farmland continued at a steady pace, but agricultural output at the end of 1994 stood at about half of what it had been in 1990.[17] Privatization of large state enterprises was much slower, in part because the law streamlining the process was not finalized until 1994.[18] Yet it appears that most of the privatization vouchers distributed by early 1995 to 2.2 million residents of Latvia were being saved for the eventual purchase of state-owned housing in which people were already living, rather than of industrial enterprises.[19] The slow pace of industrial restructuring warded off mass layoffs, keeping official unemployment figures low (see table 7.3), but the uncertainties of the situation (combined with the loss of the Soviet market) also caused a drop of industrial output by the end of 1994 to four-tenths of what it was in 1990. While it was probably true that, comparatively speaking, the continuing commitment of a succession of Latvian governments to economic reform had helped the country (along with Estonia and Lithuania) to make "the greatest progress among the former Soviet republics in the transition to a market economy,"[20] Latvians living amidst daily economic uncertainties were scarcely able to view the situation coolly as a "transition."

Finally, Latvia's small size continued to underline its vulnerability as a state, in spite of determined efforts at Baltic integration and the incorporation of Latvia into such international bodies as the United Nations, the Nordic Council, and the Council of Europe. Even among the most optimistic, Latvia's membership in the European Community and NATO was perceived to lie well into the future. As the country matured to become suitable for such additional security-enhancing memberships, the political situation in Russia (and the Commonwealth of Independent States generally) was a source of continued worry. The feeling of insecurity was fed by memories of Latvia's historical experiences, especially the realization that at the main turning points (the 1918 acquisition of independence, the Molotov–Ribbentrop Pact, the collapse of the Soviet Union) the fate of the country was largely determined by the behavior and policies of the great powers. Thus sensible strategic thinking among intellectuals concerned with the country's defense[21] did not eliminate despairing reactions in the general population to the often threatening pronouncements of Russian political leaders about the "near abroad."

A variety of legacies

The mood of uncertainty characterizing post-1991 political life in Latvia emerged as the country sought to integrate three different historical legacies. The first – the most distant in real time – was that of the interwar Republic of Latvia (1918–40), now posited as the political entity of which the post-1991 Republic of Latvia is a continuation. The second – rather less distant – was the period of Soviet domination (1945–88) which was now more frequently than not portrayed as a period of "occupation" and consisted of the inherited institutions, laws, habits, and perceived injustices of the time when Latvia was a Soviet republic. The third was the immediate past – the 1988–91 period of the so-called "Third Awakening" – which consisted of the ideas, energies, promises, and people from an era when all Latvians (though not necessarily all residents of Latvia) appeared to be united against a common foe.[22]

Because the 1991 Republic had emerged from a relatively pacific "revolution," the past in all these guises remained active in post-1991 life. Except for the Soviet framework, little else had been swept away for a fresh start: the Supreme Soviet, filled with activists of the Latvian Popular Front (founded in 1988), was the "transition government" that led the country until the election of the fifth Saeima in 1993 (the fourth had been elected in 1931); Soviet-era laws, institutions, and habits of mind still structured everyday life; and, by deliberate choice, many elements of the 1918 Republic were "brought back" to assert the legitimacy of the new Republic. Inevitably, these different legacies did not sit well with each other.

Interwar period of independence (1918–40)

The first period of Latvian independence entered the immediate pre-1991 years as an instrument for challenging the Latvian status quo as a Soviet Republic. Even before the May 1990 independence declaration by the Latvian Supreme Council, the 1970s and 1980s dissidents first, and then the Latvian National Independence Movement (founded in 1988), revived the use of the national colors (crimson-white-crimson) and other national symbols.[23] The May 1990 Supreme Council declaration stated explicitly that when independence came, Latvia would not be a new state but rather a continuation of the state that had been illegally incorporated into the Soviet Union in August of 1940. The declaration reactivated the 1922 Constitution (instead of writing a new one) and the specifics of the interwar political system began to be scrutinized, as if in preparation for their wholesale revival. The 1922 Constitution remained as a reference point for reforms before 1991 and was officially renewed in 1993, but almost from the beginning its role was problematic. It called for a unicameral legislature, a relatively weak president elected by the legislature, and simply did not mention numerous problems which a new 1991 state would have to deal with (local government, intersession lawmaking, specification of national language, specifics of the electoral system, a constitutional court).[24]

By 1991, Latvian public life was suffused with all manner of mnemonics of the interwar republic, virtually all of them casting its institutions in a favorable light. For the time being, however, there was little discussion of a significant problem that would have to be coped with if Latvia were now to be renewed as a democratic state. After 1918, when independence had been declared and as in the 1920s the new parliamentary republic began to function, there appeared almost immediately strong criticism, mostly from organizations on the political right, of democratic political institutions, charging that the new Latvian state was not serving as an adequate protector of the "Latvian nation."[25] That criticism grew in volume until, in May 1934, Kārlis Ulmanis, the leader of one of the major parliamentary parties, the Agrarian Union, carried out a coup, suspended the 1922 Constitution, the parliament (Saeima) and all political parties, and instituted authoritarian rule.[26] The undeniable popularity of Kārlis Ulmanis after 1934 suggests that devotion to parliamentary democracy was none too strong in all quarters of Latvia's population then. Quite literally, the interwar political legacy was a dual one: the parliamentary period (1918–34) and the authoritarian period (1930–40). The single-party dictatorships that had arrived with incorporation into the Soviet Union in 1940 and had remained the status quo until the late 1980s had been immediately preceded by six years of one-man rule by the interwar republic's undeniably popular but authoritarian last president. The authoritarian period in the interwar republic – fully known by at least the Latvian population of the 1991 Republic – was a silent but nevertheless eloquent reminder that the Latvian state had already experienced one failure of parliamentary democracy.

The Soviet period (1940–88)

The Latvian political activists of the "Third Awakening" (1988–91) were divided initially on the meaning of the "Soviet period." It was quite obviously the given reality in which virtually all of them had matured intellectually and politically, while its typical structures had served for many as the pathways of upward mobility into the nomenklatura. In the past, the only openly unambiguous condemnation of Soviet rule in Latvia had come from western émigré Latvians and from a handful of dissidents in Latvia from the late 1960s onward. The unambiguous condemnation theme was picked up earliest by the Latvian National Independence Movement (in 1988), while the Latvian

Popular Front normally used much more restrained language. By 1990 and the independence vote in the Supreme Council, however, the momentum for total separation had become overwhelming, and public expression of doubts about this ultimate goal among ethnic Latvians were rare. Among the non-Latvians – the Russians, Belorussians, Ukrainians, and others – opinion, predictably, was very divided, and opposition to independence manifested itself as the Interfront movement, which championed an undissolvable USSR.[27] To Latvians, the logic of their own argument was unassailable: if the country had been illegally occupied in 1940, then the past half-century of Soviet (and Russian) domination had all been a giant exercise in illegality, no matter what benefits the period had brought to individuals; and the only logical concluding step was the restoration of Latvian independence and the dismantling of all "imposed" institutions and arrangements. The Soviet period had produced a Latvia in which the Soviet military was a highly visible presence (Riga containing the headquarters of the Baltic Military District), the proportion of Latvians in the country was dropping toward the fifty-percent mark, and the Russian language was replacing Latvian in most important domains of life. The June 1988 plenum of all Latvian "creative societies" – the event that initiated the "Third Awakening" – directed to the authorities a long list of grievances reminiscent of the *cahiers de doleance* preceding the French Revolution of 1789. That the Baltic Republics of the Soviet Union were at least economically more "advanced" than most other union republics, and the reasons why that was so, was not an important discussion point at that moment.

The "Third Awakening" (1988–91)

Soviet-period dissidence (late 1960s to early 1980s) in Latvia was not great enough numerically to become a foundation upon which later challenges to Moscow's authority could be built.[28] It was the Gorbachev years that were given by Latvians the name "Third Awakening" so as to link their perestroika-era political activism to the "first national awakening" (1850s–80s) and the "second" (in the immediate post-1918 years).[29] During 1986–87 several environmentally-minded Latvian journalists, by successfully marshaling public opinion in opposition to a new hydroelectric plant on the Daugava River, discovered that some decisions of even such august bodies as the Moscow Politburo could now be reversed. The use of the seemingly permissive policy of glasnost' to marshal public opinion continued during 1988 and 1989 and produced, among other things, massive commemorative demonstrations on significant days of Latvian history (though not Soviet history): March 25, the anniversary of the 1949 deportation of some 30,000 "kulaks"; June 13, the anniversary of the 1941 deportation of some 10,000 persons deemed threatening to the Soviet regime; August 23, the anniversary of the signing of the Molotov-Ribbentrop Pact, which assigned Latvia to the Soviet sphere of interest; November 18, the anniversary of the 1918 proclamation of independence.[30] The same impulse led to the founding in 1988 of the Latvian Popular Front, ostensibly to support Gorbachev's perestroika policies, as well as of the Latvian National Independence Movement, which, in contrast to the LPF, began almost immediately to champion the idea of an independent Latvia. The Front claimed a membership of 110,000 (perhaps 90 percent Latvian) in 2,300 local chapters; the Independence Movement was considerably smaller but more cohesive ideologically.[31]

The March 1990 regular elections of the Latvian Supreme Soviet gave the "reformers" their first opportunity to flex their muscles in the formal political arena, and their efforts were successful. The election produced a majority of deputies in the Supreme Soviet (134 of 170 seats) who were already members of the LPF and the Latvian National Independence Movement, or were sympathetic to these two movements. After being elected, some forty of these deputies formally renounced their membership in the Communist Party and joined the LPF.[32] On May 4, 1990, the Supreme Soviet (now renamed the Supreme Council) passed a resolution stating as the ultimate goal of its work the eventual achievement of full independence. In the period from May 1990 to September 1991, this dominant coalition of reformers – working in the Supreme Council, its sixteen standing committees, the Cabinet of Ministers, nineteen ministries, and thirteen state boards and commissions – continued to produce a body of laws and regulations predicated on the idea of eventual independence. The government began to think of itself as a de facto transitional government, to be changed at some time in the future when total separation from the USSR was achieved.

These "Awakening" years also saw momentous organizational transformations of various kinds – certainly the collapse of the Latvian Communist Party and possibly also the beginnings of "civil society." Immediately after the Supreme Council vote on independence in May 1990 the Party split into moderate (led by Ivars Kezbers) and pro-Moscow (led by Alfrēds Rubiks) factions; in addition, the decline in party membership, having started in 1988, continued rapidly. The new ("informal") organizations were numerous and varied: they included renewed groups (such as the Riga Latvian Association, founded in 1868; the Boy Scouts; and the university fraternities), entirely new entities (such as business enterprises), and reinvigorated entities (such as nearly defunct congregations of the Latvian Lutheran Church). Almost every social, cultural, and political organization that had been closed by the Ulmanis regime in 1934 (such political parties as the Latvian Social Democrats and the Agrarian Union) or disbanded by the Soviet regime in

1940 tried to revive itself (many unsuccessfully). These years also witnessed the beginnings of the growth of private business enterprises, the number of functioning enterprises (excluding farms) reaching 56,242 by the end of 1995.[33] Also, by that date some 200 non-governmental organizations were registered in Latvia, though the growth of free trade unions remained minimal.[34]

In the post-1991 period, Latvian memories of the "Third Awakening" tended to emphasize the successes when united action produced intended results. Demonstrations with hundreds of thousands of participants showed the unity of the Latvian *tauta* (people; see note 83) moved by shared ideals. Unity was evident as well in the friendly reception accorded to Latvians who had fled westward in 1944 (just before the return of the Soviet Army to Latvia) and were now, in large numbers, supporting personally and materially the idea of a renewed independent Latvia. Perhaps the most significant memory of national (that is, Latvian) unity came from the troubled days of January 1991. Then, in response to the attack by the Soviet Army on the television station in Vilnius, Lithuania, Latvians by the thousands erected barricades around the most important public buildings in Riga and for two weeks stood watch in preparation for an armed attack (which never came). In the post-1991 years the "time of the barricades" was remembered with affection but also sadness, because the common purpose symbolized by the barricades is deemed now to have disappeared.[35]

Renewed independence within a transition (1990–93)

In retrospect, it is clear that the transition to post-communism in Latvia began at one level in May 1990, when the Supreme Council declared the country to be "in transition" out of the Soviet Union and then sought to negotiate with Moscow how the exit should be made. At another level, the fifteen months following May 1990, turned out to be, without anyone realizing it at the time, a transition in the full sense of the word, made so by the events of August 1991. While the Supreme Council believed itself to be working toward a peaceful separation, in reality it had been laying the groundwork for the renewed state. From March 1990 until June 1993 (when the Council was replaced by a newly elected parliament [Saeima]), the leadership of two individuals – Anatolijs Gorbunovs, the council chair – and Ivars Godmanis, the prime minister – bridged the late Soviet and full independence periods. Gorbunovs, a former ideological secretary of the Latvian Communist Party's Central Committee and now *ex officio* [as chair of the Supreme Council] also the head of state, maintained high popularity ratings among both the Latvian and the minority nationality populations. He managed to stand above the fray of everyday politics and became a useful symbol of institutional continuity.

Godmanis, by contrast, was an academic – a physics professor at the University of Latvia and a relative newcomer to political life, which he had entered by becoming active in the Popular Front in 1988. As the presiding officer of the Cabinet of Ministers, he became from May 1990 the lightning rod of all the dissatisfactions that governmental action and inaction generated, and his popularity ratings, among Latvian and non-Latvians alike, were on a continuous downslide.

When the August 1991 coup occurred in Moscow, the Latvian government in Riga was ready with a quick response. The Supreme Council quickly amended the 1990 declaration to read that as of August 22, 1991, Latvia was an independent sovereign republic with its internal affairs guided by the February 1922 Constitution.[36] The Council was now faced with the tasks of maintaining the reform momentum of the pre-August 1991 months and of adapting political and social institutions to the new circumstances. The new political context in which these tasks had to be carried out included the stresses and strains that had already manifested themselves in the Supreme Council, caused by the myriad problems reform was creating throughout a general population that could now express its continuous criticism in the daily press.[37] The political question at the end of 1991 and beginning of 1992 was how long the Supreme Council could retain its 1990 mandate. Most of the citizenry showed no signs of challenging the Council's legitimacy: there was, after all, no other "government" to be had at the moment. But the development of political opinion was now unfettered, as was the possibility of differing opinions becoming embodied in new movements, groups, coalitions, and parties.[38]

From 1990 onward the Council had to work simultaneously on numerous reform fronts while at the same time revising the pre-1940 basic documents that were slated to become the fundamental laws of the land: principally the Constitution of 1922 but also the Civil Law of 1937. Beyond this assignment, there were the immediate pressures to revoke or change Soviet-period laws, regulations, and practices to conform with "models" promised by the Popular Front since 1990: a free-market economy with a social "safety net," a secure new monetary system, economic linkages with both western and eastern markets, a wage and salary structure reflecting performance, a free press and freedom of organization, a less specialized and less coercive educational system, and a "civil society" that would be autonomous and, if need be, could provide countervailing power to the central government.[39] In addition, from August 1991 on, the government had to create a diplomatic service and a civil service; ensure that foreign diplomats had access to Riga properties to establish embassies; and develop recruiting mechanisms for an army, border guards, and customs officials. All of these changes had to be brought about by a relatively small number of knowledgeable persons who, at the personal level, were themselves going through intellectual transformations of various kinds.

The 1991 Latvian state had not been created by revolutionaries sweeping aside an easily identifiable old politico-economic elite, as had been the case in 1918–1920 when Latvians replaced Russians and Baltic Germans in virtually all high-level positions. This time, the only part of the old elite that had been decisively extruded from power were the members of the pre-1991 pro-Moscow Latvian Communist Party. The new elite was a patchwork of ex-Communists and former members of the Latvian nomenklatura, early anti-Communists such as Eduards Berklāvs (purged in 1959, together with some 2,000 other members, by Khrushchev for "national-communist" activities and now the leader of the Latvian National Independence Movement) and very recent ones. It also included many energetic and ambitious persons who had remained outside the Party and the government but had developed considerable administrative and political talents in other state structures such as the university system, collective farms, the Academy of Sciences, and the media.[40]

Though in terms of statehood, Latvia had entered a new phase in 1991, the residents of Latvia at that crucial moment were still surrounded by the immediate past. The highest political authority, the Supreme Council, was an institution of the Soviet period; and the Council's presiding officer (Gorbunovs), had been a functionary in the Latvian Communist Party. The country's currency was still the Soviet ruble; and most of its labor force, in spite of some pre-1991 decentralization and the existence of privatization laws, was employed in state-owned and state-managed enterprises. Though the Supreme Council had been dominated by reformers for the past fifteen months, their reform labors remained woefully incomplete (the 1922 Constitution, for example, was still being amended and revised to fit the new circumstances).[41] The new state also had an estimated 45,000 Soviet soldiers within its borders, and the leaders of its erstwhile "home" – the Soviet Union – were still struggling to find a formula by means of which the "Union" could be preserved as a single, undivided entity.

The collapse of the Soviet Union at the end of 1991 removed in Latvia for the time being the fear of any immediate reincorporation into that entity, and the reformers in the Supreme Council could turn inward. But the politics of reform was now no longer simply a matter of official institutions issuing decrees. The government had been legislating for some eighteen months already, and its policies were heartily disliked by segments of the population. The August 1991 events left the large Russian (and other Slavic) part of the population in Latvia uneasy about its future in the new state, for example, while others looked to the government for a fast resolution of the problems created by the fifty-year "Soviet occupation." A spectrum of attitudes was becoming identifiable. On the "right," critics of the Council underscored what to them was an unacceptably large number of the former nomenklatura in high places in the new regime and, correspondingly, the low number of persons who had refused "compromises" with the old system. The argument on the "right" was that the main purpose of the new state was to ensure the preservation of the Latvian *tauta* and that those who had "compromised" earlier could not be entrusted with so serious a task. Now that Latvians – the "basic nation" (Latv. *pamattauta*) – had regained control of the country that bore their name, the government had to be the instrument for ensuring that control remained in Latvian hands.[42] For the "left," the most pressing issue was the political and economic future of the Slavic-language-speaking minorities, primarily the Russians. Opinion on the left could no longer realistically question the *fait accompli* of an independent Latvia (though fringe groups continued to do so), but it did argue that the government's primary responsibilities were to ensure legal "equality" (including citizenship) for all residents of the country and continued employment of the labor force. By and large, the opinions on the wings of the political spectrum were voiced most loudly outside the Supreme Council, although they were articulated by individuals within the Council on occasion. By and large also, the wings of the spectrum had a distinct "national" coloration, with the activists on the "right" being Latvians and those on the "left," though not exclusively non-Latvians, having their base of support in the Slavic-language population. The arguments of both wings presupposed a dominant role for the central government, at least in the economy but also in many domains of social and cultural life. In this respect, the "wings" were in line with the political philosophy of the interwar Latvian republic, which remained unapologetically statist during the parliamentary period (1918–34) and especially so during the Kārlis Ulmanis's authoritarian rule (1934–40).

Expressing numerous and varied positions in the middle of the political spectrum were the pragmatically inclined, in and out of the government. Their policies (in government) and arguments (outside the government) were grounded in the demonstrable and unavoidable need to address and solve problems pressing in from all sides. Their guidelines were the preservation of independence and the implementation of reforms that would result in a "westernized" Latvia. The problems that needed addressing ranged from the simplest and most easily solvable (for example, exclusive use of the Latvian language in parliamentary discussions) to the most complex (such as privatization of state industrial enterprises).

As the early months of 1992 passed, another problem began to overshadow all others, namely, the legitimacy of the Supreme Council itself. It was, after all, a Soviet-period structure, and, though elected, it had lost since March 1990 a number of its members through withdrawal and resignation.

To the opinion on the political "right" the Council's origins were suspect; to the opinion on the left, its representativeness was questionable. By declaring in August 1991, the 1922 Constitution as the country's basic law, the Council had bound itself to a parliamentary election in the near future, presumably in 1992. Throughout that year, however, the election date continued to be postponed in expectation of the passage of a citizenship law that would finally define the "political community," that is, citizens and therefore voters. The hope that such a law could be passed quickly was abandoned in the fall, and the Godmanis government settled for a temporary solution, defining the "political community" as those who would have become citizens at the time of the election, which was then set for the late spring of 1993. In the discussions surrounding the electoral procedures, the new parliament-to-be was designated as the fifth Saeima, the parliament elected in 1931 and dismissed by Kārlis Ulmanis in 1934 having been the fourth. Just as the laws of the renewed republic were to be infused with legitimacy by the 1922 Constitution, so the principal law-making body would receive its legitimization by being connected with the interwar parliamentary tradition. The absence of a definitive citizenship law, however, meant that a substantial number of adult residents of Latvia (most of them ethnic Slavs) would not be able to vote in the parliamentary election and would have to depend on others among the citizens to represent their interests. The Constitution called for a Saeima of 100 deputies, and the electoral procedures specified that a candidates' list receiving less than 4 percent of the total vote would not receive any seats.

The 1993 parliamentary elections

The election campaign did not begin in earnest until mid-spring of 1993, and became intense after the Council set the election date as June 5–6. The relatively liberal election rules from the pre-1934 period were retained, as was the minimum of 4 percent of the vote for a party or grouping to receive representation. The array of groupings and parties that eventually put forward candidate lists numbered twenty-three (see table 7.4), and contained virtually every identifiable viewpoint on the Latvian political spectrum. The campaign was sprightly with relatively little extremism in evidence, but its short duration as well as the large number of parties did not allow most of them to develop a clear identity or a distinctive platform. All the contestants, save the Popular Front, were sharply critical of the Godmanis government; and all stated, in different variations and with different emphases, unobjectionable goals: economic development, continued privatization, vigilance with respect to sovereignty, and integration with the rest of Europe.[43] Public interest in the

Table 7.4 *Parliamentary elections in Latvia, 1993*

Party or political group	Votes	Percent of vote	Seats in Saeima[a]
Latvia's Way	362,479	32.3	36
Latvian National Independence Movement	149,455	13.4	15
Harmony For Latvia–Revival for the Economy	124,282	12.0	13
Latvian Agrarian Union	119,134	10.6	12
Equal Rights Movement	64,495	5.8	7
For Fatherland and Freedom	59,994	5.4	6
Christian Democratic Party	56,136	5.0	6
Democratic Center Party	n.a.	4.8	5
Latvian Popular Front	29,349	2.6	–
The Green Party	13,387	1.2	–
Russian National Democratic List	13,008	1.2	–
Democratic Labor Party	10,512	.9	–
"Latvia's Luck"	9,842	.8	–
Our Land	9,274	.8	–
Economic Activity League	8,400	.7	–
Social Democratic Workers' Party	7,432	.6	–
Anti-Communist Union	5,969	.5	–
Republican Platform	5,071	.4	–
Conservatives' & Farmers' Party	2,800	.3	–
Independence Union	1,966	.2	–
Latvian Liberal Party	1,517	.2	–
Latvian Unity Party	1,017	.1	–
Liberal Alliance	523	.05	–

Note: [a]Since the Latvian Saeima has 100 seats, the absolute number of seats also equals the percentage of seats.

Sources: *Diena*, June 8, 1993, p. 1, *Baltic Independent*, June 11-17, 1993, p. 4; *The Baltic Observer*, June 11-17, 1993, p. 13.

campaign remained acute, and 89 percent of the eligible voters participated in the election.

Seven of the competing parties obtained more that 4 percent of the total vote for Saeima representation and the deputies from these parties became, for a time, the new political elite. Pride of place went to Latvia's Way, which had merged in its candidates' list such popular figures from the Supreme Council as Gorbunovs and Georgs Andrējevs, then foreign minister; as well as political leaders of the Latvian émigré community such as Gunārs Meierovics, the chairman of the World Federation of Free Latvians. Meierovics had the additional appeal of being the son of Zigfrids Meierovics, the first foreign minister of the interwar republic who had obtained western *de jure* recognition of the new state after 1918.

Other successful electoral groups included the Agrarian Union, which announced itself as the continuation of the interwar party that had played a major political role in the parliamentary period (and was also the party of Kārlis Ulmanis); the Latvian National Independence Movement, which become the mainstay of the political "right" during the recent changes; and the somewhat clumsily named Harmony for Latvija–Revival for the Economy Party, which was led by Jānis Jurkāns, a former foreign minister in the Godmanis government, who had formed the Harmony Party in large part to give voice to the interests of the non-Latvian minorities.

Remarkably, the Latvian Popular Front – the font of all reformist thinking in recent years – was excluded from the Saeima, having received only 2.6 percent of the vote, perhaps because its list contained the name of Ivars Godmanis, the now very unpopular prime minister. The "Russian" voice in the Saeima was represented by Jurkāns party as well as by the Equality Party; further to the right of the Latvian National Independence Movement was the For Fatherland and Freedom party; and the moderates were helped by the small Christian Democrats party.

The new Saeima met for the first time on July 6 and, following the 1922 Constitution, elected from among its deputies both a Saeima president (the unflaggingly popular Gorbunovs), and a president (and also head of state) for the country, Guntis Ulmanis. Between them Gorbunovs and Ulmanis represented continuity with both the period of the Supreme Council, which Gorbunovs had headed since 1990; and with the interwar republic, because Guntis Ulmanis was the grandnephew of Kārlis Ulmanis, the interwar republic's last president. Somewhat later in July, Latvia's Way and the Agrarian Union agreed to form a minority coalition cabinet, which could command forty-eight votes if party discipline were maintained and a majority if additional votes could be recruited from smaller groupings. The cabinet was headed by Valdis Birkavs of Latvia's Way, and included among its thirteen ministers three persons from the Latvian diaspora: the minister of defense, Valdis Pavlovskis (United States), the minister of welfare, Jānis Ritenis (Australia), and the minister of justice, Egīls Levits (Germany). The Saeima and the cabinet immediately began to work on the tasks inherited from the Supreme Council, among which the most important were the citizenship law and the continuing presence of the Russian Army.

As had been the case with the Godmanis transition government, the Birkavs government after 1993 was blamed for virtually all that happened "on its watch." Its most controversial decisions concerned the withdrawal of the remaining Russian troops in Latvia, and the treaty that was signed with Russia in spring 1994, detailing the timing of the withdrawal and the disposition of demobilized Russian military personnel, especially officers. The treaty was interpreted by many (especially on the right) as a cave-in to outside pressure from the West, and this was reflected in the public opinion polls about the government's performance. Unless the Birkavs government resigned, however, or unless there was a new Saeima election (next scheduled in 1995), frustrated voters had to find other means to express their unhappiness.

The Latvian Saeima elections resulted in a parliament that differed sharply from those elected by the other two now-independent Baltic peoples – the Lithuanians and Estonians – in their first post-August 1991 parliamentary elections in the fall of 1992.[44] In Lithuania, the Lithuanian Popular Front (Sajudis) suffered an embarrassing defeat that gave an absolute majority in the Sejmas to the Lithuanian Democratic Labor Party (the former independent Communist Party) and its leader Algirdas Brazauskas, who in February 1993, also became Lithuania's first popularly elected president. In Estonia, the September 1992, Riigikogu elections resulted in a right-of-center three-party majority and led to the formation of a cabinet (by Prime Minister Mart Laar) most members of which were of a new political generation (born in the late 1950s) and, with a few exceptions, had been too young to develop any blamable connections with the pre-1991 communist establishment. The new Latvian political elite, however, was a merger, and the leaders of the new government, through their personal histories, reflected virtually every aspect of the recent political experiences of the Latvian *tauta*. Latvia too now had a center-right coalition majority in the Saeima, but the center, Latvia's Way, was far larger than its right-wing partner, the Agrarian Union; moreover, the center had a substantial infusion of persons who in the past had first been orthodox communists, then reform communists, and then ex-communists. The country's new president, Guntis Ulmanis, had suffered deportation and had to take another surname for a while to hide his relation to the former interwar president.[45] Moreover, the cabinet had three ministers from the Latvian émigré communities of the western world. The transfer of power from the old Supreme Council to the new Saeima was entirely uneventful, with Latvia's Way immediately entering discussions about possible cabinet coalitions with the less numerous parties. Deputies from all the smaller parties quickly became integrated into the ongoing work of the Saeima committees and their public statements on issues before the Saeima were from the beginning responsible and constructive in tone.

The municipal elections of 1994

On May 29, 1994, there was a successful round of municipal elections in which the political groupings of the "right" did particularly well in urban areas and Latvia's Way did very badly. It should be remembered that non-citizens could not participate in local elections, so that most of the voters were likely to be Latvians (over 18 years of age). Moreover, just 58.5 percent of the eligible voters nationwide participated (50.5 percent in Riga).[46] Still, the parties of the right received a surprisingly large proportion of the total vote. In Riga, sixteen lists of candidates were put forward for the 60-seat municipal council, and the three largest winners were the Latvian National Independence Movement/Green coalition (22 seats), a new entrant called the Saimnieks (master; head of farmstead) party (11), and For Fatherland and Freedom (6). All other parties were awarded four or fewer seats each, with Latvia's Way receiving only two seats. The fact that for several years the Riga City Council would be dominated by voices of the political right (which also selected the city's mayor, that is, the president of the city council) was a meaningful result. Riga, with its 856,000 inhabitants (about one-third of the country's population) and the headquarters of all major news media, dominates the political culture of Latvia; and the activities of the Riga City Council share the spotlight in the Riga media with those of the national government. Thus the Latvian National Independence Movement, as well as the For Fatherland and Freedom Party, had not only demonstrated staying power but had also acquired an instrument for demonstrating their practical capabilities. Being able to govern Riga was not quite the same as governing the country, but the job was certainly next to national government in terms of complexity and responsibility.

Of the three big winners in Riga, the Saimnieks party, led by Ziedonis Čevers, the interior minister of the erstwhile Godmanis government, was an interesting new entrant in the political campaign, because its leaders seemed to be arguing for the desirability of apolitical leadership. The Saimnieks platform – as befitting municipal elections – focused almost entirely on local urban problems, claiming that their solution could be brought about only by well-versed technical experts. It should also be noted that the Equality Party won the next largest number of council seats (4) after the first three parties The Equality Party ran unapologetically as a defender of the "rights" of non-Latvians, who at this date still comprised some 65 percent of the city's total population. Since most non-citizens could not vote, and most of the Riga non-Latvian population were non-citizens, support for Equality was understandably low. To the political right, however, the fact that such parties as Equality and Jānis Jurkāns's Harmony Party (which also emphasized tolerance for non-Latvians and received two seats in the Riga Council) were just below the primarily Latvian parties in terms of political strength was a warning. A liberalized citizenship law (and thus further enfranchisement), they thought, would enhance the political weight of the non-Latvian population and probably would lead to policies not in the best interests of the Latvian *tauta*.

Fall of the Birkavs government

During the second half of its year in office, the Birkavs government did manage to bring to fruition a citizenship law, which was passed by the Saeima in a special summer session on July 28, 1994. The Latvian government had also negotiated an agreement with Russia that all Russian troops, save a handful left guarding the Skrunda radar facility, would be withdrawn from Latvia by August 31. On both issues, compromise was necessary: the citizenship law (after an earlier version containing quotas was vetoed by President Ulmanis and sent back to the Saeima) finally excluded quotas for non-Latvians, and the troop agreement included a promise by the Latvian government to safeguard the social welfare of the "retired" Russian military officers in Latvia. The new citizenship law – affecting some 400,000 residents of Latvia – now permitted in 1996 the start of the naturalization process of all non-citizens born in Latvia, and from 2003 on the same process for all non-citizens born outside Latvia. Though Western observers were pleased that these difficult controversies had been "resolved," no such pleasure was exhibited by large segments of the Latvian population.[47]

In the Saeima, the fragility of the Latvia's Way coalition with the Agrarian Union was demonstrated in mid-July 1994, when the three Union ministers in the thirteen-person cabinet withdrew. Birkavs promptly announced his own resignation and the end of his cabinet. These events were not entirely unexpected, because the Agrarian Union had expressed repeatedly dissatisfaction not only with the citizenship law and the troop agreement but also with Latvia's Way's policy on imported agricultural goods. The Unionists wanted high import tariffs in order, they said, to protect the Latvian farmers in a time of transition; Latvia's Way, on the other hand, was striving to implement free-market policies and to reduce subsidies. Subsequent events not only underlined the unresolved state of the "farm problem" but eventually also the relative weakness (at the national level) of the parties of the right. President Ulmanis (himself a Unionist), called upon the Latvian National Independence Movement to accept the task of forming a new cabinet. Andrejs Krastiņš, a prominent MP in the Movement's ranks, negotiated with the other members of the so-called National Bloc (the Movement, For Fatherland and Freedom, the Agrarian Union, the Democrats, the Christian Democrats) but was unable to form a cabinet acceptable to the Saeima. Consequently, Ulmanis had to turn again to Latvia's Way (which still had the plurality of seats in the Saeima) to try again. On September 15, the Saeima voted in favor of a new cabinet led by Māris Gailis of Latvia's Way, by a vote (89 deputies voting) of 49 for, 33 against, and 7 abstaining. The new cabinet was supported by the Latvia's Way MPs, the Union of Economists, and the Harmony Party. In opposition were the National Bloc and the Equality Party.

Krastiņš, on the right, commented that the document Gailis issued to present his cabinet's plans for the future was authored by "Karl Marx, Vladimir Ilyich Lenin, and Hans Christian Andersen."[48] Though in the subsequent twelve months there were a number of controversial issues – several strikes by professional organizations (primary and secondary school teachers, medical personnel) and the "bank crisis" of June 1995[49] – the Gailis government dealt with these without precipitating a confidence vote in the Saeima.

Preparing for the 1995 parliamentary elections

As these events suggest, tracking the processes of democratization in post-1991 Latvia is all the more difficult because of the absence in these years of corner-turning political events that would constitute a definitive sign either of full acceptance or full non-acceptance of democratic values. At both the national and local levels, elections took place as prescribed in the Constitution, turnout for them was relatively high, and ministerial offices have been turned over to successors in an orderly fashion. No coups or attempted coups occurred, and most of the political groupings that in the 1993 parliamentary election received less than the 4 percent (of the total vote) required for representation, started in early 1995 to prepare for the September election, though sometimes in different coalitions than those they had formed for the 1993 competition. Incumbents and aspirants to power had a larger stage upon which to display their talents. Although the election (or reelection) campaigns were not noticeably media-driven, the opportunities for self-promotion were greater. The number of magazines and other periodicals in Latvia (virtually all privatized) had increased from 182 in 1993 to 213 in 1994 and the number of newspapers from 242 in 1993 to 257 in 1994.[50] By 1995, there were some fifteen private radio and television companies. There were also several new radio stations and at least two new television channels, though for most people the principal source of information was probably Latvian State Television.[51]

The fact that nineteen political groups (coalitions and formally registered political parties) submitted candidates lists for the September 30–October 1, 1995 election suggested that there had not been any appreciable drop of interest within the political class in vying for political power. Only a handful of the parties and groups came into being for the sole purpose of competing for the 1995 election. The vast majority had been part of the political class at least since 1991, some were formed in the years of the "Third Awakening," and a few were renewed versions of parties that harked back to the first period of independence (1918–40) and, in one case – the Latvian Social Democratic Workers Party – to 1904. Thus by 1995, the political future of democratization in Latvia was not likely to involve persons other than those currently active in the parties, their leadership, and their parliamentary "fractions" (the party members representing the party in the Saeima; Latv. *frakcijas*). With a couple of important exceptions (noted below), the political leaders who in the near future were likely to be in the position of helping or hindering democratization already held political power or were actively seeking it. Yet what kind of political sentiment and leadership would eventually emerge from the population of the approximately 300,000 resident voting-age non-citizens of Latvia (mostly Russians) was not clear at this juncture.

The stability of the well-known parties was evident in a survey of voters' opinion several days before the election, when 76.0 percent of those with the right to vote said that they would participate in the election. Among those who were willing to commit themselves, 12.9 percent said that they would vote for Latvia's Way and 12.6 percent for the Democratic Party Saimnieks. After these two leaders, there was a sharp drop: 6.9 percent for Fatherland and Freedom, 5.9 percent for the Latvian Unity Party (a newcomer, see below), 5.8 percent for the Latvian National Independence Movement, 4.5 percent for Latvia (Joachim Siegerist's party) and 4.0 percent for the Agrarian Union. Opinion favoring the other parties fell in each case below 3 percent (that is, substantially below the new 5 percent cutoff for parliamentary representation). Yet fully 33.8 percent of that proportion said that they had not yet made up their minds.[52] These figures suggested that longevity in the public arena had produced a following: of the high-scoring parties (above 5 percent) – the Unity Party – was the only recent arrival among the top five. But the very high proportion of "undecideds" gave to the prognostication of all the leading parties a worried tone.

In the months just before the election, public opinion polls also made clear that economic issues were foremost in the voters' minds as "the most serious problems in Latvia."[53] The first three major problems (on a list of twenty-five) were low wages, the need to renew local industry, and unemployment. Crime and unprofessional politicians were fourth and fifth, followed by low pensions, high costs of communal services, and agriculture. High prices of goods and corruption concluded the list of the ten most important problems. "Patriotic" issues scored low: defense (no. 24), presence of Russian military personnel (no. 23), border and customs problems (no. 19), the citizenship question (no. 21). Material inequality among groups in the population scored moderately high (no. 11), but education moderately low (no. 15). Environmental issues stood in the bottom half of the list (no. 18). Judging by these rankings, the political parties were well advised to address the issues of family-level economic well-being, criminality, and quality of leadership. Yet the worries depicted in surveys of this kind were difficult to translate into specific attention-grabbing proposals that would clearly differentiate one party from another.

This problem of differentiation was serious not only for voters but also for analysts, first, because there were so many parties, and second, because the usual right-center-left division was somewhat of a simplification. Nonetheless, in the interview cited earlier, the former Minister of Justice Egīls Levits suggested that the 1995 campaign was demonstrating the existence of something like a right-to-left spectrum.[54] Where each part of the spectrum began and ended, however, was difficult to determine because of coalitions and shared attitudes. For example, parties in all three categories (right/left/center) tended to favor a strongly activist central government: the "right" to protect the Latvian tauta, the "left" to ensure egalitarian treatment of all citizens, and the "center" (e.g. Latvia's Way) because it judged the "private sector" and "civil society" to be insufficiently strong for the present "transition" situation. Also, the "right" did not have a monopoly of the idea that Latvia should be a "national" state: this notion was shared by virtually all the parties with the exception of those few (Equality, the Russian Citizens Party) which believed that Latvia's most promising future lay in the creation of a "two-community state" (two official languages, the right to dual [that is, Latvian and Russian] citizenship). All the parties without exception declared their loyalty to the principles of political democracy, and a number – regardless of their position in the political spectrum – believed that the national president should be popularly elected (rather than elected by the Saeima, as prescribed in the 1922 Constitution).

The most important change in the rules for the 1995 election was the increase of the minimal proportion for parliamentary representation to 5 percent. It was hoped that this would reduce the number of parties in the Saeima. In addition, the regulations governing the 1993 elections had required no disclosure of party financing, but the law for 1995 election did. The somewhat meager information gleaned from the party reports that were due on September 1, 1995 (see table 7.5) suggests, first, that the law's reporting requirements were too imprecise, and, second, that the parties were reluctant to yield precise information or did not know what was required of them. Six parties did not report by the required date. Information from those that did confirmed the advantages of incumbency: Latvia's Way, the dominant force in the government since 1993, was also the best financed party.[55] Two parties – the Economists and Harmony – reported substantial donors of the "corporate" variety, Harmony benefiting from a large contribution by a well-known Russian businessman in Latvia. Most parties relied heavily on individual contributions and membership fees. Since these individual donations were not distinguished with respect to size, however, it

Table 7.5 *Declarations of income of parties in 1995 Latvian parliamentary elections*

Party	Amount in party accounts as of Aug. 16, 1995	Largest source of party income
Latvia's Way	49,543	individual contributions (196,127 L)
For Latvia (Siegerist)	16,339 L	individual contributions (55,738 L)
Economists (TPA)	17,014 USD 676 L	contribution from Solvtrans Corp. (20,000 USD)
DP Saimnieks	8,645 L	not given
Harmony	2,925 L	contribution from Vladimir Kuleshov (1,000,000 USD)
LNIM	2,397 L	individual contributions (37,230 L)
Latvian Popular Front	1,867 L	not given
Christian Democratic Party	1,391 L	not given
Agrarian Union	1,277 L	from bank credit (1,111 L)
LDDP	948 L	individual contributions (3,003 L)
Fatherland and Freedom	628 L	not given
Unprotected Party	384 L	individual contributions (230 L)
Socialist Party	115 L	membership dues
Justice	36 L	membership dues (409 L)
Democratic Party	1 L	candidate fees (1,373 L)

Source: Adapted from Nellija Locmele, "Latvijas partijas atzistas truciguma" [Latvia's Parties Confess to Poverty], *Diena*, September 7, 1995, p. 3.

was not possible to analyze party position in relations to the interests of the contributors.

Parties of the "right"

Preparation for the 1995 campaign brought into coalition, in November 1994, two of the oldest political groups on the Latvian political stage, namely, the Latvian National Independence Movement and the Greens. The Movement, founded in July 1988 simultaneously with the Latvian Popular Front (see below), did not formally register as a political party until June 1994. In 1995 it had about 2,130 members and in the 1993 election received enough votes to obtain 15 deputies in the Saeima. During the 1988–1991 period, the Movement remained intransigent on the question of national sovereignty and independence, and its indefatigable leader, Eduards Berklāvs, the highest-ranking Communist to be purged in 1959 for "bourgeois nationalism,"[56] remained active from 1988 onward. The Movement's coalition partner, the environmentalist Green Party, founded in January 1990 and having 228 members in 1995, proved to have much less political potential.[57] In the early years the Greens had to compete with the Latvian Popular Front, and had difficulty retaining the loyalty of environmentally conscious activists.[58] The vote for the Green Party in the 1993 elections fell far short (1.2 percent) of the necessary 4 percent required for Saeima representation.

Through its bloc of deputies in the 1993 Saeima, the Latvian National Independence Movement had accumulated considerable experience in governing, unlike the Greens who had no parliamentary representation. The two parties, however, were linked ideologically. The Movement, in an elaborate 1995 platform, featured the need for the Latvian state to guarantee the continued existence of the Latvian nation,[59] while the Greens tended to see ecological questions as needing to be solved in order for the Latvian nation to have a healthy environment.[60] Unlike Western Europe, where ecopolitics has tended to merge with the politics of the left, in Latvia the association between environmental protectionism and nationalism was strong from the beginning and continued to be very close.

Chronologically speaking, the Latvian Popular Front was as old as the Latvian National Independence Movement, both having been founded in 1988. On October 8–9 of that year the First Congress of the Latvian Popular Front took place, with some 1000 delegates representing, it was said, about 110,000 dues-paying members (perhaps 90 percent of them Latvians) in 2,300 local chapters.[61] The Congress revealed the spirit of the times: some one-third of the participants were Communist Party members, and there was good representation from the environmentalists, the dissidents, the more radical independence-minded, religious groups, and the "creative" intelligentsia. Because of its umbrella-like nature, the Front could not satisfy the more radically inclined Latvians, for whom mere "republic sovereignty" within the USSR was a compromise. The Front paid the price for not formally becoming a party until 1994, as large numbers of its parliamentary and extraparliamentary supporters shifted to better organized party formations. In the 1993 parliamentary election, the Front received an insufficient proportion (2.5 percent) of the total vote to be represented in the Saeima. With a 1995 membership of 2,025 persons, the Front was hardly a spent force, but it had failed to establish itself as a distinct entity. Its 1995 platform, having become stridently nationalistic, maintained that "unfortunately, after the achievement of independence, the political and economic power in the state was taken over by circles the mainstays of which are members of the nomenklatura and persons from the shadow economy. The politics of these persons are subordinated to the interests of a narrow group of parvenus."[62] Though the Latvian Popular Front had been the political school through which virtually all currently active Latvian political leaders had passed, it had now moved to the periphery of effective politics.

The organization called For Fatherland and Freedom was formally registered as a political party in January 1995, even though its origins are to be found much earlier, in the first days of the "Third Awakening," when activists sought to establish a directly lineal relationship between current political ideals and the interwar republic. Then, in 1990, the so-called "Congress Movement" attempted to create something like an alternative government to the Supreme Council by holding congresses of interwar citizens (and their offspring); in this thinking, all institution of the Soviet-period were illegitimate. This atmosphere generated a number of small party-like formations, among them the so-called "18 November Union" and "Fatherland." These two groups then produced the coalition known as For Fatherland and Freedom for the 1993 election. For Fatherland and Freedom has shown itself to have had more staying power than many of the splinter formations of the right. In 1995, it had 670 members and the 1993 election gave it six seats in the Saeima. Although its 1995 platform was well-rounded and addressed straightforwardly the same problems as other platforms, the party continued to be preoccupied more than most with the consequences of the "Soviet occupation."

The organization that in 1995 called itself For Latvia and claimed to be "national movement," earned an unsavory reputation in an earlier incarnation in the 1993 election. The 1995 For Latvia party was registered in November 1994, and was led by four Saeima deputies who were elected under the aegis of the Latvian National Independence Movement but were expelled from the Movement in 1994. In the 1993 election, the Movement's ranks included Joachim Siegerist, a right-wing activist from Germany who claimed to have Latvian parentage. He and his supporters were perhaps the most blatantly populist campaigners in the 1993 elections, seeking to appeal to the ranks of the many Latvians whose standard of living had plummeted during the ongoing transition. Siegerist and his second-in-command, the Latvian historian Odisejs Kostanda, were both elected to the Saeima in 1993, but their subsequent activities became embarrassing to the Movement. Siegerist promised repeatedly to learn the Latvian language (knowledge of which is required by the internal rules of the Saeima), but did not; moreover, he repeatedly missed Saeima sessions and was finally expelled from the Saeima in 1995. Although For Latvia claims to have some 12,000 members (which would make it the largest Latvian political formation), these numbers cannot be verified. In 1995 For Latvia appeared to be animated by a total rejection of the Soviet past and its platform embodied that spirit. At the same time, though, the promises it made to the electorate presupposed a highly activist and interventionist government, which fact linked this party to the statism of the interwar republic.[63]

The 1995 campaign included several small parties of the right, none of which had parliamentary representation and were not expected to obtain it. The Union of Latvian Farmers, because of its larger and more prominent namesake – the Agrarian Union, had little success in manifesting a presence. Another 1995 coalition (formed in June) – Our Land and the Anti-Communist Union – accused the Saeima of having violated the 1922 Constitution (and thus of having carried out a coup d'etat) in passing the citizenship law without putting it to a popular vote. The Latvian National Democratic Party had 437 members but in 1995, as was the case with all the splinter parties, had trouble establishing a clear identity. Yet another coalition between the Political Union of the Unprotected[64] and the Latvian Independence Party brought together two groups neither of which had been represented in the 1993 Saeima.

The two common themes among all the parties of the "right" in the 1995 campaign were (1) that the Latvian state should have as its first priority the protection of the Latvian nation; and (2) that the "merged elite" (reform Communists, former communists, non-communists, émigré Latvians) whose members have wielded political power since 1991 had in fact produced a debacle, or, at best, endangered the survival of the Latvian nation in its own state. Yet none renounced the renewed 1922 Constitution. By contrast with the 1920s, when the right proclaimed increasingly loudly that the parliamentary system "wasn't working," the charges from the larger parties of the right in 1995 tended to be not against the system but against the Soviet-era heritage that was said to have populated the system with persons insufficiently loyal to the present needs and future survival of the Latvian tauta. Latvia's close proximity to Russia left the former open to efforts by that regional superpower to re-create a new "empire" in the old Soviet space, through manipulating the sentiments and loyalties of the Slavic-language citizens of Latvia.[65] The emphasis on "national endangerment" made it unlikely that this sensibility would diminish in the near future, because even though the "Soviet period" would recede into the more distant past, the geographical location of the country would not change.

Parties of the "center"

The center in Latvian politics since the election of 1993 was dominated by Latvia's Way, the electoral coalition that came into being in February of that year. It included prominent persons from the Supreme Council (the transition government), the Popular Front, and from the Latvian western diaspora. Receiving 36 seats in the 1993 parliamentary elections, Latvia's Way formally became a political party in October 1993, and continued as the main force in Latvian politics from that point onward.[66] In 1995, the party had 387 members and 110 candidate members. In July 1993, Latvia's Way went to the right to form a coalition cabinet with the Agrarian Union, and governed until July 1994, when the Birkavs cabinet resigned. Latvia's Way then found a coalition partner in the small Economists party, and the resulting cabinet was headed until the fall of 1995 by Maris Gailis. Even though Latvia's Way from 1993 on had to govern without ever having an absolute majority in the Saeima, it was the only political grouping that could fairly claim to have had a plurality in both the Saeima and the public opinion polls. Because it has had the responsibility of governing for the past three years, the party in 1995 sought to project an image of stability, responsibility, and, not least, know-how. The collapse of the Birkavs coalition in 1993, the failure of the right to assemble a cabinet acceptable to the Saeima then, and the subsequent successes of the Gailis government permitted Latvia's Way to paint itself as a political force essential not only to good governing but to any sensible governing of the country. Moreover, as coalitions formed and re-formed on both the left and right and as other parties renamed themselves, Latvia's Way developed an image of permanence, attracting for that reason voters who might disagree with specific items in its platform.[67] Even though there were signs in 1995 that the party's popularity was diminishing, its most important leaders (Gorbunovs; Gailis, then prime minister; Birkavs, the former prime minister and then foreign minister; and Jānis Ādamsons, then interior minister) remained personally very popular, with very high name-recognition in public opinion polls.

The direct beneficiary of the Ulmanis legacy (strong leadership and economic recovery) from the interwar period was the Latvian Agrarian Union, which in the 1995 election was in coalition with the Latvian Christian Democratic Union and the Lettgallian Democratic Party. This coalition was formed in April 1995. The Agrarian Union (not to be confused with the Latvian Farmers Party [see above]) was renewed in April 1991, and linked itself directly with its predecessor of the interwar years.[68] Before it was disbanded in 1934 by its leader Ulmanis, the interwar Union dominated Latvian politics, supplying three of the four presidents of Latvia, and ten of the thirteen prime ministers in the period 1917–1934. Though its political base was the Latvian rural population, the party's leadership then consisted principally of middle-class professionals. The post-1991 Union had some 3800 members, which made it the largest political organization in the country. In the 1993 election, the Union obtained 12 deputies in the Saeima. The politics of the Union naturally focused on Latvia's rural population (about 35 percent of the total), which sought income guarantees as well as some degree of state protection against foreign agricultural imports. In most other economic and non-economic matters, its 1995 platform was close to that of Latvia's Way but agricultural protectionism continued to be the stumbling block for any future coalitions between these two parties.[69]

Of the Union's coalition partners, the Christian Democratic Party was founded in March 1991, with some 650 members. In the 1993 elections it obtained 6 seats in the Saeima. Drawing on the example of Christian Democratic parties in western Europe (especially Germany), the Latvian Christian Democrats cast their political program in light of what they understood to be Christian morality, thus lending to the 1995 coalition program an emphasis (and a tone) it would normally not have. The Letgallian Democratic Party did not exist in the 1993 election; it was founded in February 1994 and in 1995 had 256 members. As its name suggests, the Lettgallian Party brought to the coalition a regional element that has been missing in post-1991 Latvian politics but was strongly present in the interwar parliamentary period. Letgallia (Latv. *Latgale*) is the easternmost of the four large regional subdivisions of Latvia (Vidzeme, Kurzeme, Zemgale, Latgale), and its past was substantially different from the rest of Latvian-inhabited territories (a distinctive dialect, domination by Poland until the late eighteenth century, serf emancipation forty years later than in the other Latvian lands, considerable economic underdevelopment in the interwar years). Letgallia's Latvian population is predominantly Roman Catholic, and it also has a very high proportion of Slavic-language inhabitants, especially in such cities as Daugavpils and Rezekne. The coalition's 1995 platform included specific mention of the need to preserve and enhance the special cultural features of Letgallia.

The Latvian Liberal Party was founded January 1990, by a small group of entrepreneurially-inclined persons in the Latvian Popular Front. In the 1993 parliamentary elections it received less that 4 percent of the total vote and therefore was not represented in the Saeima. In 1995 it had some 300 members. Apart from its emphasis on the need to promote entrepreneurialism within a reformed free-market economy, this party had not registered a strong presence in the political arena and it was doubtful that in the 1995 election it would receive the necessary minimum 5 percent of the popular vote to have parliamentary representation.

Parties of the "left"

Of all the political groups on the Latvian spectrum, the parties of the left have had the most difficult time, first, in making themselves "respectable," and, second, in overcoming the fragmentation that seems to be more pronounced here than on the right. Because of both the distant and the recent past, the "left" possesses an image of "friendliness" toward the Slavic populations of Latvia and toward Russia. Russification policy under the pre-1918 Tsarist regime, and, in the Soviet period, the industrial-development policy that brought hundreds of thousands of Russians and other Slavic peoples into Latvia, introduced into Latvian history the belief that a succession of Russian governments practiced "cultural genocide" against the Latvian people.[70] As a result of this history, the "left" has been saddled (perhaps unfairly) with the task of having to explain (and to apologize for) the fact that some 45 percent of the country's population is non-Latvian, and that most of the cities in the country (including Riga) have populations in which the majority is non-Latvian. Much of the activist energy producing the Popular Front movement after 1988 had to do precisely with this issue, and one of the first successes of the Popular Front – even before the 1990 independence declaration – was the 1989 decree by the Supreme Council making the Latvian language the official language of the state.

By 1993–95 many voters saw the left as prepared to "compromise" on the issue of language (that is, on the question of Latvian culture), and as insufficiently worried about the emergence of a "two-nation state" (Latv. *divu kopienu valsts*). This was inferred from the left's urging "more humane" treatment of the "national minorities" through faster naturalization and through reforms of the administrative offices (especially the Naturalization and Citizenship Office) with which the "minorities" come into contact. An early "dissident" on this question – Jānis Jurkāns – stepped down in 1993 from the post of foreign minister after concluding that these issues were being swept aside, and founded the electoral coalition called Harmony for Latvia – Economic Rebirth, which in the 1993 Saeima election received 12 percent of the vote and 13 seats. It ran on a platform that accentuated the need to find ways to integrate the Slavic-language populations into Latvia. In February 1994, however, Jurkāns' coalition fragmented, producing the National Harmony Party, which in 1995 had about 400 members and five seats in the Saeima, and the Union of Economists, which inherited five seats in the Saeima from the split and presented a separate list for the 1995 election. The Harmony Party's 1995 platform was all-encompassing, but with respect to foreign policy it stressed the need for a balanced approach to east and west and urged unspecified "partnership relations" with Russia. It also expressed the belief that Latvia would face a major social crisis in the future if the "Russians" were not integrated into Latvian society.[71]

In the 1995 election, as in 1993, the "left" looked to benefit from the deterioration in living standards, which, the "left" parties charged, could have been avoided by a wiser policy than the Godmanis-Birkavs-Gailis governments had followed. While they supported Latvia's currency reform,[72] they continued to question the slow pace of currency emission[73] and the under- and unemployment created by the withdrawal of subsidies to state industry.[74] The Latvian intelligentsia was particularly unhappy over the diminution of central government support for education and research, and charged the government with following a deliberate policy of "systematic elimination of scientific work."[75] The main universities – the University of Latvia and the Riga Technical University – had to continue their work with flat or reduced budgets, which meant an increase in student-faculty ratios as well as a considerable amount of "moonlighting" on the part of staff and faculty.

These policies, identified in 1995 with Latvia's Way as they had once been identified with the Godmanis transition government, had brought wrenching changes, but the parties of the left had difficulty criticizing the government's policies of "economic reform" without seeming to be calling for a return to the centrally planned system. Perhaps the most pointed criticism had come from a group that emerged in the 1994 municipal elections and by 1995 was called Democratic Party Saimnieks. Founded with that name in April 1995, this party merged two smaller groupings: the Democratic Party (formerly the Democratic Center Party, founded in 1992) and the parliamentary group called Saimnieks, founded in March 1994. The membership of DP Saimnieks in 1995 was around 758. In 1994 DP Saimnieks had five deputies in the Saeima, who were the former Democratic Center party deputies elected in 1993. The two leaders of DP Saimnieks were Ziedonis Čevers, the former interior minister of the transition Godmanis government and Juris Celmiņš, the former head of the Saimnieks faction. The political platform of DP Saimnieks focused more than anything else on the economic situation in Latvia and proposed a moderate statism as a solution.[76] The name of the party appeared to have been designed to connote seriousness of purpose and decisiveness. The term itself – *saimnieks* – historically meant "head of farmstead," which was an important quasi-public office in the estate economies in which virtually all Latvians (being enserfed peasants) resided until the mid-nineteenth century. The *saimnieks* was responsible for the wise management of the farmstead and for all the persons on it; without his leadership the farmstead would not survive. Kārlis Ulmanis, the interwar authoritarian president, was frequently called the *Saimnieks* of Latvia, and the party's current name might just be a bow in the direction of interwar authoritarian statism.

A similarly "moderate left" party in 1995 was the Union of Economists ("Economist"). Founded in March 1994, by a split within the political organization called Harmony-Economic Revival, this segment of the Jurkans group perceived that questions of economic development were being sidelined by the search for "social justice" for the Slavic-language population, and therefore sought an independent organization. The Economist in 1995 had 300 members and 5 deputies in Saeima (of the 13 who were elected by the still-undivided Jurkans party in the 1993 election). Its 1995 platform disowned what it called the "extremist liberalism" of Latvia's Way and called for guidance by the central government of economic reform. Its ultimate goals appeared to be close to those of western European welfare-state social democrats, in that the role of the private sector was not only recognized but thought to be necessary.

The economic plight of large segments of the Latvian population created a niche in the political spectrum of parties claiming that economic reform had unnecessarily sacrificed the welfare of vulnerable people. The most prominent voice in the 1995 election speaking with these accents, besides the National Harmony Party, was the electoral coalition Work and Justice. The coalition was established in May 1995, and it comprised three parties with very different pedigrees. The partner with the most notorious past was the Latvian Democratic Labor Party which emerged in 1990, after the split in the ranks of the of the Latvian Communist Party.[77] These renamed "reform Communists" were then led by Ivars Ķezbers, who remained a visible and active member, though the Party's leader was Juris Bojārs, who was forbidden from running for the Saeima in 1993, and remained excluded in 1995, by the law prohibiting former employees of the KGB (Bojārs held the rank of major in the KGB) from running for public office. The second partner had a less tainted past. The Latvian Social Democratic Workers Party was renewed in Latvia in 1989 and is the oldest Latvian political party, having been founded in 1904. The third member of the coalition – a junior member – is the Party of Cheated Persons ("Justice"), which was founded in February 1994. In 1995 the Democratic Labor Party had over 1,000 members; the Social Democrats 380 members; and Justice 352 members. The Social Democrats presented a list in the 1993 elections but received only .7 percent of the vote and hence obtained no seats in the Saeima. The Party of the Cheated, as the name suggests, was in 1995 a collection of disaffected and alienated persons hurt by the economic transformations. The coalition's platform announced, among other things, that it was "against communism, national extremism, and the subordination of state and society to the selfish interests of those greedy for power and property."

The presence of such prominent former Communist Party members as Ķezbers and Bojārs among the politically active kept alive the question of how such persons should be viewed and how their present actions should be interpreted. But the highly visible political position of such former high-ranking Party members as Latvia's Way's Anatolijs Gorbunovs made impossible a blanket condemnation of all former nomenklatura members active in current politics. Even though the 1995 Work and Justice coalition included the Social Democrats, who were a major presence in the interwar republic and therefore added an air of respectability to the coalition, the presence of the former communists gave to the whole coalition a faintly foreign tinge.

Prominent figures from the recent communist past were brought into the 1995 election by the Latvian Unity Party, which was founded in December 1992 as an organization, and presented a list for the 1993 election, but received less that 4 percent of the vote. The party seems to have been given a new lease on life by the presence on its list of Alberts Kauls. Before 1991, Kauls was the controversial former director of "Adaži," the model kholkhoz that was often cited by Gorbachev as a case study of acceptable economic reform. Kauls, however, appeared to have been a backer of the pro-Moscow wing of the Communist Party in the events of January 1991 – the time of the barricades in Riga. Because of this background, Kauls was excluded by law from becoming a candidate in 1995. In the meantime, the Unity Party, as befitting its name, featured in its program controlled economic development as a unifying force of the population of Latvia. A small and relatively unknown party of the left – the Democratic Party – was founded after the 1993 election (in August) but now claimed to have 2,378 members. Known popularly as Family Party and led by Marģers Martinsons, the DP concentrated its political rhetoric on the "Latvian family" and the need for state action to save it.

The 1995 election lists of these parties contained virtually no non-Latvian names, which fact was noted by several other parties of the left who claimed to be ethnically more representative of those who do not have the franchise. Representation of the interests of the Latvian Slavic population in the 1993 election was claimed by the Equality Party, which became the core of a new Latvian Socialist Party founded in January 1994, and in 1995 claimed a membership of about 1000. In 1993, The Equality Party elected six members to the Saeima, and, given the large numbers of Slavic-speakers who remained without citizenship (and therefore without voting rights), the Socialists were likely to attract attention from those who wanted to speed up naturalization in order to increase their political strength. In the 1995 election, the Socialists proposed for the presidency of Latvia Alfrēds Rubiks, the erstwhile 1990–91 leader of the pro-Moscow wing of the Latvian Communist Party – a move that was seen as a calculated insult. But the Socialists could no longer claim to be the sole voice of the disenfranchised "Russians," because in 1995 they had a rival in the Latvia's Russian Citizens Party, founded in January 1995, with about 700 members. The Russian Citizen's Party claimed for itself the right to speak for the Russian-language population and found it unacceptable that parties with predominant non-Russian membership were presuming to do so: "The realization of our program rests upon this premise – the rescue of the Latvian nation (Latv. *nācija*) is the business of that nation itself. This goal can be reached if Latvians unify and consolidate. Such unity is made more difficult if the Saeima has Latvian deputies who arrive with the help of Russian voters, and by means of creating Latvian parties oriented toward Russian voters. The Russian Citizens Party thus puts forward its candidates to promote the unity of Latvians."[78] Whatever else the further enfranchisement of the Russian population might be projected, such language suggested additional fragmentation on the left.

With respect to forming a unified force, the parties of the left thus faced numerous problems. The communist past was still too recent for all of the nomenklatura members to be forgiven for it; the former communists were not natural allies of the historic Social Democrats; voters who were economically afflicted might not have been searching for a permanent home on the left; and such parties as Harmony found themselves challenged on ethnic grounds for diverting to Latvian parties the votes that should go to explicitly Russian ones. Moreover, only two of the parties of the left – Saimnieks and the Economists – showed an inclination to enter coalitions with the most prominent center party, Latvia's Way. Nonetheless, given the economic circumstances in which most Latvians lived in 1995, the parties of the left seemed currently a more palatable option to many Latvian voters than they had seemed in 1993.

The 1995 parliamentary elections

This greater palatability of the left parties was in fact reflected in the outcome of the 1995 parliamentary election (September 30–October 1), but "through a glass, darkly." The early results confused the international media. A very short story in the *New York Times* on November 3 (p. 4) was headlined "Rightists in Latvia Gain," whereas the *Baltic Observer*, which in an editorial a week before the election declared that a vote for the parties of the right constituted a vote against democracy, engaged in some wishful thinking by headlining the results "Latvia Turns to the Left." *Diena*'s (October 2) headline located the leftward turn in the rural areas ("The Countryside Turns to the Left"), whereas the totally confused *Le Monde* in Paris reported that the election had been "won" by a party called Saimnieks, which "is an anti-communist and nationalist-ultraconservative formation led by Joachim Siegerist."

As table 7.6 shows, the Latvian electorate in fact turned both right and left, and away from the center. The participation rate fell to 71.9 percent from 89.9 percent in the 1993 election, and among those who voted opinion was more fragmented than in 1993. Then, with a representation threshold of 4 percent, seven parties were represented in the Saeima, whereas in 1995, with a 5 percent threshold, nine parties were. None of the represented parties were within reach of a majority, and none the four "big" winners – Saimnieks (18 seats; moderate left, see above), Latvia's Way (17 seats; center), National Movement For Latvia – Siegerist's Party (16 seats; populist right), and For Fatherland and Freedom (14 seats; moderate right) – received enough representation to be an obvious candidate for forming a cabinet. By comparison with pre-election projections, the biggest surprise lay in the success of Joachim Siegerist's party, which obtained twice the popular vote projected for it and thus immediately became a political force to be reckoned with. Voices in the Latvian media despaired over so large a vote for a party led by a man who spoke little Latvian, had been expelled from the previous Saeima for non-attendance, and combined in his public activities various philanthropic ventures with crude political showmanship (distributing bananas to his supporters in the 1993 election). By comparison with the composition of the fifth Saeima, both the "right" and the "left" were stronger, but the "center" weaker. On the "right," Siegerist's Party (an offshoot of the Latvian National Independence Movement with no representation in the fifth Saeima, now had 16 seats; Fatherland and Freedom gained 9 seats; whereas the Movement itself, now with 8 seats, had lost five. The "right" would be represented in the sixth Saeima with 38 seats, a gain of 15 from the fifth Saeima. In the "center," Latvia's Way had lost sixteen seats, and the Agrarian Union (together with the Greens) three, leaving the "center" with twenty-four seats or a loss of nineteen seats from the fifth Saeima. The "left" now had two previously unrepresented parties – Saimnieks – with eighteen seats and the Unity party with eight seats; the Socialists (the Equality party in the fifth Saeima), which gained one vote; and the Harmony Party (Jurkāns's party), which lost six seats from its fifth Saeima total. The "left" would thus be represented with thirty-eight seats in the sixth Saeima, or a gain of twenty from the fifth Saeima.

With the parties fragmented, attention immediately shifted to President Guntis Ulmanis (still a member of the Agrarian Union), because it was now his task to initiate the formation of a cabinet. With a coalition cabinet inescapable, the nine represented parties began to form "blocs." A "National Bloc" (Latvian National Independence Movement, For Fatherland and Freedom

Table 7.6 *Parliamentary elections in Latvia, 1995*

Party or political group	Votes	Percentage of vote	Seats in Saeima[a]
Democratic Party *Saimnieks*	144,573	15.3	18
Latvia's Way	138,132	14.6	17
National Movement for Latvia	141,945	15.0	16
For Fatherland and Freedom	109,574	11.6	14
Latvian Unity Party	68,281	7.2	8
Latvian National Independence Movement/Greens	58,140	6.1	8
Latvian Agrarian Union	57,857	6.1	7
Socialist Party	53,288	5.6	6
Harmony Party	52,899	5.6	6
Coalition Work and Justice	43,539	4.6	–
Political Union Economist	14,231	1.5	–
Latvian Farmers' Union	12,741	1.3	–
Russian Citizens' Party	11,871	1.2	–
Popular Front	11,007	1.1	–
Independence Party	9,469	1.0	–
Our Land and Anti-Communist League	4,978	.5	–
Democratic Party	2,507	.2	–
Liberal Party	2,122	.2	–
National Democratic Party	1,336	.1	–

Note: [a]Since the Latvian Saeima has 100 seats, the absolute number of seats equals the percentage of seats.

Source: *Baltic Observer*, October 5-11, 1995, p. 1.

and the Agrarian Union) had already signed a coalition agreement before the election and was thus in a better position to demonstrate cohesion.

The "left" moved quickly to follow suit and on October 4, Saimnieks, Unity, and the Harmony Party signed a coalition agreement, becoming a "left bloc." To everyone's surprise, on the following day Joachim Siegerist announced that his party would "join" the "left" coalition. Latvia's Way and the Socialists for the time being remained outside the two 'blocs' and announced their intention to negotiate further.

Ulmanis's task proved difficult because any proposed cabinet would have to receive at least fifty-one votes in the Saeima to become viable; moreover, he was determined not to permit Siegerist's party to dictate the outcome. The first cabinet – from the "right bloc," with Māris Grīnblats from For Fatherland and Freedom as prime minister – failed to receive a majority (forty-nine for, fifty-one against), as did the second – from the "left bloc," with Ziedonis Čevers from Saimnieks as prime minister (fifty for, forty-five against, five abstaining). Ulmanis then sought the help of a non-partisan – Andris Šķēle, formerly a deputy minister of agriculture and now a successful entrepreneur. Šķēle's proposed cabinet received on December 22 a seventy-vote majority (twenty-four against, six not voting or absent) in the Saeima. The cabinet contained four members each from Saimnieks (vice-prime minister, interior, finance, local government) and For Fatherland and Freedom (economics, education and science, welfare, justice); three from Latvia's Way (foreign affairs, environment and regional development, transportation); two from the Latvian National Independence Movement (defense, special tasks); and one each from the Unity Party (agriculture) and the Agrarian Union (culture). In the inter-party negotiations, the "blocs" had collapsed: there had taken place a general acceptance of the idea of compromise of party principle to obtain a share of power. The Socialists, Jurkāns's Harmony Party, and Siegerist's Movement for Latvia retained their Saeima representation, of course, but were left out of the cabinet entirely. If the "grand coalition" parties maintained discipline in Saeima votes, however, the votes of the excluded opposition would not matter.

How extensively the parties "compromised" their basic principles to obtain seats in the cabinet was not obvious. After the cabinet began its work, For Fatherland and Freedom continued the effort to gather signatures to a petition to force a reconsideration of the 1994 naturalization law, and the Agrarian Union continued to talk in terms of agricultural protectionism. Representatives of the former "left bloc" promised to leave the Bank of Latvia (and its tight money policy) alone, but continued to worry over "safety net" questions. Prime Minister Andris Šķēle promised to deliver a kind of "state of the country" address, which, he said, would contain a detailed and accurate description of Latvia's problems, primarily economic ones. Insofar as Šķēle was brought into the government by a president who faced reelection (by the Saeima) in mid-1996, the fates of the "grand coalition" and the president would be intertwined for the first half of 1996.

The future of democratization in Latvia

From the foregoing it is possible to argue, first, that, as a process, democratization in Latvia is continuing and is not threatened in the immediate future with derailment.[79] The political system twice showed itself capable of handling highly competitive elections (1993, 1995); of transferring power peacefully; and, in 1995, through agreement by all major parties, of constraining (that is, keeping out of the government [cabinet]) a political party – Siegerist's For Latvia movement – which, though supported by

142,000 voters, had an exceptionally vague platform and was widely believed to have an irresponsible and potentially anti-democratic leadership.

Second, the current array of major political parties appears to have stabilized, permitting adequate representation in the Saeima of all elements of a right-center-left spectrum of opinion. The turnover of peripheral (though not necessarily extremist) parties will most likely continue, and minor parties will also continue to gain seats in the Saeima. But the 1995 election showed clearly that coalition-building, even among parties of seemingly irreconcilable views, was entirely possible, suggesting that the view of compromise as surrender-of-principle may be fading. Whether the gradual enfranchisement of the Russian population of non-citizens will simply expand support for existing parties of the left or generate entirely new parties (such as the Russian Citizens Party in 1995) is not clear at the moment.

Third, the merged political elite that came into being in the immediate pre-1991 years, served in the transition government to 1993, and continued to occupy leading positions after 1993, has demonstrated its ability to govern. This remains true in spite of the disenchantment prevalent in the population of Latvia, because that disenchantment stems both from the perceived failures of existing leaders and from the unrealizability of the high expectations accompanying the reestablishment of the Latvian state. Because of the country's relatively small population size and correspondingly small intelligentsia, there is no unidentified substitute government or substitute elite outside existing political structures, arguing greater suitability or threatening to wreak havoc. The new merged elite has not exhibited tendencies to monopolize power: there has been a steady in- and outflow of new and talented persons, and the impulse to "cleanse" the merged elite of "Soviet-era" functionaries appears to be abating.

Fourth, the political import of the ethnic/nationality cleavages in the population of Latvia may not be as great as critics have feared. It is, for example, not demonstrably true that non-Latvians in Latvia are incapable of showing approval of Latvian political leaders: in a May 1995 poll five of eight political leaders given positive ratings by Latvians and five of eleven given positive ratings by non-Latvians were the same persons – all Latvians.[80] The efforts of For Fatherland and Freedom to force the Saeima to readdress the 1994 Citizenship and Naturalization Law and to reintroduce quotas are not guaranteed success.[81] Moreover, there are some signs – small to be sure – that the Russian population is becoming used to the idea of socio-political "integration." From 1993 onward, there has been a growing tendency among Russian parents to send their children (and grandchildren) to Latvian-language kindergartens and primary schools (when they could opt for Russian-language facilities).[82]

Fifth, a succession of Latvian governments have successfully sought incorporation of Latvia into international structures where human rights doctrines are taken seriously and by which, therefore, Latvian policies can expect to be judged on that basis. Admittedly, this clashes with the strongly held beliefs among the parties of the 'right' that the institutions in a renewed Latvian state should be used to ensure the cultural (and indeed physical) survival of the Latvian "nation" (Latv. *tauta*).[83] But from 1991 onward there has also been a growing realization that such "ethnic" or "national" protectionism clashes with the equally valued goal – that of "entering Europe" – where worries over cultural endangerment are not taken as seriously. The fear of "cultural endangerment" will not disappear, but its political effects are likely to be modified through such incorporation. Barring the catastrophes that would follow the breakdown of the democratization process in its eastern neighbors, the process in Latvia is likely to continue.

NOTES

1 Levits quote from *Diena*, 9 September 1995, p. 2; first *Diena* quote from *Diena*, 1 August 1995, p. 2; second *Diena* quote from *Diena*, 3 October 1995, p. 2.
2 "Latvian Democratization Gets Mixed Reviews," Opinion Research Memorandum, Office of Research, US Information Agency, 10 December 1993.
3 Brigita Zepa, "Baltijas valstis vakar, šodien, rīt," *Socioloģijas un Politoloģijas Žurnāls*, no. 5 (December 1994), 17.
4 *Statistical Yearbook of Latvia 1995* (Riga: Central Statistical Bureau of Latvia, 1995), p. 15.
5 Ibid. p. 12.
6 Ibid., p. 114.
7 *Iedzīvotāju dabiskā kustība un migrācija Latvijas Republikā 1989. gadā* (Riga: Valsts Statistikas Komiteja, 1990), p. 15.
8 *Statistical Yearbook of Latvia 1995*, p. 65.
9 Ibid., p. 20.
10 Ibid. p. 95.
11 Imants Paeglis, "Latvia: A Sluggish Pace for Economic Recovery," *Transition* 1, no. 22 (1 December 1995), 50.
12 Brigita Zepa, "Latvijas iedzīvotāju sociālā pašidentifikācija 1991–1995," *Socioloģijas un politoloģijas žurnāls*, no. 6 (July 1995), 6–8.
13 *Likumpārkāpumi un sabiedrībai nevēlamas parādības* (Riga: Central Statistical Bureau of Latvia, 1995), p. 7.
14 A Vilks, "Cīņa pret noziedzību vārdos un darbos," *Diena*, 9 October 1995, p. 2, 15.
15 Tālavs Jundzis, *Latvijas drošība un aizsardzība* (Riga: Junda, 1995), pp. 265–626.
16 *Statistical Yearbook of Latvia 1995*, p. 193.
17 Andris Grūtups and Edmunds Krastiņš, *Īpašuma reforma Latvijā* (Riga: Mans Īpašums, 1995).
18 "Latvia," *Nations in Transit* (New York: Freedom House, 1995), p. 89.

19 Imants Paeglis, "Latvia: A Sluggish Pace for Economic Recovery," p. 51; *Latvijas statistikas gadgrāmata 1995*, p. 22.

20 Gertrude Schroeder, "Economic Transformation in the Post–Soviet Republics: An Overview," in *Economic Transition in Russia and the New States of Eurasia*, ed. Bartlomiej Kaminski (Armonk, NY: M. E. Sharpe, 1996).

21 Jundzis, *Latvijas drošība un aizsardzība*. Jundzis was defense minister of Latvia from 1991 to 1993.

22 Jānis Stradiņš, *Trešā Atmoda* (Riga: Zinatne, 1992).

23 Andrejs Plakans, "Return of the Past: Baltic Area Nationalism of the Perestroika Period," *Armenian Review* 43 (1990), 109–26.

24 The problems surrounding the choice to renew the 1922 Constitution and the subsequently demonstrated inadequacies of the document for the 1991 republic are discussed at length in *Satversmes reforma Latvijā: par un pret* (Riga: Institute of Latvia, 1995). At the end of 1995 the Constitution was still in the process of being reformed.

25 In the interwar republic, the Social Democratic Party defended parliamentary democracy, while the far left – the Bolsheviks – emigrated to Soviet Russia (later the USSR).

26 Edgars Dunsdorfs, *Kārļa Ulmaņa dzīve* (Stockholm: Daugava, 1978), pp. 299–426, examines in detail Ulmanis's authoritarian government.

27 Romuald Misiunas and Rein Taagepera, *The Baltic States: Years of Dependence 1940–1980* (Berkeley and Los Angeles: University of California Press, 1993; expanded edition), p. 320.

28 Aleksandras Shtromas, "The Baltic States as Soviet Republics: Tensions and Contradictions," in *The Baltic States*, ed. Graham Smith (New York: St. Martin's Press, 1994), pp. 86–117, reviews the various kinds of dissident movements, but somewhat overstates the Latvian case. In Latvia, dissidents from the pre-1988 period were in fact frequently marginalized rather than lionized in the post-1988 years.

29 Stradiņš, *Trešā Atmoda*, p. 7.

30 Misiunas and Taagepera, *The Baltic States: Years of Dependence*, pp. 303–11.

31 Plakans, *The Latvians*, pp. 172–73.

32 *Kā Latvijā izveidot tautvaldību un uzcelt labklājības valsti – Latvijas Demokrātiskās Darba Partijas (LDDP) Programma*, ed. Juris Bojārs (Riga, 1994), p. 32.

33 Neither statistics nor systematic accounts relating to this revival of "informal" organizations are available. The statistic about business enterprises is from the *Monthly Bulletin of Latvian Statistics*, no. 10 (Riga: Central Statistical Bureau, 1995), p. 66.

34 "Latvia," *Nations in Transit*, p. 86.

35 In popular thinking, this unity was all the more precious because of repeated instances of fragmentation and division in the country's twentieth-century political history.

36 Plakans, *The Latvians*, pp. 182–83.

37 Dzintra Bungs, "The People's Front of Latvia at the Crossroads," *Report on the USSR*, 22 November 1991, pp. 24–27.

38 Jan Ake Dellenbrandt, "The Reemergence of Multi-Partism in the Baltic States," in *The New Democracies in Eastern Europe: Party Systems and Political*

Cleavages, ed. Sten Berglund and Jan Ake Dellenbrandt (London: Edward Elgar, 1992), pp. 75–105.

39 Brian van Arkadie and Mats Karlsson, *Economic Survey of the Baltic States* (New York: New York University Press, 1992), pp. 117–34.

40 See Ulrich-Joachim Schulz-Torge, *Who Was Who in the Soviet Union* (Munich: K. G. Saur, 1992), for a listing of the governmental political elite in the Supreme Council.

41 Andrejs Plakans, "The Republic of Latvia and the Renewed Constitution of 1922," in *The New Political Institutions of Eastern and East-Central Europe*, ed. Carlos Fuentes Juberias (Spanish translation, forthcoming, 1997).

42 The quotation marks around the terms "right" and "left" in this description are meant to indicate that these terms describe general orientations rather than absolute positions.

43 These stances generally reflected the mood of the voting population. See "Latvian Political Parties Appeal to Constituencies Dissatisfied with Reforms, but are Pro-Free Market." Opinion Research Memorandum, Office of Research, US Information Agency, Washington, DC, 25 March 1993.

44 See Toivo Raun, "Post-Soviet Estonia 1991–1993," *Journal of Baltic Studies* 25 (1994), 73–80; Alfred Erich Senn, "Lithuania's First Two Years of Independence," *Journal of Baltic Studies* 25 (1994), 89–98.

45 See Ulmanis's recently published autobiographical sketch, *No tevis jau neprasa daudz* (Riga: Liktenstasti, 1995), pp. 68–96.

46 *The Baltic Observer*, 2–8 June 1994, pp. 1, 4.

47 The negative attitudes among Latvians on the question of immediate citizenship for non-citizens (primarily Russians) in mid-1993 were still alive in segments of the population in 1995, as witnessed by the ongoing effort in 1995 by a prominent political party, For Fatherland and Freedom, to reopen the question through a constitutionally permitted referendum (see "Ethnic Majority in Latvia Reluctant to Enfranchise Ethnic Russians," Opinion Research Memorandum, Office of Research, US Information Agency, Washington, DC, 1 March 1994).

48 *Baltic Independent*, 23–29 September 1994, p. 1.

49 This "crisis," which consisted of the failure over 1994–95 of sixteen of twenty-eight private deposit banks, climaxed in May–June 1995 with the failure of Latvia's largest private bank, "Banka Baltija." The Banka Baltija failure affected some 250,000 depositors, and its directors (one Latvian and one Russian) have been accused of deliberately causing the crash by fast and loose (and shady) dealing with businesses and governmental institutions in Russia.

50 *Statistical Yearbook of Latvia 1995*, p. 154.

51 "Latvia," *Nations in Transit*, p. 86.

52 *Diena*, 27 September 1996, p. 2.

53 The poll explicated here was carried out in early July, 1995, by the research institute "Latvijas fakti" and surveyed 1,025 adult citizens of Latvia. Each was asked to rank the three most important problems in Latvia from a list of 25 problems. Reported in *Diena*, 27 September 1995, p. 2.

54 Interview with Levits, *Diena*, 9 September 1995, p. 2.

55 One Latvian observer has argued that "true democracy" in Latvia will not exist unless all parties have equal access to campaign funding, and that the current

system advantages those parties which have wealthy patrons. See Juris Kalniņš, "Reala un iedomāta demokrātija," *Neatkarīgā Cīṇa*, 20 June 1995, p. 2.

56 Gints Apals, "Die Nationale Unabhängigskeitsbewegung Lettlands (1988–1991)," *Acta Baltica* 29, no. 30 (1992), 9–28.

57 Misiunas and Taagepera, *The Baltic States: Years of Dependence*, pp. 304–5.

58 See Dainis Īvāns's recently published autobiography, *Gadijuma karakalps* (Riga: Vieda, 1995), pp. 159–205. Īvāns was the chairman of the Latvian Popular Front from its founding to 1991.

59 S. Āboliṇa, "LNNK pirmsvēlēšanu kampaṇa," *Socioloǧijas un politoloǧijas žurnāls*, no. 6 (June 1995), 25–26.

60 See the document collection *Tauta, Zeme, Valsts: Latvijas Nacionālās Neatkarības Kustība dokumentos* (Riga, 1995), pp. 116–26.

61 Erich von Noltein, "Die 'Volksfront Lettlands': Entstehung, Programm, und Statuten (Dokumentation)," *Acta Baltica* 27 (1990), 191–224.

62 *Laiks*, 19 August 1995, p. 8.

63 Andris Indāns, "Tautas kustības Latvijai pirmsvēlēšanu kampaṇas stratēǧijas analīze," *Socioloǧijas un politoloǧijas žurnāls* no. 6 (June 1995), 29–31.

64 Sanita Vanaga, "Maznodrošināto politiskās pirmsvēlēšanas kampaṇas analīze," *Socioloǧijas un politoloǧijas žurnāls*, no. 6 (June 1995), 33–34.

65 A recent survey found that "although knowledge of the Latvian language is mandatory for acquiring Latvian citizenship, of those [Slavic-language inhabitants of Latvia] who are preparing to become citizens only 48 percent say that they know Latvian well, 44 percent say they know it a little, and 8 percent admit to not knowing it at all." (Brigita Zepa, "Kādā valodā runās un pret kuru valsti būs lojāli Latvijas pilsoṇi," *Neatkariga Cīṇa*, 19 June 1995, p. 4). The Latvian fear is that the "Russians" in Latvia, after becoming citizens, will retain primary loyalty to Russian-language culture and by extension to the Russian state.

66 *Latvijas Ceļs: Programma* (Riga 1995).

67 I. Odīte, "Savienības Latvijas ceļš vēlēšanu kampaṇas analīze," *Socioloǧijas un politoloǧijas žurnāls*, no. 6 (June 1995), 18–21.

68 *Latvijas zemnieku savienības vēsture*, ed. H. Strods (Riga: Preses nams, 1995), pp. 173–219, describes the re-founding and current history of the Agrarian Union.

69 V. Zitars, "Latvijas Zemnieku Savienības vēlēšanu kampaṇas analīze," *Socioloǧijas un politoloǧijas žurnāls*, no. 6 (June 1995), 23–25.

70 For an expression of this argument, see the published papers of a June 1991 conference, *Komūnistiskā totalitārisma un genocīda prakse Latvijā* (Riga: Zinatne, 1992). The conference was organized jointly by the Latvian Institute of History, the Scientific Association "Latvia and the World's Latvians," and the Riga Club of the Politically Repressed.

71 Māris Brandts, "Tautas Saskaṇas Partija pirms 6. Saeimas vēlēšanām," *Socioloǧijas un politoloǧijas žurnāls*, no. 6 (June 1995), 32–33.

72 See the panel discussion "The Economic Transformation of the Baltic States," *Journal of Baltic Studies* 23 (1992), 299–306.

73 *Latvia: the Transition to a Market Economy* (Washington, DC: The World Bank, 1993).

74 Zigrida Gosa, "Unemployment in Latvia Today," *Humanities and Social Sciences: Latvia*, no. 2 (1995), 89–99. See also *Ziņojums par Latvijas tautsaimniecības attīstību* (Riga: Ministry of Economics, 1994), pp. 47–48.

75 Jānis Stradiņš, "Latvia on the Crossroads of History," *Humanities and Social Sciences: Latvia* 1 (1993), 8.

76 I. Strode, "Demokrātiskās partijas Saimnieks priekšvēlēšanu kampaņas analīze," *Socioloģijas un politoloģijas žurnāls*, no. 6 (June 1995), 26–28.

77 Karen Dawisha and Bruce Parrott, *Russia and the New States of Eurasia: The Politics of Upheaval* (New York: Cambridge University Press, 1994), p. 145, misidentify Latvia's Way as the "the succcessor of the reformist wing of the Latvian Communist Party." It is rather the Democratic Labor Party that is the direct linear successor of the reform Communists.

78 *Laiks*, 2 September 1995, p. 8.

79 Cf. Dawisha and Parrott, *Russia and the New States of Eurasia*, p. 145: "On balance, the Baltic states appear to have the best chances for a successful transition to democracy." Juris Dreifelds, *Latvia in Transition* (Cambridge: Cambridge University Press, 1996), pp. 175-77, sees some dangers in the proportional representation electoral system, which tends to produce parliamentary gridlock.

80 *Socioloģijas un politoloģijas žurnāls*, no. 6 (June 1995), 17.

81 *Tēvzemei un Brīvībai – Dibināšanas lēmums, statūti, programma* (Riga, 1995), pp. 21–71.

82 Ilmārs Mežs, "Pārmaiņas Latvijas iedzīvotāju ētniskajā sastāvā 20. gadsimtā," *Latvijas Zinatņu Akadēmijas Vēstis*, no. 5-6, Part A (1995), p. 36–37. See also Anda Miķelsone, "Jomazāk skolēnu, jo mazāk skolu," *Diena*, 23 March 1996, p. 3.

83 The Latvian term *tauta* is the equivalent of the German term *Volk* and has no precise English translation. Latvia as a state (*valsts*) contains a nation (*nācija*), which in turn contains several tautas (Latvians, Russians, Ukrainians, Jews, etc.).

8   Democratization in Lithuania

Richard J. Krickus

On March 11, 1990, a newly elected Lithuanian government reclaimed the independent status it lost when the Red Army occupied the country in 1940. Mikhail Gorbachev said the declaration was illegal and tried to force Vytautas Landsbergis, the Lithuanian "president," to rescind it. Landsbergis refused and Gorbachev imposed an economic embargo upon the small Baltic country. When that failed to influence Landsbergis, Gorbachev launched a *coup d'etat* against the Lithuanians on January 13, 1991 ("Bloody Sunday"). Fourteen people were killed, but the Soviet forces stopped short of storming the parliament building and removing Landsbergis from power. "Bloody Sunday" precipitated a chain of events which ultimately led to the demise of the USSR in December 1991, the resurrection of the badly demoralized democratic movement in Russia, and a new union treaty which spawned the anti-Gorbachev Putsch of August 1991.

Today Lithuania is struggling to build an open society and the purpose of this paper is to evaluate the problems and prospects of Lithuania's achieving that goal. Toward this end, a pivotal question must be addressed. What are the prospects of Lithuania building a democratic society based upon the rule of law, multiple political parties, universal suffrage, a free press, and a viable civil society in which unions, ethnic organizations, and business enterprises and other voluntary associations operate independently of the state?

To begin our assessment we must first look at the legacies of Lithuania's past: the major elements of Lithuanian nationalism over the centuries, the revival of the Lithuanian ideal in modern times, the formation of an independent state after World War I, the experience of almost a half century of Soviet rule, and the factors that led to the Lithuanian restoration of independence in 1990.

Legacies of the past

From an ancient to a modern state

A Lithuanian state, ruled by King Mindaugas, appeared as early as the thirteenth century. Later the Lithuanians would shed their paganism to embrace Christianity and join the Polish in a commonwealth dominated by the larger nation. With "Poland's" third partition in 1795, most Lithuanians, who lived in the country's hinterland, would become subjects of the Russian Czars. A smaller number residing on the Baltic coast would be ruled by German masters. In spite of centuries-long foreign occupation, the memory of an independent state would never fully recede from the Lithuanian collective conscious. In contrast to the Estonians and Latvians, who did not enjoy their own states until the twentieth century, this legacy would provide the Lithuanians with a sense of national solidarity and collective self-confidence, which helps explain why they were the first to bolt from the USSR in 1990.[1]

In the nineteenth century there was a revival of the Lithuanian national idea. It was advanced by a series of events: by Lithuanian participation in two insurrections against the Russians in the 1830s and 1860s; by the Lithuanian language's resurrection; by the development of a new generation of Lithuanian intellectuals; and by the appearance of Lithuanian Catholic clergy who operated independently of the Polish hierarchy. In league with the new intelligentsia, the activist clergy resisted the Czar's campaign to Russify the Lithuanians and force them to join the Russian Orthodox Church.

The collapse of the Romanov Dynasty and Germany's defeat produced a modern Lithuanian state in February 1918. But from 1919 to 1920, the Lithuanians fought their "war for independence" against a Red Army led by the Lithuanian Bolshevik, Vincas Kapsukas, a rogue Polish army, and a German-Russian force led by German generals. Soviet Russia recognized Lithuania on July 12, 1920 and renounced all previous claims to its territory.

Although they had never experienced a democratic political culture, and their experience with modern political institutions was stunted by Czarist authoritarianism, the Lithuanians had organized political parties in the last part of the nineteenth century. The parties reflected the diversity of political attitudes that existed elsewhere in Europe. In addition to a Lithuanian nationalist party, Tautininkai, there was a Social Democratic Party, a Christian Democratic Party, a Peasants Party and several other parties which would operate in the newly formed parliamentary system.

In the early 1920s, Lithuania had a significant minority population comprising 20 percent of the country's 2.4 million residents. The largest minority were the Jews, who accounted for about 7.1 percent of the population or 170,400 people. Many lived in Kaunas, which had become the nation's capital in 1920 after a rogue Polish general, Lucijian Zeligowski, occupied the Vilnius region, where a sizeable Jewish population resided. Lithuania's Jews used their influence in international circles to promote an independent Lithuania. According to Istvan Deak, "the new democratic regime granted special rights to all ethnic minorities, and thus also the Jews. A ministry of Jewish affairs was set in Kovno (Kaunas) as well as a Jewish national council."[2] But during World War II an estimated 140,000 to 143,000 Jews were murdered by the Germans with the complicity of some Lithuanians.

The second largest minority were the Germans, who amounted to 4.1 percent of the population, or close to 100,000 people, most of whom lived in Memel, which the Lithuanians occupied in 1923 and renamed Klaipeda. In March 1939 Hitler entered the coastal city via the battleship Deutschland and reclaimed it for the Third Reich. Few Germans remained in Lithuania after World War II.

Before 1939, the Poles accounted for 3 percent of the population, or about 60,000 people, with a far larger number living in eastern Lithuania, which was under the control of Poland. Polish occupation of the Lithuanians' ancient capital and pressure from the Polish leader Marshall Jozef Pilsudski to join Poland in a federation fractured relations between the two countries which were on the brink of war on more than one occasion during the interwar period. In 1939, Stalin returned Vilnius and the eastern portion of the country to the Lithuanians. After the war, many Poles fled the advancing Red Army while others were repatriated to Poland.

Lithuania's democracy did not last long. "In 1926, a Populist–Social Democrat coalition took power, dependent for support on the ethnic minorities, including the Poles. Concessions to the Poles in the field of education, at a time when Poland was closing Lithuanian schools in the Vilnius area, allowed the Right to allege treason."[3] In December 1926, the army, supported by Catholic activists, toppled the government. The nationalist party, Tautininkai, would form a ruling coalition with the Christian Democrats. Antanas Smetona and Augustinas Voldermaras, who had been leaders in the country's fight for independence but later had been excluded from power, were appointed president and prime minister. A year later Smetona broke with the Christian Democrats, dissolved the parliament and wrote a new constitution which provided for a strong presidency. He also had a falling-out with the Vatican in 1931 as the latent secular-clerical fissures among Lithuanian nationalists became manifest.

In 1934, Voldemaras, who led an ultra-nationalist organization, "Iron Wolf," was arrested when he led a coup against the government. Smetona himself had autocratic tendencies and he characterized the Tautininkai as the country's "ruling party"; aping both Germany and Italy he formed a nationalist youth group, "Young Lithuania." But Lithuanian autocracy was relatively benign and did not rest on a police state and oppress ethnic minorities as was typical of Europe's fascist states.

Soviet rule

Lithuania's independence was doomed in 1939 with the signing of the Molotov-Ribbentrop Pact and a revision in the agreement which awarded Lithuania to the Soviet Union. On October 10, 1939, Lithuania was forced to sign a security treaty with the Kremlin, which permitted the stationing of Soviet troops in the country. On June 14, 1940, Moscow presented the Lithuanians with an ultimatum which demanded that Vilnius allow an even larger number of Soviet forces to be based in the country, and the next day the Soviet occupation of Lithuania began. After a phony election was conducted in July, Lithuania was incorporated into the USSR on August 3, 1940.

Stalin's agents began arresting "anti-Soviet" suspects in 1940 but on the eve of the June 1941 German attack on the Soviet Union, Stalin ordered the arrest and deportation of thousands of Lithuanians. In the wake of the Soviet retreat, a provisional Lithuanian government was established but it was dismantled after the Germans occupied the country.

During World War II, Lithuania lost almost one-third of its prewar population as a result of the Holocaust, in fighting the Germans and Soviets, through mass deportations to the Soviet Gulag and Germany, and flight from Nazi and Soviet oppression. Many Lithuanians resisted the Soviet Union's reoccupation of their country from 1944 to 1953 at a loss of 30,000 to 50,000 lives.[4]

The resistance movement, and slower rates of industrial development, helped restrain the massive migration of Russian settlers to Lithuania which the Estonians and Latvians experienced. The Lithuanians also were spared the heavy hand of Moscow because the Lithuanian Communist Party chief, Antanas Sniečkus (1940 to 1974), enjoyed a close ideological affiliation with Stalin. Sniečkus brutally oppressed "anti-Soviet" dissent and conducted the mass exile of Lithuanians to the Soviet Gulag with alacrity. Consequently Stalin allowed Sniečkus greater control of Lithuanian affairs than he granted other republic leaders and the Lithuanian Communist Party attracted cadres who retained stronger nationalist ties than their counterparts in Estonia and Latvia.[5] Furthermore because Lithuania had a more homogenous population than its two Baltic cousins (about 80 percent of the population was ethnic Lithuanian) and could provide manpower for the new Soviet enterprises, Russian settlement was minimized. Consequently the Lithuanians displayed a high level of ethnic consciousness even during the Soviet era. After

Armenia, Lithuania was the second most homogeneous of the USSR's republics, and after the Georgians and Armenians, the Lithuanians were least likely to change their ethnic identity through intermarriage.[6]

The diaspora

While Lithuanian culture was under assault in the old world it was maintained by a diaspora in the new one. About 35,000 Lithuanians settled in the United States (another 15,000 in Canada), joining a Lithuanian-American community which had first arrived in the nineteenth century. In 1940, members of the first wave of immigration had lobbied President Franklin Delano Roosevelt not to recognize the Soviet occupation of the Baltic states, and they later helped reverse a war-time agreement which returned Lithuanian displaced persons (DPs) to the USSR.[7]

After Lithuania's occupation, Stasys Lozoraitis, who had served as the country's foreign minister until 1938 – and was Lithuania's envoy in Italy at the time – functioned as the chief diplomatic representative of the former government, although no "government in exile" was formally established. After his death in 1983, his son Stasys served in the same capacity. Meanwhile, the DP's established a global network of cultural and social organizations to sustain their language and culture. During the Cold War, the 800,000-strong Lithuanian-American community publicized the harsh Soviet occupation of Lithuania and helped secure the release of prisoners of conscience such as the Lithuanian sailor Simas Kudirka. They also provided moral support to Lithuanians who never stopped resisting Soviet occupation of their country.

Growing opposition

After Stalin's death, deportees to the Gulag (most began to return home in the mid-1950s), ex-resistance fighters (the "forest brethren"), and Catholic activists provided limited resistance to Soviet rule. They published a number of underground publications but the most extensive was *The Chronicles of the Catholic Church of Lithuania*. It began circulating in the early 1970s and in spite of KGB efforts to halt it, the *Chronicles* only stopped publication in 1988 when glasnost made it unnecessary.[8]

The Catholic civil rights activists based their protest on Moscow's violations of the Soviet and Lithuanian constitutions, and international laws to which the USSR was privy, such as the UN Declaration on Human Rights. From the outset, then, the Lithuanian independence movement was advocating a law-based, democratic society, and the nexus between national self-determination and democracy would sustain the efforts of future protest movements in the country.

The Catholic civil rights activists would receive assistance from Russian dissidents such as Andrei Sakharov and Sergei Kovalev and Jewish "refusedniks." And Viktoras Petkus, a Catholic activist, would join Tomas Venclova, a Lithuanian poet and son of a prominent communist, Eitanas Finkelšteinas, a Jewish scientist and activist, and Father Karolis Garuckas, a priest, in forming a Lithuanian Helsinki Watch Group in the late 1970s. However, it would lose its effectiveness with the death, arrest, and exile of its members.

In 1987, Antanas Terleckas led the Liberty League, which had been organized in camera, in street demonstrations protesting the Molotov–Ribbentrop Pact, the Soviet occupation, and Stalin's deportations. Like the "old dissidents" in Latvia and Estonia, their counterparts in Lithuania provided a moral example of resistance which later would goad more fainthearted men and women into acts of protest. With the encouragement of Mikhail Gorbachev, and the example of popular front movements in Estonia and Latvia, the Lithuanians formed their own reformist organization – Sajūdis – in June 1988. The man who would become the leader of that organization was Vytautas Landsbergis, a musicologist whose family had been long active in Lithuanian national life – during the renaissance of the late nineteenth century and the independence period between the wars – and whose wife, Gražina, had been a deportee.[9] Landsbergis had never joined the communist party but he refrained from openly opposing the Soviet system. He was encouraged by two young philosophers at Vilnius University, Arvydas Juozaitis and Mečys Laurinkus, to help form a Lithuanian popular front movement.

Members of the Sajūdis "Initiative Group" elected June 3, 1988 included many communists; for example, Algimantas Cekuolis, editor of *Gimtasis krastas*, Bronius Genzelis, the head of the communist party at Vilnius University, Romualdas Ozolas, a philosopher and advisor to the party's Central Committee, and Kazimiera Prunskiene, an economist who would become a deputy prime minister for the Communist government in July 1989. Out of the 36 founding members of Sajūdis, 17 were members of the Lithuanian Communist Party. They were soon joined by technocrats and administrators from Kaunas who saw Sajūdis and Gorbachev's reforms as vehicles to press for Lithuanian independence. "The fate of Sajūdis over the next three years was to be its gradual takeover and radicalization by representatives from Kaunas who were often also members of the technical or scientific intelligentsia: men like Audrius Butkevičius, a doctor and later Defense Minister, Algirdas Saudargas, a physicist and later Foreign Minister, and Aleksandras Abišala, a former Komsomol official and engineer, and later Prime Minister."[10]

Although some Poles and Russians joined Sajúdis, about 97 percent of the delegates to the founding congress in October 1988 were ethnic Lithuanian. After several Sajúdis activists travelled to the United States and met with emigree leaders there, the North American diaspora – which first viewed Sajúdis with skepticism – began to provide money and equipment to its leaders and, indirectly, access to North American journalists and government officials. The neo-Stalinists in the Lithuanian Communist Party (LCP) tried to deny Sajúdis activists access to the political process but in a summer 1988 visit to Lithuania, Aleksandr Yakovlev, pressed them to work with the "perestroika movement."

It was through Sajúdis sponsored mass rallies and demonstrations in 1988 and 1989 that hundreds of thousands of Lithuanians were mobilized into a national resistance movement. Sajúdis provided them gifted leaders and an organizational structure to initially support Gorbachev's reforms, but later to vent their hostility toward the Soviet regime.

With Gorbachev's help, Algirdas Brazauskas, a communist reformer, was selected the LCP first-secretary in the fall of 1988 to replace Ringaidas Songaila, who opposed Gorbachev's efforts to democratize the party. (His predecessor, Petras Griškevičius, had died of a heart attack on November 14, 1987, soon after members of the Lithuanian Artists' Union defiantly deposed their leaders.) Brazauskas was a skillful politician popular with the Lithuanian people and under his stewardship the party endorsed many of the proposals which Sajúdis had advocated; making Lithuanian the national language, allowing the Catholic Church to function unencumbered by the state, and giving Lithuania control of its economy.

But Brazauskas was moving too slowly for the Lithuanian people, who urged him to follow the Estonian example and demand sovereignty for Lithuania, a position which Landsbergis had championed. The LCP reformers did not keep pace with Sajúdis which won favor with a majority of the population. As a consequence, Sajúdis-supported candidates captured 36 of 42 seats for the election to the All-Union Congress of People's Deputies (CPD) in March 1989.

This was a setback for Brazauskas but he realized a far greater defeat awaited him if the Lithuanian Communist Party lost the 1990 elections for the Lithuanian Supreme Soviet. In contrast to Lithuania membership in the CPD – where the delegation had little influence – this election would determine who controlled the Lithuanian government and held the reins of power in the country. Candidates elected to the Lithuanian Supreme Soviet (Parliament) would gain the political and legal legitimacy to exercise the right of secession which was provided for by Article 71 of the Soviet constitution. (Although Landsbergis and his colleagues argued they were not bound by Soviet law because of the country's forceful incorporation into the USSR.)

To woo the voters, Brazauskas began to press Moscow for greater autonomy from the Communist Party of the Soviet Union (CPSU). If the LCP remained tethered to the CPSU, Brazauskas feared Sajūdis would sweep the elections to the Lithuanian Supreme Soviet in February–March 1990.

By seeking an independent LCP, Brazauskas earned the enmity of hardliners in the CPSU Politburo, such as Igor Ligachev. Nonetheless, in December 1989 Brazauskas and 80 percent of the LCP's membership broke with the CPSU and formed an independent Lithuanian Communist Party. The pro-Soviet communists (under the leadership of Mykolas Burokevičius, a professor of communist history and member of the LCP Politburo) then formed a rump party, the "night party," which would lobby Moscow to spurn the communist reformers and crush the "bourgeois nationalists" in Sajūdis.[11]

The restoration of independence

In the February 24 elections and the run-offs on March 4 and 10, Sajūdis-backed candidates won 80 percent of the seats to the parliament. Altogether there were 472 candidates; ethnic Lithuanians numbered 401, Russians 30, Poles 30, Belarussians 6, plus several Jews. Sajūdis elected 99 deputies, the pro-independence communists captured 25 seats, the Moscow loyalists 7 seats, and independents 5 seats; the remaining seats were in dispute. The moderates in Sajūdis realized that Brazauskas and the independent communists (who would call their party the Lithuanian Democratic Labor Party or LDLP after December 1990) continued to enjoy popular support and dominated the country's ministries and economic enterprises, so they did not run a viable candidate against him in the parliamentary election. Lieven contends that the pro-independence communists would have won more seats if they had ignored a gentleman's agreement not to challenge Sajūdis candidates in the same electoral districts.[12]

In the race for chairman of the new Lithuanian Supreme Council, Vytautas Landsbergis, the Sajūdis chairman, defeated Algimantas Brazauskas by a margin of 91 to 38. Kazimira Prunskiene was chosen as prime minister and Brazauskas filled one of the two deputy-prime minister posts while Romualdas Ozolas filled the other one.

Both Landsbergis and the Sajūdis activists, and Brazauskas and the independent communists had supported Lithuanian independence, but the question of just when and how it would be achieved had not been determined before the election. Brazauskas, and many Lithuanians, favored a step-by-step approach as the most realistic and prudent policy to follow. They believed Moscow would deem any outright declaration of independence as illegal and disband any Lithuanian parliament which dared challenge Soviet rule.

Landsbergis indicated prior to the election that he favored a quicker road to independence than Brazauskas's protracted step-by-step approach, but he provided no specific timetable. On the eve of the legislature's first plenary session he decided to restore Lithuanian independence as soon as the new Parliament was constituted. Speculation about his decision to act immediately rests on several factors. Stasys Lozoraitis, believing President Bush would extend diplomatic recognition to Lithuania, urged him to do so. Lieven argues that Landsbergis choose the quick road to independence to win the support of the Kaunas radicals for his election as parliamentary chairman ("president"). But Landsbergis himself has said that he favored quick action because once Gorbachev was chosen president of the USSR by the CPD in March 1990, he would use his new powers to abort a Lithuanian restoration of independence. Among other things, he would write a new law of secession which, for all intents and purposes, would block the Lithuanians from seceding from the union.[13]

On March 11, the Lithuanian Supreme Council voted to restore the independence of Lithuania. Gorbachev responded by declaring the move illegal and warned Lithuania would suffer economic chaos by disengaging from the Soviet Union. He also threatened to return the country's borders to their 1939 status, namely, Lithuania would lose both the Baltic port of Klaipeda and much of eastern Lithuania – including Vilnius – to Belorussia.

Landsbergis responded that the Soviet constitution did not apply to Lithuania since it had been forcefully incorporated into the Soviet Union in violation of international law. After refusing to kowtow to Gorbachev's threats, Landsbergis emerged from the pack of independence leaders as the first among equals.

The Bush administration, fearing the Lithuanian crisis might prompt hard-liners to depose Gorbachev and revive the Cold War, held that since Lithuania did not control its borders it did not fulfill the requirements of a sovereign state. Chancellor Helmut Kohl also feared that the crisis could sabotage efforts to reunify the divided Germany and he urged Landsbergis to resolve his differences with Gorbachev through negotiations.

Gorbachev, in a January 1990 visit to Lithuania, had tried to talk the resolute Balts out of bolting from the Union, but he failed to move either the independence leaders or their supporters. Henceforth, he realized that if the Lithuanian rebellion was not crushed, the Soviet empire itself was at risk. Separatists in other non-Russian republics, following the Lithuanians' lead, had proclaimed their sovereignty, if not outright independence. After Soviet troops had occupied some key installations, arrested draft dodgers, and openly made a show of military power to no avail, Gorbachev imposed an embargo upon the recalcitrant Lithuanians. When that ploy failed, and Gorbachev feared losing American economic aid – he would join President

Bush in a May Washington Summit – he agreed to lift the embargo if Landsbergis imposed a moratorium on independence. The latter agreed to freeze, but not rescind, the declaration of independence and to begin negotiations with Moscow. The negotiations did not go anywhere since the two governments never ever agreed upon the ground rules. Besides, Gorbachev had no intention of settling the showdown short of Lithuanian capitulation.

By the fall of 1990 Gorbachev had turned his back upon reformist allies, such as Aleksandr Yakovlev, and sought support among CPSU reactionaries. He appointed as prime minister, Valentin Pavlov, as vice-president, Gennady Yanayev, and as minister of interior, Boris Pugo. All of these men – in addition to the KGB chief, Vladimir A. Kryuchkov and the defense minister, Dmitri T. Yazov – opposed perestroika and demanded that decisive action be taken against Landsbergis.

In December 1990, the Russians democrats were divided and demoralized when Eduard Shevardnadze, the foreign minister, warned in a resignation speech that a dictatorship was imminent. Landsbergis met with President Bush on December 10 and said that Moscow was prepared to use force against the Lithuanian government. He urged Bush to use his influence with Gorbachev and prevent Moscow from taking oppressive measures. Landsbergis knew that Gorbachev would strike early in 1991 when the American-led coalition was poised to expel Saddam Hussein's forces from Kuwait.[14]

On January 7, 1991, Gorbachev received a request from Burokevičius to impose presidential rule in Lithuania where he contended that the human rights of citizens were being violated and the lives of communists were at risk. The next day leaders in the pro-Moscow organization Edinstvo – comprised largely of pro-Soviet Russians and Poles – and the "night party," with the KGB's and military's support, conducted anti-government demonstrations. They lent credence to Burokevičius' charge that things were out of control in Lithuania. That same day Prime Minister Prunskiene resigned when the Parliament rejected her request to raise prices to fight inflation, the very move which provided Edinstvo with the pretext to launch its protest rallies.[15]

Similar demonstrations were conducted throughout the week to justify Gorbachev's declaration of presidential rule. As tensions mounted Landsbergis tried in vain to talk to Gorbachev and early in the morning of January 13, Soviet paratroopers, spearheaded by the KGB's special Alpha unit, took control of the Vilnius TV tower. In the process thirteen Lithuanians protesting the takeover and one KGB officer were killed. For still unexplained reasons, the expected attack on the parliament where Landsbergis and 60 deputies and many staffers gathered, never materialized. On February 9, 1991, the Lithuanian people rebuked Gorbachev's claim that only a radical minority favored independence when nine out of ten people (accounting for 85 percent of the potential electorate) voted in favor of an independent and democratic Lithuania.

The failed coup against Landsbergis led to the resurrection of the Russian democratic movement, which conducted a massive anti-Gorbachev demonstration in March. Then Gorbachev joined Yeltsin and other republic leaders in the "nine plus one" agreement in April; upon ratification in August, it would dramatically reduce the authority of the Communist Party and the power ministries, pass authority to the republics, and presumably allow the Baltic states to leave the union. This prompted the putsch against Gorbachev on August 18, which failed when Yeltsin and his supporters at the Russian White House used tactics the Lithuanians had deployed in blunting the Bloody Sunday coup. Its failure set into motion a train of events which culminated in the collapse of the Soviet Union in December 1991.

The status of political parties and elections since independence

Immediately after the March 11, 1990 restoration of independence, the Lithuanian government had begun to write a new constitution, but the basic law which functioned under the Soviet system was followed in the interim. A law on political parties, however, was established on September 25, 1990. It gave Lithuanian citizens the right to form parties if they had at least 400 founders along with a party program and a founding congress. Parties had to register with the Ministry of Justice and provide their list of candidates not later than thirty-five day prior to elections. Parties with a foreign affiliation were illegal.

To widen political participation, "public movements" – that is nonparty organizations – could register with the Ministry of Justice and nominate their candidates for the Parliament, if they had 1,000 signatures and if they did so not later than two months before the election. Individuals could run in single-district races if they complied with the same requirements as public movements. Alterations were made in the law of political parties in 1994 and 1995 to compel candidates to run under party labels.

Between the fall of 1991, when Lithuania achieved formal international recognition, and the summer of 1992, the Sajúdis-led legislature debated and passed a privatization law to build a free market economy. The opposition, comprised of the deputies in the Labor Party and those belonging to the Polish Union, warned against acting too precipitously. The Sajúdis deputies, representing a majority in Parliament, were political amateurs and products of an authoritarian political culture. They split into several factions and proved incapable of providing a coherent legislative agenda to meet the country's mounting economic and social problems.

The Kaunas radicals disagreed with the Vilnius intellectuals and reformed communists, among other things, over the wisdom of maintaining close relations with Moscow. To prevent legislative initiatives they opposed, deputies frequently refused to provide the quorums necessary to conduct legislative business. The dispute among the Sajúdis bloc resulted in some Kaunas parliamentarians organizing the "National Progress Faction" which operated much like an opposition. In summer 1992, for example, Zigmas Vaišvila, a faction member and a deputy-premier, accused his own prime minister, Gediminias Vagnorius, of being incompetent and corrupt.

Vagnorius resigned in mid-June after a vote of no-confidence and he was replaced by Aleksandras Abišala, a scientist from Kaunas. Abišala displayed a keen mind and under his stewardship the government operated more effectively. But the old apparatchiks, who still ran the bureaucracies, were recalcitrant about implementing government policies that threatened their influence.

Frustrated, Landsbergis decided that early elections were in order, even though the legislature had three years remaining in its term. Also, he favored a new constitution which would give greater powers to the president; much like those enjoyed by the French president. As a consequence of both initiatives, he hoped to break the gridlock that had prevented decisive governmental action and had alienated many voters.

A referendum, calling for a new constitution with a strong president, was conducted in the spring of 1992, and 70 percent of those who voted favored it. Given these results, Landsbergis was optimistic about winning the fall elections.

But there was a more pessimistic interpretation of the vote and its significance. "Only 57.5 percent of a bewildered and disgruntled electorate turned up to vote. This meant that although 69.4 percent of these approved a presidency, and only 25.6 percent opposed it, the result was well short of the 51 percent of all eligible voters required under Lithuanian law. Five percent cast invalid ballots, in some cases as a means of showing approval of a presidency in principle, but dislike of Landsbergis' candidacy and the methods used to push through the presidential scheme."[16]

The Left's return

By summer 1992, there were other signals that Landsbergis was in trouble – although given the monumental role that he had played in the country's independence drive and the courageous leadership he had provided during the fateful days of January 1991, many of his admirers would not accept this fact. The leadership he had provided in the drive for independence had won him a honored place in Lithuanian history, but the nationalist phase of Lithuania's post-Soviet period had expired. Landsbergis's opponents claimed he had attempted to pro long it by fostering cool relations with Russia and rejecting a treaty of friendship with Poland. But unlike Estonia and Latvia, where the presence of a large Russian population fueled nationalist passions, the Lithuanians faced no equivalent internal threat to their sovereignty or culture.

At this point, Lithuanians were preoccupied with economic problems and many were angered by austerity measures Aleksandras Abišala had adopted. One prominent success story was the quick privatization of 90 percent of the country's dwellings. This was one economic initiative where the Lithuanians led, rather than followed, the path of Estonia and Latvia. Despite such successes, many people agreed with Arvydas Juozaitis (one of the original Sajūdis leaders who broke with Landsbergis) that Landsbergis had "authoritarian tendencies," while still others said he simply did not possess the ability to address the practical problems that Lithuania faced as it moved from a command to a free-market economy. After all, he spent his life studying music, and what did he know about economic affairs?

The major reasons why Landsbergis's stature had diminished in the eyes of many Lithuanians, of course, were economic. The collapse of the Soviet economy and subsequent disruptions in commercial relations with Russia and other former Soviet republics fostered an economic down-turn. When Lithuania no longer could purchase fodder from Russia and Ukraine to feed livestock, millions of cows were slaughtered or exported. Industrial output also plunged. In 1991 there was a 13.1 percent decline in Gross Domestic Product (GDP) and a year later a 37.1 percent dip in GDP (see table 8.5 below). Most Lithuanians suffered a decline in living standards as inflation surged to over 1,000 percent in 1992 and fears about job security and the viability of pensions soared.[17]

Against this backdrop of economic decline, voters turned from Sajūdis in the October 25, 1992 parliamentary elections. The figures in table 8.1 include the seats decided in the follow-up election which occurred two weeks later. The table demonstrates the extent of political fragmentation in the Lithuanian polity. Altogether seventeen parties competed for seats and joined forces in some districts, while opposing one another in other ones. After the election, the Lithuanian Democratic Labor Party (LDLP) and candidates running on the Forum of Lithuanian Future line would cooperate as a faction in the Seimas with a total of seventy-three seats; so would the candidates running for the Sajūdis Coalition and Charter of the Citizens of Lithuania with a total of twenty-seven seats; and so would those elected under the banner of the Christian Democratic Party, the Lithuanian Democratic Party and the Union of Political Prisoners with a total of seventeen seats.

Table 8.1 *Parliamentary elections in Lithuania, 1992*

Party	No. of votes	% of votes	No. of seats	% of seats
Lithuanian Democratic Labor Party	817,332	42.61	68	48.2
Sajudis Coalition	393,502	20.52	24	17.0
Christian Democrats	234,368[a]	12.22	9	6.4
Social Democrats	112,410	5.86	7	5.0
Forum of Lithuanian Future	66,027[b]	3.44	5	3.5
Non-party candidates	–	–	5	3.5
Lithuanian Democratic Party	–	–	4	2.8
Union of Political Prisoners	–	–	4	2.8
Polish Union	39,773	2.07	3	2.1
Lithuanian National Union List	36,916[c]	1.92	3	2.1
Charter of the Citizens of Lithuania	–	–	3	2.1
Center Movement	46,910	2.45	2	1.4
Independents	–	–	1	.7
Lithuanian Christian Democratic Union	–	–	1	.7
Union of Political Prisoners of Lithuania	–	–	1	.7

Notes: [a]This figure represents the combined votes of the Lithuanian Christian Democratic Party, Union of Political Prisoners and Deportees of Lithuania, and the Lithuanian Democratic Party, which in some districts ran on a common list. [b]This figure represents the votes of the Alliance of the Christian Democratic Union of Lithuanian Youth (Young Lithuania). [c]This figure represents the combined votes of the National Union Party plus the Independent Party. Number of eligible voters: 2,549,952; Votes cast: 1,918,027; Voter turnout: 75.2%

Source: *Statistical Yearbook of Lithuania 1994–95* (Vilnius: Methodical Publishing Centre, 1995), p. 66.

If Labor had run candidates in all of the electoral districts, its margin of victory would have been even higher. Seventy-one seats were chosen in single-seat districts via a majority vote, and seventy seats were allotted for candidates running on party lists through a system of proportional representation. Parties receiving less than 4 percent of the vote were not represented in the Seimas. This requirement, however, did not hold for members of ethnic minority groups, so while the Polish Union only captured 2.07 percent of the vote, it received three seats.

Landsbergis, unlike most incumbents, survived the election, perhaps because he did not run as an individual candidate but as part of the Homeland Union (LHU) list which was the new name designation for the conservatives allied with him. Candidates running under the banner of small parties, such as the Liberals, won not a single seat.

Widespread economic discontent was not the only reason why the left returned to power in Lithuania in 1992. During the independence drive the leadership had opposed transforming Sajúdis from a popular front movement into a formal political party with branches and a cadre operating throughout the country, initially to assuage Moscow's fears about organizing an anti-Soviet party and later because Sajúdis could not achieve the unity necessary to build a formal political organization. Meanwhile in the Seimas, "The functions ordinarily performed by political parties were taken over by parliamentary factions with sharply differing programs. And since most of the Supreme Council deputies had no formal party obligations, they felt free to join to leave factions at will and to vote as they pleased."[18]

The LDLP was a real party, with branches in every part of the country often administrated by full-time workers. Its members controlled most local governments, large industrial enterprises and collective farms, and the liberal professions. For Lithuanians, whose living standards were in decline, Brazauskas and his party were seen as having the widespread governmental experience so obviously lacking on the right. Voters responded favorably to his claim that, "We have the people in charge with common sense who do not rely on fairy tales or fantasies to govern."[19]

Unlike the North American diaspora, many Lithuanians in Lithuania considered Brazauskas a patriot who had played a pivotal role in ending Soviet rule. For others he was attractive because he reputedly had retained good relations with his former colleagues in Moscow, and could negotiate deals with them that Landsbergis spurned. Most voters agreed with Brazauskas that close economic ties with Russia and other former Soviet Republics were vital to Lithuania's economic development. Because of his reputed capacity to negotiate effectively with the Russians, Brazauskas could exploit issues that should have worked in Landsbergis's behalf. A good example was the measures Landsbergis took which ultimately resulted in the withdrawal of former Soviet troops from Lithuania in August 1993 – that is, on Brazauskas's watch. Landsbergis organized support for a referendum in spring 1992 which asked the electorate to express its opinion about the status of former Soviet troops in Lithuania. Landsbergis said that 60,000 troops remained, that they posed a security threat, and that their presence suggested that Lithuania did not enjoy sovereign control of its territory. Brazauskas asserted that only 30,000 remained, that they did not represent a threat to Lithuania, and that it was ill-advised to demand their immediate removal since Russia did not have the resources to relocate them. The electorate disagreed and voted overwhelmingly in favor of their withdrawal.[20] Nonetheless Labor won a thumping victory in the 1992 Seimas election.

Labor also enjoyed another success. In an October 2, 1992 referendum a new constitution was approved by 85 percent of those voting; the turnout

Table 8.2 *Presidential elections in Lithuania, 1993*

	A. M. Brazauskas		S. Lozoraitis	
Voter group	Votes received	% of voter group	Votes received	% of voter group
Lithuanian voters	1,211,070	60.1	767,437	38.1
Voters abroad	1,005	15.2	5,485	83.1
Total	1,212,075	60.0	772,922	38.2

Notes: Number of eligible voters: 2,568,026 (2,560,466 in Lithuania, 7,550 abroad); Votes cast: 2,019,015 (2,012,420 in Lithuania, 6,595 abroad); Voter turnout: 78.6% (78.6% in Lithuania, 87.3% abroad).

Source: *Statistical Yearbook of Lithuania 1994–95* (Vilnius: Methodical Publishing Centre, 1995), p. 67.

amounted to 53 percent of the potential electorate. It established a parliamentary democracy with a unicameral legislature (as existed previously) and a president with strong powers in the area of international affairs. The prime minister had full responsibility over his cabinet and could not be removed by the president without approval of the Seimas.

Landsbergis, realizing he could not win the presidential election, choose not to oppose Brazauskas. Under the urging of leaders in the Christian Democratic Party and the Social Democratic Party, Stasys Lozoraitis, now the Lithuanian ambassador in Washington, threw his hat into the ring. Lozoraitis had never sought public office and he was reluctant to accept the invitation to run as president. But since there was no one else available, and believing that a competitive election would enhance Lithuanian democracy, he agreed to run. He received overwhelming support from the Lithuanian diaspora, which loathed the idea that a "communist" would become president of the newly independent government in their old homeland: members of the diaspora gave him on 83.1 percent of their ballots, which amounted to 5,485 votes (see table 8.2).

Brazauskas won 60 percent of the vote (1,212,075) representing 47.2 percent of the total electorate in the February 14, 1993 elections. Lozoraitis got 38.2 percent of the total vote (772,922) representing 30.1 percent of the total electorate. Considering that he was political amateur, that he entered the race late, and that he lacked a political base in the country, Lozoraitis's showing was not all that bad. Although he beat Brazauskas only in the city of Kaunas and the raion of Kaunas, he won a victory of sorts. By making the race competitive and challenging his opponent's policies, he advanced the cause of political pluralism in Lithuania.[21]

Contrary to the international economic community's fears that the Labor government would halt the country's drive toward a free market economy and perhaps even re-nationalize some industries, it won plaudits from the World Bank and Western economic consultants for adopting policies which adhered to fiscal and monetary austerity.

Labor falters

By 1995, the Lithuanian electorate was unhappy with the Labor Party which now was blamed for Lithuania's economic difficulties, pervasive corruption – especially associated with privatization – and the Mafiya's criminal activities and open defiance of public order.

This disenchantment with Labor helped explain what appeared to be the restoration of the right and center after the results of the spring 1995 municipal elections were posted (see table 8.3).

The municipal elections involved 1,488 seats on twelve city councils and forty-four municipal districts through a proportional representation system with a threshold of 4 percent as a prerequisite for representation. Altogether seventeen parties had entered the contest.

Right–wing parties captured more than half the total seats: for example, Homeland Union ran first with almost 30 percent, while the Christian Democrats ran third with 16.9 percent.[22]

Labor ran second with 19.9 percent and their allies the Farmers' Party ran fifth with 6.9 percent. The Polish Union Action Group For Elections – a satellite of the Polish Union which holds seats in the Seimas and has cooperated closely with Labor – received 4.5 percent of the municipal vote.

The centrists did not do as well. For example, the Social Democrats, who have earned the "centrist" appellation because they have sought votes from the middle class and have not supported Labor, ran sixth with only 4.8 percent of the turnout. Other parties of the center, such as the Center Union, which has two of the most popular politicians in the country as its leaders – Romualdas Ozolas and Egidijus Bickauskas – gained 4 percent of the national vote, and the Liberal Union, failing to meet the 4 percent threshold, received no municipal representation. Anti-system parties on the right did not do well except in isolated areas; for example, in Kaunas, Young Lithuania, an ultra-nationalist party got 12,751 votes and five seats, surpassing the Christian Democratic Party, which won 12,284 votes and four seats there. On the left, the threat of an anti-system party disappeared when the neo-Soviets discredited themselves during "Bloody Sunday" and the "August 1991 coup." Two of the leaders of the pro-Soviet Lithuanian Communist Party, Mykolas Burokevičius and Juozas Jermalavičius, were arrested by Lithuanian agents

Table 8.3 *Municipal elections in Lithuania, 1995*

Party	No. of votes	% of votes	No. of seats	% of seats
Labor Party (LDLP)	180,059	19.9	297	20.0
Homeland Union (LHU)	288,434	29.1	426	28.6
Christian Democrats (LCDP)	154,055	16.9	247	16.6
Social Democrats (LSDP)	47,866	4.8	72	4.8
Democratic Party (LDP)	5,281	0.6	9	0.6
National Union (LNU)	15,807	3.3	49	3.3
Center Union (LCU)	40,922	5.5	74	5.0
Liberal Union (LLU)	15,070	2.7	40	2.7
Farmers' Party (LFP)	52,216	6.9	104	7.0
Union of Political Prisoners and Deportees (LUPPDP)	11,245	3.8	56	3.8
Polish Action Group for Elections (LPAGP)	71,310	4.5	69	4.6
Independence Party (LIP)	287	0.1	2	0.1
National Progressive Party (LNPP)	10,024	0.9	14	0.9
Lithuanian Republican Party (LRP)	6,265	0.3	5	0.3
Lithuanian Green Party (LGP)	2,435	0.2	0	0
Young Lithuania (YLP)	28,079	1.1	16	1.1
Lithuanian Freedom Union (LFUP)	18,057	0.4	6	0.4

Sources: *Lithuania Situation Update: 1995 Municipal Elections* (Washington: International Republican Institute, 1995), pp. 13–29; *Statistical Yearbook of Lithuania 1994–95* (Vilnius: Methodical Publishing Center, 1995), p. 68.

in Minsk in 1994 and were returned to Lithuania, where they are presently awaiting trial. Since the Lithuanian neo-Stalinists were discredited by their involvement in the January and August 1991 coup attempts, proponents of a Lustration law could not garner public support for one after independence. Meanwhile, fringe parties like the Union of Political Prisoners and Deportees, which had attracted mostly older voters who had suffered exile to the eastern USSR during the Stalinist era, could be expected to grow weaker over time as nature took its course. It is uncertain, moreover, whether regional parties such as the National Union (with its base in the Kaunas area) will gain wider appeal.

The 1995 municipal elections were a disappointment since only 44.9 percent of the electorate voted. This represented a 20 percent drop from the local elections of 1990, the national elections in 1989 and 1992, and the presidential elections of 1993 where the turnout exceeded 70 percent.

Taking stock of political parties in the mid-1990s

Declining voter turn-out, while disappointing, has been countervailed by other positive indicators of political development in a country which has only been independent for five years. The municipal elections indicated that there were three political parties with a national infrastructure, a sizeable membership, and leaders capable of managing the party apparatus and reaching out to the electorate through effective campaigning.

The Labor Party has 8,000 members and leaders with extensive political and governmental experience. It has local party organizations throughout Lithuania which have operated since the Soviet era. In addition to Brazauskas (who as president cannot be active in party affairs), there are the party chairman, Adolfas Šleževičius (until early 1996) and its faction leader, Gediminas Kirkilas. The Farmer's Party, which can be fairly identified as an appendage to Labor, has a membership of only 400 but its leaders have belonged to the communist party cells which operated in the old collective farm system. One of Labor's major problems, however, has been its inability to attract younger leaders to its ranks.

The Homeland Union has a membership of 16,000 and a grass-roots network that operates nationally. Landsbergis is the party chairman and Andrius Kubilius, the faction leader. The party has developed a network of party activists many of whom were associated with Sajūdis. In the municipal election, Homeland proved effective in identifying potential voters and getting them to the polls. Perhaps it was these newly acquired skills – and not expanding support among the electorate – which accounted for its success in 1995. The party, which has been deemed uncompromising, demonstrated a more pragmatic bent soon after the municipal elections. In Siauliai, it passed over the leader of its local party branch for mayor in favor of a former communist, who once held that post, to provide experienced leadership in Lithuania's fourth largest city.[23] But the conservatives have a youth problem as well; after their back-to-back defeats in 1992 and 1993, many young people, who had been attracted to politics in the fight for independence and the early Landsbergis years, returned to private life. Since then, however, the Homeland Party has been building a youth organization and it has achieved some level of success in recruiting young people to its ranks.

The Christian Democratic Party, which was founded in 1904, was a major political force in the interwar period. It was reconstituted in 1990 and five years later had a membership of 8,500 and a national political infrastructure. Povilas Katilius is both party chairman and parliamentary faction leader. Although the extent of assistance provided by the Catholic Church is uncertain, priests have actively supported the party and have urged their flock to do the same. Like the Homeland Union, the party has widespread support among the North American diaspora. Because of their showing in the last municipal elections, some pundits believe the Christian Democrats are poised to lead a coalition government in the near future. But party activists have conceded that their party's popularity is not unrelated to its opposition status and never having had to endure the risks of governance.

Consequently, there is a division in its ranks between "conservatives" and "progressives" which goes beyond how closely the party should be aligned with the Catholic Church. The conservatives oppose the progressive's desire to make a real push to win the 1996 elections for the Seimas. They fear losing popularity once the party takes responsibility for running a country stricken by daunting economic problems.[24]

Two other parties have leaders with extensive political experience: the Center Union with Bickauskas and Ozolas, and the Social Democrats with Aloyzas Sakalas. But neither party has been able to attract more than 4 to 5 percent of the electorate's votes.

In comparing the Lithuanian political spectrum with political alignments in other European democracies, the left–right dichotomy has little meaning. Insofar as there is a coherent "left" and "right," the lines of division are not decisively marked by collectivist economic policies in the first case and free-market policies in the second one. Representatives of the business community, for example, see only marginal differences between the two when it comes to economic policy; many politicians of both tendencies are suspicious of capitalism and favor price controls, subsidies, and protective tariffs. In 1994, the conservatives supported an (abortive) referendum which would have compensated people who had lost money in failed credit unions or other financial institutions.

Those on the right, who have rallied around Landsbergis, and those on the left, who have done the same around Brazauskas, really differ over other issues; for example, one's perception of the Soviet era, the wisdom of Lithuania's breaking with the Soviet Union, relations with Russia today, and the nature of Lithuanian national life. In the last instance, the question is whether Lithuania should attempt to reclaim the prewar pastoral society including close association with the Catholic church or should it try to create a new, secular society?

Polls indicate that the key words to describe rightist tendencies are "Catholic state," a characterization of the Soviet era as a "dark period" and a favorable "orientation toward the West." By contrast leftist tendencies include "secular state," "Russia is not an enemy," and support for "social guarantees."[25]

One can find direct links between former Soviet apparatchiks and Labor, nationalists and the Homeland Union, and devout Catholics and the Christian Democrats. But both left wing and right wing parties have drawn from a broad cross-section of the population; for example, workers have voted for all three parties. Personalities also have been an important factor. Landsbergis and Brazauskas have been the two most dominant political figures on the political scene since the late 1980s and each enjoys hard-core support amounting to 15–20 percent of the electorate.

There are few data available regarding the financing of party organizations. By law, parties are obliged to make their funding sources public, but they have been derelict in doing so. One limited investigation of party finances has revealed that in 1993 Labor claimed it had garnered $127,000 in campaign contributions while the Homeland Union reported $184,000 and the Social Democrats $67,000. None of the three provided information about the sources of the contributions.[26]

Mass attitudes

What do Lithuanians think about the Soviet legacy? What do they think about the institutions and politicians who have governed them in the post-independence period? What issues concern them most? What do answers to all of these questions tell us about popular support for political pluralism in Lithuania as the country approaches the twenty-first century?

Lithuanians, to a greater degree than Estonians and Latvians, look favorably upon the past and therefore may be categorized as slightly more "reactionary." In one survey, 27 percent of the Lithuanian respondents approved of the old regime and disapproved of the current one, in contrast to 20 percent and 14 percent respectively of the Latvian and Estonian respondents. Existing fears about the presence of a large Russian population in both Latvia and Estonia may serve as a prism through which respondents from both countries view the past and account, in part, for this finding. But the pollster Vladas Gaidys believes that religion also has a bearing on the Lithuanian attitude toward the recent past. Because of their Catholic tradition, they are more inclined to support the status quo and fear change more than their Protestant Baltic cousins. Specifically, it accounts for their inbred resistance to change, respect for authority, and pre-capitalist economic ideas.[27]

When asked their views of the old economy, 80 percent of the Lithuanian respondents gave it a positive rating, while 61 percent of the Estonians and 63 percent of the Latvians gave the same response. Conversely, in evaluating their current economy the Lithuanians gave a 73 percent negative rating in contrast to 31 percent for the Estonians and 63 percent for the Latvians. And when asked whether they were nostalgic for the old system 67 percent of the Lithuanians asked said yes in contrast to 28 percent for the Estonians and 49 percent for the Latvians.[28]

Lithuanians, however, frequently gave more positive views about political matters than their two neighbors. For example, 41 percent of a Lithuanian sample said it "is foolish" to be afraid of participating in politics whereas the response for Estonians was 26 percent and Latvians 30 percent.[29] Also, Lithuanians have demonstrated a more liberal attitude toward political participation on the part of all ethnic groups than have Estonians and Latvians. Only 2 percent of Estonians and Latvians respectively said that "any former Soviet citizen now living in this country" should have a right to vote, whereas 11 percent of Lithuanians responded positively. While 37 percent and 31 percent of Estonians and Latvians disagreed with the statement that "when jobs were scarce . . . priority should be given to the indigenous population rather than Russians," 46 percent of the Lithuanians disagreed.[30] It is noteworthy, however, that when asked their opinion about the future of their political system, fewer Lithuanians had a positive view, 69 percent, than Estonians and Latvians, who scored 92 percent and 74 percent respectively.[31]

This finding corresponds with the generally pessimistic mood of the Lithuanian electorate in the mid-1990s. The vast majority of Lithuanians from all walks of life and both elites and masses had a dim view of the Seimas and Prime Minister Adlofas Šleževičius's government. It was seen as corrupt and incompetent. Over half of the Lithuanian people indicated that they were skeptical of the country's political institutions and no more than 30 percent claimed to trust the cabinet of ministers, parliament, the police, courts and local governmental jurisdictions.[32]

Reports of political corruption surfaced when Sajúdis was in power, but since the left's return, the press has published numerous stories about rip-offs involving public officials. For example, *Lietuvos rytas* revealed that Romasis Vaitekunas, the minister of interior, was driving a Mercedes-Benz 600L which had been stolen in Germany. But even after the story was published, he continued to use the car for his purposes. Then beginning in the summer of 1995, Romualdas Ozolas claimed that Prime Minister Šleževičius had misused his office to enrich himself through a number of privatization schemes.

Ozolas could not back his accusations with concrete evidence but in December 1995, charges of widespread corruption were given added legitimacy when two of the country's largest banks, Innovation and Litimpeks, were forced to halt business because of economic mis-management. The presidents of both banks were arrested and the country's central bank board chairman, Kazys Ratkevicus, was fired. Later it was learned that Prime Minister Šleževičius and the minister of interior, Vaitekunas, had withdrawn their savings accounts from the banks which had paid them interest far above the going rate of return. This prompted both the foreign minister, Povilas Gylys, and the defense minister, Linas Linkevičius, to offer their resignations in protest. Brazauskas refused to accept their resignations and suggested that Slezevičius should resign instead. The prime minister refused to comply but on February 8, 1996, he was ousted when a majority of the Seimas gave him a vote of no confidence.[33] He was replaced by Mindaugas Stankevičius, the minister for administrative reforms and local government affairs.

Finally, after the economy the number one concern of most Lithuanians is crime; 75 percent say so. Since 1990, the number of actual crimes reported has increased in all major cities: for example, in Vilnius from 9,087 in 1990 to 11,694 in 1994, and in Kaunas the numbers run from 6,107 in 1990 to 7,192 in 1994. But since independence, crime rates have fluctuated depending upon the offense. In 1995, for example, while rapes dropped by 35.5 percent over the previous year, murders soared by 37 percent. But the type of crime which involves a larger share of the population, thefts, increased by 26.5 percent.[34]

Civil society

Demographic data indicate several constants in Lithuanian society for most of this century. For example, ethnic Lithuanians have represented approximately 80 percent of the population since the 1920s, and about the same percentage has been Roman Catholic. But three massive demographic changes have occurred during the Soviet era: a rural to urban migration, a decline in agricultural employment, and rising levels of educational attainment (see table 8.4). In the 1950s, about seven out of every ten Lithuanians lived in rural areas, but by the 1980s, only 32.3 percent did. And with 67.7 percent of the population residing in urban areas, compared with 30.9 percent in the 1950s, it is clear that most Lithuanians now work in manufacturing, the liberal professions, and the service sector.

A stable democratic system involves more than formal democracy, free parties, elections and the like; stable democracies also enjoy high rates of economic growth and low rates of economic inequality. Economic prosperity provides all elements of society with the means to organize and influence the political process and to acquire a substantial level of political efficacy. As table 8.5 indicates, the Lithuanian economy suffered a steep decline beginning in 1990, when the GDP fell by 5.0 percent; it continued to slide in 1991 by 13.1 percent, in 1992 by 37.7 percent, and in 1993 by 24.2 percent. But by 1994, the European Bank for Reconstruction and Development estimated a 1.7 percent increase in GDP and forecast a 5.0 percent upturn in 1995. In addition, the Bank reported improvement in the inflationary picture as inflation slowed to an annual rate of 35 percent during

Table 8.4 *Demographic trends in Lithuania since the 1950s*

	1950s	1970s	1980s
Percentage of population	(1951)	(1979)	(1989)
Rural	69.1	40.0	32.3
Urban	30.9	60.0	67.7
Average annual rates	(1951–61)	(1971–79)	(1980–90)
of population growth (%)	0.9	0.8	0.8
Age distribution (%)		(1979)	(1989)
15–24	n.a.	16.8	15.3
25–49	n.a.	34.4	34.6
50–59	n.a.	10.7	11.8
Over 60	n.a.	14.5	15.7

Sources: New World Demographics, *First Book of Demographics for the Republics of the Former Soviet Union, 1951–1990*; US Department of Commerce, *Statistical Abstracts of the United States*; Paul S. Shoup, *The East European and Soviet Data Handbook*; UNESCO, *Statistical Yearbooks*; United Nations, *Demographic Yearbooks*.

1995, in contrast to the 1,000 plus inflation rate of 1992. Also, in 1994, 61.5 percent of the work force was engaged in private activity and the private sector accounted for 62.3 percent of the country's GDP. Moreover, the investment firm of Coopers and Lybrand reported that in 1993 and 1994 there was an increase in exports and imports while the Litas has functioned as a stable convertible currency, pegged to the US dollar, for several years.[35] Notwithstanding gains in the economy's macro performance, the micro picture has been bleak. Most Lithuanians, 77 percent, deem the economy the country's most critical problem. In a 1994 poll, 20 percent of a sample said their living standards were "rising," 7 percent responded their situation was "stable" and they were "satisfied," 8 percent said "stable but dissatisfied," and 64 percent reported their living standards were "falling." According to government statistics, in January 1995 an unemployment rate of 5.2 percent had been reported but by November of that year it had reached 7.1 percent.[36]

Many educators and liberal professionals, who had enjoyed comparatively high wages as well as prestige and perks under the old economy, have suffered as their schools and other publicly funded institutes and research centers have lost state funding. The same holds true for public employees operating at all levels of government and workers in large Soviet-era enterprises. Moreover, economic anxiety is linked with underemployment and a decline in state subsidies.

Table 8.5 *Indicators of economic trends in Lithuania since 1989*

	1989	1990	1991	1992	1993	1994	1995[a]
GDP	1.5	-5.0	-13.1	-37.7	-24.2	1.7	3.0
Industrial output	n.a.	n.a.	n.a.	-50.9	-42.7	2.0	2.0
Rate of inflation	2.1	8.4	224.7	1,020.5	409.2	72	35
% Labor force unemployed	n.a.	n.a.	0.3	1	2.5	4.2	6.6
GNP per capita	n.a.	n.a.	n.a.	n.a.	3,240	n.a.	n.a.
% Workforce in private activity[b]	20.0	22.3	29.8	41.3	54.2	61.5	n.a.
% GDP from private sector[b]	n.a.	n.a.	16.0	37.0	57.0	62.3	n.a.

Notes: GDP – % change over previous year; Industrial output – % change over previous year; Rate of inflation – % change in end-year retail/consumer prices; Rate of unemployment as of end of year; GNP per capita – in US dollars at PPP exchange rates. [a] Estimate. [b] Non-state sector.

Sources: European Bank for Reconstruction and Development, *Transition Report 1995: Economic Transition in Eastern Europe and the Former Soviet Union* (London: EBRD, 1995); European Bank for Reconstruction and Development, *Transition Report Update, April 1996: Assessing Progress in Economies in Transition* (London: EBRD, 1996).

Since 1991 agricultural production has declined and tens of thousands of Lithuanians working in that sector have earned subsistence incomes. Privatization in agriculture has been completed and with the dismantling of the Soviet farm system, Lithuanian agriculture has been marked by cooperative enterprises and small private farms. An estimated 25 percent of the work force remains in the agricultural sector and if related enterprises are included – food processing, and so forth – the percentage soars to 40 percent. This last figure indicates that the economy has a long way to go before it can be considered a "developed" economy and meet the requirements for membership in the European Union.[37]

Although some private farms have done well – and with privatization improvements have been made in food processing and the marketing and distribution of farm products – many other enterprises are poorly managed because the horrible work habits of the Soviet era persist. Also, most people making a living in agriculture have been farm laborers who have performed narrow tasks, not farm entrepreneurs who have experience in both managing and working farms.

Of course, most of the estimated one-fifth of the population of 3.7 million living on pensions – amounting to 742,000 – have been especially hurt by the new economy. High rates of inflation have reduced the worth of pensions and older people wishing to rejoin the labor force have had difficulty finding work because of their age and lack of appropriate skills.

Anecdotal evidence suggests that the younger generation has enjoyed disproportionate gains in the new economy. Young people have actively participated in the "underground economy" for which no data exist; for example, they have been involved in the large scale sales of metals – and other commodities – secured at low prices from the inventory of Soviet enterprises (including material from Russia) and smuggled abroad for high prices at great profit for everyone involved in the process.

Other segments of society that have improved their economic status include government officials, administrators of privatized factories and farms, and those with good political contacts who have exploited the privatization process. Meanwhile, some highly educated people have done well in joint-ventures or programs sponsored by international bodies and NGOs.

Richard Rose has warned that macroeconomic income data may present a much too pessimistic picture of the economic status of the average Lithuanian family. He asserts there are numerous "micro-economies" in all of the Baltic states. "[W]e can also observe a division between officially recorded and unofficial economies and between monetized and non-monetized activities, producing a total of eight different types of 'economies,' including at least four at the micro-economic level."[38]

Also, it is a mistake to assess living conditions by looking at macro-economic data and official income data associated with the monetized economy. "The collapse of the command economy has greatly expanded the scope of economic activities outside state control, including opportunities to make money in 'second' economies, typically as a supplement to household income."[39] Most Lithuanian families depend upon more than one salary to meet their financial obligations, and in addition to two or more people working, many Lithuanians work at more than one job. Most families have ameliorated their economic plight through non-monetarized activities; for example, they secure a large amount of food through friends or relatives in agriculture, or their own plots. And the plight of "subsistence farmers" may be exaggerated since many farmers also work in non-agricultural employment.

The status of associations and social and economic groups

Since Lithuania is in transition from a command to a market economy, the status of group life is also in flux.

Non-governmental organizations

One measure of a healthy civil society is membership in nongovernmental organizations and other private associations. In Lithuania, "Actual membership counts for nongovernmental and charitable organizations remain difficult to collect, as most groups refrain from building formal memberships in a reaction against the Soviet-era practice of forced membership." (This phenomenon should also be considered when assessing membership in political parties.) Nonetheless, as of mid-1994 Freedom House counted "749, including 74 charitable funds, 65 professional associations and 31 political organizations."[40]

Business associations

Among business associations, the largest is the Confederation of Industrialists, which is comprised of firms formerly associated with the Soviet-era Industrialists' Association. Its members include privatized enterprises and it is organized to maintain old ties with the East and to forge new ones in the West. A second organization, the Businessmen's Association, is comprised of enterprises established since 1992.[41]

There are no data available describing the political activities of such business organizations but it is plausible to surmise that they are less visible in Lithuania than in the West because most entrepreneurs prefer to use their contacts to secure favorable treatment on a bilateral basis. For example, Bronislovas Lubys, who heads the Confederation of Industrialists, was the director of the giant Lithuanian chemical complex Azotas during Soviet rule, and he was selected by Brazauskas to be prime minister until he was replaced by Šleževičius in March 1993. Thus, as is true in other former communist lands in Europe, nomenklatura capitalism is alive and well in Lithuania.

The small business community has begun to organize to influence the political process and to forge alliances with local authorities. For example, Rita Dapkus, who ran the parliament's press office during the fateful days of "Bloody Sunday," is an officer in a new association of restaurant owners in Vilnius. Its target is the Seimas where national legislation effects the operation of the food business. Dapkus has lamented that both "left and right-wing deputies" are ignorant about the workings of a free market economy. Also domestic and foreign investors report that there has been no progress in the war on corruption; bribes must be offered at all levels of government to start a business – for example, to rent or purchase property, secure a license, and arrange other matters part of normal business operations.[42]

Terry D. Clark reports that the new business class has begun to forge alliances with local political authorities. In Šiauliai, "dire economic straits have encouraged a political-economic coalition between new entrepreneurs and the city council chairman; they are working toward revitalizing the local economy with a free-enterprise zone built around the former Soviet army air base northwest of the city."[43] As the economy becomes less dependent upon government and centralized planning mechanisms, the free market is likely to promote alliances between local business interests and government.

Agricultural organizations

Only a minority of farmers have organized agricultural associations. The first wave of farmers to respond favorably to Landsbergis' campaign to privatize agriculture formed the Farmer's Union. But two groups have opposed his agricultural drive; the Land Owner's Union, which is also an organization of private farmers, has complained about the schedule of land distribution and property rights. The Peasant's Union, a far larger organization comprised of administrators and employees of the old collective and state farms, has charged that the privatization of agriculture has occurred without proper planning.

Organized crime

The transition to a capitalist economy has not only disrupted the lives of workers and agricultural and industrial enterprises, it has fostered widespread organized criminal activity. As long as the economy is undergoing rapid and unregulated transition, government policy will be ad hoc and often counterproductive, corruption will persist, and organized crime will continue to play a pivotal role in business affairs. It is conventional wisdom among journalists and political observers that the Mafiya controls or influences many newly created enterprises. Therefore, such criminal behavior should not be assessed as a "social" problem alone but a major economic problem.

Extortion is a thriving business in the new "capitalist" economy and mobsters have bombed establishments where their owners have refused to provide protection money. In 1993, there were 150 reports of bombings in Lithuania, 31 in Vilnius alone.[44]

Even more disturbing than property damage are the numerous murders which have been perpetrated by the mob, mostly in places where the criminals have clashed over turf – in Vilnius, Kaunas, Klaipeda, and the Baltic resort city of Palanaga. In other instances, business people, who refused to pay for protection, have been targets, as well as journalists and their newspapers.

Even though ordinary citizens may not be directly affected by the mob, they pay higher taxes and more for goods and services as a result of organized crime. Most Lithuanians believe the mob could not flourish without the help of corrupt public officials. This conviction represents a major blow to building a civic culture based upon public trust. But another allegation about the Mafiya is equally disturbing. Some Lithuanian officials believe that the old Soviet KGB has worked closely with criminal organizations, and that this unholy alliance poses a threat to the country's security.[45]

Clearly, Lithuania has been a corridor through which nuclear material has passed. The passage of nuclear materials, and drugs, has been the subject of attention in the American press and it explains why the US Federal Bureau of Investigation has taken an interest in criminal activities there.

Unions

The prospects for labor unions will remain precarious as long as the economy experiences dramatic disruptions – encouraging growth in sectors of the economy that are difficult to organize, such as services, and decline in other areas where unions are strongest, such as manufacturing. According to an American source, there are three trade union organizations in Lithuania today:

(1) "The successor to the old Communist trade union confederation, the 'Lithuanian Trade Union Center,' is still dominated by elements of the old union apparat and barely functions as an organization, despite continuing to claim a large nominal membership. By one estimate," its "membership declined (since independence) from 270,000 to 250,000 in 1994."

(2) "The 'Unification of Trade Unions' is a confederation that developed from a group of branch unions that left the official union confederation in 1989 over issues of Lithuanian independence and relations with the Communist Party." It has had close links with the Social Democratic Party. Its membership has declined from 110,000 to 80,0000 in 1994 "when it became an affiliate of the International Confederation of Free Trade Unions."

(3) "The third significant trade union organization . . . is the 'Lithuanian Workers Union' (LDS) . . . The LDS leadership recognized the necessity of changing to a market-based economy, but wants to ensure that the transition is accompanied by a strong social safety net . . . Despite growing unemployment and other adverse conditions, in 1994 the LDS achieved a growth in membership, from approximately 130,000 to 140,000."[46]

Lithuanian observers of the labor union scene assert that the membership claims of all three union associations are grossly inflated.[47] Indeed, in this instance as well in most other ones, the quality of data and reporting systems typical of older democracies does not exist in Lithuania and what is available must be used with caution. Even when the personnel collecting information have appropriate skills, rapid changes in society undermine its utility, or the absence of a common basis for comparison precludes comparative analysis.

Clearly when the economy was in a free fall, the work force of large enterprises declined and this contributed to the plight of Lithuania's labor movement. The average monthly wage is US$131 and as Aldona Balsiene, the head of LDS, reports, even workers belonging to unions find it difficult to pay their dues. Moreover, the newly privatized enterprises are small, largely service oriented and traditionally difficult to organize. At the same time, they operate largely outside of the open economy.

Wage subsidies provided by government and Soviet-era enterprises are declining and Balsiene believes the real rate of joblessness may be as high as 20 percent. Also, because women suffer more from lay-offs, the LDS has formed a women's labor organization which has claimed two to three thousand members.[48]

Ethnic groups

While the employment picture remains troubling, Lithuania can take satisfaction in the absence of serious ethnic conflict. In 1989 the Lithuanian government passed a citizenship law with the "zero option." It allowed persons who had lived and worked in the country on a continual basis to become citizens within two years of the law's adoption. The largest ethnic minorities are the Russians, representing 8.4 percent of the population, and the Poles, accounting for 7 percent of the population. Ethnic Lithuanians have comprised roughly 80 percent of the country's population since the 1920s, while minority groups have accounted for the rest (although Russians have replaced Jews and Germans since the end of World War II). (Figures outlining the contemporary breakdown of Lithuania's population by nationality are contained in table 8.6.) Skeptical about Lithuanian independence, a number of Russians supported the Soviet-dominated Edinstvo (the International Front or "inter-front" Movement), which actively opposed Sajūdis and supported the failed January 13, 1991 coup. Some Russians were Sajūdis activists, such as Nikolai Medvedev, who was elected to the Supreme Council, and many supported independence although they favored the step-by-step approach associated with Brazauskas. Unlike the Polish community, organizations in the Russian community have been cultural and not political.

In keeping with polls indicating that Russians have been more favorable to the Soviet system than their Lithuanian counterparts, they have given most of their votes to the "left" – that is, Labor – since independence. Whereas 16 percent of the ethnic Lithuanians claim to support Labor, 37 percent of the

Table 8.6 *Ethnic composition of the population of Lithuania, 1995*

Ethnic group	Population in 1,000s	Percent
Total population	3,717.7	–
Lithuanians	3,022.4	81.4
Russians	310.9	8.4
Poles	259.2	7.0
Byelorussians	55.9	1.5
Ukrainians	37.7	1.0
Jews	5.9	0.1
Other	25.7	0.7

Source: *Statistical Yearbook of Lithuania 1994–95* (Vilnius: Methodical Publishing Centre, 1995), p. 39.

ethnic Russians are so inclined. And while 7 percent of the Lithuanians have admitted to being communist party members, the figure for Russians in Lithuania is 22 percent. And Russians, by a 21 to 5 percent margin over Lithuanian respondents, have agreed with the observation, "We would be better off if we were still part of the Soviet Union."[49]

The Russians' political quiescence perhaps can be attributed to Lithuania's liberal citizenship law and the conviction that they see Labor as representing their political interests. Also, employment and income figures comparing Russians and Lithuanians have shown no differences in status. And a majority of Russians, 59 percent, claim that "This country offers better chances than Russia for rising living standards in the future." And by a 45 percent to 27 percent margin they have agreed that "Conditions for people like me are worse in Russia than here."[50]

The Russian community has begun to demonstrate a heightened level of political awareness. Pyotr Frolov of the Lithuanian Russian Community supports a new party which would represent the interests of Lithuania's minorities – the Party For Lithuania's National Minorities.[51] Also, *Echo litvy*, the Russian-language newspaper, has advocated the Russian community create a new umbrella organization to qualify for funding (the amount was not given) which has been earmarked by the Russian Federation for Russians in the "near abroad" areas. It would not be a formal political party but it would enhance the political prospects of the Russian community once it had been formed.[52]

Like many Russians, Poles had misgivings about Lithuanian independence, and in the Vilnius region and places like Šalčininkai, the Polish apparatchiks actively opposed it. They also supported the coup attempts of January and

August 1991. As a consequence, after independence, Landsbergis removed Polish officials from office in two jurisdictions and replaced them with his appointees.[53]

Currently more ethnic Poles than ethnic Lithuanians, by a margin of 13 percent to 7 percent, claim to still "believe in communism."[54] But Poles like Czesła Okinczyć joined Sajúdis and were elected to parliament in 1990, and others, like the publisher Romuald Mieczćkowski, also supported independence.

The Polish community has also formed political organizations. The most significant has been the Polish Union, which has three seats in the Seimas. Led by Jan Senkiewicz, the Polish Union clashed with the Labor government when it demanded that the Union had to become a formal political party if it wanted to participate in the municipal elections of 1995. (Senkiewicz wanted to maintain the Union's status as a social organization.) To comply, a Polish Action Group For Elections was formed and it won sixty-nine seats – doing best in Vilnius and municipal districts in the city's environs and the cities of Šalčininkai, Drúskininkai, and Trakai. It achieved majority status in two regional councils while it took two-fifths of the seats in Vilnius.[55] In 1995, Okinczyć announced he would form a political party which – on the basis of his past association with Sajúdis – probably means one adopting a less radical stance than the Polish Union.

Poles have developed political organizations, while the Russians have not, because the Polish community is indigenous to eastern Lithuania, and during the interwar years relations between Lithuanians and Poles were fractious. Consequently, given their special status, Poles believe their demands have greater legitimacy than those of the Russian "migrants."

The Polish community, however, is divided over how hard it should press for instruction in Polish, the establishment of a Polish university, and the celebration of Polish culture in society at large. In part, this division represents the appearance of cross-pressures in the political system and is a sign of pluralism. It is noteworthy that Wanda Mieczkowski, whose husband, Romuald, is the editor of the Polish newspaper *Znad willi*, is an officer in the Women's Party which was established by the former prime minister, Kazimiera Prunskiene. (Presently nine women serve in the Seimas and the party wishes to increase that number. The party has not yet been tested in the electoral arena and some deem it a front for Labor; clearly, it is a vehicle to thrust the former prime minister back into the political fray.) Ms. Mieczkowski owns a highly regarded cafe-art gallery. For Poles who have experienced economic success, traditional communal concerns play a less important role in their lives than was true of the past, when Soviet apparatchiks exploited ethic discord to sustain their power.[56]

The Church

The role of the Roman Catholic Church in post-Soviet Lithuania is unclear. During the Soviet occupation, many Lithuanians displayed their nationalistic sentiments by identifying with the Church whose clergy and faithful had been cruelly oppressed by Soviet authorities. But some Lithuanians, who once expressed themselves in this manner, are much cooler toward the church, which many progressive Catholics believe is too rigid and dogmatic. Like Catholics in other modern democratic societies, liberal Catholics in Lithuania do not believe that the church should be involved in secular affairs such as abortion. Unlike Poland, the church in Lithuania has refrained from injecting its dogma into public life but it has not been a bystander either.

The church's leader, Arch-Bishop Audrys Backis, has had difficulty working with members of the clergy whose Catholicism has not reflected Vatican II reforms. He has prohibited priests from engaging in political activities but not all of his subordinates have obeyed his dictates. For example, some spoke in favor of Lozoraitis in his presidential race against Brazauskas and others have been overt in supporting the Christian Democrats. The church has clashed with the Labor government over the return of church property, which was extensive before World War II.

The Catholic Church, however, continues to enjoy support among the Lithuanian people as 75 percent of them say they have confidence in the Catholic Church; only the media enjoy wider popular support.[57] Similar to the heightened level of political awareness among Christian fundamentalists in the United States, Lithuanians who are devout Catholics are more likely to participate in politics and to express a high level of political efficacy than their secular-minded brethren.[58]

The media

The press in Lithuania has moved from a "controlled" press to the status of "independent," although its operations have been distorted by economic difficulties and attempts at intimidation.

All of the major dailies including *Lietuvos rytas*, the largest and most profitable newspaper, have lost circulation. For example, *Lietuvos rytas'* pre-independence level of 500,000 declined to 75,000 in 1995; and the paper is expensive – it costs the equivalent of fifty cents. But *Lietuvos rytas* and *Respublika* are independent papers, unlike *Lietuvos aidas* and *Diena* which are controlled by the Homeland Union and Labor.[59] And there are newspapers published in both Polish (*Znad willi*) and Russian (*Echo litvy*).

Print journalists have demonstrated great courage in reporting on the activities of organized crime and corruption. In 1993, an editor for

Respublika, Vitas Lingys, was shot dead in broad daylight outside of his apartment because he had refused to stop publishing articles about the mob. Allegedly he had linked gangs in Vilnius to a Russian mob operating in New York City's "Little Odessa." In the summer of 1995, Boris Dekanidze, the leader of the Vilnius Brigade, a Georgian-Jewish gang, was tried and executed for ordering the hit.[60]

On November 16, 1995, an annex to *Lietuvos rytas* was bombed after it published a series of articles on corruption and the government's failure to fight crime. The campaign had included a front page story with photos depicting prisoners partying in their cushy refuge in a prison not too far from Vilnius. There were no casualties but the building had to be destroyed.[61] The very next weekend *Respublika*, *Lietuvos rytas*, and *Lietuvos aidas* all ran identical front page stories accusing the government of failing to protect the press in Lithuania and tolerating crime and corruption.

The status of the electronic media, radio and TV, is precarious. In addition to state-owned Radio 1 and Radio 2 there are several independent radio stations, including the popular Polish-language *Znad willi*, and while they have extensive listening audiences, all of them are in financial difficulty. "Television remains the primary source of information and the most important medium, in terms of impact on public opinion."[62] As of 1994, there were four national TV channels, one state-owned, a second private and carrying programs from Russia's Ostankino station, a third private and carrying Lithuanian-language programs, and the fourth private and featuring largely Polish-language shows. The existence of state-operated stations, therefore, has not been a serious problem. The most difficult problem facing the private stations is securing the financial revenues necessary to stay in business.

But in spite of financial difficulties and a law restricting investigative reporting – because the private lives of public officials are not deemed of public import – the press has inspired greater confidence among the Lithuanian population than any other institution. In one poll, 82 percent of the respondents said that had "a great deal of confidence" in the press.[63]

The military

Like other institutions in Lithuania, the military continues to reflect practices associated with the recent past; for example, an officer corps which was trained in the "Soviet manner," where the mistreatment of enlisted personnel persists and professional soldiers do not look favorably upon civilian oversight of their activities. But few foreign observers believe the Lithuanian military represents a threat to democracy. Because of its association with the Red Army, it has little popular support and it is not a force around which anti-democratic forces can be mobilized. Only 38 percent of the Lithuanian population expresses confidence in their military. By contrast the figure is 50 percent in Estonia and 85 percent in Poland.[64]

As a result of membership in the Partnership for Peace (PFP), the Baltic Peace-Keeping Battalion, and military-to-military operations with Nordic and NATO forces – including service in the former Yugoslavia – both the Lithuanian officer corps and enlisted personnel have been exposed to units that exemplify civilian control of the military and practices which inculcate soldiers with democratic values.[65]

Whatever their reservations about the prospects, most Lithuanians want to "rejoin Europe." Lithuania, in addition to PFP, belongs to the Organization on Cooperation and Security in Europe, the Council of Europe, the North Atlantic Cooperation Council and has observer status in the West European Union. Also, Lithuanian nationalism has remained closely entangled in the minds of most Lithuanians with membership in the western community of nations. Most Lithuanian leaders realize that should their country's experiment with democracy fail, Lithuania would lose its moral legitimacy in the eyes of the Western democracies and that set-back would make it vulnerable to Russian chauvinists who claim Lithuania belongs in the Russian sphere of influence. A majority of Lithuanians, 53 percent, believe the "Russian state" is a threat to Lithuania's "peace and security."[66]

Foreign relations

Lithuania has achieved a number of breakthroughs in its relations with its neighbors while it has ameliorated old wounds at home. Vilnius and Moscow have negotiated the withdrawal of troops from Lithuania, an agreement over military transit through Lithuania to Kaliningrad, and a most favored nation trade accord. In 1994, Lithuania signed a Treaty of Friendship with Poland under which Warsaw recognized Vilnius as Lithuania's capital and renounced any claims to Lithuanian territory. It also signed a similar agreement with Belarus.

In contrast to the cool relations among the Baltic states during the interwar period, the three democracies have cooperated since the "popular front" era. But as independent countries their interests often clash, and to resolve such differences, they now coordinate their activities through the Baltic Parliamentary Assembly, a Council of Baltic Presidents, and a Baltic Council of Ministers.

Lithuania has enjoyed especially warm relations with the Scandinavian countries which have been generous in providing all manner of assistance. For example, Denmark helped organize the Baltic Battalion and is the only

European member of NATO which has openly advocated Baltic membership in that organization.

Finally, in 1994 the Lithuanian government made a public appeal to the Jewish community for forgiveness for the killings of Jews during the Holocaust.

Notwithstanding these foreign policy successes, Lithuania's major international problem is a Russia which will be stricken by revolutionary upheaval for years. As a consequence, it is plausible that chauvinists bent on restoring an imperial Russian state, which includes the Balts, could gain power. It is the fear of Russia's disintegration, not so much the threat of outright Russian aggression, which explains why Lithuanians deem membership in NATO as both vital to safeguarding their independence and sustaining their fledgling democracy.

Simultaneously, the Lithuanians realize that economic crisis represents their greatest internal threat; so membership in the European Union is not only vital to their economic welfare but to their democracy's health. In the winter of 1995–96, some Lithuanian parliamentarians expressed greater concern about being denied access to the EU than to NATO's foot dragging on the enlargement issue. This concern was spawned by Helmut Kohl's observation that the Baltic democracies had not reached a stage of economic development warranting EU membership.[67]

Conclusions

Lithuania has achieved mixed success in its drive towards democracy and a free-market economy.

By whatever measuring sticks one employs, the Lithuanians are far ahead of other former Soviet republics in developing a democratic electoral process. Since the restoration of the Lithuanian state in 1990, several national and two municipal elections have been conducted in an orderly, peaceful, and honest fashion. No group has been denied citizenship, the right to vote, or the opportunity to create an electoral organization. The incumbents have accepted defeat without any attempt to abort the transfer of power and, once in positions of authority, the new leadership has refrained from retaliating against the opposition.

The status of the country's political parties is more problematic. While several of them have developed country-wide networks and demonstrated the capacity to mobilize voters in national campaigns, there are far too many parties – at last count over twenty of them. The most serious shortcoming of Lithuania's political parties, however, is their failure to address the country's daunting problems through the governmental process. What is more, they – and the executive agencies – have been derelict in conducting legislative oversight of laws once they have been passed. The 1995 banking crisis was largely a result of the Bank of Lithuania's dismal oversight of commercial lending institutions.

In assessing the performance of Lithuanian political elites and popular attitudes toward them, one cannot ignore the persistence of *Homo sovieticus*. During the Soviet era, people were forced to lie, cheat, and steal to survive economic hardship and protect their families from arbitrary punishment at the hands of the authorities. The Soviet apparatchiks manipulated the legal system to safeguard their power and privileges and today many Lithuanians view law as an instrument the powerful manipulate to promote their welfare at the expense of ordinary folk.

The persistence of the Soviet political culture contributes to the tendency of politicians to engage in personal attacks upon their opponents and make vicious, groundless charges about their rivals' motives. *Homo sovieticus* explains why those in power make decisions in secret, dictate terms, and deem compromise a sign of weakness and not a prudent attempt to advance a political program in an open society.

Many of the imperfections of Lithuanian democracy are associated with the absence of a strong civil society undergirded by a large secure middle class. Consequently public policy initiatives which emanate from civil society are inchoate. Without well-organized interest groups the public lacks the ability to shape the policy process and to influence the administration of public law through grassroots pressure.

Perhaps most Lithuanians may be deemed "middle class" if one uses educational and social criteria to make that designation, but the country's middle class is unstable because of the dire economic circumstances of its members.

Lithuania has begun to build an economic infrastructure which includes a stable convertible currency, extensive privatization, and steady progress in the war against inflation. Its price liberalization policies have won praise from international economic bodies such as the World Bank and the International Monetary Fund. It also has a well educated labor force, considerable technical and scientific expertise, and Western oriented business elites, although their ranks are small at present. As the economy matures and the middle class flourishes, interest groups will develop and begin to function much as they do in other democracies. Membership in NGOs will expand as the memory of forced participation in "voluntary associations," typical of the Soviet era, recedes from the consciousness of the population.

Presently, however, Lithuania has failed to match the economic performance of its Baltic neighbors. In 1994, while per capita income was $6,690 in Estonia, and $4,374 in Latvia, it was only $3,771 in Lithuania.[68] Foreign economic analysts attribute slower growth rates to Lithuania's failure to move more aggressively toward a wider free market. The country's most valuable assets, such as transport, energy, ports, and communications, remain state owned and operated.

The next disruptive stage in the economy's transition will involve the closing of old unprofitable enterprises and labor force reductions, shrinkage in agriculture, and the elimination of wage and price subsidies. To make matters worse, Lithuanian consumers and state agencies have failed to pay their energy bills. The Lithuanian Director of Energy, Rimvydas Ruksenas, has warned that the winter of 1996–97 may be a cold one because of this situation. He says that energy prices are unrealistic and must be raised by as much as 50 percent to avoid an energy short-fall. It is uncertain how long Gazprom, the Russian supplier, will wait to get paid before it completely cuts off supplying natural gas and oil to Lithuania.[69]

To add to the population's woes is a budgetary crisis which has caused the government to experience difficulty in meeting financial obligations. By late spring 1996, the government made a 48 percent reduction in spending. "The government has temporarily stopped financing all public construction and the purchase of vehicles, computers, and other pieces of equipment. Salaries and pensions have not been paid on time."[70]

Should the economic situation deteriorate further – as the country continues to grapple with the dislocations of an historical economic transformation – Lithuanian democracy will be put to a stiff test.

One institution, the free press, has already passed the test. Although under assault, Lithuania's journalists have not been silenced. Furthermore, a new law is being enacted to replace the existing one which has placed restrictions on journalists probing the private lives of politicians to uncover evidence of corruption.

The greatest threat to the viability of the Lithuanian print and electronic media has been a paucity of financial resources. Consequently, some commentators are convinced that even the newspapers which have refused to buckle before the Mafiya or the government frequently run stories which are nothing less than paid advertisements. Nonetheless, the Lithuanian media continue to serve as a vital democratic asset. Perhaps their greatest achievement to date was the pivotal role they played in the removal of Prime Minister Slezevičius from office.

That incident was a victory for the Lithuanian people and their faith in democracy as well. It demonstrated to a skeptical citizenry that in a democratic Lithuania, public opinion can have an impact upon the political process. An aroused public expelled a powerful official from office; in the old Soviet days when politicians blatantly ignored public opinion, such an outcome was unthinkable.

Democratic foundations in Lithuania are shaky and will be buffeted by protracted economic hard times, but unlike other parts of the former Soviet Union, it is unlikely that anti-democratic forces will gain power. Organizations which resort to violence will not attract significant popular support to their ranks. Nor is the military a likely candidate for an anti-democratic coup. In addition to lacking popular appeal, both its officers and men have begun to absorb democratic values and practices through extensive military-to-military programs with Western military establishments.

Political instability in Russia and the likelihood that chauvinists will gain power there, of course, explains why the Lithuanians want to join NATO. Western leaders must remember: if the Baltic peoples conclude they are left to fend for themselves in a region which will be stricken by upheaval for years – and one where a powerful but disoriented neighbor exists – the resultant anxiety could place democracy at risk in all three societies.

Finally, American commentators should be careful lest they unfairly apply criteria of democratization to the former communist lands of Europe, or ignore cultural differences which may explain why democratic institutions will evolve differently in the Baltic countries than in the United States. For example, party identification is in decline in many democracies (including the United States). In contrast, voter turn-out in Lithuania exceeds that in the United States at all levels of the political system. What is more, fragmented families and communities, declining unions and other entities vital to civil society are all visible in most Western democracies and this trend is not peculiar to Lithuania (witness the decline of the American labor movement).

Lithuanian political elites may be criticized for not moving expeditiously toward capitalism but they have cause to question the wisdom of embracing the same free-market paradigm which has contributed to economic inequality in the United States. The Anglo-American brand of capitalism is far too radical for people living in democratic societies in many parts of Europe and Asia. The communitarian ethos is stronger in the Baltic countries than in the United States. Therefore the evolution of civil society in Lithuania is not as likely to display the same passion for privatism and individualism which are the hallmarks of American society.

Epilogue: the Right's return

The first round of the Seimas election conducted on October 20, 1996 returned Landsbergis's Homeland Union Party to power. The party list results, determined by proportional representation and involving 70 seats, were as follows:

– The Homeland Union Party got 29.11 percent of the vote and received thirty-two seats;

– The Christian Democratic Party got 10.20 percent of the vote and received eleven seats;

– The Democratic Labor Party got 9.94 percent of the vote and received eleven seats;

– The Center Union got 8.30 percent of the vote and received nine seats;

– The Social Democratic Party got 6.81 percent of the vote and received seven seats.[71]

Only Landsbergis and the former conservative prime minister, Gediminas Vagnorious, received the majority vote necessary to capture a seat in the first round of the single mandate race. But the Homeland Union candidates, on the basis of first round results, are expected to do well in the second round. Landsbergis enjoys a hard core bloc of at least 20 percent of the electorate and his party demonstrated an impressive capacity to attract its voters to the polls. This ability, Labor's image of corruption, a disappointing turn-out of 53 percent, and the fact that any party in power will suffer as long as Lithuania is going through its daunting transition from communism to an open society, explain the right's victory.

In contrast to the 1992 parliamentary elections, when the Central Movement (as the Center Union was then called) won two seats, it secured nine seats in the first round in 1996 and probably will win a few more in the next one. The same can be said for the Social Democrats, who captured seven seats in 1992, a number they reached by the first round in 1996. The centrist parties, however, did not attract that vast pool of voters not identifying with any party. They picked up votes from those Lithuanians who once supported the Labor Party – which was discredited by it image of corruption as exemplified by the December 1995 bank scandal and former Prime Minister Slezevicius's role in it – but hardly enough to challenge the front-running Homeland Union.

The far right National Party of Young Lithuania got 3.60 percent of the vote and did not reach the 5 percent necessary to win seats; this also held true for Prunskiene's new Women's Party, which got 3.6 percent, and the Election Action of Lithuanian Poles, which got 3.0 percent. As was true of the past, Poles were less likely to vote than ethnic Lithuanians, and like the Russians they were unhappy about moving the bar of representation from 4 to 5 percent for parties and 5 to 7 percent for party coalitions. In four predominantly Polish districts of eastern Lithuania, a less than 40 percent turnout invalidated the races; they will be repeated six months later. But all of the fringe parties mentioned are likely to win one of the seventy-one seats in the single-mandate district voting to be held on November 10, 1996.

It is conceivable that Homeland Union can win a majority of the Seimas on its own; but it is more likely that it will form a coalition with the Christian Democrats and the Centrists if necessary. But just days before the election,

Landsbergis lashed out at Center Union leaders Romualdas Ozolas and Egidijus Bickauskas for reneging on a pledge to work with the conservatives in forming a government after the second round of the election.

Meanwhile, President Brazauskas is likely to prepare for his 1998 bid for reelection by claiming that he is above party politics. Until then, the right and left in Lithuania will have to endure a condition of cohabitation.

After the first round of the election, Landsbergis said, "Our main goal is to restore confidence. In doing so we are going to attack corruption and implement a clean-hands policy in government." If a new conservative coalition government can achieve those objectives it will help accelerate Lithuania's drive toward democratization.[72]

NOTES

1 See Alfred Erich Senn, *The Emergence of Modern Lithuania* (New York: Columbia University Press, 1959).

2 For data on Jews in the 1920s, see *Lietuviškoji Tarybine Enciklopedija Vyriausioji* Vol. 12 (Vilnius: Enciklopedija Redakicija), p. 519. For Deak citation, see Istvan Deak, "Surviving the Holocaust: The Kovno Ghetto Diary," *New York Review of Books*, 8 November 1990, p. 54. For data regarding Jews killed during the Holocaust, see Daniel Jonah Goldhagen, *Hitler's Willing Executioners* (New York: Knopf, 1996), p. 423.

3 Anatol Lieven, *The Baltic Revolution* (New Haven: Yale University Press, 1994), p. 66.

4 For a discussion of the Soviet period, see Romuald J. Misiunas and Rein Taagepera, *The Baltic States: Years of Dependence 1940–1990* (Berkeley, CA: University of California Press, 1993).

5 Aleksandras Shtromas, "The Baltic States as Soviet Republics," in *The Baltic States*, ed. Graham Smith (New York: St. Martin's Press, 1994), p. 100.

6 For treatment of Lithuania's ethnic homogeneity, see Barbara Anderson and Brian Silver, "Some Factors in the Linguistic and Ethnic Russification of Soviet Nationalities," in *The Nationalities Factor in Soviet Politics and Society*, ed. Lubomyr Hajda and Mark Beissinger (Boulder, CO: Westview Press, 1990), p. 119; and in the same book, Romuald J. Misiunis, "The Baltic Republics," p. 206.

7 For a discussion of the Lithuanian diaspora and US policy toward Lithuania after its annexation in 1940, see Antanas J. Van Reenan, *Lithuanian Diaspora: Konigsberg to Chicago* (Lanham, NY: University Press of America, 1990).

8 For a comprehensive discussion of the Catholic civil rights activists and their samizdat, *The Chronicle of the Catholic Church in Lithuania*, see V. Stanley Vardys, *The Catholic Church, Dissent, and Nationality in Soviet Lithuania* (New York: Columbia University Press, 1978).

9 See Alfred Eric Senn, *Lithuania Awakening* (Berkeley, CA: University of California Press, 1990).

10 Lieven, *Baltic Revolution*, p. 226.

11 Ibid., p. 235.

12 Ibid., p. 237. Also, author's interviews with Stasys Lozoraitis, Fall 1992, and Vytautas Landsbergis, Summer 1994.

13 For a discussion of the Lithuanian restoration of independence and the American reaction, see Richard J. Krickus, *Showdown: The Lithuanian Rebellion and the Break-up of the Soviet Empire* (London: Brassey's Press, 1996).

14 Alfred Eric Senn provides a detailed analysis of the events leading up to and including Bloody Sunday in his *Gorbachev's Failure in Lithuania* (New York: St. Martin's Press, 1995).

15 Ibid., p. 127.

16 Lieven, *Baltic Revolution*, p. 260.

17 Coopers and Lybrand, *Lithuania: A Business and Investment Guide* (Vilnius, 1995), pp. 1, 2.

18 Saulius Girnius, *RFE/RL*, 6 December 1993, p. 6.

19 *Philadelphia Inquirer*, 14 February 1993.

20 Author's interviews with Algimantas Brazauskas and Vytautas Landsbergis, January 1992.

21 For data pertaining to the 1993 presidential election, see *Statistical Yearbook of Lithuania* (Vilnius: Methodical Publishing Centre, 1995), p. 67.

22 Author's interview with Christopher Shields, who conducted programs on developing democratic political parties in Lithuania for the International Republican Institute, Summer 1995. The data provided here, and the analysis of political parties, come from the Institute's *Lithuania Situation Update: 1995 Municipal Elections* (Washington: International Republican Institute, 5 April 1995).

23 Terry D. Clark, "An Emerging Urban Regime: A Case Study of Siauliai," unpublished manuscript.

24 Author's interview with Aidas Polubinskas, a member of the Christian Democratic Party, Summer 1995.

25 Vladas Gaidys, "Lithuania between State and Market," paper presented at Catholic University of Lublin, 26–28 May 1994, p. 9.

26 Author's interview with Arturas Racas, reporter for *Lietuvos rytas*, who collected this information, Winter 1995–96.

27 Author's interview with Vladys Gaidys, a pollster, Summer 1995.

28 Richard Rose, *New Baltics Barometer II: A Survey Study* (Glasgow: Centre for the Study of Public Policy, University of Strathclyde, 1995), pp. 19, 14.

29 Ibid., pp. 21–22.

30 Ibid., pp. 22, 47.

31 Ibid., p. 25.

32 *Baltic Independent* (Tallinn), 14–20 July 1995.

33 Ibid., 12–18 January 1996.

34 *Statistical Yearbook*, p. 82.

35 Coopers and Lybrand, *Lithuania*, pp. 1, 2.

36 For attitudes about Lithuania's greatest problems, see *Lithuanian Political Culture*, a research report summary conducted by the Institute of International Relations and Political Science, Vilnius University, sponsored by the Friedrich Naumman Foundation in December, 1994, p. 5. For opinions about living standards, see Gaidys, "Lithuania Between State and Market," p. 5.

37 Author's interview with Eric Branich, American consultant on coop-farming in the Baltic states, Summer 1995.
38 Richard Rose, "Similarities and Differences in Micro-Economic Conditions of Nationalities in Baltics States," paper presented at Stockholm School of Economics conference, Riga, Latvia, 17–18 August 1995, p. 4.
39 Ibid., p. 5.
40 Freedom House, *Nations in Transit: Civil Society, Democracy and Markets in East Central Europe and the Newly Independent States* (New York: Freedom House, 1995), p. 92.
41 Ibid.
42 Author's interview with Rita Dapkus, Summer 1995.
43 Terry D. Clark, "A New Grass-Roots Partnership," *Transition*, 15 March 1995, p. 34.
44 *Baltic Independent*, 24–30 March 1995.
45 Author's interview with Colonel Ignas Stankovičius, Summer 1994.
46 Report of the AFL-CIO Free Trade Union Institute, "Assistance to the Lithuanian Workers' Union – 1995," undated, pp. 1–2.
47 Author's interview with Rimantas Dagys, Social Democratic Deputy, Summer 1995.
48 Author's interview with Aldona Balsiene, Summer 1995.
49 Rose, *New Baltics Barometer II*, pp. 43, 56, 33.
50 Centre For The Study of Public Policy, University of Strathclyde, Press Release, "Baltic Peoples Agree On Rights And Obligations But Split Two Ways About Who Should Be Citizens," Table 7.
51 *Baltic Independent*, 16–22 December 1994.
52 Ibid., 18–24 August 1995.
53 For a discussion of Lithuania's "Polish question," see Stephen R. Burant, "Polish–Lithuanian Relations: Past, Present, and Future," *Problems of Communism* (May–June 1991). See also Richard J. Krickus, "Lithuania's Polish Question," *Report on the USSR*, 29 November 1991.
54 Poll findings provided by Vladys Gaidys, Summer 1995.
55 *Lithuania: Situation Update*, p. 23.
56 Author's interview with Wanda Mieczkowski, Summer 1995.
57 *Baltic Independent*, 14–20 July 1995.
58 These are provisional findings which Egle Laumenškaite of the Center for Religious Studies at Vilnius University has shared with me.
59 Saulius Girnius, "Ahead of the Censors, but Feeling the Economic Strain in the Baltic States," *Transition*, 6 October 1995, p. 16.
60 Sherry Ricchiardi, "Killing The Messenger," *American Journalism Review*, November 1995, pp. 19–25.
61 Author's interview with Marius Laurinavičius, editor at *Lietuvos rytas*, January 1996.
62 "Ahead of the Censors," p. 16.
63 *Baltic Independent*, 14–20 July 1995.
64 David G. Gibson, "High Public Confidence in the Church," *Transition*, 5 April 1996, p. 29.

65 Author's interviews with Linas Lincavičius, minister of defense, and Colonel Ignas Stankovicius of the "international section" of the Defense Ministry, Summer 1994.
66 Rose, *New Baltics Barometer II*, p. 34.
67 Author's interviews with two Homeland Union Deputies, Andrius Kubilius and Emmanuelis Zingeris, January 1996.
68 *Washington Post*, 28 March 1996.
69 *Baltic Times*, 25 April–1 May 1996.
70 Saulius Girnius, "Caretaker Government Faces Financial Crisis," *Transition*, 17 May 1996, p. 40.
71 *Respublika*, 22 October 1996.
72 *Baltic Times*, 24–30 October 1996.

9 Democratization and political development in Estonia, 1987–96

Toivo U. Raun

Introduction

The following study of political development in Estonia on the eve of the Soviet Union's demise and the early postindependence era focuses on the question of democratization and closely related issues. It stresses the role of the country's previous evolution, especially the experiences of the interwar independence era and the Soviet period, in shaping how Estonia dealt with the political challenges it faced in the years 1987–96. The key theme of the period under review is the non-violent nature of Estonia's democratization process despite ethnic tensions and economic uncertainty. Emboldened by Moscow's weakness and events in Eastern Europe, Estonia quickly turned to the restoration of independence as the only viable option for its future and, along with the other two Baltic states, played a significant role in the coming collapse of the USSR in the years 1988–91. For the period 1991–96 the study assesses the evolution of the new political system, analyzing the Constitution of 1992 and the functioning and interaction of the legislative and executive branches. The electoral system and citizen participation in the electoral process are also analyzed. Political parties in Estonia in the early 1990s have struggled to define their role and to establish strong ties with voters; by 1995–96 there were signs that stable and relatively large parties were beginning to emerge. Finally, the role of various social and economic factors in the process of democratization is examined, including the issue of ethnic relations and the impact of Estonia's successful economic reforms.

In view of Estonia's strategic geopolitical location on the southern shore of the Gulf of Finland, its role as a historical crossroads in the Baltic region is not surprising. Despite Russian and Soviet hegemony during much of the modern era, the formative influences in historical times in such key areas as education and religion came from the German states and Scandinavia. Thus, Estonia retained a "pre-Russian" identity in terms of cultural background, and tsarist attempts at integration of the Estonian areas into the Russian cultural and political world came far too late to be successful. During the twentieth century, especially in the interwar era and in the decades after 1956, Estonia developed a strong connection to Finland that also served as a counterbalance to great power influences from both east and west.

Demographic and social trends

Although the first modern censuses in the region that became the Republic of Estonia in 1918 took place only in the late nineteenth century, there is every indication that the ethnic composition of the area had been stable for centuries, and it remained so until World War II. The ethnic Estonian proportion of the population was 89.8 percent in 1881 and 88.2 percent in 1934.[1] However, as seen in table 9.1, the decades of Soviet rule had a drastic impact on the population mix in Estonia. It is ironic that the upheavals of World War II and postwar Stalinist border manipulation actually raised the Estonian share of the population to an estimated 97 percent in 1945 (within postwar borders).[2]

Nevertheless, a rapid decline in the native proportion began in the late 1940s, overwhelmingly as a result of massive in-migration by Russians and other East Slavs (especially to Tallinn and northeastern Estonia) combined with Stalin-era deportations of tens of thousands of Estonians to remote parts of the Soviet Union. Although most surviving Estonian deportees returned after 1956, the immigration of East Slavs continued, and by 1989 only the Latvians, among the union republic nationalities, had suffered a comparable weakening of their demographic position. These population shifts had a profound impact on Estonian thinking under Soviet rule. Estonian dissent in the 1970s and the early 1980s focused on national and cultural survival, and it is hardly coincidental (when the opportunity presented itself during the reform era of Mikhail Gorbachev) that Estonia was the first Soviet republic to pass a language law in January 1989.[3] Mainly because of out-migration by Russians, Ukrainians, and Belorussians in the first half of the 1990s, the Estonian proportion of the population began to rise once again, increasing to 64.2 percent in 1995 (see table 9.1) and 64.6 percent in 1996. Given the high death rates and low birth rates of recent years (trends that will be difficult to reverse in the near future), a negative rate of natural increase among all ethnic groups in the country will likely prevail for some time.[4]

Tables 9.2 and 9.3 provide an overview of other demographic trends in Estonia. Table 9.3 focuses on the process of urbanization in Estonia in the twentieth century as well as the proportion of Estonians and Russians, the two largest ethnic groups represented in the cities, during census years. In

Table 9.1 *Major ethnic groups in Estonia: number (in 1,000's) and percentage of total population*

	1934[a]		1959		1970		1979		1989		1995[b]	
	No.	%	No.	%	No.	%	No.	%	No.	%	No.	%
Estonians	993.5	88.2	892.7	74.6	925.1	68.2	947.8	64.7	963.3	61.5	958.0	64.2
Russians	92.7	8.2	240.2	20.1	334.6	24.6	408.8	27.9	474.8	30.3	428.4	28.7
Ukrainians	–	–	15.8	1.3	28.1	2.1	36.0	2.5	48.3	3.1	39.6	2.7
Belorussians	–	–	10.9	0.9	18.7	1.4	23.5	1.6	27.7	1.8	23.1	1.6
Finns	1.1	0.1	16.7	1.4	18.5	1.4	17.6	1.2	16.6	1.1	14.5	1.0
Jews	4.4	0.4	5.4	0.5	5.3	0.4	5.0	0.3	4.6	0.3	2.9	0.2
Germans	16.3	1.5	0.7	0.1	7.9	0.6	3.9	0.3	3.5	0.2	1.7	0.1
Latvians	5.4	0.5	2.9	0.2	3.3	0.2	4.0	0.3	3.1	0.2	2.8	0.2
Swedes	7.6	0.7	–	–	–	–	–	–	–	–	–	–
Others	5.4	0.5	11.5	1.0	14.6	1.1	17.9	1.2	23.8	1.5	20.6	1.4
Total[c]	1,126.4	100.1	1,196.8	100.1	1,356.1	100.0	1,464.5	100.0	1,565.7	100.0	1,491.6	100.1

Notes: [a]Prewar borders. [b]Estimate. [c]Due to rounding off totals are not always 100.0%.

Sources: Egil Levits, "Die demographische Situation in der UdSSR und in den baltischen Staaten unter besonderer Berücksichtigung von nationalen und sprachsoziologischen Aspekten," *Acta Baltica*, 21 (1981), 63–4; *Eesti arvudes 1920–1935* (Tallinn: Riigi Statistika Keskbüroo, 1937), p. 12; Riina Kionka, "Migration to and from Estonia," *Report on the USSR* 2, no. 37 (1990), 20; Kalev Katus, "Rahvus: sakslane; elukoht: Eesti," *Aja Puls*, no. 22 (1990), 10; Ene Tiit, "Eesti rahvastik ja selle probleemid," *Akadeemia*, 5 (1993), 2118; *Rahvastikustatistika Teatmik*, no. 3 (1995), 22-23, 26-27.

Table 9.2 *Demographic trends in Estonia since the 1950s*

	1950s	1970s	1980s
Percentage of population	(1951)	(1979)	(1989)
Rural	50.4	30.6	28.5
Urban	49.6	69.4	71.5
Average annual rates of	(1951–61)	(1971–79)	(1980–90)
population growth (%)	1.0	0.7	0.7
Age distribution (%)	(1959)	(1979)	(1989)
15–24	14.3[a]	15.1	13.8
25–49	34.8	35.7	34.8
50–59	11.9	11.3	12.3
Over 60	15.1	16.3	16.8
Levels of education[b] (%)		(1979)	(1989)
Primary	n.a.	28.3	18.0
Secondary	n.a.	58.0	66.6
Post-secondary	n.a.	9.8	13.6

Notes: [a]Ages 16–24. [b]Indicates attainment of completed or partial education at each level among persons over 15 years of age.

Sources: US Department of Commerce, *Statistical Abstracts of the United States*; Paul S. Shoup, *The East European and Soviet Data Handbook*; UNESCO, *Statistical Yearbooks*; United Nations, *Demographic Yearbooks*; *Itogi vsesoiuznoi perepisi naseleniia 1959 goda: Estonskaia SSR* (Tallinn: Gosstatizdat, 1962), p. 18; *Eesti Vabariigi maakondade, linnade ja alevite rahvastik*, vol. 1 (Tallinn: Eesti Vabariigi Statistikaamet, 1990), p. 92.

contrast to the gradual movement to the cities in the interwar independence era, the urban population increased at an astonishing rate during the Stalin years, corresponding to what can rightly be called the forced industrialization of Estonia. The pace of urbanization slowed down substantially in the post-Stalin period and reached culmination in the 1980s. In the first half of the 1990s, a slight decline began, reflecting above all the out-migration of Russians and other non-Estonians, and this trend can be expected to continue for the foreseeable future.

With regard to ethnic composition, the Estonian proportion in the cities, which had begun a steady increase in the nineteenth century, reached a historical peak in the 1930s and during World War II. Thereafter, a precipitous fall in the Estonian share took place during the decades of Soviet rule, even more rapidly than in the republic as a whole, since the great majority of East Slavic immigrants settled in the cities, especially Tallinn and northeastern Estonia. In the first half of the 1990s, once again reflecting the

Table 9.3 *Ethnic composition of urban population in Estonia, 1922–95*

	Urban residents as % of total population	% of urban residents[c] Estonians	Russians
1922[a]	25.0[c]	82.3	8.1
1934[a]	28.7[c]	85.5	7.0
1940[b]	33.6[d]	n.a.	n.a.
1945[b]	31.3[d]	n.a.	n.a.
1950[b]	47.1[d]	n.a.	n.a.
1959[a]	56.4[e]	61.9	30.8
1970[a]	64.7[e]	57.5	33.9
1979[a]	69.4[e]	54.8	36.6
1989[a]	71.5[e]	51.2	39.0
1995[b]	70.0[f]	53.3	38.0

Sources: [a]Census data. [b]Estimate according to postwar borders. [c]Toivo U. Raun, *Estonia and the Estonians*, 2nd ed. (Stanford: Hoover Institution Press, 1991), pp. 248–9. Estimate for 1995: *Postimees* (Tartu), 20 January 1996, p. 3. [d]Rein Taagepera, "Baltic Population Changes, 1950–1980," *Journal of Baltic Studies*, 12 (1981), 40. [e]*Statistika Aastaraamat 1994* (Tallinn: Eesti Statistikaamet, 1994) p. 45. [f]*Statistika Aastaraamat 1995* (Tallinn: Eesti Statistikaamet, 1995), p. 40.

out-migration of Russians and other non-Estonians, the Estonian proportion of the urban population showed a slight increase for the first time since World War II. In 1995, 91 percent of the non-Estonians in Estonia lived in the urban areas while 9 percent resided in the countryside; for Estonians, the corresponding figures were 60 percent urban and 40 percent rural.[5] In the 1930s, nearly two-thirds of the working population in the country was engaged in agricultural occupations, but this proportion shifted drastically under Soviet rule, falling to 26.5 percent (including forestry) in 1960 and further to 13.5 percent in 1980. The share of industrial workers in the labor force peaked at about 35 percent in the late 1960s; thereafter, the major occupational growth areas were services, health, and education.[6]

Historical background

Even a cursory overview of the background to recent political developments in Estonia must begin with the Estonian national movement in the second half of the nineteenth century, when the territory that became twentieth-century Estonia formed the northern half of the Baltic Provinces of the Russian Empire. With some important variations the Estonian case followed a similar pattern to that of others in central and eastern Europe at the time.[7] Two distinctive features, in particular, stand out, especially in view of their significance for later developments: a very high level of literacy, clearly related to Estonia's Protestant (Lutheran) religious heritage,[8] and an important tradition of social mobilization, especially through the establishment of grass-roots cultural and economic organizations, beginning in the 1860s when tsarist policy on such local initiatives was relaxed.[9]

Given the authoritarian nature of the tsarist regime, opportunities for political participation were limited, but the extension – in 1877 – of the 1870 municipal reform to the Baltic Provinces afforded the growing Estonian middle class a new arena in which to acquire political experience. By the early twentieth century Estonian elites increasingly gained control of northern Baltic urban governments, including the future capital of Tallinn in 1904.[10] The Revolution of 1905 permitted Estonian aspirations for cultural and political autonomy in a democratized Russian federation to come out into the open, setting the tone for Estonian political goals until the end of the tsarist regime.[11] Participation in the four State Dumas (1906–17), especially the experience of the electoral process itself, provided yet another opportunity for Estonian political education in the waning years of the Russian Empire.

Before the collapse of the Soviet Union in 1991, the key period in Estonia's previous political development was the interwar independence era (1918–40). In contrast to the other regions of the former USSR, Estonia and the other two Baltic states were able to establish and maintain an independent existence for a significant length of time following the fall of the tsarist regime. Aided by a favorable location on the Baltic Sea, Estonia received important support from Scandinavia and Great Britain at key points in its struggle for independence in the aftermath of the Russian Revolution, and the collapse and temporary weakness of both Germany and Russia afforded a unique window of opportunity. Nevertheless, these external factors cannot be viewed in isolation from the internal readiness of a maturing Estonian national movement to take advantage of the situation.[12]

As elsewhere in East Central Europe, the record of the interwar era in Estonia was mixed, but these years did signify the beginning of a modern civic culture that to a large extent survived the subsequent tribulations of Soviet rule. The Constitution of 1920 reflected the democratic idealism of the immediate postwar period and established a strictly parliamentary system with no independently elected executive. Instead, the Riigikogu (State Assembly) selected the riigivanem (literally "state elder") who served both as prime minister and head of state. The principle of the sovereignty of the people was emphasized in provisions for referendum and legislative initiative by demand of 25,000 voters as well as the requirement that constitutional amendments be approved only by referendum. The Riigikogu was elected for a three-year term by universal male and female suffrage by voters twenty years of age and older.[13]

This system worked reasonably well in the economically stable 1920s, although critics on the right decried the virtual non-existence of the executive branch. However, the uncertainties caused by the Depression in the early 1930s raised political passions to new heights. In 1933, frustrated by the country's economic problems and exasperated with the ineffectual parliament, Estonian voters overwhelmingly approved a presidentialist constitution proposed by a powerful mass movement on the far right of the political spectrum, led by the League of Veterans of the Estonian War of Independence (*Eesti Vabadussõjalaste Liit*). The leadership and most active support for this movement came from the urban middle class, which especially feared loss of status in uncertain times. In March 1934, before elections under the Constitution of 1933 could be held, Prime Minister Konstantin Päts of the Farmers' Party carried out a bloodless coup that ushered in an authoritarian regime lasting until the eclipse of Estonian independence in June 1940. Päts's main constituency was clearly in the rural areas, but – like the Veterans – he also had significant appeal among business and military circles. By the standards of the 1930s Päts's rule was relatively mild, and he even amnestied nearly all of his opponents on both the right and the left in 1938.[14] In 1937, Päts had the third constitution of the interwar era drawn up, creating the illusion of renewed participation with a bicameral legislature (political parties remained illegal), but actually strengthening the presidential system even further. Although the extent to which civic culture struck deep roots in the liberal democratic era can be debated, it is clear that Päts's authoritarian regime stunted Estonia's political evolution in the late 1930s.[15]

Following the restoration of independence in August–September 1991, as the Estonian Constitutional Assembly deliberated in the ensuing months, it explicitly took into account the country's constitutional development in the 1920s and 1930s as it assessed future options.[16] Some political parties active in Estonia in the late 1980s and early 1990s, especially those representing the rural population, have emphasized their continuity from forerunners or namesakes in the interwar era, but the majority have regarded themselves as entirely new entities.[17] In most cases, it was felt that too much had changed since 1934, when political parties in a democratic system were last legal, to focus on the continuity factor.

Legacy of the Communist era

Although there is no doubt that the nearly five decades of Soviet rule had a highly negative impact on Estonian political culture, the more intriguing questions involve the extent to which elements of the pre-Soviet legacy survived and to what degree non-Soviet influences penetrated the ostensibly closed system and reached the population of Estonia. In the postwar Stalin era the idea of independence was kept alive by an Estonian guerrilla movement, the so-called "forest brethren" (Est. *metsavennad*), based in the thickly wooded parts of the country.[18] The guerrillas had no illusions about defeating Soviet power on their own, but they sought to hold out until the Western powers pressured the USSR to permit the restoration of an independent Estonia. Although the movement failed to achieve its objectives, it could not have lasted for nearly a decade without substantial support from the Estonian population at large.

The early post-Stalin years in Estonia witnessed a cultural rebirth from the wasteland of Stalinism, Khrushchev's experimentation with economic decentralization, and the emergence of the illusory hope that some form of political autonomy would be possible within the Soviet system. The invasion of Czechoslovakia in 1968 and the recentralizing tendencies that increasingly appeared in the Brezhnev era dashed hopes for evolutionary change and, as elsewhere in the Soviet Union, gave rise in Estonia to a dissent movement. On an all-Union scale Estonian dissent in the 1970s and early 1980s certainly displayed above-average activism, including appeals to the United Nations for the restoration of Estonian independence.[19] However, the number of individuals willing to risk the consequences of outright opposition remained perforce limited since the threat of murderous repression still existed in the post-Stalin era, as the imprisonment and subsequent death of the dissident Jüri Kukk illustrates.[20]

The rapid emergence of grass-roots activism and initiative in the Gorbachev era raises the larger question of what processes were transpiring in Estonian society in the immediately preceding years. Any thorough answer to this question must await the results of considerably more research than is now available, but a useful beginning can be made by focusing on the impact of the so-called "Letter of the Forty," a signed, open letter sent in October 1980 to three Soviet newspapers by forty leading Estonian intellectuals, some with strong communist credentials. Written in response to the rough treatment youthful demonstrators received at the hands of the police, the letter emphasized the troubled ethnic relations in Estonia and the declining status of the Estonian language in public life, education, and the media. It sought to explain Estonian sensitivity regarding the issues of language and culture and concluded that "the native inhabitants of Estonia . . . [should] always have the final word on the destiny of their land and people."[21]

What is noteworthy here is that the authors, who included writers, academicians, actors, and artists, among others, felt driven to take a public stand at the seeming low point of Estonian morale in the late Brezhnev era in order to avoid a "repeat" of the events of 1940 when Estonian leaders failed to put up any resistance to Soviet pressure. They also were clearly emboldened by the success of Solidarity in Poland only a few months earlier in 1980. Even more striking was the response within Estonian society. The letter circulated in literally thousands of samizdat copies, and the signers, who apparently were protected from any harsh repression by their numbers and high profile, were lionized at public appearances and at more intimate gatherings.[22] In view of the intrusive nature of Soviet rule, it would be difficult to argue that any substantial elements of a civil society (in the sense of autonomous structures operating outside state control) existed in Estonia around 1980, but the widespread response evoked by the Letter of the Forty suggests that the pre-1940 legacy had not been eclipsed and that civic culture in Estonia was not dead but perhaps only being held in reserve.

A unique feature of the decades of Soviet rule in Estonia was the window on the West that the republic had through its close ties to Finland. Finnish visitors began arriving in Estonia in the early post-Stalin years, and by 1965 a regular boat connection was opened between Tallinn and Helsinki, a highly unusual relationship for the USSR with a capitalist country. Finnish tourists brought Western newspapers and literature, including some works by Estonian exile writers living in the West. Academics and other intellectuals were able to establish contacts with colleagues in Finland and were often able to keep abreast of developments in their field in the West. Most importantly, Finnish television was available in the northern third of Estonia, providing daily access to Western news reports and programming. The Estonian and Finnish languages are linguistically close enough that a native speaker of Estonian can gain at least a passive knowledge of Finnish by very little effort. The Soviet authorities presumably tolerated the Estonian-Finnish connection because of Finland's neutral political stance and the hard currency revenue brought by Finnish tourists. At the very end of the Brezhnev era a campaign that began in the local Estonian press against the negative influence of Finnish television was quickly called off, suggesting ambivalence among Soviet officials and perhaps reflecting a loss of confidence in the existing system among the established elites.[23]

Periodization and overview, 1987–96

Estonia's political evolution towards democratization since 1987 can be divided into three periods: (1) the pre-transition years (Spring 1987–August 20, 1991), characterized by a broad movement for renewed self-determination that began with the goal of autonomy within a reformed Soviet system, but which moved rather quickly in the direction of complete independence; (2) a relatively brief period of transition (August 20, 1991–September 20, 1992), covering the thirteen months between the failed Soviet coup – and the international recognition of the restoration of Estonian independence – and the first democratic elections for parliament and president which took place soon after approval of a new constitution in June 1992; and (3) an era of democratic consolidation (September 20, 1992 to the present) when the new constitution was actually put into practice and the division of powers between the various branches of government began to take concrete shape, most importantly in the evolving relations between the Riigikogu and the president.

Perhaps the key theme in Estonia that needs to be stressed throughout the eight-year period under review is the non-violent nature of the transition from Soviet rule to a developing democratic system despite the existence of considerable ethnic tensions and much economic hardship. A number of factors contributed to the peacefulness of this process. First, the role of Estonia's previous historical development and inherited traditions should be noted. The use of violence was never part of modern Estonian political culture, even during the authoritarian Päts regime of the 1930s. In the twentieth century Estonians looked above all to Scandinavia, especially Finland, as a model of evolutionary and stable political development. Under Soviet rule Estonians showed particular admiration for non-violent reform movements in Eastern Europe, especially the Prague Spring and Solidarity. Second, the ethnic tensions in the country are a problem of recent origin. As noted above, Estonia was virtually a monoethnic entity in 1945. Since Russians and other non-Estonians are overwhelmingly recent immigrants, there are no deep-seated historical antagonisms to contend with among the various ethnic groups in contrast to several other parts of the postcommunist world such as the Balkans or the Caucasus. In this situation the credit for the avoidance of violence should go to Estonians and non-Estonians alike.[24]

Third, it is clear that the potential for violence was greatest during the pre-transition years at the end of the Gorbachev era as the Soviet system was in the process of collapse. After August 1991 time was on the side of non-violent development, as indicated by public opinion polls that increasingly showed declining tensions between Estonians and non-Estonians. For example, a comparison of two polls taken in December 1988 and February 1993 indicates that the proportion of Estonians classifying ethnic relations as "poor/very poor" declined from 55 percent to 12 percent while among non-Estonians it fell from 39 percent to 9 percent. Similarly, in November–December 1994, 83 percent of ethnic Russians polled in Estonia said they had never had any sort of conflict with Estonians, and only 7 percent felt they had ever suffered any discrimination.[25]

Equally significant in contributing to the peaceful transition in Estonia was the favorable foreign policy situation the country enjoyed. Estonia had no territorial problems or serious disputes of any kind with its Baltic neighbors, Latvia and Lithuania. Indeed the movements for independence in the late 1980s fostered a new spirit of cooperation among the Baltic peoples, in striking contrast to the interwar era and the crisis year of 1939–40. Before the restoration of independence the strongest vehicle for this cooperation was the popular front movements in the three Baltic republics. After August 1991 the Baltic governments and parliaments established formal institutions of partnership such as the Baltic Assembly and the Baltic Council of Ministers.[26] Estonia also benefitted from the positive attitude of the Scandinavian states towards the restoration of Baltic independence and the strong Scandinavian engagement in supporting Baltic integration with the West. In contrast to the earlier twentieth century, especially the decades of Soviet rule when they adopted a hands-off policy toward their Baltic neighbors, the Scandinavian states now began to view the fate of the Baltic countries as an integral part of their own security. The presence of three Nordic countries (Denmark, Sweden, and Finland) in the European Union by January 1995 also strengthened the Baltic lobby for eventual membership in this key international organization.[27]

The broader international context was favorable as well since Estonia and the other two Baltic states received significant backing from the major European powers, the United States, and leading international organizations. Although there was much ambivalence on the Baltic question among Western leaders while Gorbachev was still in power, the Baltic states clearly received the strongest international support for their political aspirations among former Soviet republics, mainly because of their previous membership in the international community during the 1920s and 1930s. Most importantly, Western diplomatic aid and lobbying with Moscow helped keep any potential Soviet or Russian interventionism at bay, and it was a key factor in promoting the Estonian-Russian agreement on the final withdrawal of ex-Soviet troops from Estonia on August 31, 1994.[28] Estonian membership in such organizations as the Conference on Security and Cooperation in Europe (as of October 1991) and the Council of Europe (as of May 1993), especially the testimony of experts from these bodies, also helped deflect Moscow's criticism of the treatment of the ethnic Russian community in Estonia. Finally, although relations with Moscow remained unsettled in the late 1980s and the early 1990s, the weakness of the imploding Soviet Union and the postcommunist Russian state (recalling a similar situation at the time of the Revolution of 1917 and its aftermath) meant that Estonia was able to assert its independence with relative equanimity and avoid being drawn or forced into the Commonwealth of Independent States.

Following the withdrawal of ex-Soviet troops, the major unresolved issue between Estonia and Russia in the postindependence years was the border question. A quick solution of the problem – if Estonia had agreed to yield the great majority of the disputed territory – might have been possible in the early months after August 1991, but Estonian public opinion was not yet ready to make such sweeping concessions. In the ensuing years Russian foreign policy assumed a more intransigent stance, while Estonian public opinion moved in the opposite direction, as it increasingly recognized the consequences of reacquiring lands populated almost entirely by non-Estonians. Estonian politicians also became more willing to accept the current border, with some minor adjustments, since it could then be secured more effectively against smugglers and organized criminal elements and a resolution of the border issue would make Estonia a more viable candidate for membership in the European Union. The major sticking point was sharply divergent views of the Peace of Tartu between Estonia and Soviet Russia in February 1920. The Estonian side sought affirmation of Estonian independence through the Russian side's acceptance of Article 2 of the treaty according to which Russia renounced any claims to Estonia in perpetuity. On the other hand, the Russian side maintained that the Peace of Tartu had lost its validity in 1940, suggesting a desire to keep its options open for the future.[29] Nevertheless, although clearly an irritant, the border issue did not destabilize Estonian-Russian relations, and it did not pose an obstacle in practice to the process of democratization in Estonia.

The Independence Movement, 1987–91

The first signs of social mobilization during the glasnost era in Estonia appeared in the form of environmental protests in Spring 1987, especially by students at Tartu University, against the threat of expanded phosphate mining in northern Estonia, and by the anniversary of the Molotov–Ribbentrop Pact on August 23 of that year, Estonian dissidents had organized a major demonstration that publicly questioned the legitimacy of Soviet rule for the first time.[30] However, more characteristic of the early glasnost period was a proposal in September 1987 by four intellectuals for self-management and autonomy in the Estonian economy, that is, radical economic reform *within* the Soviet system.[31]

By 1988, political organizations outside the Communist Party itself began to appear in Estonia. In terms of size and influence the most important was the Popular Front of Estonia (PFE), the first organization of its kind in the Soviet Union. Led by reformist communists, the PFE began with the rather modest aim of channeling the reawakening civic energies of the population and pushing the leadership of the Communist Party of Estonia (CPE) towards fundamental reform, and it sought to play a stabilizing and centrist role in the republic's re-emerging political life.[32] Two other notable political forces that appeared in 1988 were on opposite sides of the spectrum. Led by former dissidents, the Estonian National Independence Party unequivocally advocated the restoration of Estonian independence, stressing the illegality of Soviet rule according to international law. In contrast, the International Movement of

Workers of the ESSR (Intermovement, for short), based to a large extent in the huge all-Union enterprises in Estonia and led by their managers, decried the allegedly nationalist character of the PFE and claimed to represent the Russian and Russophone population of the republic.[33]

During the second half of 1988, the CPE was swept along by the reformist impulses encouraged by the Popular Front, especially after Vaino Väljas replaced the Brezhnev-era appointee Karl Vaino as first secretary in June. Väljas proved instrumental in engineering the nearly unanimous passage of a declaration on sovereignty (that is, the primacy of republican laws over all-Union ones) by the ESSR Supreme Soviet in November, the first such resolution in the Soviet Union.[34] After this high point, however, the CPE's role began to wane as the goal of the movement for change moved increasingly from autonomy to complete independence.

In February 1989, a rival grass-roots movement to the PFE, the Estonian Citizens' Committees, appeared on the scene, backed by the Estonian National Independence Party, the Estonian Heritage Society (founded in December 1987 for the purpose of reconnecting Estonians with a past from which they had been increasingly cut off under Soviet rule), and the Estonian Christian Union. The Citizens' Committees, representing the right wing of the emerging Estonian political spectrum, feared that the Popular Front would make too many concessions to Moscow and the existing authorities, leading to a watering down of the concept of Estonian independence. Basing its activity on the principle of legal continuity from the Republic of Estonia of the 1920s and 1930s, the Citizens' Committees organized a massive voluntary registration campaign of citizens of pre-1940 Estonia, that is, individuals who were citizens of independent Estonia and their descendants. By February 1990, the movement had registered over 70 percent of the ethnic Estonian population as citizens and clearly helped push public opinion toward the goal of full independence.[35]

Beginning in early 1989, new opportunities for political mobilization appeared with the emergence of increasingly freer elections, as traditional Soviet practice began to fade or was simply ignored. At the end of March, the first republicwide, multicandidate elections in the history of the Estonian SSR were held in order to select delegates to the new Congress of People's Deputies in Moscow. For the 36 available seats there were 119 candidates, of whom 61.5 percent were Estonians. Although no longer compelled to vote, a striking 87.1 percent of the electorate participated, and Estonians, mainly those associated with the Popular Front, won 29 of the 36 seats (80.6 percent).[36] Further experience in pluralistic electoral politics followed shortly thereafter in local government elections in December 1989, the vote for representatives to the non-Soviet Congress of Estonia in February–March 1990, and elections to the Estonian SSR Supreme Soviet in March 1990.

Events elsewhere in the Soviet bloc, especially the withering away of the Brezhnev doctrine in Eastern Europe in summer 1989, and Moscow's vacillation on any genuine autonomy as well as its intemperate threats following the massive Baltic demonstration on the fiftieth anniversary of the Molotov–Ribbentrop Pact in August 1989 also fueled Estonian sentiment for independence.[37] The competition between the Popular Front and the Citizens' Committees during 1989 already revealed the basic fault line in Estonian politics between what may be called the *fundamentalists*, who argued on the basis of principle and demanded the strict return to the status quo before Soviet rule, and the *pragmatists*, who proceeded from the concrete situation confronting them and were willing to make compromises in a less than ideal world. By October 1989, the Popular Front explicitly endorsed independence, mirroring the shift in public opinion on this issue. From September 1989 to May 1990, support for independence among ethnic Estonians increased from 64 to 96 percent; among non-Estonians it grew from 9 to 26 percent.[38]

The early months of 1990 witnessed a crucial struggle over who should lead the movement for renewed independence in the next phase. On the one hand, the campaign of the Estonian Citizens' Committees culminated in elections (only citizens of pre-1940 Estonia and their descendants could vote) at the end of February to the non-Soviet Congress of Estonia, an alternative parliament that quickly claimed the moral and legal right to negotiate independence. On the other hand, the Popular Front, which dominated the newly and relatively democratically elected ESSR Supreme Soviet (four seats were reserved for the Soviet military in Estonia), argued that Moscow would be more willing to negotiate with an existing institution.[39] On March 30, the Supreme Soviet (now more appropriately translated from the Estonian Ülemnõukogu as "Supreme Council") declared the beginning of a transition period "lasting until the formation of the constitutional organs of state power of the Republic of Estonia."[40] In the event, the two bodies agreed to cooperate initially, and there was substantial overlap in their composition. However, the Supreme Council possessed the clear advantage of commanding administrative and legislative authority within the existing system, and it dominated the day-to-day political life.

For his part, Gorbachev refused to negotiate seriously on the issue of Estonian or Baltic independence, clearly fearing the consequences of any territorial changes in the USSR, and a long stalemate occurred between Tallinn and Moscow, to be ended only by the abortive August 1991 coup. Before that, there was one final poll in March on the issue of restoring independence after Estonia had boycotted Gorbachev's all-Union referendum on the future of the USSR a few weeks earlier. All permanent residents were eligible to participate, and the result was a 77.8 percent "yes" vote, including nearly all ethnic Estonians and perhaps 30 percent of the non-Estonians.[41] Ironically, the failed August coup resolved the impasse between Estonia and the waning Soviet Union. On August 20, the Supreme Council unilaterally affirmed Estonian independence since, as it noted, the coup had rendered bilateral negotiations with the Soviet Union impossible. Following talks with representatives of the Congress of Estonia, it was agreed that both the Congress and the Supreme Council would send representatives to a Constitutional Assembly "for the purpose of drafting the Constitution of the Republic of Estonia and presenting it to the people for a referendum." Parliamentary elections were to be held in 1992 on the basis of the new constitution.[42]

During 1990, especially following the meaningful elections to the Congress of Estonia and the new Supreme Council early in the year, the political spectrum in Estonia began to fill out. It now made sense to compete in the political area since the existing authorities were no longer able or willing to block spontaneous political activity. The new parties and groupings on the right were typically closely associated with the Congress of Estonia while those in the center or on the moderate left were often offshoots of the Popular Front. The major political casualty in 1990 was the CPE, which was stripped of its official "leading role" in public life by the Supreme Soviet in February and then lost over half of its membership – mainly ethnic Estonians – during the following year. By January 1991, what remained of the party formally split into pro-independence and pro-CPSU branches.[43]

In view of the delicacy of the issue, the pre-independence Estonian government postponed treatment of the citizenship question for fear of committing itself to a long-term policy while the status of the large non-Estonian population in the country remained unresolved. Following the restoration of independence, in November 1991, Estonia reinstated its 1938 citizenship law, meaning that all individuals who were citizens in June 1940 and their descendants, regardless of ethnic background, were automatically considered citizens. However, since nearly all Russians and other non-Estonians in 1991 were immigrants, those desiring citizenship had to go through a three-year naturalization procedure (counting from March 30, 1990, when Estonia declared the start of a transition period to renewed independence), including demonstration of a modest level of competence in Estonian.[44] In practice, this solution meant that the great majority of non-Estonians were excluded from voting in national elections at least until April 1993.

The Constitution of 1992

As noted above, the Constitutional Assembly was created during the crisis of the August 1991 coup through negotiations between the Supreme Council and the Congress of Estonia at a time when the need for unity in the face of threatening developments in Moscow seemed paramount. After further talks each institution elected 30 members from its ranks to the Constitutional Assembly, resulting in the following approximate breakdown: Popular Front – c. 20, national radicals – c. 20, moderates and reform communists – c. 13, and ethnic Russians (all from the Supreme Council) – 7.[45] Before the August agreement some members of the Estonian National Independence Party, the leading force in the Congress of Estonia, supported the strict restoration of last constitution of pre-1940 Estonia (the Päts constitution of 1937) as a logical application of the principle of legal continuity. However, the undemocratic aspects of the 1937 Constitution (for example, a provision allowing the president to appoint one-fourth of the members of the upper house of parliament and giving him considerable influence over the rest of its composition) and its strongly presidentialist character rendered its renewal problematic. The compromise of August 20 essentially meant that the Constitutional Assembly would create a new document although it would draw on the models and experience of the 1920s and 1930s.[46]

The Constitutional Assembly began its deliberations in September 1991 and accepted as a working document – by a bare majority – a draft based on the Constitution of 1920, but purged of its extreme parliamentarism. Most of the changes made in the next few months were intended to satisfy the sizeable minority of delegates who wanted a stronger executive branch. In mid-December the amended draft was made public and comments invited. The Assembly took into account two recommendations that repeatedly appeared: (1) it changed the name of the head of state from riigivanem (as used in the 1920 Constitution) to president, and (2) as a one-time compromise, it allowed the first presidential election to be direct.[47] On June 28, 1992, 66.3 percent of the eligible voters (that is, citizens of Estonia 18 years of age and older) went to the polls and approved the new constitution and an accompanying law of implementation by an overwhelming margin: 91.2 percent "yes" and 8.8 percent "no."[48]

The Constitution of 1992, drawing on the liberal democratic tradition of the 1920s, assigned political supremacy to a revived Riigikogu, a unicameral parliament with 101 members elected for a four-year term. The Riigikogu possesses ultimate authority over all key political decisions, including legislation, treaties with foreign countries, the appointment of the prime minister and other leading officials, the longevity of governments, and – in case of need – declaration of a state of emergency in the country. Aside from the one-time compromise noted above in the 1992 elections, parliament also elects the president by a two-thirds majority vote for a five-year term. The president, who must be a citizen by birth and at least 40 years of age, may not be elected for more than two consecutive terms. It was the intention of the Constitutional Assembly's majority that the powers of the president be more ceremonial than real, but it is noteworthy that he represents the country in international relations, has the first two choices in nominating a prime minister, can force parliament to reconsider legislation, can initiate amendments to the constitution, and acts as the supreme commander of the national defense. The judiciary is independent of the legislative and executive branches, but both the president and the Riigikogu participate in the appointment of judges to the State Court and to lower ones. The Constitution of 1992 also contains an extensive section (48 articles) entitled "Fundamental Rights, Liberties, and Duties," including the basic freedoms outlined in the bill of rights in the US Constitution.[49]

Evolution of the political system since 1992

Following the September 1992 parliamentary and presidential elections, the new political system began to evolve in practice. As agreed beforehand, both the Supreme Council and the Congress of Estonia liquidated their existence in the last days of September, and the new Riigikogu assumed power on September 30. During its first working session on October 5, parliament elected the writer and former foreign minister Lennart Meri (b. 1929) president (discussed below) since no candidate had received a majority in the popular vote. Meri nominated Mart Laar (b. 1960), the head of the most successful electoral alliance – Fatherland – with 28.7 percent of the seats in the Riigikogu (see table 9.4), as the candidate for the post of prime minister. He was able to form a three-party coalition (Fatherland, the Moderates, and the Estonian National Independence Party) with fifty-three seats and was sworn into office on October 21.[50]

Laar's cabinet represented a new, often very youthful political generation that with few exceptions was also free of any previous communist past. In contrast, its predecessors in the transition period following August 1991 tended to be dominated by reformist ex-communists such as Edgar Savisaar (b. 1950), a Popular Front leader and prime minister from April 1990 to January 1992, and Tiit Vähi (b. 1947), prime minister during January–October 1992.[51] Despite only commanding a bare majority in the Riigikogu and plagued by splits within Fatherland, the Laar government managed to stay in office for nearly two years until September 28, 1994, setting a record for longevity in comparison to its predecessors in the previous democratic era (1920–34). The vote of no-confidence against Laar

Table 9.4 *Riigikogu elections in Estonia, 1992*

Party or electoral alliance	Votes	% votes[a]	Seats	% seats
Fatherland[b]	100,828	22.0	29	28.7
Secure Home[c]	62,329	13.6	17	16.8
Popular Front	56,124	12.3	15	14.9
Moderates[d]	44,577	9.7	12	11.9
Estonian National Independence Party	40,260	8.8	10	9.9
Independent Royalists	32,638	7.1	8	7.9
Estonian Citizen	31,553	6.9	8	7.9
Union of Estonian Pensioners	17,011	3.7	0	–
Farmers' Union	13,356	2.9	0	–
Greens[e]	12,009	2.6	1	1.0
Estonian Entrepreneurial Party[e]	10,946	2.4	1	1.0
Left Alternative[f]	7,374	1.6	0	–
Others	29,242	6.4	0	–
Total	458,247	100.0	101	100.0

Notes: [a]5 percent threshold for representation as a party. [b]Five-party alliance. [c]Three-party alliance, including Estonian Coalition Party. [d]Estonian Social Democrats and Estonian Rural Center Party. [e]Received one seat by direct election. [f]Former Estonian Communist Party.

Source: *Vabariigi Presidendi ja Riigikogu valimised 1992: Dokumente ja materjale* (Tallinn: Eesti Vabariigi Valimiskomisjon, 1992), pp. 96–8, 138–39.

in the Riigikogu was 60–27, as the opposition cited his "incorrect handling of state affairs" as the main reason – for example, a controversial arms deal with Israel and the secret sale of surplus Russian rubles to Chechnia.[52] Although the government crisis lasted more than five weeks, largely because the Riigikogu rejected President Meri's first nominee for prime minister as being too close to the policies of the previous government, constitutional procedures were strictly followed throughout the transition. On November 4, Andres Tarand (b. 1940) of the Moderates, previously minister of the environment in the Laar cabinet, formed a new government based on the same parties as represented in the previous coalition. With regular parliamentary elections scheduled for early March 1995, all parties in the Riigikogu preferred to see Tarand leading a caretaker cabinet for the next few months rather than face the prospect of special elections.[53]

Following the Riigikogu elections on March 5, 1995 (see table 9.5), President Meri once again turned to the leader of the senior partner of the winning electoral alliance, in this case Tiit Vähi of the Estonian Coalition Party, as his nominee for prime minister. With a solid forty-one seats in

Table 9.5 *Riigikogu elections in Estonia, 1995*

Party or electoral alliance	Votes	% votes[a]	Seats	% seats
Coalition Party & Rural Union[b]	174,248	32.2	41	40.6
Estonian Reform Party[c]	87,531	16.2	19	18.8
Estonian Center Party[d]	76,634	14.2	16	15.8
Fatherland & Estonian National Independence Party	42,493	7.9	8	7.9
Moderates[e]	32,381	6.0	6	5.9
Our Home is Estonia[f]	31,763	5.9	6	5.9
Rightists[g]	27,053	5.0	5	5.0
Better Estonia & Estonian Citizen	19,529	3.6	0	–
Future of Estonia Party	13,907	2.6	0	–
Justice[h]	12,248	2.3	0	–
Others	22,912	4.1	0	–
Total	540,699	100.0	101	99.9

Notes: [a]5 percent threshold for representation as a party. [b]Alliance of five parties, two of which ran under Secure Home in 1992. [c]New party, including some members splitting off from Fatherland and Moderates. [d]Successor to Popular Front. [e]Estonian Social Democrats and Estonian Rural Center Party. [f]United People's Party of Estonia, Russian Party in Estonia, and Estonian Russian People's Party. [g]New party, split off from Fatherland. [h]Former Estonian Communist Party.

Sources: *Riigikogu Postimees* (Tartu), 21 March 1995, pp. 1, 8–9, 15; *Postimehe valimisteatmik 1995* (Tartu: "Postimees," 1995), pp. 31–32, 42, 47, 59–60.

parliament behind him, Vähi first approached the second-largest group in the new Riigikogu, the Estonian Reform Party (nineteen seats), but negotiations broke down over differences in economic policy. He then formed a two-party coalition with the Estonian Center Party (sixteen seats), which was sworn into office on April 17.[54] However, the new cabinet lasted less than six months, falling on October 11, the victim of a taping scandal involving Edgar Savisaar, its interior minister and the leader of the Center Party. A former prime minister and one of Estonia's most prominent politicians, Savisaar admitted taping conversations with other leading political figures, but refused to resign, arguing – without presenting any facts – that this practice was not unusual in the country. Especially damaging was the fact that the tapes were found on the premises of a shadowy private security agency, run by two former KGB agents, who had previous ties to Savisaar. In the end, Prime Minister Vähi dismissed Savisaar and then resigned himself, citing the damage to Estonia's image as a democratic state.[55]

Noting Vähi's appropriate solution to the crisis and recognizing the leading role of his Coalition Party in parliament, President Meri turned to him once more to form a new government. A quick agreement was achieved with the Reform Party, and the new cabinet, commanding 60 seats in the Riigikogu, took office on November 6. It remained to be seen, however, how stable the new governing coalition would be, given the continuing differences in economic policy priorities between the Reform Party and the Rural Union.[56] Thus, Estonia had four governments during the first three years of the functioning of the 1992 Constitution, and despite being buffeted by scandal more than once, the system worked relatively smoothly. In the long run, the taping scandal may contribute to the strengthening of democracy by encouraging politicians to abide by a stricter ethical code.

Clearly the most intriguing question in the evolution of the new political system in Estonia was the issue of parliamentary versus presidential power. Despite the intentions of the makers of the constitution, the Riigikogu found it difficult to play its assigned leading role in national politics, largely because of fragmentation and splits among the various political parties and blocs. Fatherland, initially the strongest force in the Laar government, split into three groups, illustrating the problem of electoral alliances successfully gaining votes, but finding it hard to agree on policy. In the Riigikogu elected in March 1995, fully fourteen parties were represented among 90 members (eleven of the 101 legislators had no party affiliation). Eleven of these parties had seven or fewer members of parliament, and six had only two each.[57]

As would be expected, the major beneficiary of this parliamentary weakness was the presidency. Starting in spring 1993, President Meri began to play an activist role in the legislative process, for example, forcing the Riigikogu to reconsider and effectively make changes in the controversial law on aliens in June–July 1993. In January 1994, Meri and the government clashed over Meri's reluctance to confirm some of the ministerial changes proposed by Prime Minister Laar, causing a temporary constitutional stalemate. Meri was forced to back down, but his action was another example of his seeking to interpret the constitution in order to enhance presidential powers.[58] Finally, Meri has also played a highly visible role in foreign policy, most notably in the strikingly successful negotiations with Boris Yeltsin at the end of July 1994 over the final withdrawal of ex-Soviet troops from Estonia.[59] After only a few years, constitutional traditions were still in the process of formation, but the early experience had shifted at least some power to the executive branch.

Electoral system and elections, 1992–96

Following experimentation with various approaches to parliamentary elections in the last few years of Soviet rule, Estonia established a new system for Riigikogu elections that stresses proportional representation and draws on the models of Finland and Germany. It combines the choice of individual candidates with the use of party or electoral alliance lists, drawn up by a given organization's leadership. Thus, each voter picks an individual candidate, but unless that candidate can win an individual mandate (a relatively rare occurrence: seventeen in 1992 and fifteen in 1995), the rank order set by the party or electoral alliance is all that matters.[60]

In general, candidates can be elected to the Riigikogu in one of three ways. First, there is the possibility of direct election, if a candidate is able to equal or surpass the "simple quota" in his electoral district. The simple quota is obtained by dividing the number of valid votes (each voter casts one vote for one candidate listed on the district ballot) in an entire district by the number of seats allocated to it.[61] Thus, for example, in District 1 in 1995, the simple quota was 5,314.25 (42,514 valid votes divided by 8), and two strong candidates exceeded this number, leaving the six remaining seats to be decided by other means.[62] Second, a candidate may be elected at the district level, if the total number of votes for his party exceeds one or more simple quotas and if he is near the top of his party's district list and received a total of individual votes equal to or surpassing 10 percent of the district's simple quota (thus, 531 in District 1 in 1995). There is the further restriction that only those parties or electoral alliances that achieved the threshold level of 5 percent of the national vote are eligible for distribution of seats at the district level. In 1995, thirty-four candidates received "district-level" seats (twenty-four in 1992). Third, a candidate may obtain a "compensation mandate" on the basis of national party or alliance lists, once again subject to the 5 percent threshold on the national level. The candidates in this category are typically the least popular with the voters, and they usually gain a seat in parliament because of their relatively high ranking on a given party's national list, a decision made by the party leadership. In both 1995 (fifty-two seats) and 1992 (sixty seats), the lion's share of mandates was allocated in this way. This method of distribution, a complex procedure using modified d'Hondt divisors, obviously favors the largest party.[63] Thus, Fatherland received 22.0 percent of the votes, but twenty-nine seats (28.7 percent) in 1992 while the Coalition Party and Rural Union obtained 32.2 of the votes, but fully forty-one seats (40.6 percent) in 1995.

The results of the two post-independence Riigikogu elections are presented in tables 9.4 and 9.5. In 1992, seventeen parties and electoral alliances along with 628 candidates competed for seats in parliament. In 1995, the number of parties and alliances was virtually the same (sixteen), but the number of candidates doubled (1,272).[64] In the two elections, the number of parties or alliances that achieved representation in the Riigikogu declined from nine to seven, suggesting at least some movement toward stabilization. The trend was also away from fringe or protest parties (for example, Estonian Citizen and the Independent Royalists), but the right side of the spectrum in parliament was more fragmented in 1995 than in 1992. Considerable voter dissatisfaction has been expressed with regard to an electoral system that requires voting for an individual, but allocates most seats by closed party lists and one that allows some candidates with a tiny popular vote to be elected.[65] Some minor adjustments were made between the two parliamentary elections, but the large parties in the Riigikogu have little incentive to make major changes. A positive sign was that the proportion of voters who remained unrepresented in parliament (that is, neither the candidate they voted for nor the party of that candidate achieved representation) declined from 14.6 percent in 1992 to 12.6 percent in 1995 (see tables 9.4 and 9.5).

A key difference between the two elections was the considerable growth in the number of eligible voters from 661,074 in 1992 to 766,626 in 1995, an increase of 16.0 percent. This change reflected the growing number of Russians and other non-Estonians who were acquiring citizenship, and it obviously made possible the electoral success in 1995 of Our Home Is Estonia (six seats), a Russian-based alliance.[66] Although their votes comprised just over 1 percent of the total cast, it is noteworthy that Estonian citizens permanently residing abroad (mainly World War II exiles and their descendants in the United States, Canada, and Sweden) did have an impact on the election.[67] Without the votes from abroad, the Rightists would have fallen short of the 5 percent national threshold, and the Fatherland-Estonian National Independence Party alliance received over 9 percent of its total vote from outside Estonia.[68]

As noted above, in view of the considerable sentiment in the country for direct election of the president, the Constitutional Assembly agreed to a one-time exception to the 1992 Constitution and permitted a popular vote in the first presidential elections in September 1992. However, if no candidate received a majority in the direct vote, the Riigikogu would decide between the two top vote-getters by a simple majority vote. As a further exception, candidates for this first election were nominated by the voting public; in order to achieve nomination a candidate had to obtain the signatures of 10,000 eligible voters. Four candidates were nominated: Lennart Meri, writer, diplomat, and former foreign minister in one of the transition governments; Lagle Parek (b. 1941), a former dissident and the only woman in the race; Arnold Rüütel (b. 1928), chair of the outgoing Supreme Council – the position he also held in the Estonian SSR Supreme Soviet since 1983; and Rein Taagepera (b. 1933), an exile political scientist teaching at both the University of California, Irvine and Tartu University.[69] The results of the popular vote were as follows: Rüütel – 41.8 percent, Meri – 29.5 percent, Taagepera – 23.4 percent, and Parek – 4.2 percent. Despite his communist past, Rüütel enjoyed wide popularity, especially in the rural areas. However, it seems clear that Taagepera, the candidate of the Popular Front, pulled enough votes away from Rüütel to force the election into the Riigikogu. Here, given the electoral victory of Fatherland and other groups on the right side of the spectrum, Meri's election was all but assured. Meri received fifty-nine votes to Rüütel's thirty-one (eleven ballots were invalid, presumably blank).[70]

As another one-time exception to the 1992 Constitution, the first president's term was slated to last four years instead of five. Thus, the next presidential elections were scheduled for fall 1996 according to the following format. To be nominated, a candidate must have the support of one-fifth of the members of parliament. For election, a two-thirds majority of the Riigikogu is required, but if no victor emerges in three rounds of voting, an Electoral College, consisting of the Riigikogu and at least one member of each local government council in Estonia, is convened. The decision in the Electoral College is made by majority vote of those present.[71] It is note-worthy that public opinion has continued to support the direct election of the president, for example, a striking 86 percent of those queried in a poll in December 1995, and it is possible that a constitutional amendment on this issue will be passed in the near future. However, such a change could only go into effect with the third post-independence presidential term, beginning in 2001.[72]

Estonia held its second presidential elections of the post-independence era in August and September 1996. As stipulated in the constitution, the process began in the Riigikogu, where two candidates were nominated: the incumbent president, Lennart Meri, and his main rival from the 1992 elections, Arnold Rüütel. However, the required two-thirds majority (that is, 68 votes of a possible 101) proved impossible to attain since a considerable number of parliamentary representatives abstained. In the three rounds of voting held in the Riigikogu on August 26–27, Meri garnered 45, 49, and 52 votes, respectively, while Rüütel's totals were 34, 34, and 32. Thus, the process moved to the Electoral College, consisting of the 101 members of parliament and 273 representatives of local government bodies, for a total of 374 electors. Here, two rounds of voting were slated with only a simply majority required, but new candidates could be nominated by 21 electors each. The voting in the Electoral College was held on September 20, and three new candidates appeared on the ballot: Tunne Kelam (b. 1936), deputy speaker of the parliament and a leading member of the Fatherland Union; Siiri Oviir (b. 1947), deputy chair of the Center Party; and Enn Tõugu (b. 1935), an academician working in Sweden. In the first round, the results were as follows: Meri – 139, Rüütel – 85, Kelam – 76, Tõugu – 47, and Oviir (the only female candidate) – 25. For the second round, only the top two vote-getters remained, and Meri finally emerged victorious by a bare majority, obtaining 196 votes to Rüütel's 126. As in the Riigikogu, a substantial share of the electors refused to support either candidate (44 abstentions and 6 invalid ballots).[73]

Although Meri had far outdistanced any rivals in public opinion polls before the election, his support in the Riigikogu was considerably weaker, probably because of his rather imperial style and some resentment at his attempts to expand the powers of the presidency. Meri may also have been hurt by renewed charges of alleged KGB connections, although he probably benefited from Edgar Savisaar's last-minute attempt to force Meri to withdraw from the race, which was widely perceived as unseemly and inappropriate. It also became clear during the electoral process that a two-thirds majority would be difficult for even a highly popular candidate to obtain. Had the second round of voting in the Electoral College not produced a majority for Meri, the whole process would have started all over again in the Riigikogu, creating a situation that would have bordered on a constitutional crisis. In a post-election interview Meri vowed to improve his relations with parliament, but some Riigikogu members were already calling for setting specific limits on presidential powers. Above all, it was clear that there would be much more public debate on the procedures for electing the president, and the experience of the 1996 elections added fuel to the arguments of those who either wanted to simplify the process or move toward direct election.[74]

The first local government elections according to the new constitution were held in October 1993. Only citizens could run for election, but in a concession to the large number of non-citizens in Estonia at the time, all permanent residents eighteen years of age and older who had resided in a given locality for at least five years were granted the right to vote.[75] The results of the local elections were a clear setback for the governing parties in the Riigikogu, who at the time had been in power on the national level for almost exactly one year. Although most candidates were associated with local political organizations or "parties," those running under the Fatherland banner did poorly, especially in the larger cities, while the opposition Estonian Coalition Party fared best among nationwide groups. The turnout was low compared to national elections – 52.6 percent of the eligible voters (see table 9.6) – but non-Estonians participated much more actively than Estonians, probably because this was the first opportunity for many to vote in the post-Soviet era. In Tallinn, two mostly ethnic Russian groups captured 42 percent (twenty-seven of sixty-four) of the seats in the city council. Nevertheless, in Tallinn and elsewhere in Estonia, moderate Russian candidates proved more successful than those who openly opposed Estonian statehood.[76] The local elections can be seen as a first step in the process of integrating non-Estonians into the country's body politic.

Table 9.6 *Voter participation in major elections and referenda in Estonia, 1989–95*

Political institution or referendum	Date	Eligible voters participating (%)
1. USSR Congress of People's Deputies	March 26, 1989	87.1
2. Congress of Estonia	February 24– March 1, 1990	71.0
3. Estonian SSR Supreme Soviet	March 18, 1990	78.2
4. Referendum on independence	March 3, 1991	82.9
5. Referendum on new constitution	June 28, 1992	66.8
6. Riigikogu	September 20, 1992	67.8
President	September 20, 1992	68.0
7. Local government assemblies	October 17, 1993	52.6
8. Riigikogu	March 5, 1995	68.9

Source: Tiina Raitviir, "Valimised ja referendumid 1989–1995: Osavõtuaktiivsus," *Päevaleht* (Tallinn), May 30, 1995, p. 6.

Citizen involvement in politics

Six multicandidate and/or multiparty elections along with two referendums took place in Estonia during the six years from March 1989 to March 1995. Table 9.6 provides an overview of these events as well as the level of participation in each electoral opportunity.

Leaving aside the local government elections of 1993 as a special case, it is clear that a considerable post-Soviet decline occurred in voter activism. Two factors in particular most likely contributed to this trend. First, after August 1991, much less appeared to be at stake for ethnic Estonian voters, since independence had already been gained. The especially high level of participation in the elections to the USSR Congress of Deputies in March 1989 is best explained by its being the first opportunity for a genuine choice by the voters. Second, the rapid changes taking place and economic difficulties many people experienced during the early independence years had a disorienting effect and probably contributed to some voter alienation.[77] Nevertheless, the overall voter turnout in Estonia in the first years after the restoration of independence was comparable to that in recent elections in the much more experienced democracy of neighboring Finland.[78]

On a regional basis in Estonia, a noteworthy reversal took place between the elections before and after August 1991. In the years 1989–91 the rural areas were without exception more active participants than the urban ones, largely because ethnic Estonian voters – who had a greater interest in the issues of the day – dominated the countryside in terms of numbers. On the other hand, in the post-Soviet years, during which the role of non-Estonian voters has been limited (except in 1993), the cities have proven considerably more activist than the rural districts. In both Riigikogu elections Tallinn clearly led the way in voter turnout, although Tartu, Estonia's second-largest city and a university town, trailed curiously far behind. In the rural districts a consistent trend throughout the six-year period was a low level of activism in the economically least developed regions. The most likely explanation for this trend is the relative sense of hopelessness with regard to the future among many people in the poorer areas of the country.[79]

Political parties

The political landscape in Estonia in the late 1980s and early 1990s was significantly influenced by two major legacies: the brief liberal democratic tradition of the interwar period and the long decades of one-party rule under communism. Even the earlier tradition was not completely unsullied. Along with a positive image of multiparty democracy, there also existed the negative view of a system that ultimately failed to work and appeared to break down through bickering and the pursuit of narrow interests. As elsewhere in the Soviet bloc, communist rule in Estonia fostered a profound cynicism about political parties among all sectors of the population.[80]

Given this heritage, it is not surprising that a well-functioning and stable party system, complete with organic links to the rank-and-file members of society, has yet to emerge in Estonia. Indeed, in a December 1992 poll, political parties ranked virtually at the bottom of a list of institutions that people had confidence in. Only 10 percent of Estonians and 5 percent of non-Estonians had faith in parties. Similarly, popular identification with political parties was also low. In April 1993, the rate of identification with a party in Estonia (13 percent) was minuscule compared to the European Community average (56 percent in 1992) and lagged well behind the level of the Visegrád countries except for Poland. The difference between Estonians (17 percent) and non-Estonians (7 percent) in Estonia, however, was noteworthy.[81]

A major consequence of these attitudes was a striking multiplicity of political parties that dominated the political scene during the first years of independence. In May 1994, the Riigikogu passed a new law on political parties intended to limit their numbers by requiring a minimum membership of 1,000 Estonian citizens for registration and the right to compete in national elections. Nevertheless, up until the March 1995 parliamentary elections, a membership of 200 sufficed; thus, the full impact of the law would not be felt until the next scheduled Riigikogu elections in 1999. The law also stipulated that any registered party unable to gain representation in two consecutive parliaments would be struck from the official list and forced to end its activity as a political party.[82] By the latter part of 1995, however, a growing interest in political mergers developed, for example, the formal unification of Fatherland and the Estonian National Independence Party as the Fatherland Union (*Isamaaliit*) in December 1995. To some extent this was a marriage of necessity, since both parties had done poorly in the last Riigikogu elections, but it also reflected a major new trend in Estonian politics. A new consolidated Moderate Party, as opposed to the looser existing political alliance, also appeared to be in the offing between the Social Democrats and the Rural Center Party. In short, the Scandinavianization of the Estonian party system (that is, the emergence of at most five to six stable major parties), a goal long expressed by a number of political observers in Estonia, seemed considerably closer to reality by early 1996.[83]

The lack of stability among political parties and the inability to consolidate into larger, more viable units in the early years of independence also resulted from several other factors. The strong grass-roots organizing tradition in modern Estonian history has not (yet) carried over into the political realm in the early postcommunist era; the great majority of parties have been established by a small number of elites rather than from below. A considerable number of parties were not based on a worldview or a broad perspective on a range of issues, but focused typically on a single problem or two.[84] Furthermore, it is understandable that the bewildering pace of change and the range of issues that a society in transition from communism has to deal with have militated against any rapid progress toward stable political parties.

The absence of established political traditions that are widely respected or that remain in the living memory of broad sections of society has contributed to a certain ideological instability in Estonia and a distorted political spectrum. Very few parties have been able to develop clearly defined ideological positions and draw the logical conclusions from them. Thus, after the March 1995 parliamentary elections in the negotiations over formation of a new coalition government, all sorts of combinations seemed possible. For example, the Estonian Center Party held serious talks with *all* other parties in the Riigikogu except the Rightists.[85] Following the collapse of communism the left was so discredited that no party with any serious ambitions for electoral success would have dared to associate itself with that side of the political spectrum. The only party that has openly done so is the official successor to the Communist Party of Estonia, the Estonian Democratic Labor Party, but it has paid a heavy price for this association, having obtained only 2 percent of the vote in the two Riigikogu elections in 1992 and 1995. Socialism as well was disgraced in the public eye. Thus, the Estonian Social Democratic Party has twice formed an electoral alliance called the "Moderates" and has tended to play down any left-leaning aspects of it program. In short, all Estonian parties in the two post-Soviet parliaments have claimed to be rightist or centrist, but these terms are not very meaningful in any objective sense in the current Estonian context.[86]

In many ways, the basic fault line in Estonian politics that emerged in 1989 between the pragmatists, led by the Popular Front, and the fundamentalists, associated with the Congress of Estonia, has continued to the present day despite the disappearance of these two broad popular movements. The current pragmatists, who can be placed at the center of the political spectrum or slightly to the left of it, are represented by the powerful electoral alliance of the Coalition Party and Rural Union as well as the Estonian Center Party. The leading figures in these organizations were typically managers and administrators during the Soviet era, holding positions that usually required Communist Party membership (twelve of the fifteen ministers in the current Vähi cabinet were former CPE members).[87] Their political opponents have referred to the pragmatists as "formers" (Est. *endised*), that is, recycled communists whom it is risky to trust with the business of governing. However, it is noteworthy that the pragmatists rarely held top political or ideological posts (Arnold Rüütel of the Rural Union is the main exception). As would be expected, the present-day fundamentalists are concentrated on the right side of the spectrum and are represented in the current Riigikogu – in rather fragmented form – by the Estonian Reform Party, Fatherland and the Estonian National Independence Party, and the Rightists.[88] In the years since September 1992, parties on both sides of the fault line have been part of the ruling coalition, and it is not surprising that the experience of governing has narrowed the gap between the various Estonian political forces. Although all major parties were fully committed to democratization and a Western-style market economy, the fundamentalists continued to favor a radical Thatcherite approach whereas the pragmatists emphasized the importance of maintaining a broad social safety net.

As noted above, the fringe or protest parties on the right declined in importance between the 1992 and 1995 elections, and unless they can unite several diverse groups, they probably have little political future. On the left side, Vaino Väljas, who retained a measure of personal popularity for his role in the reforms of the early glasnost era, chaired the Estonian Democratic Labor Party, the CPE's successor, in the early postcommunist era, and the party's new leaders have argued that socialism remains a powerful idea.[89] However, given its past role, the party has little likelihood of electoral success among Estonians, although the growing number of ethnic Russian voters could enhance its prospects in future parliamentary elections.

The entry of Our Home is Estonia, an electoral alliance of three disparate ethnic Russian groups, into the Riigikogu was the surprise result of the 1995 elections. Pre-election polls gave the Russian-based alliance no more than 3 percent of the vote and thus little chance for representation. Nevertheless, although no exact figures are available, the ethnic Russian and Russophone share of eligible voters had risen to slightly over 10 percent by the eve of the elections. The most likely explanation for the surprising result may be the reluctance of Russian voters to reveal their support for a Russian party to Estonian pollsters. However, it clear that not all eligible non-Estonian voters supported Our Home is Estonia. Of the major competitors, the Center Party proved most successful with non-Estonian voters, especially in northeastern Estonia, presumably because of its advocacy of a strong social safety net and the popularity of its leader, Edgar Savisaar, among non-Estonians. Our Home is Estonia is clearly a unique political entity in the Riigikogu. Its main goal is to represent the interests of the ethnic Russian community in Estonia, but it is also loyal to an independent Estonia and its established constitution. As a marriage of convenience for electoral purposes, Our Home is Estonia has no ideological unity since the three parties involved include a moderate Russian nationalist group, a centrist one, and a small group of heirs to the Intermovement.[90]

The Russian presence in the Riigikogu has served as a further means to relieve ethnic tensions in Estonia. Our Home is Estonia has played the role of a constructive opposition and found its niche as an advocate for the interests of the Russian and Russophone population. For example, it has sought to make the attainment of Estonian citizenship easier for non-citizens, calling for a less demanding language test, and it has strongly supported the cause of Russian-language education in Estonia.[91] In short, a Russian voice in the parliament has made the concerns of the non-Estonian population considerably more visible to Estonian politicians and public opinion.

Political evolution of society

In view of the large Russian presence in Estonia created by Moscow's policies under Soviet rule, the ethnic factor remained a key issue throughout the period under review. In the initial post-independence years, most Russians in Estonia were cut off from politics since the Intermovement was banned, and few had yet become citizens. Nevertheless, as soon as it was possible, growing numbers of non-Estonians became citizens, or at least learned Estonian, especially among the younger generation, thus beginning the process of integration into Estonian society. In January 1995, a new citizenship law replaced the previously restored 1938 legislation, raising the residency requirement to six years, but only for new immigrants. Our Home is Estonia, the Russian fraction in parliament, criticized the new law for not making the acquisition of citizenship easier, pointing out the social tensions created by the existence of large numbers of non-citizens.[92] However, by November 1995 it was estimated that about 25 percent of non-Estonians were already citizens, a little over half by descent and the rest by naturalization, and the monthly rate of newly acquired citizenship was increasing. On the other hand, Estonia also had a relatively large number of citizens of Russia (about 82,000 in January 1996), and the largest group among non-Estonians could not yet decide what choice it should make on this question.[93] In sum, it was clear that the process of political and social integration would take time, and serious challenges remained, especially in the urban areas of northeastern Estonia such as Narva where the population was 85.9 percent Russian and only 4.0 percent Estonian in 1989.[94] Despite some emigration in the early 1990s, there was every indication that the great majority of non-Estonians were in Estonia to stay.[95]

Although Johan Laidoner, Estonia's top military leader in the interwar era, allied with and served the Päts regime during the 1930s, he was clearly in a subordinate role to the civilian government. This tradition continued in the postindependence years, especially since the Soviet authorities had been highly suspicious of Estonian and other Baltic officers and rarely allowed them to rise very far in the ranks of the armed forces. In this situation the new Estonian government was hard pressed to find suitable leaders for its fledgling military force. In May 1993, a solution to this dilemma appeared with the appointment as commander-in-chief of Aleksander Einseln, a retired US army colonel who was born in Estonia in the late interwar era and then fled as a child with his family during World War II. His stated goal was to bring Western practices to the reborn Estonian military and purge it of any Soviet legacy. Einseln had some success in this task, but he also showed increasing frustration, culminating in a public row with the minister of defense in the latter part of 1995 over how the military was being run. He was also saddled with ultimate responsibility for a scandal involving the illegal sale of weapons by a high-ranking member of his staff. In December 1995, President Meri relieved Einseln of his duties, largely, it seems, because of the need to maintain civilian control of the military – a key element in NATO's requirements for countries seeking membership.[96]

Along with Einseln, four ethnic Estonians residing in the diaspora served as ministers in several cabinets during the years 1992–95, including the ministries of foreign affairs, defense, energy, and finance. However, it is noteworthy that between April 1995 and December 1996 none was represented in the government.[97] Among the 101 representatives in the Riigikogu elected in 1992, there were two diaspora Estonians, including Jüri Toomepuu, the largest vote-getter in the elections and leader of the right-wing fringe party Estonian Citizen. In the following Riigikogu, elected in 1995, no Estonians from abroad achieved representation.[98] Thus, by 1995, there was a clear decline in diaspora participation in Estonian politics, punctuated by General Einseln's dismissal at the end of the year. This trend reflected a certain alienation between the two communities that was perhaps inevitable given the long period of separation during Soviet rule.

The role of women in Estonian politics has been limited historically, and it is likely to remain so for the foreseeable future. The proportion of female representatives in the two post-Soviet parliaments was only 12 percent in each, and as noted above, Lagle Parek finished a distant last with just over 4 percent of the vote in the 1992 presidential race. As Valve Kirsipuu, a leading female member of the Estonian Reform Party, recently suggested, Estonians of either sex are reluctant to entrust women with leadership positions. Opinion polls indicate that women are far less interested than men in involvement in politics, and as elsewhere in the former communist world, women in Estonia typically bear a double burden of working both outside and inside the home. Female candidates have been most successful at the local level; in the 1993 municipal elections they won 24 percent of the seats.[99]

Compared to other former Soviet republics, Estonia took bold and rapid steps in the economic sphere, especially as the first to introduce its own currency, the kroon (crown), in June 1992 and thus escape the "ruble zone." The government of Prime Minister Mart Laar pursued an aggressive free-market policy, eliminating subsidies and price controls, and it still managed to bring inflation under relative control, for example, annual rates of 36, 42, and 28 percent in 1993, 1994, and 1995, respectively (see table 9.7).[100]

Estonia also managed to escape trade dependence on Russia relatively quickly, and by late 1992, Finland had become its leading trading partner. Overall, Estonia's economic development compared favorably not only to that of other former republics, but also to that of former Warsaw Pact countries. For example, in 1994, Estonia ranked above all these countries, including the Czech Republic and Hungary, with regard to foreign direct investment per capita and as percentage of GDP.[101] Thus, effective economic reforms were set in place by the first postindependence government, and they have endured despite several changes of government since fall 1994.

Despite the macroeconomic successes and positive evaluations from international agencies and observers, the recent economic changes have also substantially heightened inequality of income and wealth as well as social divisions. Perhaps the greatest antagonism has developed between the cities and the countryside, as the rural areas (30 percent of the population) have remained bitter at not sharing in economic progress and resented the rise of urban nouveaux riches. For various reasons, for example, complications raised by legal claims and the slowness of land surveys, the privatization of rural land has hardly begun with only 2 percent in private hands in summer 1995.[102] Furthermore, regional socioeconomic differences are growing and appear to have an impact on voting patterns. Another major gap in society that has widened in recent years is a generational one, especially between

Table 9.7 *Indicators of economic trends in Estonia since 1989*

	1989	1990	1991	1992	1993	1994	1995[a]
GDP	-1.1	-8.1	-11.0	-14.2	-6.7	-3.2	4
Industrial output	0.6	n.a.	n.a.	-35	-18.7	-3.0	n.a.
Rate of inflation	6.1	23.1	210.5	1,076	89.8	48	29
% Labor force unemployed	n.a.	n.a.	n.a.	0.9	2.1	1.8	1.8
GNP per capita	n.a.	n.a.	n.a.	n.a.	6,860	n.a.	n.a.
% Workforce in private activity[b]	n.a.	n.a.	10.5	15.0	n.a.	n.a.	n.a.
% GDP from private sector[c]	n.a.	n.a.	n.a.	45.0	50.6	58.0	n.a.

Notes: GDP – % change over previous year; industrial output – % change over previous year; rate of inflation – % change in end-year retail/consumer prices; % of labor force unemployed – end of year; GNP per capita – in US dollars at PPP exchange rates. [a]Estimate. [b]Pure private sector. [c]Non-state sector.

Sources: European Bank for Reconstruction and Development, *Transition Report 1995* (London: EBRD, 1995), pp. 182, 194, 196, Table 3; European Bank for Reconstruction and Development, *Transition Report Update, April 1996: Assessing Progress in Economies in Transition* (London: EBRD, 1996); *Statistika Aastaraamat 1995* (Tallinn: Eesti Statistikaamet, 1995), p. 205; *Statistika Aastaraamat 1993* (Tallinn: Eesti Statistikaamet, 1993), p. 175; *Statisticheskii ezhegodnik Estonii 1990* (Tallinn: Olion, 1991), p. 157; *Baltic Observer* (Riga), February 15–21, 1996, p. 11.

younger workers, who have benefited the most from the new economic system, and retired persons on fixed incomes, who have been hardest hit by free-market prices. There is no doubt that the rural population and the older generation voted massively against the parties of the Laar government in the 1995 Riigikogu elections.

Among various interest groups in society, urban businesspeople and managers have been most successful in influencing the country's political agenda, as indicated by the recent electoral victory of the Estonian Coalition Party and the rise of the Estonian Reform Party (perhaps because the latter had the resources to outspend all its rivals in 1995).[103] In contrast, organized labor, especially with the collapse of the left, found itself with virtually no money or political power. Between 1992 and 1995, the major agricultural groups were essentially shut out of the corridors of power under the Fatherland-led coalition government. However, the Rural Union's alliance with the Coalition Party brought it into the current Vähi government, and the agricultural sector's voice is being heard more, for example, Vähi's recent promise to push land reform.[104]

Although it has had no direct role in politics, organized crime, dominated by various non-Estonian groups, has certainly presented a serious problem for the Estonian authorities. For example, during the first eleven months of 1995, seventeen substantial bombs were set off in Tallinn alone, resulting in six deaths. Most of these appeared to reflect a struggle for power and turf between the mainly non-Estonian underworld groups. Nevertheless, some of the bombs, for example, one at the entrance to the municipal court, were clearly intended to intimidate the authorities, perhaps in connection with the trial of seven underworld figures for the murder of two police officers in December 1994. The Estonian press reacted strongly to these events, calling for resolute measures by the government. The political impact of organized crime in Estonia has remained indirect, but each postindependence government has faced the challenge of dealing with its destabilizing activity. None has been very successful.[105] Although the endemic corruption characteristic of the Soviet era was less prevalent in Estonia than in other parts of the USSR, graft has remained a serious problem, especially among government officials who had their formative experience under the previous regime. It is striking that the penalties for taking or offering bribery in a 1993 law were less stringent than those in a Soviet-era one passed in 1990, and if anything, corruption has increased in recent years. Estonian reformers have called for passage of new laws that follow Western norms in dealing with corruption, but it seems clear that overcoming the legacy of the communist era in this regard will require a considerable period of time.[106]

Television, radio, and the press in Estonia have all been substantially privatized, especially newspapers and magazines, and the range of information and opinion available is quite broad. Several Estonian television stations are available with a range of programming, but only one offers newscasts (in both Estonian and Russian). In addition, Finnish, Russian, and other foreign channels are accessible to a considerable proportion of the population. In 1996, three Estonian-language daily newspapers – *Eesti Päevaleht* (The Estonian Newspaper [Tallinn]), *Postimees* (The Courier [Tartu]), and *Sõnumileht* (The Newsletter [Tallinn]) – competed on the national level. It is noteworthy that *Postimees*, despite its provincial location in southern Estonia, had the largest circulation and readership among dailies. None of the three is associated with a particular political party, although a preference for one or more of the larger parties is noticeable to an observant reader. During the 1995 parliamentary election campaign, all the major parties received extensive coverage in the leading dailies, but the smaller ones were largely ignored.[107]

The postindependence years witnessed a flowering of religious pluralism in Estonia. Already in 1992, there were forty-five religious groups operating in the country.[108] However, nearly all remained small in numbers, and even the two traditional major churches, the Lutheran and the Orthodox, exercised little influence in public or political life. Although the great majority of Estonians were officially associated with Lutheranism from the Reformation to the onset of Soviet rule, before 1918 the church was mainly in the hands of the Baltic German elites, and it never gained the prestige that comparable institutions enjoyed in many other parts of Eastern Europe.

Conclusion

Among former Soviet republics, Estonia was as well placed as any to take advantage of the collapse of communism and begin the process of transition to a democratic political system. The memory of the first independence period in the interwar era remained alive through a modern oral tradition, and Estonia acquired a unique window on the West via Finland during the post-Stalin decades that kept it relatively abreast of the external world. Making use of its non-violent political tradition, the country managed to navigate the potentially perilous transition years in a civilized manner. Nevertheless, building a new democratic system proved to be a daunting task. Although the post-August 1991 years witnessed a number of notable achievements, including a functioning democratic constitution and the holding of regular elections on schedule, the rapid pace of change and the economic upheaval of recent years have been disorienting and fostered a lingering alienation from politics. Above all, the most lasting legacy of Soviet rule – the drastically changed ethnic composition of the country – has militated against any rapid solution to the problem of political integration.

How far has democratic consolidation proceeded in Estonia? By 1996, there was little doubt that the ethnic Estonian population regarded the new political system as legitimate and overwhelmingly accepted the democratic rules of the game. At the same time, polls indicated that the non-Estonian population increasingly identified with Estonia, even if the majority had not yet sought Estonian citizenship. The most workable solution to the challenge of further democratic consolidation would focus on the process of integration, as opposed to assimilation, that is, encouraging non-Estonians to develop a multiple identity – retaining their ethnic roots, but also learning to participate and function in the Estonian political environment.

NOTES

1 Toivo U. Raun, *Estonia and the Estonians*, 2d ed. (Stanford, CA: Hoover Institution Press, 1991), p. 247.

2 Kalev Katus, "Eesti rahvastiku tulevikujooned," *Looming*, no. 2 (1994), 249. In January 1945, the Soviets unilaterally transferred about 5 percent of the territory of the Estonian SSR (formed in August 1940 after the forcible annexation of the independent Republic of Estonia) to the Russian SFSR. These lands, which remained under dispute between Estonia and Russia during the first half of the 1990s, were located east of the Narva River and in the Petseri (Russian Pechory) region in the southeast. The great majority of the population thus transferred was non-Estonian, but thousands of ethnic Estonians in the Petseri area did become residents of the RSFSR. See Raun, *Estonia and the Estonians*, p. 181 and Toivo U. Raun, "The Petseri Region of the Republic of Estonia," *Jahrbücher für Geschichte Osteuropas*, 39 (1991), 531.

3 See Toivo U. Raun, "The Estonian SSR Language Law (1989): Background and Implementation," *Nationalities Papers* 23 (1995), 515–34.

4 *Rahvastikustatistika Teatmik*, no. 3 (1995), 22-3, 26-7; *Postimees* (Tartu), 11 October 1996, p. 9; *Sõnumileht*, 10 January 1996, p. 6. It is noteworthy that the proportion of babies born to ethnic Estonian mothers has increased considerably since the late 1980s (from 58.6 percent in 1987 to 72.8 percent in 1994) while the Estonian share of the deaths in the republic dropped from 72.0 percent to 66.3 percent during the same period. These trends are also contributing to a gradual increase in the ethnic Estonian proportion of the total population. See *Statistika Aastaraamat 1995* (Tallinn: Eesti Statistikaamet, 1995), pp. 51, 60.

5 *Postimees* (Tartu), 23 December 1995, p. 7.

6 Raun, *Estonia and the Estonians*, p. 127; *Eesti NSV rahvamajandus 1970. aastal* (Tallinn: Statistika, 1971), p. 235; *Narodnoe khoziaistvo Estonskoi SSR v 1980 godu* (Tallinn: Eesti Raamat, 1981), pp. 203–204; *Statisticheskii ezhegodnik Estonii 1990* (Tallinn: Olion, 1991), pp. 238–39.

7 See, for example, Toivo U. Raun, "The Latvian and Estonian National Movements, 1860–1914," *Slavonic and East European Review* 64 (1986), 66–80.

8 According to the 1881 census, in the northern half of the Baltic Provinces ethnic Estonian literacy (reading only) for the population 14 years of age and older was 93–94 percent for males and 96–97 percent for females. Toivo U. Raun, "The Development of Estonian Literacy in the 18th and 19th Centuries," *Journal of Baltic Studies* 10 (1979), 122.

9 Ea Jansen, "Voluntary Associations in Estonia: The Model of the 19th Century," *Proceedings of the Estonian Academy of Sciences: Humanities and Social Sciences* 43 (1993), 115–25.

10 Toomas Karjahärm, "Eesti linnakodanluse formeerumisest 1870-ndate aastate lõpust kuni 1914. aastani (linna- ja duumavalimiste materjalide põhjal)," *Eesti NSV Teaduste Akadeemia Toimetised: Ühiskonnateadused* 23 (1973), 256–57, 262.

11 Toivo U. Raun, "1905 as a Turning Point in Estonian History," *East European Quarterly* 14 (1980), 327–33; Toivo U. Raun, "Estonian Social and Political Thought, 1905–February 1917," in *Die baltischen Provinzen Russlands zwischen den Revolutionen von 1905 und 1917*, ed. Andrew Ezergailis and Gert von Pistohlkors (Cologne: Böhlau, 1982), pp. 59–72.

12 Evald Uustalu, "Die Staatsgründung Estlands," in *Von den baltischen Provinzen zu den baltischen Staaten: Beiträge zur Entstehungsgeschichte der Republiken Estland und Lettland, 1917–1918*, ed. Jürgen von Hehn, Hans von Rimscha, and Hellmuth Weiss (Marburg/Lahn: J. G. Herder-Institut, 1971), pp. 275–92.

13 Henn-Jüri Uibopuu, "The Constitutional Development of the Estonian Republic," *Journal of Baltic Studies* 4 (1973), 12–15.

14 Raun, *Estonia and the Estonians*, pp. 116–23; Tönu Parming, *The Collapse of Liberal Democracy and the Rise of Authoritarianism in Estonia* (London: Sage, 1975), pp. 50–51.

15 Rein Ruutsoo, "Eesti omariiklus ja rahvuslik areng 1918–1940," in *Eesti rahvas ja stalinlus*, ed. Kaarel Haav and Rein Ruutsoo (Tallinn: Olion, 1990), p. 56.

16 Rein Taagepera, "Estonia's Constitutional Assembly, 1991–1992," *Journal of Baltic Studies* 25 (1994), 211–12.

17 *Postimehe valimisteatmik 1995* (Tartu: Postimees, 1995), pp. 32–67.

18 For contrasting recent views on the numerical strength of the guerrillas, see *Vastupanuliikumine Eestis 1944–1949*, ed. Evald Laasi (Tallinn: Nõmm & Co., 1992), p. 116 and Mart Laar, *War in the Woods* (Washington, DC: Compass Press, 1992), p. 155.

19 See V. Stanley Vardys, "Human Rights Issues in Estonia, Latvia, and Lithuania," *Journal of Baltic Studies* 12 (1981), 275–98.

20 Kukk died in March 1981 in a labor camp, apparently as a result of forced feeding during a hunger strike. On Kukk, see Rein Taagepera, *Softening Without Liberalization in the Soviet Union: The Case of Jüri Kukk* (Lanham, MD: University Press of America, 1984).

21 "Open Letter from the Estonian SSR," Appendix II in Vardys, "Human Rights Issues," pp. 292–96 (quotation on p. 295).

22 Sirje Kiin, Rein Ruutsoo, and Andres Tarand, *40 kirja lugu* (Tallinn: Olion, 1990), pp. 8, 12, 39, 67–70.

23 Raun, *Estonia and the Estonians*, p. 214.

24 Toivo U. Raun, "Ethnic Relations and Conflict in the Baltic States," in *Ethnic Nationalism and Regional Conflict: The Former Soviet Union and Yugoslavia*, ed. W. Raymond Duncan and G. Paul Holman, Jr. (Boulder, CO: Westview, 1994), pp. 171–74, 177.

25 Aksel Kirch, Marika Kirch, and Tarmo Tuisk, "Russians in the Baltic States: To Be or Not To Be?" *Journal of Baltic Studies* 24 (1993), 178, 182–3; *Postimees* (Tartu), 18 April 1995, p. 9.

26 Walter C. Clemens, Jr., *Baltic Independence and Russian Empire* (New York: St. Martin's, 1991), pp. 123–44; *Postimees* (Tartu), 14 June 1994, p. 1.

27 *Helsingin Sanomat*, 9 June 1994, p. A2, and 10 October 1994, p. A11; *Eesti Sõnumid* (Tallinn), 3 July 1995, p. 1.

28 *New York Times*, 27 July 1994, p. A1.

29 *Postimees* (Tartu), 3 February 1995, p. 3, and 6 January 1996, p. 2; *Helsingin Sanomat*, 29 May 1994, p. C1; *Rahuleping Eesti ja Venemaa vahel/Mirnyi dogovor mezhdu Rossiei i Estoniei* (Tartu: Bergmann, 1920; reprinted Tallinn: Valgus, 1989), p. 3.

30 Rein Taagepera, "Estonia's Road to Independence," *Problems of Communism* 38, no. 6 (1989), 15–16; "*Glasnost* in the Baltic: Summer Demonstrations," *Baltic Forum* 4, no. 2 (1987), 3.

31 Toivo Miljan, "The Proposal to Establish Economic Autonomy in Estonia," *Journal of Baltic Studies* 20 (1989), 154–60.

32 *Rahvakongress: Eestimaa Rahvarinde kongress 1.–2. oktoobril 1988* (Tallinn: Perioodika, 1988), pp. 19–21.

33 Tiina Raitviir, "Eesti poliitiliste jõudude tekkimine ja ümberkujunemine," *Hommikuleht* (Tallinn), 30 June 1994, p. 5; *Homeland* (Tallinn), 27 July 1988, p. 2. Despite its claims, the Intermovement's support among Estonia's Russophone population (in Russian, *russkoiazychnyi* or "Russian-speaking," i.e., those non-Estonians – including both ethnic Russians and others – who habitually spoke Russian as their primary means of communication) appeared to be limited. For example, in a poll at the end of 1988 only 15 percent of the Russophones in Estonia backed the movement (*Homeland* [Tallinn], 15 March 1989, p. 2), and another poll in April 1989 indicated that the Intermovement had the support of 10.9 percent of the non-Estonian population (Toomas Ilves, "Reaction: The Intermovement in Estonia," in *Toward Independence: The Baltic Popular Movements*, ed. Jan Arveds Trapans [Boulder, CO: Westview, 1991], p. 79).

34 *Homeland* (Tallinn), 23 November 1988, pp. 1–2.

35 Riina Kionka, "The Estonian Citizens' Committee: An Opposition Movement of a Different Complexion," *Report on the USSR* 2, no. 6 (1990), 30–33.

36 Rein Taagepera, "A Note on the March 1989 Elections in Estonia," *Soviet Studies* 42 (1990), 331–32, 336–37.

37 *Baltic Forum* 6, no. 2 (1989), 77–79.

38 *Homeland* (Tallinn), 18 October 1989, pp. 1–2, and 25 October 1989, pp. 1–2; *Estonian Independent* (Tallinn), 30 May 1990, p. 3.

39 *Homeland* (Tallinn), 21 March 1990, p. 1, 28 March 1990, pp. 1, 4, and 4 April 1990, p. 1.

40 *Perestroika in the Soviet Republics: Documents on the National Question*, ed. Charles F. Furtado, Jr. and Andrea Chandler (Boulder, CO: Westview, 1992), pp. 102–103.

41 *Estonian Independent* (Tallinn), 7 March 1991, pp. 1, 3.

42 *Baltic Independent* (Tallinn), 30 August–5 September 1991, p. 3.

43 Tiina Raitviir, "Eesti poliitiliste jõudude tekkimine ja ümberkujunemine," *Hommikuleht* (Tallinn), 1 July 1994, p. 5.

44 Dzintra Bungs, Saulius Girnius, and Riina Kionka, "Citizenship Legislation in the Baltic States," *RFE/RL Research Report* 1, no. 50 (18 December 1992), 38–39.

45 Taagepera, "Estonia's Constitutional Assembly," pp. 216–17. The Congress of Estonia had 464 members and the Supreme Council 101. The 43 delegates who belonged to both bodies could choose, if elected, which one they would represent in the Constitutional Assembly.

46 Ibid., pp. 214, 216.

47 Ibid., pp. 220, 223, 225, 227–28.

48 *Baltic Independent* (Tallinn), 3–9 July 1992, p. 1.

49 *Eesti Vabariigi põhiseadus/Republic of Estonia Constitution* (Tallinn: Eesti Vabariigi Riigikantselei, 1993); *Eesti Vabariigi põhiseadus/Eesti Vabariigi põhiseaduse rakendamisseadus* (Tallinn: Riigi Teataja, 1994), pp. 28–30.

50 *Eesti Krooonika 1993*, ed. Jaan Laas (Tallinn: AS Esintell, 1993), pp. 107–108. The number of representatives in the three-party coalition grew from fifty-one to fifty-three because of two quick defections from the Estonian Citizen, one each

to Fatherland and the Estonian National Independence Party (*Baltic Independent* [Tallinn], 16–22 October 1992, p. 7).

51 *Kes on kes Eesti poliitikas 1988–1992* (Tallinn: Eesti Entsüklopeedia, 1992), p. 83 and *passim*.

52 *Baltic Independent* (Tallinn), 30 September–6 October 1994, pp. 1, 3. The arms deal with Israel, which was negotiated in January 1993 and cost Estonia about $50 million, was criticized for several reasons: the expense, the questionable quality of some of the arms actually sent, and the lack of consultation with parliament. The so-called "ruble affair" took place between December 1992 and March 1993 and involved the secret sale – under still unexplained circumstances – of most of about 2.3 billion rubles that had been withdrawn from circulation following the introduction of the Estonian kroon in June 1992. In return, Estonia received some $1.9 million, or about 27 percent less than the prevailing exchange rate at the time. The difference presumably went to the facilitators of the deal; no one has yet accused Laar or a key adviser of personally profiting from the affair. However, critics have suggested that at the very least it was unseemly for a country that is striving to become a European state governed by law (German *Rechtsstaat*) to have engaged in such secret trafficking at the highest level of government. See *Postimees* (Tartu), 7 December 1995, p. 4; *Eesti Ekspress* (Tallinn), 12 January 1996, pp. A1,2.

53 *Baltic Independent* (Tallinn), 11–17 November 1994, p. 3. Although the normal term for members of parliament is four years according to the 1992 Constitution, as a one-time exception the first Riigikogu was limited to a mandate of "up to three years." Since the new constitution also called for regular parliamentary elections to be held on the first Sunday in March in an election year (following the custom established in the 1920s and 1930s), the actual term of the first Riigikogu proved to be two and a half years. *Eesti Vabariigi põhiseadus/Eesti Vabariigi põhiseaduse rakendamisseadus*, pp. 11, 28.

54 *Baltic Independent* (Tallinn), 14–20 April 1995, p. 3, and 21–27 April 1995, p. 1.

55 *New York Times*, 18 October 1995, p. A8; *Baltic Independent* (Tallinn), 13–19 October 1995, pp. 1, 3; *Helsingin Sanomat*, 6 October 1995, p. C3, 10 October 1995, p. C2, and 12 October 1995, p. C3; *Eesti Päevaleht* (Tallinn), 29 November 1995, p. 3. After his dismissal as minister, Savisaar resigned as head of the Center Party and announced that he was leaving politics. However, he did not resign his seat in parliament and quietly returned to that position after a two-month absence. The taping affair remained under investigation in early 1996.

56 *Baltic Independent* (Tallinn), 27 October–2 November 1995, p. 1; *Baltic Observer* (Riga), 2–8 November 1995, pp. 1, 5, and 9–15 November 1995, pp. 1, 4.

57 *Helsingin Sanomat*, 23 September 1994, p. C3; Rein Taagepera, "Estonian Parliamentary Elections, March 1995," *Electoral Studies* 14 (1995) p. 329; *Riigikogu Postimees* (Tartu), 21 March 1995, p. 15.

58 Taagepera, "Estonia's Constitutional Assembly," p. 231; *Helsingin Sanomat*, 23 September 1994, p. C3; *Baltic Independent* (Tallinn), 9–15 July 1993, p. 1, 16–22 July 1993, p. 1, and 14–20 January 1994, pp. 1, 3. The 1992 Constitution was rather vague on the issue of appointment of ministers. Article 90 states: "Changes in the composition of those appointed to the Government of the Republic shall be made by the President of the Republic, on proposal by the

Prime Minister" (*Eesti Vabariigi põhiseadus/Republic of Estonia Constitution*, p. 29).

59 *Helsingin Sanomat*, 27 July 1994, p. B1.

60 Taagepera, "Estonian Parliamentary Elections," pp. 328–29; *Riigikogu Postimees* (Tartu), 21 March 1995, pp. 1–7; *Vabariigi Presidendi ja Riigikogu valimised 1992* (Tallinn: Eesti Vabariigi Valimiskomisjon, 1992), p. 93.

61 The number of seats in a given district is obtained by first dividing the total number of registered voters (766,626 in 1995) by 101 (the number of seats in the Riigikogu) in order to derive the national quota (7,590.356 in 1995). Then, the number of registered voters in a given district (e.g., 58,131 in 1995 in District 1) is divided by the national quota (resulting in the number 7.6585 in District 1). This figure is rounded up or down. Thus, District 1 was allocated 8 seats in 1995. *Postimehe valimisteatmik*, p. 119.

62 *Riigikogu Postimees* (Tartu), 21 March 1995, p. 15.

63 *Postimehe valimisteatmik*, pp. 127–30; *Riigikogu Postimees* (Tartu), 21 March 1995, pp. 7, 15; Taagepera, "Estonian Parliamentary Elections," pp. 328–29. The current Riigikogu Electoral Law is available in English in *Legal Acts of Estonia*, no. 1 (9 February 1995), pp. 12–32.

64 Individual candidates could run for parliament, and thirteen did so in 1995 (twenty-six in 1992). However, the odds are clearly against individual candidates, and none was successful in either election. *Postimehe valimisteatmik*, pp. 5, 93.

65 *Postimehe valimisteatmik*, pp. 5, 30, 76–93; Taagepera, "Estonian Parliamentary Elections," pp. 329–30.

66 *Postimehe valimisteatmik*, pp. 119, 121.

67 The votes of Estonian citizens abroad were counted in the electoral district of their last place of permanent residence in Estonia (or that of their parents or grandparents). See *Legal Acts of Estonia*, no. 1 (9 February 1995), p. 13.

68 *Postimees* (Tartu), 7 June 1995, p. 7. Of the 6,647 votes cast by Estonians abroad, 58.7 percent went to the Fatherland-Estonian National Independence Party alliance. The Reform Party trailed as a distant second with 12.6 percent, and the Coalition Party and Rural Union alliance – the overall victor in the elections – came in third with only 7.1 percent. Thus, Estonian voters abroad were much more supportive of the right side of the political spectrum than were those in Estonia itself.

69 *Vabariigi Presidendi ja Riigikogu valimised*, pp. 110–15.

70 Ibid., pp. 116–26.

71 *Eesti Vabariigi põhiseadus/Eesti Vabariigi põhiseaduse rakendamisseadus*, pp. 15, 29.

72 *Postimees* (Tartu), 9 January 1996, p. 3; *Eesti Ekspress* (Tallinn), 19 January 1996, p. A4.

73 *Baltic Times* (Riga), 29 August–4 September 1996, pp. 1, 4; 26 September–2 October 1996, pp. 1, 4.

74 *Postimees* (Tartu), 20 September 1996, pp. 2-3; *Helsingin Sanomat*, 21 September 1996, p. C7; *Baltic Times* (Riga), 29 August–4 September 1996, pp. 1, 4, and 26 September–2 October 1996, pp. 1, 4.

75 *Eesti Vabariigi põhiseadus/Eesti Vabariigi põhiseaduse rakendamisseadus*, p. 26.

76 *Baltic Independent* (Tallinn), 22–28 October 1993, pp. 1, 4. For full results of the local government elections, see *Kohaliku omavalitsuse volikogu valimised 17. oktoobril 1993* (Tallinn: Eesti Vabariigi Riigikogu Kantselei valimiste osakond, 1994).

77 Tiina Raitviir, "Valimised ja referendumid 1989–1995: Osavõtuaktiivsus," *Päevaleht* (Tallinn), 30 May 1995, p. 6.

78 Voter turnout in the last two Finnish parliamentary elections was 71.8 percent in 1995 and 72.1 percent in 1991. *Helsingin Sanomat*, 21 March 1995, p. B2; Sten Berglund, "The Finnish Parliamentary Elections of March 1991," *Scandinavian Political Studies* 14 (1991), 337.

79 Tiina Raitviir, "Valimised ja referendumid 1989–1995: Osavõtuaktiivsus," *Päevaleht* (Tallinn), 31 May 1995, p. 6, and 2 June 1995, p. 5; *Vabariigi Presidendi ja Riigikogu valimised*, pp. 60–90; *Riigikogu Postimees* (Tartu), 21 March 1995, p. 16.

80 Rain Rosimannus, "Political Parties: Identity and Identification," *Nationalities Papers*, 23 (1995), 37–38.

81 Ibid., 30–31, 33.

82 Tiina Raitviir, "Maailmavaatetud Eesti parteid," *Eesti Ekspress* (Tallinn), 17 February 1995, p. A10; *Riigi Teataja*, Part I, no. 40 (6 June 1994), 1180–83.

83 *Postimees* (Tartu), 25 August 1995, p. 7; *Sõnumileht* (Tallinn), 13 December 1995, p. 2.

84 Raitviir, "Maailmavaatetud Eesti parteid"; Rosimannus, "Political Parties," 38–39.

85 *Eesti Sõnumid* (Tallinn), 20 April 1995, p. 2.

86 Jaan Kaplinski, "Arenguparadoksid ja pluralism Eestis," *Eesti Sõnumid* (Tallinn), 16 May 1995, p. 2; *Eesti Sõnumid* (Tallinn), 3 February 1995, p. 2.

87 Tiina Raitviir, "Maailmavaatetud Eesti parteid 2," *Eesti Ekspress* (Tallinn), 23 February 1995, p. A14; *Valitsuse Postimees* (Tartu), 18 April 1995, pp. 2–3.

88 Raitviir, "Maailmavaatetud Eesti parteid 2."

89 *Eesti Ekspress* (Tallinn), 12 January 1996, p. A10.

90 *Eesti Sõnumid* (Tallinn), 27 February 1995, p. 1; *Eesti Ekspress* (Tallinn), 10 March 1995, p. A10; Taagepera, "Estonian Parliamentary Elections," p. 330; *Helsingin Sanomat*, 7 March 1995, p. C2; *Postimees* (Tartu), 8 March 1995, p. 6.

91 *Postimees* (Tartu), 18 January 1996, p. 3.

92 *Legal Acts of Estonia*, no. 6 (16 June 1995), pp. 163–74; *Estoniia* (Tallinn), 1 August 1995, p. 1.

93 *Postimees* (Tartu), 17 November 1995, p. 7; 6 January 1996, p. 5.

94 *Eesti Vabariigi maakondade, linnade ja alevite rahvastik*, I (Tallinn: Eesti Vabariigi Riiklik Statistikaamet, 1990), pp. 32–3. Narva was 64.8 percent Estonian in 1934 (Raun, *Estonia and the Estonians*, p. 207), but its ethnic composition changed drastically during World War II and Stalinist rule.

95 In the seven years between the last Soviet census of January 1989 and the end of 1995, it is estimated that the ethnic Russian population in Estonia declined by about 52,000 or 11 percent. See *Statistika Aastaraamat 1995*, pp. 40, 46; *Sõnumileht* (Tallinn), 10 January 1996, p. 6.

96 *Helsingin Sanomat*, 4 December 1995, p. C1; 26 September 1995, p. A5.

97 *Valitsuse Postimees* (Tartu), 18 April 1995, p. 7; *Baltic Times* (Riga), 5-11 December 1996, pp. 1, 8.
98 Toomepuu (like Einseln, a US Army veteran) received 16,904 votes in 1992, but only 3,635 in 1995. See *Postimehe valimisteatmik*, p. 9; *Riigikogu Postimees* (Tartu), 21 March 1995, p. 6.
99 *Eesti Päevaleht* (Tallinn), 17 June 1995, p. 9; Tiina Raitviir, "Naised ja poliitika," *Õhtuleht* (Tallinn), 23 July 1993, p. 10; *Helsingin Sanomat*, March 3, 1995, p. C2; Maureen Sharp, "Political Life Is a Masculine Life in Estonia," *Baltic Observer* (Riga), 23-29 November 1995, p. 19.
100 *Transition Report 1995* (London: European Bank for Reconstruction and Development, 1995), p. 194; *Baltic Observer* (Riga), 15-21 February 1996, p. 11.
101 *Baltic Independent* (Tallinn), 21-27 July 1995, p. B2.
102 *Helsingin Sanomat*, 5 March 1995, p. C2; *Postimees* (Tartu), 17 July 1995, p. 3.
103 Taagepera, "Estonian Parliamentary Elections," p. 330. It should be noted that no legislation had been passed on disclosure of campaign expenditures before the March 1995 elections, and information on this issue remained fragmentary (*Nations in Transit: Civil Society, Democracy, and Markets in East Central Europe and the Newly Independent States* [New York: Freedom House, 1995], p. 50).
104 *Postimees* (Tartu), 3 July 1995, p. 2.
105 *Eesti Päevaleht* (Tallinn), 16 October 1995, p. 2; *Sõnumileht* (Tallinn), 10 November 1995, p. 1.
106 *Sõnumileht* (Tallinn), 8 November 1995, p. 2; *Eesti Päevaleht* (Tallinn), 17 October 1995, p. 2.
107 *Baltic '95 Media Book: Estonia* (N.p.: Baltic Network Oy, n.d.), *passim*; *Eesti Ekspress* (Tallinn), 21 April 1995, p. A13.
108 Jaan J. Leppik, "Uususundid Eestis," *Vikerkaar*, no. 6 (1992), 57.

Appendix

Research guidelines for country-studies

Factors influencing the formation of political groups and parties

1. What are the key elements of the precommunist historical legacy of each country? Did the country have any precommunist experience of democracy, and have any elements of the postcommunist polity, such as particular government structures, intermediary associations, and political parties, been modeled on precommunist patterns?

2. What are the key elements of the legacy of the communist era? How has the political and social evolution of each country in the late communist era (e.g., the emergence or nonemergence of a significant dissent movement) affected the postcommunist formation of societal interest groups and parties?

3. How did the nature of the transition from communism (e.g., gradual versus abrupt; peaceful versus violent; internally – versus externally – precipitated) affect the formation of intermediary associations and parties in the early postcommunist period?

4. In the postcommunist selection of government leaders, what has been the importance of competitive elections and other forms of citizen political participation compared with threats of violence and the use of violence? Have military officers or the political police played a significant role in the selection process?

5. What political forces and calculations shaped the late-communist and especially the postcommunist electoral legislation and the timing of elections?

6. In brief, what are the main social and ethnic cleavages in postcommunist society?

7. In brief, what have been the pattern and pace of postcommunist economic change, and which social groups have been the winners and losers?

8. How has the presence or absence of violent conflict inside the country or with other states affected the inclination and ability of political parties or other organizations with political agendas to mobilize social groups in support of internal democratization?

The political evolution of society

9. Which types of political associations or actors have become most prominent in each country's political life? (For example, political parties, state sector managerial lobbies, trade unions, business organizations, professional associations, religious organizations, clans, paramilitary units, criminal groups, etc.) How has the public perception of political parties and what they claim to represent affected citizens' attitudes toward the political system? What is the relative importance of parties as vehicles for new elites intent on accumulating political power and wealth? What alternative vehicles have been used or preferred?

10. How have attempted marketization and privatization affected the political strength and behavior of business and managerial groups? Have labor groups formed or formally affiliated themselves with political parties, and what role have they assumed in the financing of elections and the control of the media?

11. How have attempted marketization and privatization affected the political strength and behavior of agricultural groups? Have these groups formed or formally affiliated themselves with political parties, and what role have they played in elections?

12. How have attempted marketization and privatization affected the political strength and behavior of organized industrial labor? Have labor unions sponsored or become affiliated with political parties? In their political programs and behavior (e.g., strikes), what is the relative importance of preserving democracy versus improving economic welfare?

13. What has been the political impact of organized criminal groups? Are associations or political parties linked with organized crime? How has the public perception of the role of organized crime affected citizens' attitudes toward the political system?

14. What do existing survey data show about the level of public support within the country for democratization? Do attitudes toward democratic governmental institutions, political compromise, participation in elections, and membership in

political parties and intermediary associations differ significantly between younger and older citizens? Do attitudes on these matters differ substantially between major ethnic groups? Similarly, are there significant attitudinal differences between men and women over democracy and the various forms of political participation? How has the performance of the postcommunist economy affected public attitudes toward democracy?

15. Have the media become a channel for the expression of a range of societal interests independent of the preferences of the government? How has control of the media affected the conduct of elections and other forms of political participation?

Political parties and the party system

16. How strong are the country's political parties and party system? Since the end of communism, has the country's party system been characterized only by the creation of ephemeral parties, or do patterns of leadership, electoral results, and survey data indicate that some stable parties have emerged?

17. How have the structure and durability of political parties been affected by the electoral law(s) and by laws – if any – on campaign finance? How have parties been affected by the timing of elections – including regional versus countrywide elections?

18. How have the cohesion and durability of political parties been affected by the structure of government – in particular, the existence of a parliamentary versus a presidential system, of a unitary versus a federal state, and the amount of discretionary power in the hands of a state bureaucracy independent of the top governmental authorities?

19. To what extent have the renamed communist parties actually changed (a) their attitudes toward liberal democracy (b) their political leadership, and (c) the interests that they represent? What role has been played by electoral competition in any changes that have occurred?

20. Apart from communist successor-parties, have anti-democratic parties or social movements based on clericalism, fascist traditions, or radical nationalism developed?

21. Among the major parties, what proportion consists of parties that are: a) disloyal or loyal to democratic procedures b) ethnically or religiously based c) based primarily in one geographic region d) willing to endorse political violence, and e) linked with paramilitary forces?

22. Has the party system facilitated or obstructed the creation of governments able to formulate and carry through reasonably coherent policies? How has the capacity of postcommunist regimes to formulate and implement policies affected citizen support of democratization and marketization processes?

Index

Abišala, Aleksandras, 295, 301, 302
AFD (Alliance of Free Democrats, Hungary), 110, 115, 117, 120, 122, 123, 125, 129–30, 137, 140–1, 142
age distribution
  Estonia, 337
  Hungary, 116
  Latvia, 248
  Lithuania, 313
  Slovakia, 206
agriculture
  Czech Republic, 154, 159
  Lithuania, 314
    organizations, 317
  Slovakia, 206, 207, 220
Albania, 4
Almond, Gabriel, 50, 51
Antall, József, 125, 128, 135, 139, 143
Armenia, 4, 10, 294
Association of Slovak Workers, 232, 234
authoritarianism/authoritarian regimes, 5, 6–7, 11–12, 21, 24, 26
  and the international environment, 9
  political participation in, 12, 13
  and postcommunist democratization, 45
  support for, in Poland, 96–7
Azerbaijan, 8, 9, 10

Backis, Archbishop Audrys, 322
Balcerowicz, Leszek, 92, 100
Balsiene, Aldona, 319
Baltic states
  cooperation among, 343–4
  and democratization, 10, 20
  see also Estonia; Latvia; Lithuania
Barankovics, István, 114
Belarus, 6, 7, 9, 11, 14, 16, 19, 25
Berklāvs, Eduards, 259, 271
bicameralism, and the Czech

Constitution, 184
Bickauskas, Egidijus, 330
Bihari, Mihály, 136
Birkavs, Valdis, 274
  government of, 263, 263–5, 266–7, 277
Bojārs, Juris, 278, 279
Bollen, Kenneth, 41
Boross, Péter, 125
Bosnia Herzegovina, 20
Brazauskas, A. M., 264, 296–7, 304, 305, 306, 309, 311, 316, 322, 330
Bulgaria, 5, 15
Bunce, Valerie, 11
Burokevičius, Mykolas, 297, 299, 306
Bush, George, 298, 299
business associations
  Czech Republic, 159
  Estonia, 365
  Latvia, 257
  Slovakia, 220
Bútora, Martin, 205
Bútorová, Zora, 219

Čalfa, Marian, 155
capitalism
  and Lithuania, 328
  see also business associations
Čarnogurský, Ján, 222
Catholic church
  in Hungary, 113
  in Lithuania, 291, 294–5, 309, 322
  in Poland, 13, 23, 67, 73–4, 86–7, 88, 91, 94, 99
  in Slovakia, 200
CDPP (Christian Democratic People's Party, Hungary), 115, 117, 128, 137, 143
Central Asia, 9